S0-BXX-529

ZAGATSURVEY®

2007

LONDON RESTAURANTS

Local editors and coordinators: Sholto Douglas-Home and Susan Kessler

Staff editor: Troy Segal

Published and distributed by
ZAGAT SURVEY, LLC
4 Columbus Circle
New York, New York 10019
Tel: 212 977 6000
E-mail: london@zagat.com
Web site: www.zagat.com

Acknowledgments

We thank Kirsty Aitken, Deborah Bennett, Primula and John Birch, Karen Bonham, Caroline Clegg, Ricki Conway, Alex, Louis and Tallula Douglas-Home, Rosanne Johnston, Lady Judge, Larry Kessler, Rena and Bob Kiley, Le Cordon Bleu (London), Pamela and Michael Lester, Leuka 2000, Margaret Levin, Thomas Lewis, Anne Semmes, Steven Shukow, Alexandra Spezzotti, Peter Vogl, Susan and Jeffrey Weingarten and Annette Wilkinson. We are also grateful to our assistant editor, Victoria Elmacioglu, as well as the following members of our staff: Maryanne Bertollo, Reni Chin, Larry Cohn, Andrew Eng, Schuyler Frazier, Jeff Freier, Natalie Lebert, Mike Liao, Dave Makulec, Becky Reimer, Thomas Sheehan, Joshua Siegel, Carla Spartos, Sharon Yates and Kyle Zolner.

The reviews published in this guide are based on public opinion surveys, with numerical ratings reflecting the average scores given by all survey participants who voted on each establishment and text based on direct quotes from, or fair paraphrasings of, participants' comments. Phone numbers, addresses and other factual information were correct to the best of our knowledge when published in this guide; any subsequent changes may not be reflected.

© 2006 Zagat Survey, LLC
ISBN 1-57006-804-6
Printed in the United States of America

Contents

About This Survey

Here are the results of our *2007 London Restaurant Survey*, covering 1,005 establishments as tested, and tasted, by 5,273 local restaurant-goers. To help you find London's best meals and best buys, we have prepared a number of lists. See Most Popular (page 9), Top Ratings (pages 10–16), Best Buys (page 17), Prix Fixe Bargains (page 18) and 40 handy indexes (pages 175–235).

This marks the 27th year that Zagat Survey has reported on the shared experiences of diners like you. What started in 1979 as a hobby involving 200 of our friends rating NYC restaurants has come a long way. Today we have over 250,000 active surveyors and now cover dining, entertaining, golf, hotels, resorts, spas, movies, music, nightlife, shopping, theatre and tourist attractions. All of these guides are based on consumer surveys. They are also available by subscription at zagat.com, and for use on PDAs and mobiles.

By regularly surveying large numbers of avid customers, we hope to have achieved a uniquely current and reliable series of guides. More than a quarter-century of experience has verified this. If understood properly, these guides are the industry's report card, since each place's ratings and review are really a free market study of its own customers.

This year's participants dined out an average of 2.4 times per week, meaning this *Survey* is based on roughly 657,000 meals. Of these 5,000-plus surveyors, 39% are women, 61% men; the breakdown by age is 13% in their 20s; 32%, 30s; 21%, 40s; 19%, 50s; and 15%, 60s or above. Our editors have synopsised our surveyors' opinions, with their comments shown in quotation marks. We sincerely thank each of these people; this book is really "theirs."

We are especially grateful to our editors and coordinators, who have been with this guide since its first edition: Sholto Douglas-Home, London restaurant critic for over 15 years and an international marketing executive, and Susan Kessler, cookbook author and consultant for numerous lifestyle publications in the U.K. and U.S.

Finally, we invite you to join any of our upcoming *Surveys* — to do so, just register at zagat.com. Each participant will receive a free copy of the resulting guide when it is published. Your comments and even criticisms of this guide are also solicited. There is always room for improvement with your help. Just contact us at london@zagat.com.

New York, NY
6 September, 2006

Nina and Tim Zagat

What's New

London's dining scene is booming, and with a rise in action comes a rise in prices: the average cost of a meal went up 3.3%, to £38 (about $70 or 55€), from 2005, making the city more expensive than Paris (about £36 or 52€ per meal) and New York (about £20 or 30€). So, not surprisingly, 68% of surveyors say they're spending more when eating out, compared to two years ago. Yet an even greater number – 77% – say they're eating out as often, or even more than before. Herewith, some news on the places they're patronising.

For Members Only: London can be a tough town if you're trying to nab a table, especially last minute: 39% of surveyors say they routinely book a few days ahead. That may be why the number of private clubs around town is blossoming. As we go to press, Soho House's Nick Jones is scheduled to open High Road House in Chiswick, with a brasserie, bar and even bedrooms. Early next year, The Ivy (already Theatreland's unofficial club) plans to make its upstairs members-only.

Hotel Havens: Once considered dull dining venues, hotels have smartened up – witness the lavish revamp of Brown's – and are now hot places for chefs to strut their stuff. One such is Christopher Galvin (Galvin Bistrot de Luxe), who's opened Galvin at Windows atop the Hilton Park Lane. Theo Randall, ex-chef at the River Café, aims to unveil a venue in late 2006 at the InterContinental at Hyde Park Corner, while Mayfair's Grosvenor House will team with top toque Richard Corrigan of Lindsay House on an eatery next year.

Smoking Extinguished: It's been a long time in coming, but the government's plan to prohibit smoking in public spaces looks set to become law in summer 2007. The news will be welcomed by surveyors, nearly three-fourths of whom claim that a restaurant's smoking policy affects, to some degree, their choice of where to eat; 20% name it the single biggest irritant about dining out.

Old Faces, New Venues: Autumn arrivals are due from chef Tom Aikens – Tom's Kitchen in a former Chelsea pub – and the Chor Bizarre team – Tamarai, an Asian restaurant/club in Covent Garden. The ever-popular Wolseley is launching a Lower Regent Street offshoot called Rex, whilst renowned Paris chef, Joël Robuchon, is debuting a branch of his L'Atelier in Theatreland. The varied nature of these newcomers testifies to the increasingly rich range of restaurants in London today.

London   Sholto Douglas-Home
6 September, 2006

Ratings & Symbols

Name, Address, Tube Stop, Phone*, Fax & Web Site

Zagat Ratings

Hours & Credit Cards

F	D	S	C

Tim & Nina's Fish Bar ◐ ☒ ⊄ ▽ 23 | 5 | 9 | £9

Exeter St., WC2 (Covent Garden), 020-7123 4567;
fax 020-7123 4567; www.zagat.com

Open seven days a week, 24 hours a day (some say
that's "168 hours too many"), this "chaotic" Covent
Garden dive serving "cheap, no-nonsense" fish 'n' chips
is "ideal" for a "quick grease fix"; no one's impressed by
the "tired, tatty decor" or "patchy service", but judging
from its "perpetual queues", the "no-frills" food and
prices are "spot-on."

Review, with surveyors' comments in quotes

Top Spots: Places with the highest overall ratings, popularity
and importance are listed in BLOCK CAPITAL LETTERS.

Hours: ◐ serves after 11 PM
  ☒ closed on Sunday

Credit Cards: ⊄ no credit cards accepted

Ratings are on a scale of **0** to **30**.

F	Food	D	Decor	S	Service	C	Cost
23		5		9		£9	

0–9   poor to fair   **20–25**   very good to excellent
10–15 fair to good   **26–30**   extraordinary to perfection
16–19 good to very good   ▽ low response/less reliable

Cost (C:) Reflects our surveyors' average estimate of the
price of a dinner with one drink and service and is a
benchmark only. Lunch is usually 25% less.

For newcomers or survey write-ins listed without ratings,
the price range is indicated as follows:

I	£20 and below	**E**	£36 to £50
M	£21 to £35	**VE**	£51 or more

---

* When calling from outside the U.K., dial international code + 44,
  then omit the first zero of the number.

Most Popular

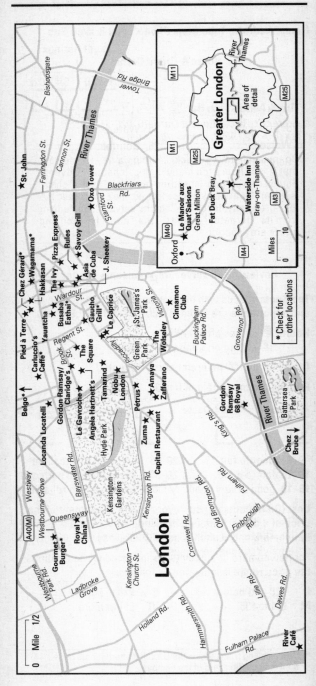

Greater London

Area of detail

M11
M25
M1
M25
M40
M3
M4

River Thames

Le Manoir aux Quat'Saisons
Great Milton

Oxford

Fat Duck Bray

Waterside Inn
Bray-on-Thames

Miles
0   10

London

River Thames

Tower Bridge Rd.
Bishopsgate
Farringdon St.
Cannon St.

★ St. John
Blackfriars Rd.
★ Oxo Tower
Stamford St.
Savoy Grill ★
★ Pizza Express*
Rules ★
★ Chez Gérard*
★ Wagamama*
Hakkasan ★
The Ivy ★ Asia de Cuba ★
★ J. Sheekey
Wardour St.
Pied à Terre ★ ★
Yauatcha ★ Busaba Eathai* ★
Regent St.
Carluccio's Caffè* ★
Gaucho Grill* ★
Le Caprice ★
St. James's Park
Cinnamon Club ★
The Wolseley ★
Buckingham Palace Rd.
Grosvenor Rd.
Belgo* ★
Locanda Locatelli ★
Gordon Ramsay/ ★ Brook St.
Claridge's ★
The Square ★
Tamarind ★
Nobu London ★
Green Park
Victoria St.
Amaya ★ ★
Zafferano
Gordon Ramsay/ ★
68 Royal
Piccadilly
Le Gavroche ★
Angela Hartnett's ★
Pétrus ★
Hyde Park
Zuma ★ Capital Restaurant ★
Bayswater Rd.
Kensington Rd.
King's Rd.
Battersea Park
Chez Bruce ▶
Kensington Gardens
Westway
A40(M)
Westbourne Grove
Queensway
Gourmet Burger* ★
Royal China* ★
Westbourne Park Rd.
Ladbroke Grove
Kensington Church St.
Cromwell Rd.
Old Brompton Rd.
Finborough Rd.
Fulham Rd.
Holland Rd.
Hammersmith Rd.
Lille Rd.
Dawes Rd.
Fulham Palace Rd.
River Café ★

* Check for other locations

Mile
0   1/2

8   subscribe to zagat.com

Most Popular

Each surveyor has been asked to name his or her five favourite places. This list reflects their choices.

1. Wagamama
2. Nobu London
3. Ivy
4. Gordon Ramsay/68 Royal
5. J. Sheekey
6. Wolseley
7. Gordon Ramsay/Claridge's
8. Square
9. Zuma
10. Rules
11. Hakkasan
12. Le Gavroche
13. Asia de Cuba
14. Pétrus
15. Le Caprice
16. Capital
17. Zafferano
18. Yauatcha
19. Fat Duck
20. Savoy Grill
21. Gaucho Grill
22. Amaya
23. Royal China
24. Le Manoir/Quat
25. Waterside Inn*
26. Gourmet Burger
27. River Café*
28. Pied à Terre
29. Pizza Express
30. Chez Bruce
31. Busaba Eathai
32. St. John
33. Locanda Locatelli
34. Tamarind
35. Carluccio's
36. Belgo
37. Chez Gérard
38. Oxo Tower
39. Angela Hartnett's
40. Cinnamon Club

It's obvious that many of the restaurants on the above list are among the London area's most expensive, but if popularity were calibrated to price, we suspect that a number of other restaurants would join the above ranks. Given the fact that both our surveyors and readers love to discover dining bargains, we have added a list of 80 Best Buys and restaurants offering bargain prix fix menus on page 17–18. These are restaurants that give real quality at extremely reasonable prices.

---

* Indicates a tie with restaurant above

Top Ratings

Excluding places with low voting.

Food

28	Gordon Ramsay/68 Royal	Capital
	Fat Duck	River Café
	Le Gavroche	Glasshouse
	Le Manoir/Quat	Gravetye Manor*
	Waterside Inn	Morgan M
27	Roussillon	Assaggi
	Pied à Terre	St. John
	Square	Club Gascon
	Chez Bruce	Foliage
	Pétrus	Quirinale
	L'Oranger	Rasoi Vineet Bhatia
	Mosimann's (club)*	L'Etranger
	Gordon Ramsay/Claridge's	Zuma
	La Trompette	Ledbury
	Nobu London	Orrery
	Enoteca Turi	Nobu Berkeley
	Hunan	J. Sheekey
	Aubergine	25 Locanda Locatelli
26	Original Lah. Kebab	Jin Kichi
	Umu*	Zafferano

By Cuisine

American
- 21 Sophie's Steak
- 20 Lucky 7
- 19 Christopher's
- 18 Bodeans
- Big Easy

Asian
- 23 Champor
- 22 Asia de Cuba
- e&o
- Eight over Eight
- 21 Cocoon

British (Modern)
- 27 Chez Bruce
- 26 Glasshouse
- Gravetye Manor*
- St. John
- 25 Clarke's

British (Traditional)
- 25 Mark's Club (club)
- Wilton's
- 24 Rib Room
- Rhodes 24
- 23 Bentley's

Chinese
- 27 Hunan
- 25 Hakkasan
- Kai Mayfair
- Yauatcha
- Four Seasons

Chophouses
- 24 Rib Room
- 23 Rules
- Guinea Grill
- 22 Gaucho Grill
- Smiths/Top Floor

Eclectic
- 27 Mosimann's (club)
- 24 Michael Moore
- 23 Lanes
- 22 Lanesborough
- Providores/Tapa

Fish 'n' Chips
- 25 Two Bros. Fish
- 23 Sweetings
- North Sea
- 21 fish!
- 20 Geales Fish

French (Bistro)
24 Racine
23 Galvin Bistrot
21 La Poule au Pot
20 Bibendum Oyster
     Le Café du Marché

French (Classic)
28 Le Gavroche
     Waterside Inn
27 L'Oranger
25 French Horn
24 Oslo Court

French (New)
28 Gordon Ramsay/68 Royal
     Le Manoir/Quat
27 Roussillon
     Pied à Terre
     Square

Indian/Pakistani
26 Original Lah. Kebab
     Rasoi Vineet Bhatia
25 Vama
     Amaya
     Zaika

Italian
27 Enoteca Turi
26 River Café
     Assaggi
     Quirinale
25 Locanda Locatelli

Japanese
27 Nobu London
26 Umu
     Zuma
     Nobu Berkeley
25 Jin Kichi

Lebanese
23 Ishbilia
22 Noura
     Fakhreldine
     Al Hamra
     Maroush

Mediterranean
25 Moro
24 Fifteen
20 Pescatori
     Eagle
19 Nicole's

Modern European
28 Fat Duck
27 Gordon Ramsay/Claridge's
     La Trompette
26 Foliage
25 Origin

Pizza
23 Osteria Basilico
     Il Bordello
21 Orso
20 Oliveto
     Made in Italy

Seafood
26 J. Sheekey
25 Wilton's
24 One-O-One
23 Bentley's
     Green's

Spanish
23 Fino
     Cambio de Tercio
22 Salt Yard
     Eyre Brothers
21 Tapas Brindisa

Thai
24 Patara
23 Nahm
22 Chiang Mai
     Churchill Arms
     Blue Elephant

Vegetarian
27 Roussillon
26 Morgan M
23 Rasa
     Food for Thought
22 Lanesborough

By Special Feature

Breakfast (other than hotels)
24 St. John Bread/Wine
     Cinnamon Club
22 Roast
21 Wolseley
20 Aubaine

Brunch
24 Le Caprice
     Quadrato
23 Lundum's
22 Cecconi's
21 Sam's Brasserie

Top Food

Business Lunch Spots
28 Le Gavroche
27 Square
26 J. Sheekey
25 Greenhouse
23 Bentleys

Cheese Boards
28 Gordon Ramsay/68 Royal
27 Square
    Pétrus
25 Tom Aikens
    Greenhouse

Child-Friendly
26 River Café
    Zuma
21 Manicomio
20 Aubaine
    San Lorenzo

Communal Tables
24 La Fromagerie
23 Baker & Spice
    Ottolenghi
21 Busaba Eathai
20 Wagamama

Gastropubs
23 Anchor & Hope
22 Churchill Arms
21 Gun
    Cow Din. Rm
    Ladbroke Arms

Hotel Dining
28 Le Manoir/Quat
    Le Manoir/Quat
    Waterside Inn
    Waterside Inn
27 Pétrus
    Berkeley Hotel
    Gordon Ramsay/Claridge's
    Claridge's Hotel
    Nobu London
    Metropolitan Hotel

In-Store Eating
23 Books for Cooks
20 Fifth Floor
19 Nicole's
18 Carluccio's
17 202

Late Night
26 Nobu Berkeley
25 Hakkasan
23 Ivy
22 Cecconi's
16 Floridita

Meet for a Drink
26 Zuma
    Nobu Berkeley
25 Hakkasan
22 Roka
21 Cocoon

Newcomers/Rated
26 Nobu Berkeley
25 Origin
23 Galvin Bistrot
    Bentley's
    Canteen

Newcomers/Unrated
    Arbutus
    Galvin/Windows
    Gilgamesh
    La Noisette
    Papillon

Offbeat
28 Fat Duck
25 Richard Corrigan
24 St. John Bread/Wine
23 Books for Cooks
22 Blue Elephant

Olde England
25 Wilton's (1742)
23 Ritz (1906)
    Sweetings (1889)
    Rules (1798)
20 Simpson's (1828)

Outdoor
26 River Café
    Ledbury
22 Smiths/Top Floor
    Le Pont de la Tour
21 La Poule au Pot

People-Watching
27 Nobu London
26 Zuma
23 Ivy
21 Wolseley
20 Cipriani

Private Clubs – Members Only

27 Mosimann's
25 Mark's Club
   Morton's
23 Harry's Bar
22 George

Private Rooms

27 Square
   Pétrus
   Gordon Ramsay/Claridge's
25 Zafferano
   Amaya

Room with a View

26 Foliage
25 Ubon by Nobu
24 Rhodes 24
22 Le Pont de la Tour
   Oxo Tower

Small Plates

26 Club Gascon
25 Origin
   Amaya
24 Maze
   Le Cercle

Sunday Lunch/Town

27 Chez Bruce
26 River Café
   Orrery
25 Yauatcha
24 Racine

Sunday Lunch/Country

28 Fat Duck
   Le Manoir/Quat
   Waterside Inn
26 Gravetye Manor
25 French Horn

Tasting Menu

28 Gordon Ramsay/68 Royal
   Fat Duck
26 Club Gascon
25 Amaya
   Tom Aikens*

Tea Service

   Berkeley Hotel
   Brown's Hotel
   Connaught Hotel
   Lanesborough Hotel
   Ritz Hotel

Theatreland

26 J. Sheekey
25 Origin
   Richard Corrigan
24 Savoy Grill
23 Ivy

Winning Wine Lists

28 Gordon Ramsay/68 Royal
27 Square
   Pétrus
25 Greenhouse
   Tom Aikens

By Location

Belgravia

27 Pétrus
   Mosimann's (club)
25 Zafferano
   Amaya
24 Rib Room

Bloomsbury/Fitzrovia

27 Pied à Terre
25 Hakkasan
23 Fino
   Rasa
   Passione

Canary Wharf

25 Ubon by Nobu
24 Quadrato
23 Royal China
22 Gaucho Grill
21 Plateau

Chelsea

28 Gordon Ramsay/68 Royal
27 Aubergine
26 Rasoi Vineet Bhatia
25 Vama
   Tom Aikens

Chiswick

27 La Trompette
22 Annie's
21 Gourmet Burger
   Sam's Brasserie
   FishWorks

City

24 Rhodes 24
23 Sweetings
   Café Spice Namasté
   Don
22 Gaucho Grill

Top Food

Clerkenwell
25 Moro
20 Eagle
   La Porchetta
18 Strada
   Sofra

Covent Garden
26 J. Sheekey
25 Origin
24 Clos Maggiore
   Savoy Grill
23 Indigo

Hampstead
25 Jin Kichi
22 Gaucho Grill
21 Gourmet Burger
   Good Earth
19 Bombay Bicycle

Islington
26 Morgan M
23 Frederick's
   Rasa
   Ottolenghi
21 FishWorks

Kensington
25 Clarke's
   Zaika
23 ffiona's
   Il Portico
   Locanda Ottoemezzo

Knightsbridge
26 Capital
   Foliage
   Zuma
24 Patara
   Racine

Marylebone
26 Orrery
25 Locanda Locatelli
   Defune
   Mandalay*
24 Michael Moore

Mayfair
28 Le Gavroche
27 Square
   Gordon Ramsay/Claridge's
   Nobu London
26 Umu

Notting Hill
26 Assaggi
   Ledbury
25 Notting Hill Brass.
23 Osteria Basilico
   Ottolenghi

Piccadilly
23 Yoshino
   Bentley's
22 Gaucho Grill
   Fakhreldine
21 Chowki Bar

Shoreditch/Spitalfields/Hoxton
24 Fifteen
   St. John Bread/Wine*
23 Canteen
22 Eyre Brothers
   Viet Hoa

Smithfield
26 St. John
   Club Gascon
22 Smiths/Top Floor
20 Le Café du Marché
   Smiths/Dining Rm.

Soho
25 Yauatcha
   Richard Corrigan
24 Red Fort
   Patara
23 Alastair Little

South Kensington
26 L'Etranger
24 Bibendum
   Patara
23 Lundum's
   Cambio de Tercio

St. James's
27 L'Oranger
25 Wilton's
24 Le Caprice
23 Green's
   Ritz

In the Country
28 Fat Duck
   Le Manior/Quat
   Waterside Inn
26 Gravetye Manor
25 French Horn

Top Decor

28 Les Trois Garçons	Levant
27 Le Manoir/Quat	Benares
Ritz	Cinnamon Club
26 Champor	Belvedere
Waterside Inn	Plateau*
Lanesborough	La Porte des Indes
Wolseley	Le Gavroche
Sketch/Gallery	Mark's Club (club)
Gordon Ramsay/Claridge's	Oxo Tower
Gravetye Manor	**24** Notting Hill Brass.
Brunello	L'Oranger
25 Hakkasan	Rules
Umu	Morton's (club)
Momo	Park, The
Taman gang	Bam-Bou
Sketch/Lecture Rm.	Annabel's (club)
Mosimann's (club)	Amaya
Blakes	Julie's
Grill, The*	Lanes*
Gordon Ramsay/68 Royal	Savoy Grill
Shanghai Blues	Foliage
Pétrus	Blue Elephant

Outdoors

Belvedere	Manicomio
Coq d'Argent	Momo
La Famiglia	Oxo Tower
La Poule au Pot	River Café
Ledbury	Smiths/Top Floor
Le Pont de la Tour	Spoon

Romance

Angela Hartnett's	Le Gavroche
Blakes	Lundum's
Club Gascon	Pétrus
Galvin/Windows	Ritz
Gordon Ramsay/Claridge's	Sketch/Lecture Rm.
La Poule au Pot	Veeraswamy

Rooms

Amaya	Ritz
China Tang	Savoy Grill
Gilgamesh	Sketch/Lecture Rm.
Hakkasan	Umu
Les Trois Garçons	Wolseley
Momo	Zuma

Views

Blueprint Café	Oxo Tower
Coq d'Argent	Rhodes 24
Foliage	Roast
Galvin/Windows	Smiths/Top Floor
Inn the Park	Ubon by Nobu
Le Pont de la Tour	Waterside Inn

Top Service

28 Gordon Ramsay/68 Royal
27 Waterside Inn
Mark's Club (club)
Fat Duck
Morton's (club)
26 Le Manoir/Quat
Mosimann's (club)
George (club)
Pétrus
Roussillon
Gordon Ramsay/Claridge's
Enoteca Turi
Le Gavroche
Capital
Square
Ritz
La Genova
25 French Horn
Quadrato
L'Oranger

Pied à Terre
Wilton's
Foliage
Gravetye Manor
Quirinale*
Ledbury
Harry's Bar (club)
Il Portico*
ffiona's
Grill, The
Angela Hartnett's
Oslo Court
24 Rib Room
Savoy Grill
Lundum's
Aubergine
Orrery
Annabel's (club)
Chez Bruce
Lanesborough

Best Buys

1. Food for Thought
2. Leon
3. Churchill Arms
4. Original Lah. Kebab
5. Little Bay
6. Gourmet Burger
7. Lucky 7
8. Books for Cooks
9. Chelsea Bun
10. Jenny Lo's Tea Hse.
11. Pepper Tree
12. Wagamama
13. Pat. Valerie
14. Mandalay
15. La Porchetta
16. North Sea
17. Busaba Eathai
18. Gallipoli
19. Two Bros. Fish
20. New Culture Rev.
21. Ask Pizza
22. Pizza Express
23. Ed's Easy Diner
24. Fire & Stone
25. Masala Zone
26. Le Mercury
27. Wong Kei
28. Ye Olde Cheshire
29. Giraffe
30. Chowki Bar
31. Ping Pong
32. Ben's Thai
33. Khan's
34. Crazy Homies
35. La Fromagerie
36. Baker & Spice
37. Chinese Exp.
38. Bodeans
39. Troubador
40. Alounak

Other Good Values

Arkansas Café
Belgo
Bloom's
Buona Sera
Carluccio's
Chuen Cheng Ku
Costas Grill
Duke of Cambridge
Eagle
ECapital
Eco
Four Seasons Chinese
Geales Fish
Ikkyu
Imli
Imperial China
Iznik
Joy King Lau
Kulu Kulu Sushi
Made in Italy
Malabar Junction
Mela
Meson Don Felipe
Mildreds
Moshi Moshi
Mr. Kong
Nautilus Fish
New World
Noto
Nyonya
Ottolenghi
Pizza Metro
Rodizio Rico
Satsuma
Seashell
Strada
Taqueria
Tas
Tootsies
Viet Hoa

Prix Fixe Bargains
(Dinner for £35 & Under)

Albannach	£32.50
Alloro	33.50
Almeida	17.50
Avenue	21.95
Banquette	21.00
Bellamy's	27.00
Blue Elephant	25.00
Brasserie Roux	24.50
Champor	26.90
Chez Gérard	16.75
Cipriani	30.00
Clos Maggiore	24.50
Crazy Homies	34.95
Embassy	22.50
Fairuz	26.95
Fifth Floor	24.50
Fino	17.95
Food Room	23.50
Galvin Bistrot	17.50
Glasshouse	35.00
Greyhound	31.00
Il Convivio	32.50
Latium	28.50
La Trompette	35.00
L'Aventure	35.00
Le Café du Marché	28.95
Livebait	18.50
Lundum's	22.50
Matsuri	35.00
Neal Street	25.00
Plateau	24.75
Racine	18.50
Rodizio Rico	18.00
Royal China	30.00
Sartoria	24.50
Sonny's	19.50
Thai Square	18.00
Wòdka	26.50
Yoshino	25.00

subscribe to zagat.com

Restaurant Directory

Abbaye
16 | 14 | 13 | £23

55 Charterhouse St., EC1 (Farringdon), 020-7253 1612;
fax 7251 5259
An "honest", "reasonably priced" Belgian-themed menu of "moules and frites like across the Channel", "all the beers in the world" and a "relaxed" attitude is what to expect at this rustic, "candlelit" Clerkenwell bistro – although to many, it's "more of a drinking place" (the "bar at the front is a better bet than the restaurant").

Abbeville, The
▽ 19 | 20 | 19 | £23

67-69 Abbeville Rd., SW4 (Clapham South), 020-8675 2201;
fax 8675 2212; www.theabbeville.com
"Cheap and undiscovered", this Clapham citizen serves "solid gastropub" Modern European–Traditional British fare, and whilst it's "not worth an expedition" from far and wide, the place makes a "great local" – "it's suitably cosy in winter and swings open half its windows in summer."

Abeno
20 | 10 | 18 | £25

47 Museum St., WC1 (Holborn), 020-7405 3211;
fax 7405 3212

Abeno Too
17-18 Great Newport St., WC2 (Leicester Sq.),
020-7379 1160
"If you've never tried okonomiyaki" (a sort of omelet-pancake) or other "Japanese street snacks", this "cramped" spot near the British Museum and its new branch "conveniently located near Leicester Square" offer a "different experience"; some opine it's "overpriced for what it is" – whilst the food "is filling, your wallet might be emptied by the end" – but "kind" "service makes up" for much.

Abingdon, The
20 | 17 | 19 | £36

54 Abingdon Rd., W8 (Earl's Ct./High St. Kensington),
020-7937 3339; fax 7795 6388;
www.theabingdon.ukgateway.net
It's "a bit hidden in residential" Kensington – so expect "blazers and pearls", "not tourists or shoppers" – but this "affluent area's" "version of a local" is "gastropubbing at its best", with "delicate", "proven offerings" from a "quality" Modern European menu, presented by "attentive staff"; although the "tab's on the pricey side", the bar "drinks are inexpensive."

Addendum ⊠
– | – | – | M

Apex City of London Hotel, 1 Seething Ln., EC3 (Tower Hill),
020-7977 9500; fax 7977 9529; www.addendumrestaurant.co.uk
Set in a spanking new hotel near the Tower of London, this two-part eatery – a weekday-only restaurant plus brasserie – is overseen by experienced chef Tom Ilic (ex Bonds); the restaurant features an upscale Modern European menu served in a smart, low-ceilinged room with

discreet leather booths, while the glass-fronted brasserie offers a cheaper selection of unfussy, light dishes.

Admiral Codrington, The   17 17 15 £32

17 Mossop St., SW3 (South Kensington), 020-7581 0005; fax 7589 2452; www.theadmiralcodrington.co.uk

"If not an admiral, at least a commodore", this "entertaining" Chelsea boozer boasts a "light-filled" rear dining room with a "unique retractable roof", as well as Modern British–Euro cooking that "goes beyond gastropub staples"; the "food and service are of variable quality", but you can always count on the front bar, with its "cosy booths", to be a "buzzy" "hangout" for "the braying classes."

Admiralty, The   19 19 20 £47

Somerset House, The Strand, WC2 (Temple), 020-7845 4646; fax 7845 4658

"In an oft-overlooked location" accessed via the "grand" Somerset House courtyard, this "stylish, high-ceilinged" dining room is "not as popular as it deserves" declare devotees of its "decent" Modern British cooking and "unobtrusive service"; but foes feel it "doesn't make the most of its setting" amongst all the "art and architecture", grousing the "good wine list" is "let down" by "large markups"

Aglio e Olio   – – – M

194 Fulham Rd., SW10 (South Kensington), 020-7351 0070

"Very much a local crowd" inhabit this "noisy" Italian "favourite" in Fulham Road; even though the "menu is always the same, the quality is constantly top" and "great value for Chelsea"; "service is patchy to say the least", but not enough to prevent devotees from dubbing it "one of London's best-kept secrets."

Agni   – – – M

160 King St., W6 (Ravenscourt Park), 020-8846 9191; www.agnirestaurant.com

Named after the Sanskrit word for 'fierce determination', this no-frills, bi-level Hammersmith debutante is "really making an effort", with "imaginative, well-presented" regional Indian dishes prepared by chef/co-owner Gowtham Karingi (ex Veeraswamy and Zaika), smoothed along by "helpful, friendly staff."

Alastair Little ●🅐   23 16 20 £44

49 Frith St., W1 (Leicester Sq./Tottenham Court Rd.), 020-7734 5183; fax 7734 5206

It may be a "quirky" venue in "unimpressive" Soho quarters, but this "perennial favourite" is "still home" to "fine" "modern fare that's retained its English character" and pleasantly "informal" service; "it may have lost a bit of its edge" "since Alastair moved on" in 2003, but it remains "a good place" (at a "good price per the quality") for a "relaxed dinner."

Albannach ☒

16 | 19 | 16 | £44

66 Trafalgar Sq., WC2 (Charing Cross/Leicester Sq.),
020-7930 0066; fax 7389 9800; www.albannach.co.uk
In a grand former bank hall with a "suitably dark, nooks-and-crannies—filled basement" bar, this "generally likeable place" is "trying hard", "serving Scottish food with a Modern European twist" and the "greatest selection of rare, slow-matured whiskies"; unfortunately, the "kilted waiters" are "rare and slow too", and the "tricky" Trafalgar Square "site doesn't necessarily attract serious diners."

Al Bustan

20 | 14 | 19 | £31

68 Old Brompton Rd., SW7 (South Kensington), 020-7584 5805;
fax 8563 1036
Simply attired it may be, but the "chef is a magician" who "transports you to Eastern realms" say fans of this "friendly" South Kensington Lebanese whose menu is heavy with "healthy options"; still, its "general appeal has gone down" among sceptics who shrug it's "overpriced for what you get."

Al Duca ☒

18 | 15 | 18 | £40

4-5 Duke of York St., SW1 (Green Park/Piccadilly Circus),
020-7839 3090; fax 7839 4050; www.alduca-restaurant.co.uk
"Leave with a smile" from this "friendly" St. James's "find" where "dependable", "well-prepared" Italian fare is served in a simple, slightly "cramped room"; if some say it "seems undistinguished" ("needs some menu changes"), the "good" prix fixes make it "popular with business types and high-end shoppers."

Al Hamra ●

22 | 16 | 18 | £38

31-33 Shepherd Mkt., W1 (Green Park), 020-7493 1954;
fax 7493 1044

Brasserie Al Hamra ☒⊄

52 Shepherd Mkt., W1 (Green Park), 020-7493 1068; fax 7355 3511
www.alhamrarestaurant.com
"The granddaddy of Mayfair Lebanese restaurants", this Shepherd Market stalwart may look "a bit old and unoriginal", but it's "always bustling" with "efficient" (mostly) servers relaying "trusted", "traditional" and "tempting" Middle Eastern fare; "great alfresco tables" make it "worthwhile on a sunny evening"; and if the "upscale" prices pose a problem, the new Brasserie-deli (with some French fare), just opposite the original, offers a more casual option.

Alloro ☒

22 | 17 | 20 | £47

19-20 Dover St., W1 (Green Park), 020-7495 4768;
fax 7629 5348
"Escape the footballers' wives and Britney wannabes" at this "elegant, grown-up" Mayfair eatery where a "good-looking crowd mixing finance and art" dine on "vibrant" Italian cooking and vino that's "pricey, but worth it" ("lin-

guine with lobster – I rest my case"); although the decor "misses a touch of personality", the "discreet service" scores a bravo.

All Star Lanes   – | – | – | M

Victoria House, Bloomsbury Pl., WC1 (Holborn), 020-7025 2676; www.allstarlanes.co.uk

Bringing a "luxury" touch to the usually "tacky" world of 10-pin bowling, this '50s-style "funky", colourful Bloomsbury newcomer makes for "a blast of a night": a veritable "grown-up playground", it offers pulsing music, two bars and a spacious dining area (overlooking the six lanes' strike zone) serving midpriced American munchies to players and spectators alike.

Almeida   19 | 18 | 18 | £41

30 Almeida St., N1 (Angel/Highbury & Islington), 020-7354 4777; fax 7354 2777; www.conran-restaurants.co.uk

"Just a quick hop from the Almeida Theatre" ("its main virtue" critics quip), this "lively" "Conran Group mainstay" "showcases" charcuterie and cheese trolleys on its Classic French menu; even if there's "no wow factor" – the "decor could do with an upgrade" and the "expensive" fare "straddles the fine line between traditional and uninspired" – it remains "Islington's most reliable upmarket" venue (and, of course, perfect pre- or post-show).

Alounak ●   21 | 11 | 15 | £20

10 Russell Gardens, W14 (Olympia), 020-7603 1130
44 Westbourne Grove, W2 (Bayswater/Queensway), 020-7229 4158; fax 7792 1219

"Cosy" and "chaotic", this "no-frills" Persian pair in Olympia and Westbourne Grove are "always lively" thanks to their "quality" fare at an "excellent price"; but with service that's "a tad overbearing", they're "not for lingering" – and "remember to bring your own" bottle as they "don't serve alcohol"; P.S. "be prepared to queue" unless you book (Russell Gardens only).

Al Sultan   19 | 14 | 16 | £36

51-52 Hertford St., W1 (Green Park), 020-7408 1155; fax 7408 1113; www.alsultan.co.uk

"Forget the unflattering decor – instead concentrate" on the "delicious Lebanese food" at this casual Shepherd Market venue with "too-close tables" but comfy banquettes; it makes a "good choice if you are dining alone", and is "perfect post-[Curzon] cinema next door."

Al Waha ●   ∇ 24 | 12 | 19 | £32

75 Westbourne Grove, W2 (Bayswater/Queensway), 020-7229 0806; www.waha-uk.com

"Hits the spot every time" say admirers of this "small, crowded" Westbourne Grove Lebanese that lacks much in the way of ambience, but makes up for it with "fantastic", "fresh-tasting flavours", served by "friendly people" who "do their best to give you a good dining experience."

AMAYA ● 25 24 21 £52
15-19 Halkin Arcade, Motcomb St., SW1 (Knightsbridge), 020-7823 1166; fax 7259 6464; www.realindianfood.com
"Creativity remains a hallmark" of this "plush", "sleek Belgravia nouveau Indian" ("owned by the Chutney Mary folks") where a "deliciously intense", "inventive menu" – "every dish is a revelation"; it's "pricey" ("take a couple of credit cards"), and some snap the "service is polite but not very knowledgeable"; still, for most the "only complaint" is that it's "hidden in a nondescript shopping mall."

Amici Bar & Italian Kitchen ● – – – M
35 Bellevue Rd., SW17 (Wandsworth Common), 020-8672 5888; www.amiciitaly.co.uk
The owners of Pomino have transformed their Wandsworth eatery into this warm, casual Italian, serving well-priced regional Roman and Tuscan dishes in an airy setting that includes a comfy bar; there's a range of menus – like the cafe-style option and an under-10 'bambino' selection – as well as a competitively priced wine list.

Anakana – – – M
1 Olivers Yard, City Rd., EC1 (Old St.), 0845-262 5262; www.anakana.co.uk
The name of this new Shoreditch industrial-chic Indian (think exposed air-conditioning ducts, lights hanging from cables) translates as 'come eat', which hints at its casual approach, as do its communal tables and no-reservations policy; happily, the "flavourful" street-style fare is "a cut above your average curry house", and served by "enthusiastic, bubbly staff"; there's a relaxed lounge as well, already attracting an "achingly hip" crowd.

Anchor & Hope ⌀ 23 12 17 £32
36 The Cut, SE1 (Waterloo), 020-7928 9898
"Get there early or expect to wait" (and wait) at this "funky" Waterloo gastropub whose "irritating no-booking policy" often means "mayhem" within its highly "homely surroundings"; but fans forgive all for the "fantastic", "superb-for-sharing" Modern British "comfort food" and "well-thought-out wine list"; "the service is relaxed, provided you go off-peak."

Andrew Edmunds 22 19 19 £34
46 Lexington St., W1 (Oxford Circus/Piccadilly Circus), 020-7437 5708
"If intimacy is your thing", this "cosy", "shabby-chic" Soho "favourite" fits the bill, with "rustic, drippy candles on tables", "warm" staff and "hearty", "unfussy" Modern European cooking at prices that "don't compromise next

month's rent"; "so maybe it's a little crammed", but fans proclaim it a "perfect date restaurant" (just "don't stay too long, or the wooden chairs might hurt your bum").

ANGELA HARTNETT'S MENU | 24 | 24 | 25 | £81 |

The Connaught Hotel, 16 Carlos Pl., W1 (Bond St./Green Park), 020-7592 1222; fax 7292 1223; www.angelahartnett.com

"Traditionalists still lament the former Connaught [restaurant], but this is a stunning replacement" assert advocates of chef Angela Hartnett, whose "imaginative" Italian-accented Modern European menu "perfects the balance of inventive and traditional" within the "classy" confines of the aubergine and green dining room; it's supplemented by a "phenomenal wine list" and "service you almost don't notice", and if it all seems "too ambitious and pretentious" to some, it's "absolute heaven" to most.

Anglesea Arms | ▽ 21 | 14 | 16 | £30 |

35 Wingate Rd., W6 (Goldhawk Rd./Ravenscourt Park), 020-8749 1291; fax 8749 1254

With no reservations taken, it's "sooo hard to get into this" "cosy" Shepherd's Bush gastropub – because everyone wants a taste of the Modern British fare that can be "hit-and-miss, but when it hits, it's incredible"; the cuisine's quality "is not matched by the service" or the "old-style dining room" ("a bit dated"), but "all 'round, it's a nice place."

Annabel's 🗷 | 21 | 24 | 24 | £72 |

Private club; inquiries: 020-7629 1096

"Rub shoulders with millionaires, royalty" and "beautiful people" at this "very discreet", "all-time classic" Berkeley Square private nightclub in a "sexy, romantic setting" with a "consistently good", albeit "ludicrously expensive" Classic British–French menu and "old-school service"; although a few think "you need a title to feel comfy here", an invitation is just "too good to pass up."

Annex 3 ●🗷 | ▽ 9 | 25 | 14 | £39 |

6 Little Portland St., W1 (Oxford Circus), 020-7631 0700; www.lestroisgarcons.com

Giving the old RK Stanley premises near Oxford Circus an "über-glam", "outlandish" overhaul – "as expected from the Les Trois Garçons" team – this "very loud" new venue combines a "kitschy" cocktail lounge with dining room; the Eclectic fare is "nothing special, but at least it's reasonably priced"; even so, most say "come for a drink, be dazzled and go have dinner somewhere else."

Annie's | 22 | 22 | 22 | £31 |

162 Thames Rd., W4 (Kew Bridge B.R.), 020-8994 6848 36-38 White Hart Ln., SW13 (Barnes Bridge B.R.), 020-8878 2020; fax 8876 8478

"A solid choice for an evening with friends" or weekend lunch, this "inviting" duo in Chiswick and Barnes with "eclectic but relaxing decor" proffers an "accomplished", "carefully prepared" Modern British menu; "you get a lot for your money", but at brunch "beware the 'babychino' crowd with screaming children."

Aperitivo 🖂   17 | 13 | 16 | £30
41 Beak St., W1 (Oxford Circus/Piccadilly Circus), 020-7287 2057; www.aperitivo-restaurants.com
Fans of the "flexible" "light-eating option" find the "Italian tapas-style" plates "become strangely addictive" at this "simple" Soho site; but a decline in scores supports sceptics who say the place is "losing it" and "deceptively inexpensive – each dish seems reasonable, but you need many to make a meal."

Arbutus   – | – | – | E
63-64 Frith St., W1 (Leicester Sq./Tottenham Court Rd.), 020-7734 4545; www.arbutusrestaurant.co.uk
Anthony Demetre and Will Smith, the ex chef and manager, respectively, of the defunct Putney Bridge, have teamed up to open this new midsize Modern European; the robust fare – think saddle of rabbit and braised pig's head – is dished up in a neatly decorated U-shaped space, with black leather banquettes and wood flooring; as befits its Soho address, there's a pre-theatre prix fixe – £15 for three courses.

Archipelago 🖂   ∇ 17 | 26 | 21 | £48
110 Whitfield St., W1 (Goodge St./Warren St.), 020-7383 3346; fax 7383 7181
"For those with an adventurous spirit", this "decidedly odd", yet strangely "romantic" Fitzrovian haunt full of "fantastic" furniture (some of "which is for sale") indeed offers a "true adventure" – thanks to an "exotic" Eclectic menu featuring crocodile, peacock and kangaroo; "weird", yes, but "tasty" – so "be inspired to be courageous in your eating."

Ark 🖂   21 | 21 | 20 | £43
122 Palace Gardens Terrace, W8 (Notting Hill Gate), 020-7229 4024; fax 7792 8787
Notting Hillers have "no need to go to the West End" for good eats when they have this "narrow" "little neighbourhood joint", which has seen an across-the-board jump in ratings thanks to "friendly staff" and a modern Italian menu that "never disappoints" – even if it is "surprisingly expensive."

Arkansas Cafe   ∇ 18 | 8 | 14 | £19
Old Spitalfields Mkt., 107B Commercial St., E1 (Liverpool St.), 020-7377 6999; fax 7377 6990
This "tacky"-lookin' Spitalfields Market haunt is dominated by "talkative American" Bubba Helberg, who "cooks up fine" carnivore delights; but if it's "high on quality BBQ, it's low on frills and service" ("more a picnic than a cafe" experience, in effect).

Artigiano
18 | 16 | 14 | £34

12A Belsize Terrace, NW3 (Belsize Park/Swiss Cottage),
020-7794 4288; fax 7435 2048; www.etruscarestaurants.com
The contemporary "upscale Italian food" comes with "lots
of choice to suit all tastes" at this "busy, buzzy" Belsize
Village "local favourite"; on the downside, "service can be
hit-and-miss" ("better weekdays than weekends"), and
whilst "skylights allow lots of light in during the day", at
night the setting seems "a little sterile."

ASIA DE CUBA ◗
22 | 23 | 19 | £50

St. Martin's Lane Hotel, 45 St. Martin's Ln., WC2 (Leicester Sq.),
020-7300 5588; fax 7300 5540; www.chinagrillmanagement.com
Like its U.S. *confrères*, this Covent Garden "minimalist"-
white, art-columned "noisy hotel resto" serves "inventive"
fusion fare "utilizing the flavours of Asia and Cuba" that's
"sophisticated without being pernickety" – even if the
"hefty" prices make it "the most expensive chain in the
world"; the "hipster" hordes insist it's still "über-cool, in
spite of its age" (it opened in 1999), but those suffering the
seven-year itch jeer it's "past its prime" – though, given
their "attitude", "the staff don't seem to have noticed."

Ask Pizza
16 | 14 | 16 | £18

219-221 Chiswick High Rd., W4 (Turnham Green),
020-8742 1323 ◗
48 Grafton Way, W1 (Warren St.), 020-7388 8108; fax 7388 8112 ◗
222 Kensington High St., W8 (High St. Kensington),
020-7937 5540; fax 7937 5540
145 Notting Hill Gate, W11 (Notting Hill Gate), 020-7792 9942
121-125 Park St., W1 (Marble Arch), 020-7495 7760; fax 7495 7760
300 King's Rd., SW3 (Sloane Sq.), 020-7349 9123
345 Fulham Palace Rd., SW6 (Hammersmith/Putney Bridge),
020-7371 0392
Unit 23-24, Gloucester Arcade, SW7 (Gloucester Rd.),
020-7835 0840 ◗
160-162 Victoria St., SW1 (St. James's Park/Victoria),
020-7630 8228; fax 7630 5218
216 Haverstock Hill, NW3 (Belsize Park/Chalk Farm),
020-7433 3896; fax 7435 6490 ◗
www.askcentral.co.uk
Additional locations throughout London
"It's not glitzy, but does exactly what it says on the tin" declare disciples of this "convenient" chain – namely, dish
up "dependable pizzas and Italian entrees" "without dent-
ing the wallet"; that doesn't stop quibblers from quipping
"don't ask, don't tell" about this place (it's that "boring").

ASSAGGI ⊠
26 | 17 | 24 | £53

39 Chepstow Pl., W2 (Notting Hill Gate), 020-7792 5501;
fax 08700 512923
Despite its digs – an "unassuming", "loud room" above a
Notting Hill pub – clients "call and beg" for bookings to

this "stunning" site, now entering its second decade of "magnificently executed Italian fare", full of "bold, robust flavours" and presented by "warm, welcoming" and witty waiters ("listening to them describe the food is half the fun"); "it's one of those rare places where each quid is worth it" – "pity it isn't twice the size, so there's more likelihood of getting a table."

Astor Bar & Grill ☒

– – – E

20 Glasshouse St., W1 (Piccadilly Circus), 020-7734 4888; fax 7734 5400; www.astorbarandgrill.com

Under the aegis of Channel 4 chairman Luke Johnson and partners, that '90s icon Atlantic Bar & Grill is "now called Astor"; its cavernous but comfortable space underneath Piccadilly Circus – perhaps "the most beautiful, original art deco room in London" – has been spruced up in louche, ruby red and tan tones, and offers a short, steak-oriented American menu; several bars and nightly DJs provide ample diversion, and the "new ownership has resulted in a step-up in service" too.

Aubaine

20 21 17 £34

260-262 Brompton Rd., SW3 (South Kensington), 020-7052 0100; fax 7052 0622; www.aubaine.co.uk

"Decorated in hip Gallic-countryside-meets-urban-minimalism" style, this bustling Brompton Cross "toddler-friendly" venue has become a "chic locals'" lunch and "weekend social scene"; they delight in the "simple" "French-to-the-core" bistro eats (but "don't try to deviate an inch from the menu – Mr. Le Chef won't have it"), deal with the "haphazard, but charming service" and indulge in takeaway from the "divine-smelling" bakery, whose wares are "worth their weight in gold (and cost about as much)."

AUBERGINE ☒

27 21 24 £70

11 Park Walk, SW10 (Gloucester Rd./South Kensington), 020-7352 3449; fax 7351 1770; www.atozrestaurants.com

"As good or even better than the 'big names'" of London dining, chef William Drabble's "magically delicate, refined" New French cuisine (including a "perfectly balanced gourmand menu") is the main draw at this "charming", if "slightly old-fashioned"-looking haunt – though the "gentle, efficient service" draws kudos too; it "has become extremely expensive", making a few fret the Chelsea trek is "not as worthwhile as it once was" – but still "perfect for a romantic dinner" or (cheaper) lunch.

Aurora ☒

22 23 23 £47

Great Eastern Hotel, 40 Liverpool St., EC2 (Liverpool St.), 020-7618 7000; fax 7618 7001; www.great-eastern-hotel.co.uk

"Relatively unknown outside the City", this "trendy hotel" eatery offers "dependable, high-end" dining on Classic French–Modern British fare within a "wonderful space" of soaring ceilings and stained-glass dome, plus "unpretentious, polite service"; there's "nothing dangerous" or edgy about the place – after all, "mostly businesspeople eat here" – but there's "never a disappointment", either; N.B. it changed hands post-*Survey*.

Automat ●   17 | 20 | 16 | £32

33 Dover St., W1 (Green Park), 020-7499 3033;
www.automat-london.com
An American "addition to WoBo (west of Bond Street)", NY architect Carlos Almada's "light, buzzy" brasserie offers a "beautifully designed" "railcar-shaped room" ("try to book a booth", "the perfect place to subtly spot the celebrity clientele") and "high-end American diner comfort food"; however, the "not impressed" huff "it's a nice idea, but relatively uninspiring", given the still "ropey service" and "marked-up"-for-"Mayfair premium slapped on the average-ish" eats.

Avenue, The ●☒   18 | 18 | 19 | £44

7-9 St. James's St., SW1 (Green Park), 020-7321 2111;
fax 7321 2500; www.egami.co.uk
With "white walls, high energy" and lots of "media people in androgynous suits", this "noisy", "airy, *très moderne*" St. James's haunt "remains reliable" for "quality", if "pricey" Modern European fare; if a few feel it "fell out of fashion a while ago", stalwarts say it's been "revived by hedge fund money" types at the "brash" bar scene that's beefed it up into a "fancy late-night gathering place."

Awana   ▽ 17 | 22 | 22 | £38

85 Sloane Ave., SW3 (South Kensington), 020-7584 8880;
www.awana.co.uk
In the low-ceilinged Chelsea site long held by Zen, Mango Tree owner Eddie Lim unveils this "attractive, modern" Malaysian serving "refined, forcefully spiced grub", including "exceptional" offerings from the 14-seat satay bar at the back of the "slick" surrounds; staff are "truly charming" – even if they do "push the drinks a bit" – but still, some wish for "more variety and better quality" in the cuisine.

Axis ☒   20 | 19 | 21 | £49

One Aldwych Hotel, 1 Aldwych, WC2 (Charing Cross/
Covent Garden), 020-7300 0300; fax 7300 0301;
www.onealdwych.com
"Underneath the hip One Aldwych Hotel" and the Strand's "madding crowds", this "streamlined", "discreet" dining room with "hot bar" "serves the working set well" with a "super" Eclectic–Modern British menu; antagonists axe it for its "aggressive decor" and cuisine that's "not capable enough for the price", but all agree it's "good pre/post theatre", thanks to the "efficient" staff.

Aziz
▽ 15 | 19 | 15 | £29

30-32 Vanston Pl., SW6 (Fulham Broadway), 020-7386 0086;
fax 7610 1661

"Atmospheric and entertaining" – "the belly-dancing
nights are an experience" – this Moroccan brings a "taste
of North Africa to Fulham" (down to the hookah pipes in
the lounge); and even if the food is often "hit-and-miss"
and the "beautiful staff" "can be slow", it makes a "great
neighbourhood spot"; P.S. there are "tasty baked goods"
for takeaway in their deli next door.

Babalou
– | – | – | M

St. Matthew's Church, The Crypt, SW2 (Brixton), 020-7738 3366;
fax 7738 3345; www.babalou.net

With "Moroccan-inspired decor that makes you forget
you're in a Downtown Brixton church crypt", this dark,
sprawling newcomer mixes dining, drinking and dancing in
equal measures, cranking up the decibels as the evening
progresses; an open-plan kitchen produces sensibly
priced "exotic" Eclectic fare, accompanied by a heavy-
duty cocktail and wine list; N.B. closed Monday–Tuesday,
but open until 5 AM on weekends.

Babylon
▽ 15 | 21 | 15 | £51

The Roof Gardens, 99 Kensington High St., W8
(High St. Kensington), 020-7368 3993; fax 7938 2774;
www.roofgardens.com

"The lovely view over the treetops of the roof gardens one
floor down is the reason to come" to Sir Richard Branson's
"cool" eatery atop a Kensington building, since the Modern
European "fare is pretty standard"; but the venue's "brilliant for a corporate event" or on "a summer night, with
dinner and dancing" (restaurant patrons are allowed access to the private nightclub Friday and Saturday).

Baker & Spice
23 | 17 | 13 | £22

47 Denyer St., SW3 (Knightsbridge/South Kensington),
020-7589 9148; fax 7823 9148
54-56 Elizabeth St., SW1 (Sloane Sq./Victoria), 020-7730 3033;
fax 7730 3188 ⊠
75 Salusbury Rd., NW6 (Queens Park), 020-7604 3636;
fax 7604 3646
www.bakerandspice.com

"They sure do cram them in" to this trio of bakery/delis
around town, whether it be to eat at the communal table or
(the "better" option) to take away the "terrific" Med
munchies, especially the "lethal" "pastries to live for"; sure,
the "prices are off the scale" and "staff could be friend-
lier", but the fact many cite these sites as "a reason to move
to the vicinity" suggests the "food compensates" for all.

Balans
16 | 15 | 18 | £25

214 Chiswick High Rd., W4 (Turnham Green), 020-8742 1435

(continued)
Balans
*187 Kensington High St., W8 (High St. Kensington), 020-7376 0115;
fax 7938 4653* ☻
*60 Old Compton St., W1 (Leicester Sq./Piccadilly Circus/
Tottenham Court Rd.), 020-7439 2183; fax 7734 2665* ☻
*239 Old Brompton Rd., SW5 (Earl's Ct.), 020-7244 8838;
fax 7244 6226* ☻
Balans Cafe
*34 Old Compton St. (Leicester Sq./Piccadilly Circus/
Tottenham Court Rd.), 020-7439 3309
www.balans.co.uk*
"Cool hanging and easy eating" sums up this chain of
"campy" all-day bistros, which are "always jammed" with
a "bevy of hunks" – though "flirty" staff welcome all; malcontents mutter the Modern British menu is "a safe bet for a
mediocre meal" – but then, most diners are gorging on the
"eye candy" anyway; P.S. 60 Old Compton Street is "open
through the night", hence "great after hitting the clubs."

Balham Kitchen & Bar   20 21 16 £30
*15-19 Bedford Hill, SW12 (Balham B.R.), 020-8675 6900;
fax 8673 3965; www.balhamkitchen.com*
"Thirtysomethings wearing black T-shirts and tatty jeans"
enjoy "especially nice" Modern British meals at this "laid-
back outpost of the Soho House group" with banquette
seating and a comfy bar; many feel it's "the best Balham
has to offer" – though "if there were more competition, it
wouldn't be so popular" scoff sceptics, citing staff that act
"too big for their boots."

Baltic ☻   21 21 19 £37
*74 Blackfriars Rd., SE1 (Southwark), 020-7928 1111;
fax 7928 8487; www.balticrestaurant.co.uk*
At this "ultracool" Southwark haunt – an 1850s coach-
builder's workshop – diners "wade through trendies"
propped up against the "proper bar in front" (with "top-
notch cocktail-makers") to reach an "airy", "wooden-
floored" dining room serving "different" dishes from a
"varied modern Polish menu"; if "heartwarming comfort
food gone chic" and "vodka is your thing, it's heaven."

Bam-Bou ⌧   21 24 18 £38
*1 Percy St., W1 (Tottenham Court Rd.), 020-7323 9130;
fax 7323 9140; www.bam-bou.co.uk*
With "lots of different nooks and crannies to hide in", this
"sumptuous-looking" "colonial" Fitzrovian townhouse is
"a find for romantic meets" amidst meals of "exotic", "interesting" Southeast Asian–Vietnamese fare, even if some
snarl "the portions are on the small side" and the "service
a bit too slow"; P.S. the "top-floor bar is a great way to
pass the time" – just "watch out for the stairs, as they're
lethal after a few drinks."

Bank Aldwych
18 19 17 £39

1 Kingsway, WC2 (Holborn), 020-7379 9797; fax 7240 7001;
www.bankrestaurants.com
"Although it hasn't got the buzz it once did", "you can always bank on" this "large" "solid performer" in Aldwych "for client entertaining" (even at breakfast), as it couples "reliable" Modern European fare and "big, well-spaced tables that offer adequate privacy" stalwarts say; in contrast, more demanding depositors decry it as "loud and bright", "but not brilliant" – especially since the service, whilst "quite slick", "can be slack."

Bankside
∇ 17 16 15 £32

32 Southwark Bridge Rd., SE1 (London Bridge), 020-7633 0011;
fax 7633 0011
1 Angel Ct., 30 Throgmorton St., EC2 (Bank), 0845-226 0011 ⊠
www.banksiderestaurants.co.uk
The Modern British bites are "not groundbreaking, but dependable" summarise surveyors about this casual, "busy" Southwark site (handy for the Tate Modern), with a "noisy new branch in the City"; however, the "good value" is somewhat compromised by a "franchisey feeling" and staff that seem "stripped of English-language skills."

Bank Westminster & Zander Bar ⊠
16 16 16 £36

45 Buckingham Gate, SW1 (St. James's Park), 020-7379 9797;
fax 7240 7001; www.bankrestaurants.com
Armed with "allegedly the longest bar in London – or is it Europe?" this "posh" Modern European in Victoria can be "a good venue for business" or pre-theatre, as staff do a "quick turnaround"; alas, whilst "not bad value for money, the meals are not memorable" – "a bit too trendy without the creativity" – and the conservatorylike dining room feels "cold."

Banquette ●
∇ 24 21 23 £41

Savoy Hotel, The Strand, WC2 (Covent Garden/Embankment),
020-7420 2392; fax 7592 1601; www.marcuswareing.com
Overlooking the Savoy Hotel's entrance court, this tiny 1950s diner-style eatery "seems a little outta place" (not to mention hard to locate), but it's "a good find" for a "quiet, casual business lunch" or pre/post-theatre; the Eclectic fare is "pretty solid", especially on the "excellent set menu", and comes courtesy of "outstanding service."

Barnsbury, The
∇ 23 15 17 £24

209-211 Liverpool Rd., N1 (Angel), 020-7607 5519; fax 7607 3256;
www.thebarnsbury.co.uk
"Just up the road from the Angel tube" station is this "absolute gem – cosy by the fire when it's cold, breezy in the garden when it's warm"; the Modern British cuisine comes "with originality and flair", "exceeding expectations for a

pub" ("gastropub-plus!"); P.S. "unique lighting" – chandeliers made from goblets – alleviates the "sparse" decor.

Bar Shu _ _ _ E
28 Frith St., W1 (Leicester Sq./Tottenham Court Rd.), 020-7287 8822
In a prime corner location in Soho, this lively newcomer mixes modern design touches with antique carved wood panels and Chinese opera masks for an eclectic, exotic look; the menu offers an unusual taste of authentic, distinctively fiery Szechuan cuisine (which currently has little foothold in London), thanks to special spices shipped in from southwest China; multilingual staff are on hand to guide diners through the culinary options.

Beauberry House _ _ _ E
Gallery Rd., Dulwich Village, SE21 (West Dulwich B.R.), 020-8299 9788; www.beauberryhouse.co.uk
L'Etranger's entrepreneurial owner, Ibi Issolah, has taken over this grand property in a West Dulwich park, introducing hip decorative elements – bright orange flooring and chairs and a piercingly pink staircase – to complement the building's traditional Georgian features and terrace; supporting the "well-executed" Japanese–New French menu is a wine list leaning heavily toward Burgundy (Beauberry is a village there).

Beiteddine ● ∇ 20 18 21 £32
8 Harriet St., SW1 (Knightsbridge/Sloane Sq.), 020-7235 3969; fax 7245 6335; www.beiteddinerestaurant.com
"Excellent Middle Eastern delights" are on the varied menu at this simply decorated Lebanese in glass-fronted (hence, bright) Belgravia digs; even though the "service is very good", many opt to take it away (they'll also deliver to you).

BELGO 19 16 16 £23
50 Earlham St., WC2 (Covent Garden), 020-7813 2233; fax 7209 3212
72 Chalk Farm Rd., NW1 (Chalk Farm), 020-7267 0718; fax 7284 4842
"The old shell game still has mussel" at this "raucous", cavernous Covent Garden and Chalk Farm duo, which "continue to be the universal favourite for Belgian food" in London (though admittedly, "competition for the title isn't stiff"); you have to like "industrial decor", "cafeteria-style seating" and "servers in cheesy monk outfits" offering "standard dishes, including the ubiquitous moules frites"; but there are "more beers than you could work through in a year" and a "beat-the-clock special, [a meal] for the price of the time" you order.

Bellamy's ⧄ 17 18 19 £50
18/18a Bruton Pl., W1 (Green Park/Bond St.), 020-7491 2727; fax 7491 9990
"Very Mayfair" – down to the "upscale deli through which one enters" – pronounce patrons of this "civilised", "com-

fortable place"; the staff are "welcoming" and the French brasserie fare "solid", but it's all "the same old, same old" to sceptics, who skewer it as sort of a *salon des refusés* for those who can't get into" the hotter places.

Belvedere, The
20 25 21 £47

Holland Park, off Abbotsbury Rd., W8 (Holland Park), 020-7602 1238; fax 7610 4382; www.whitestarline.org.uk

In a "gorgeous spot" in the centre of Holland Park, this "Marco Pierre White outpost" supplies a "spectacular setting" for Modern British–New French dishes with "daily specials at admirable prices"; if a handful feel the food "never achieves the high that [the venue] seems to present", the "relaxed, friendly service" and "unsurpassed ambience" are "treat" enough.

BENARES
23 25 21 £49

12a Berkeley Sq. House, Berkeley Sq., W1 (Green Park), 020-7629 8886; fax 7499 2430; www.benaresrestaurant.com

"Thrumming with financial types", this "slightly business-y", "beautiful" Berkeley Square site displays great "attention to detail" in its "serene setting" (candles, "pools with floating flowers") and "haute Indian cuisine" "done with flair and a light touch"; it's a pity "the portions and the prices are inversely proportional", and that "depending on the night the staff can be absolutely fine" or "pushy"; still, it's a "luxurious" "escape from the usual elsewhere."

Bengal Clipper ◗
▽ 21 16 17 £31

11-12 Cardamom Bldg., 31 Shad Thames, SE1 (London Bridge/ Tower Hill), 020-7357 9001; fax 7357 9002; www.bengalclipper.co.uk

Residing "in a converted warehouse", this "upmarket" Indian is "worth the trek to Tower Bridge" for "subtle", "reasonably priced" cuisine (e.g. a £7.75 Sunday buffet) and, most nights, a piano player; all of this "makes up for the "impersonal decor" and "eccentric service" – the "numerous staff don't seem to make things faster."

Benihana
16 15 19 £40

37 Sackville St., W1 (Green Park/Piccadilly Circus), 020-7494 2525; fax 7494 1456
77 King's Rd., SW3 (Sloane Sq.), 020-7376 7799; fax 7376 7377
100 Avenue Rd., NW3 (Swiss Cottage), 020-7586 9508; fax 7586 6740
www.benihana.com

"Come to be entertained – the food is almost a side dish" at this "kitschy" teppanyaki trio where "theatrical" Japanese chefs "sing, dance" and perform "chop-chop" "cooking just for you"; "prices are slightly inflated" for such "simple" fare, and "the novelty does wear off after a while", "but the kids love it" and even adults "admit it's fun."

Ben's Thai   19 | 11 | 18 | £19

93 Warrington Crescent, W9 (Maida Vale/Warwick Ave.),
020-7266 3134; fax 7221 8799
"Perfect after several pints" at the "proper pub down-stairs", this "authentic" Asian serves "large portions of Thai food" declare devotees undaunted by the dingy de-cor; it's "nothing spectacular, but in an area with precious few good restaurants (Maida Vale), it's a decent standby."

Bentley's ◑   23 | 20 | 22 | £46

11-15 Swallow St., W1 (Piccadilly Circus), 020-7734 4756;
www.bentleysoysterbarandgrill.co.uk
"Just reopened by Richard Corrigan of Lindsay House fame", this veteran seafooder offers "a welcome oasis of civility in Piccadilly"; whilst the "new decor honours the old Bentley's style", there's now a "great ground-floor oys-ter bar" and an "elegant" upstairs that's equally "brilliant" for "business or romance"; both offer "scrupulously fresh shellfish", "lovingly prepared" "Traditional British fare" and "terrific staff"; some nights, "you might even spot the chef himself, shucking like a madman."

Berkeley Square, The ☒   21 | 19 | 21 | £57

7 Davies St., W1 (Bond St.), 020-7629 6993; fax 7491 9719;
www.theberkeleysquare.com
"Sophisticated" New French dishes are the main attrac-tion at this "upmarket" venue where "a quirky crowd keep the place abuzz" and the "expensive prices" explain the "many expense-account executives"; if the purple-toned "decor feels a little sterile", you can always "sit outside in summer and watch Berkeley Square pass by"; P.S. a Service score rise confirms the staff "have got much better."

Bertorelli   17 | 16 | 17 | £32

19-23 Charlotte St., W1 (Goodge St./Tottenham Court Rd.),
020-7636 4174; fax 7467 8902 ☒
11-13 Frith St., W1 (Leicester Sq./Tottenham Court Rd.),
020-7494 3491; fax 7439 9431 ◑
44A Floral St., WC2 (Covent Garden), 020-7836 3969;
fax 7836 1868 ◑
15 Mincing Ln., EC3 (Bank/Monument),
020-7283 3028 ☒
1 Plough Pl., Fetter Ln., EC4 (Chancery Ln.), 020-7842 0510;
fax 7842 0511 ☒
www.santeonline.co.uk
This bevy of "basic" "busy bistros" provides "all-around Italian food" and service that's usually "more hit than miss" and "reasonably priced" to boot; they're "not the place for something special", but at least the "well-located" Soho and Covent Garden branches will get you out "in time for the theatre" or still be open when the opera ends.

Bibendum ◐
24 | 24 | 22 | £55

Michelin House, 81 Fulham Rd., SW3 (South Kensington), 020-7581 5817; fax 7823 7925; www.bibendum.co.uk

"A feast for the eye and mouth", this "swanky", "star-studded" venture in the "dazzling", "art nouveau–style Michelin tyre building" is somewhere to "splurge" on "mighty tasty" New French cuisine, served by "generally excellent", if slightly "stiff" staff; maybe "prices are in overdrive", but most believe in this "Brompton Cross classic."

Bibendum Oyster Bar
20 | 19 | 18 | £39

Michelin House, 81 Fulham Rd., SW3 (South Kensington), 020-7589 1480; fax 7823 7925; www.bibendum.co.uk

"Too tempting to walk past", this "more affordable alternative" "downstairs from Mr. Bib's main restaurant" in Brompton Cross offers a "wide variety of oysters" "as fresh as the sea" and "cold" French bistro fare, plus a "wine list that suits the menu well"; but some feel the "good menu is compromised by the service and setting", which seems "stark."

Bierodrome
14 | 15 | 14 | £23

67 Kingsway, WC2 (Charing Cross/Holborn), 020-7242 7469; fax 7242 7493 🅰

44-48 Clapham High St., SW4 (Clapham North), 020-7720 1118; fax 7720 0288

173-174 Upper St., N1 (Highbury & Islington), 020-7226 5835; fax 7704 0632

"Transport yourself to Belgium with a steaming pot of mussels" and frites at these raucous Belgo spin-offs around town, which "get rammed to the rafters" with a "loud, annoying" "post-university crowd"; given the "surly service" and "unadventurous food", however, many "don't go for anything other than the beers" ("be forewarned – they pack a punch").

Big Easy
18 | 16 | 15 | £29

332-334 King's Rd., SW3 (Sloane Sq.), 020-7352 4071; fax 7352 0844; www.bigeasy.uk.com

"Awash with kids", this "little piece of the Bayou in Chelsea" serves up "huge potions – too big in fact" – of "American-style" "surf 'n' turf food", the "best live Southern rock music in London" (damn, but it's "loud downstairs") and a "relaxed atmosphere" that "feels like eating on the back porch of mama's home"; however, some grumble the staff take it a little too easy, moving "like molasses when it's busy."

Bistrotheque
∇ 21 | 16 | 22 | £35

23-27 Wadesdon St., E2 (Bethnal Green), 020-8983 7900; fax 8880 6433; www.bistrotheque.com

"Enter speakeasy-style through an unmarked door" in "far-away" Bethnal Green and discover "this hip spot, full of fashionistas" mingling with "models, bodybuilders and artists", all enjoying "good, unfussy" French bistro "comfort food" and staff who are "friendly without being syrupy"; in between the clientele and the "camp cabaret" acts in the "fabulous bar downstairs", there's "a whole evening's entertainment in one venue."

Bistrot 190 ◐   – – – M
Gore Hotel, 190 Queen's Gate, SW7 (Gloucester Rd./ South Kensington), 020-7584 6601; fax 7589 8127; www.gorehotel.com
A "real find" reveal reviewers who find themselves "pleasantly surprised" by the combination of "British comfort food" and "inventive" Med dishes, plus "attentive service", at this eatery with echoes of an English country house; housed inside a Kensington hotel, it's most handy for the Royal Albert Hall nearby.

Black & Blue   16 15 15 £28
215-217 Kensington Church St., W8 (Notting Hill Gate), 020-7727 0004; fax 7229 9359
90-92 Wigmore St., W1 (Bond St.), 020-7486 1912; fax 7486 1913
105 Gloucester Rd., SW7 (Gloucester Rd.), 020-7244 7666; fax 7244 9993
205-207 Haverstock Hill, NW3 (Belsize Park), 020-7443 7744; fax 7443 7744
"For a no-fuss" meal of "decent" American fare, this "reasonably cheap" "small chain" of "family steakhouses" will "fill your tummy, if not wow you" tender-hearted turf-eaters attest; but the "predictable" menu, "slow service" and somewhat "sterile" decor cause the caustic to call it "Black & Boring."

Blah! Blah! Blah! ⊠⇱   ∇ 21 10 17 £26
78 Goldhawk Rd., W12 (Goldhawk Rd.), 020-8746 1337; fax 7328 3138
Overlook "the basic decor and setting", and this "relaxed venue" in Shepherd's Bush may well "make a full-fledged vegetarian out of you" – so "inventive" and "well-balanced" is the "good-value" menu; throw in "helpful staff", and this BYO becomes a true "foodie treat."

BLAKES ◐   20 25 23 £58
Blakes Hotel, 33 Roland Gardens, SW7 (Gloucester Rd./ South Kensington), 020-7370 6701; fax 7373 0442; www.blakeshotels.com
"With chef Neville Campbell firmly in charge of the kitchen", creating a "beautiful marriage" of Asian and European cuisines on his Eclectic menu, this "dark", "romantic" "basement haunt" brings both a "seductive setting and seductive flavours" to South Ken; augmented with "attentive staff" and a cosy, private club–like bar area, it makes "a discreet place for dinner" – "at a price."

Blandford Street ⊠   18 | 17 | 17 | £38
5-7 Blandford St., W1 (Bond St.), 020-7486 9696; fax 7486 5067;
www.blandford-street.co.uk
As "hip as the proprietor is, he retains an old-fashioned
graciousness" at this "brightly lit" Marylebone venue with
"appealing decor" (revamped in 2005) that works for "unpretentious business lunches"; if the "quality" Modern
British–European menu can be "variable" in execution,
the "reasonably priced" set lunch menu has its fans.

Bleeding Heart ⊠   22 | 19 | 21 | £41
19 Greville St., EC1 (Farringdon), 020-7404 0333; fax 7831 1402
4 Bleeding Heart Yard, off Greville St., EC1 (Farringdon),
020-7242 8238; fax 7831 1402
www.bleedingheart.co.uk
"Hard to find, hard to leave", "hard to believe you're in
London" profess fans of this "characterful" "warehouse
conversion" in a "secluded" Holborn courtyard, thanks to
its "rich, gamey New French food", including "the best
wine and cheese lists", and "an army of waiters fresh off
the Eurostar" "with delectable accents and attitude"; the
"cosy bistro "upstairs is more casual" than the "dark"
dining room "in the cellar", but neither "ever fails to
please"; N.B. don't confuse the main restaurant with the
more visible Tavern on Greville Street.

Bloom's   16 | 9 | 14 | £22
130 Golders Green Rd., NW11 (Golders Green), 020-8455 1338;
fax 8455 3033; www.bloomsrestaurant.co.uk
It may "need sprucing up" (so would you, after some 80
years), but this Golders Green "cultural landmark" brings
out "the Jewish gastronomic community" for "lovely salt
beef" and other "kosher fare"; you have to "hold on to your
plate or it will be cleared before you finish" by the smile-
challenged staff, but this is "as good as deli-eating gets in
London" ("which ain't saying much" critics kvetch).

Bluebird Brasserie   17 | 19 | 17 | £41
350 King's Rd., SW3 (Sloane Sq.), 020-7559 1000; fax 7559 1111;
www.conran-restaurants.co.uk
"Overlooking King's Road", the Conran Group's "huge,
open contemporary canteen" with upscale food "store at-
tached" is "a nice place to hang out" as its outdoor seating makes it "great for celebrity sightings"; "location is
everything for this resto", though – the seafood-oriented
Modern British cuisine and service are "competent", but
both "could be better for the cost."

Bluebird Club and Dining Rooms ▽ 19 | 20 | 19 | £44
350 King's Rd., SW3 (Sloane Sq.), 020-7559 1129; fax 7559 1202;
www.conran-restaurants.co.uk
Now open to the public after "Tom Conran's makeover"
(he's the designer son of Sir Terence), this once-private

club features a smart, skylit dining room with new, art deco-esque touches; one of the "best places in Chelsea for Sunday lunch", it also makes a nice, albeit "quiet choice for an evening meal" of Traditional British–Modern European cuisine; N.B. there's a ground floor bar that remains members only.

Blue Elephant ●   22 | 24 | 20 | £43

4-6 Fulham Broadway, SW6 (Fulham Broadway), 020-7385 6595; fax 7386 7665; www.blueelephant.com

"Be swept out of busy London and into the tranquil Far East" at this "lavish, exotic" Thai with "the spectacular look" of a "tropical rainforest" ("complete with streams running between the tables") and dishes of "multidimensional tastes and textures" served by "attentive staff"; killjoys call it "kitschy", "overpriced" and "over-engineered" ("don't be surprised if a frog leaps onto your table"), but easy-going enthusiasts enjoy "an escapist experience in the heart of Fulham."

Blueprint Café   18 | 18 | 16 | £38

Design Museum, Butlers Wharf, 28 Shad Thames, SE1 (London Bridge/Tower Hill), 020-7378 7031; fax 7357 8810; www.conran-restaurants.co.uk

Time it right and you'll get to watch "Tower Bridge open" from this "cool" Thames-side cafe (a Conran Group venue) with "well-executed" Modern European fare; whilst detractors deem it "disappointing", especially the "irritating service", those "stunning views" save it for most.

Bodeans   18 | 13 | 15 | £20

10 Poland St., W1 (Oxford Circus), 020-7287 7575; fax 7287 4342
169 Clapham High St., SW4 (Clapham Common), 020-7622 4248; fax 7622 3087
4 Broadway Chambers, SW6 (Fulham Broadway), 020-7610 0440
www.bodeansbbq.com

Dang if it ain't "just missin' a cowboy and his lasso" to complete the "camp" Western "diner-style" digs at these three "slices of the U.S." servin' up some mighty "authentic American" BBQ to "eager expats"; maybe this "rib-sticking" stuff is "not the best, but it's the quantity that counts" (e.g. the Sunday–Tuesday 'Pig-out for a Tenner'), and the Yank "sporting games playing on the plasmas" will distract from the "erratic service."

Boisdale ⊠   19 | 18 | 18 | £44

13 Eccleston St., SW1 (Victoria), 020-7730 6922; fax 7730 0548
Swedeland Ct., 202 Bishopsgate, EC2 (Liverpool St.), 020-7283 1763; fax 7283 1664
www.boisdale.co.uk

"Not for fainthearted, fragile flowers", this tartan-clad, "most masculine" duo in Victoria and the City offer "hearty,

Traditional" British–Scottish fare alongside "gallons of whiskies" (170 in fact) and a "well-stocked humidor"; the sensitive shrink from the "too-expensive" bills and the "boorish, hooray-Henry crowd that spoil" things – though the "cool" "live jazz playing" compensates on weeknights.

Bombay Bicycle Club   19 | 16 | 17 | £30

128 Holland Park Ave., W11 (Holland Park), 020-7727 7335; fax 7727 7305
95 Nightingale Ln., SW12 (Clapham South), 020-8673 6217; fax 8673 9100
3A Downshire Hill, NW3 (Hampstead), 020-7435 3544; fax 7794 3367
www.thebombaybicycleclub.co.uk

This "emerging chain" of colonial-styled Indians (including the 21-year-old original in Clapham's "nappy valley") serves "inventive, yet reassuringly familiar" dishes from a "varied menu"; even foes who find it "marred by slow service" say their "posh takeaways" are "good value", especially when "delivered to your door."

Bombay Brasserie ●   22 | 23 | 21 | £39

Courtfield Rd., SW7 (Gloucester Rd.), 020-7370 4040; fax 7835 1669; www.bombaybrasserielondon.com

"The Raj lives on (in a good way)" at this "worldly", "expensive" South Ken venue "with an ambience right out of colonial India" and a menu that manages to cater to "purist and fashionable [tastes] at the same time"; however, rebels feel that cuisinewise, this vet's now "behind the curve", catering "exclusively to tourist-land" and "suits who don't like Indian" fare; N.B. the advent of a new chef post-*Survey* may freshen things up.

Bonds   ▽ 21 | 22 | 18 | £49

Threadneedles Hotel, 5 Threadneedle St., EC2 (Bank), 020-7657 8088; fax 7657 8100; www.theetoncollection.com

"Bowlers and black umbrellas are at home" at this elegant dining room in the boutique-y Threadneedles Hotel in the heart of the City; taking over from Tom Ilic, new chef Barry Tonks ensures an "enjoyable dining experience" on New French fare that suits the suits' "discerning palates"; N.B. breakfast only on weekends.

Books for Cooks 🗷   23 | 19 | 18 | £18

4 Blenheim Crescent, W11 (Ladbroke Grove/Notting Hill Gate), 020-7221 1992; fax 7221 1517; www.booksforcooks.com

"Sit down and eat even if you're not hungry" at the back of a "sweet little bookshop" near Portobello Road, where a "test kitchen" prepares "fresh, zingy" Eclectic dishes from recipes gleaned from the "cookbooks on display"; although the "place is too cramped to be welcoming", "rock-bottom prices" and "charming" staff make it "a must for foodies."

Bountiful Cow ☒

— | — | — | M

51 Eagle St., WC1 (Holborn), 020-7404 0200

Decorated with "antique movie posters about cows and beef", TV chef/pub owner "Roxy Beaujolais' latest endeavour" leaves little doubt about the emphasis on the Modern European menu – its "wonderful steaks" and other "great charbroiled" meats, all rather "reasonably priced"; the "lively setting" in a discreet Holborn street features "funky, modern" furnishings and an open kitchen.

Boxwood Café

21 | 20 | 20 | £54

Berkeley Hotel, Wilton Pl., SW1 (Knightsbridge), 020-7235 1010; fax 7235 1011; www.gordonramsay.com

How "refreshing to enter a Gordon Ramsay establishment without having to call months in advance" attest advocates of this "toned-down dining [room] in the Berkeley", where the Modern British menu includes "interesting", if occasionally "over-engineered", interpretations of home cooking; foes fume "it's too expensive for 'cafe' food" – but then, this is "not an actual cafe, and wouldn't appreciate you mistaking it for one" (indeed, those "in unsuitable attire" may get cold looks from the otherwise "likeable staff").

Brackenbury, The

▽ 19 | 14 | 19 | £34

129-131 Brackenbury Rd., W6 (Goldhawk Rd./Hammersmith), 020-8748 0107; fax 8748 6159

"An informal pleasure", this "established" "neighbourhood bistro" has been offering Hammersmith-ites Modern European meals for nearly two decades; and whilst some suggest it "needs to raise its game a bit further", "the lunch menu's such a good deal, it's probably worth going" out there just "to have the friendly staff serve it to you."

Bradley's

▽ 22 | 17 | 16 | £48

25 Winchester Rd., NW3 (Swiss Cottage), 020-7722 3457; fax 7435 1392

"Right around the corner" from Swiss Cottage tube station is this intimate eatery that "should be better known" for its "consistently good" Classic French–Modern British fare, including some "superb seafood"; but what fans feel is an "overlooked gem", opponents opine is "overpriced, and overstayed its welcome" after 15 years.

Brasserie Roux ●

20 | 18 | 18 | £39

Sofitel St. James London, 8 Pall Mall, SW1 (Piccadilly Circus), 020-7968 2900; fax 7389 7647; www.sofitelstjames.com

"Unfailingly reliable", "honest bourgeois food" from an Albert Roux–inspired menu draws disciples to this "hugely spacious" French brasserie in a St. James's hotel; despite the rooster-themed decor ("made me hungry for chicken"), carpers criticise the "characterless surroundings" – but you won't roux the day you try the "amazingly low-priced pre-theatre menu."

Brasserie St. Quentin
19 | 18 | 19 | £36

243 Brompton Rd., SW3 (Knightsbridge/South Kensington), 020-7589 8005; fax 7584 6064; www.brasseriestquentin.co.uk

"Every neighbourhood should have one": a "typical Paris brasserie (only a bit posher)", serving a "lovingly pre-pared" "classic menu" that, if "unlikely to surprise, [won't] let one down" either; a "recent tarting-up" has "preserved the place's comfortable Frenchness"; so, no surprise that "the same people always fill" this haunt "in walking distance of Harrods."

Brian Turner Mayfair ⊠
21 | 19 | 22 | £53

Millennium Hotel Mayfair, 44 Grosvenor Sq., W1 (Bond St./Green Park), 020-7596 3444; fax 7596 3443; www.millenniumhotels.com

"Humorous Yorkshireman", "fantastic chef" and TV per-sonality "Brian Turner delivers (at least in spirit)" some "sumptuous" Traditional British cuisine at this "sleek" ho-tel dining room with "good, discreet service"; and if the "decor does not do justice to the food" and the "food does not live up to other fine Mayfair" places, there's always the 150-label-long wine list to seek refuge in.

Brinkley's
∇ 15 | 17 | 20 | £33

47 Hollywood Rd., SW10 (Earl's Court/South Kensington), 020-7351 1683; fax 7376 5083; www.brinkleys.com

"A friendly, come-back-again feel" characterises this "ca-sual", "cheerful Chelsea" corner; and if critics "can't fig-ure out why it's so busy" – after all, the Modern British menu's "nothing special" – they need look no further than the "wines at retail prices"; P.S. "ask for the garden in summer" or even winter (it's heated).

Browns
16 | 17 | 16 | £30

47 Maddox St., W1 (Bond St./Oxford Circus), 020-7491 4565; fax 7497 4564
82-84 St. Martin's Ln., WC2 (Leicester Sq.), 020-7497 5050; fax 7497 5005
Shad Thames, SE1 (London Bridge), 020-7378 1700; fax 7378 7468
Hertsmere Rd., E14 (Canary Wharf/West India Quay), 020-7987 9777; fax 7537 1341
8 Old Jewry, EC2 (Bank), 020-7606 6677; fax 7600 5359 ⊠
9 Islington Green, N1 (Angel), 020-7226 2555; fax 7359 7306
www.browns-restaurants.com

"Good and solid for eating, if not dining", these "busy" "buzzy" haunts around town offer Traditional British fare (like the signature steak and Guinness pie) that suits those "on a budget, or families"; foes feel "the formula's getting tired" and the "staff often seem to simply not care", but it's a "nice fall-back option" for most.

BRUNELLO
20 | 26 | 20 | £62

*Baglioni, 60 Hyde Park Gate, SW7 (Gloucester Rd./
High St. Kensington), 020-7368 5900; fax 7368 5701;
www.baglionihotellondon.com*

"Love it or hate it", the "contemporary" gold-leafed decor of
this Kensington hotel dining room is definitely "impressive" –
and offers a "spacious", dramatic canvas for chef Stefano
Stecca's "authentic" "modern Italian food", "served with
style"; it "costs the earth, but it's heavenly" fun to "people-
watch" "the celebrities staying in the Baglioni."

Builders Arms
18 | 16 | 16 | £24

*13 Britten St., SW3 (Sloane Sq./South Kensington),
020-7349 9040; fax 7351 3181; www.geronimo-inns.co.uk*

"As cosy and comfortable as someone's living room", this
"shabby-chic" Chelsea-ite attracts an "attractive young
crowd", and even though it's "more of a lounge than a
place to eat", the Traditional British "posh pub" grub
"never disappoints"; what does aggravate, though, is the
"smoky atmosphere" (it'll be so "great when smoking is
stopped in 2007").

Bull, The
– | – | – | E

*13 North Hill, N6 (Highgate), 0845-456 5033; fax 0845 456 5034;
www.inthebull.biz*

"A great addition to the north London scene" – and chancing
"a location that has spelt death for many a restaurant" – is
this "homely" Highgate yearling; in pub premises dating
back to 1765, it comprises a "comfortable" ground-floor
dining room with "a wide variety" of Modern European
dishes (especially French), and relaxed first-floor bar with
floor-to-ceiling windows and an American pool table.

Buona Sera ◐
17 | 15 | 19 | £23

*289A King's Rd., SW3 (Sloane Sq.), 020-7352 8827; fax 7352 8827
22-26 Northcote Rd., SW11 (Clapham Junction B.R.),
020-7228 9925; fax 7228 1114*

Diners and "servers require special qualifications and balance" to "climb the ladders" to get to the "double-decker
tables" at these "cheerful" "little Italian bistros" in
Chelsea and Battersea; admittedly, many "go for the experience more than the food", a "steady", "if dull", selection
of "cheap" pizzas, pastas et al.

BUSABA EATHAI
21 | 19 | 16 | £20

*8-13 Bird St., W1 (Bond St.), 020-7518 8080
106-110 Wardour St., W1 (Piccadilly Circus/Tottenham Court Rd.),
020-7255 8686
22 Store St., WC1 (Goodge St.), 020-7299 7900; fax 7299 7909*

Those lines "can be long, but it's worth the wait" to get into
this "lively" Thai trio, whose "fantastically valued", "terrif-
ically fresh" and "delectably spicy" dishes "allow no grain
of rice to go uneaten"; most find the incense and dark-

wood decor "calming" and the communal tables conducive to "good conversation"; "the weak point" is the service, se hurried that the outside "queue can often take longer than the staff will allow for the meal!"

Butlers Wharf Chop House   19 | 18 | 19 | £40
*Butlers Wharf Bldg., 36E Shad Thames, SE1 (London Bridge Tower Hill), 020-7403 3403; fax 7940 1855;
www.conran-restaurants.co.uk*
"The best thing about" this Conran Group chophouse is its "pleasant" location "overlooking Tower Bridge", with a Thames-side terrace for "watching the world go by"; oth erwise, it's "ok", offering "standard" "but tasty Traditiona British favourites" that are a "reliable business-mea choice", if rather "expensive" for those not on expenses.

Café Boheme ●   19 | 18 | 17 | £27
13-17 Old Compton St., W1 (Leicester Sq./Tottenham Court Rd.) 020-7734 0623; fax 7434 3775; www.cafeboheme.co.uk
"A long-standing favourite of media types" that's "always crowded" with a "cosmopolitan" crew "hanging out", thi "lively" Soho spot sports "a bohemian attitude"; there may be "no surprises" in the "ample portions" of "more-than average" French brasserie fare, but there is an unusual for-London late-might menu that's offered until 2:30 AM P.S. "if you get a table outside in summer, hold on to it."

Café des Amis ●▨   18 | 16 | 16 | £34
11-14 Hanover Pl., WC2 (Covent Garden), 020-7379 3444; fax 7379 9124; www.cafedesamis.co.uk
It's "hard to find" down an alley, but this "wonderful bolt hole away from the crowds of Covent Garden" is an easy going bistro that's "convenient" for "a quick mea ahead of the opera" or theatre; "friendly waiters" serv "huge portions" of "reliable" New French cuisine in "comfortable" bi-level dining room, and there's a "lovel bar below" in the basement.

Café Fish   18 | 13 | 17 | £29
36-40 Rupert St., W1 (Leicester Sq./Piccadilly Circus), 020-7287 8989; fax 7287 8400; www.santeonline.co.uk
There's a "vintage canteen atmosphere" and "fish sho ambience" of tiles and tables at this "casual" Soho sea fooder where "all types" of fin fare pop up on the "tried, true Traditional British menu; the unimpressed say it's "just ok and object to the "loud piano player", but all agree it's in "great location for Shaftsbury Avenue theatres."

Café Japan   24 | 10 | 20 | £25
626 Finchley Rd., NW11 (Golders Green), 020-8455 6854; fax 8455 6854
"Wonderful sushi" and other "quality Japanese" fare are th highlights on a "reasonably priced" menu that "won't der the budget" at this Golders Green Asian; it's a "cramped

"hole-in-the-wall", but the "real-deal" food "could be right out of Tokyo"; N.B. lunch is weekends- and cash-only.

Café Lazeez ◑   17 | 16 | 16 | £30
21 Dean St., W1 (Leicester Sq./Tottenham Court Rd.),
020-7434 9393; fax 7434 0022 🖾
93-95 Old Brompton Rd., SW7 (Gloucester Rd./South Kensington),
020-7581 9993; fax 7581 8200
www.cafelazeez.com
Offering a "contemporary, healthy take on Indian food" and an "evolved" menu that goes beyond "the usual suspects", these "noisy", informal curry houses in Soho (with "edgy celebs") and South Ken (live music Wednesday–Saturday) are "good standbys" that get "crowded with beautiful young things" enjoying the late drinking hours; still, a "disappointed" handful think the "average" fare "lacks finesse."

Cafe Med   19 | 15 | 17 | £26
21 Loudoun Rd., NW8 (St. John's Wood), 020-7625 1222 ◑
370 St. John St., EC1 (Angel), 020-7278 1199
These "thoroughly decent" casual chain links in St. John's Wood and Angel are "good values" with "always solid" Eclectic-Med offerings ("the homemade chips are to die for"); if a few claim they're "nothing special", more maintain that they make for a "great family place on Sundays."

Cafe Pacifico ◑   18 | 15 | 16 | £25
5 Langley St., WC2 (Covent Garden), 020-7379 7728;
fax 7379 5933; www.cafepacifico-laperla.com
It's "Cabo San London" at this "still-rocking" Covent Garden cantina with "good, if not outstanding" Tex-Mex fare that manages to "pleasantly surprise" on occasion; but even proponents who "are in a party frame of mind" warn of the "killer tequilas" fuelling margaritas that might "make you not remember the night."

Café Rouge   14 | 15 | 14 | £24
227-229 Chiswick High Rd., W4 (Chiswick Park), 020-8742 7447;
fax 8742 7557
15 Frith St., W1 (Tottenham Court Rd.), 020-7437 4307;
fax 7437 4442
98-100 Shepherd's Bush Rd., W6 (Shepherd's Bush),
020-7602 7732; fax 7603 7710
34 Wellington St., WC2 (Covent Garden), 020-7836 0998;
fax 7497 0738
40 Abbeville Rd., SW4 (Clapham South), 020-8673 3399;
fax 8673 2299
27-31 Basil St., SW3 (Knightsbridge), 020-7584 2345;
fax 7584 4253
200 Putney Bridge Rd., SW15 (Putney Bridge), 020-8788 4257
10 Cabot Sq., 29-35 Mackenzie Walk, E14 (Canary Wharf),
020-7537 9696; fax 7987 1232

(continued)

(continued)

Café Rouge
6-7 South Grove, N6 (Highgate), 020-8342 9797
120 St. John's Wood High St., NW8 (St. John's Wood),
020-7722 8366; fax 7483 1015
www.caferouge.co.uk
Additional locations throughout London.
Fans of these "good-value", family-friendly (there's crayons and games for kids) bistros say they serve "solid fare with a European spin" and are ok for a "spur-of-the-moment" bite; but critics counter this "formulaic" "faux French" "chain acts more like a chain gang" hanging around "every London corner" with "poor food" and "painfully slow service."

Café Spice Namasté ☒   23 | 17 | 19 | £36
16 Prescot St., E1 (Aldgate/Tower Hill), 020-7488 9242;
fax 7488 9339; www.cafespice.co.uk
"Boy, can they cook" at chef-owner Cyrus Todiwala's "festive", "funky" eatery "hidden away" near Tower Bridge, where the "drop-dead" Indian menu offers "excellent, innovative" choices; service is "slow", but "helpful", and even if it's been "surpassed by more exciting" newcomers, at least that makes it "stupidly easy to get a table on weekends."

Caldesi ☒   22 | 18 | 21 | £39
15-17 Marylebone Ln., W1 (Bond St.), 020-7935 9226;
fax 7935 9228; www.caldesi.com
"Authentic Tuscan cuisine" like "mama used to make", a "well-priced wine list" that "reflects knowledge of the region" and "lovely service" in a "cosy atmosphere" make this Marylebone trattoria a "joy"; P.S. just up the street the owners run a small bistro, Café Caldesi, as well as Cucina Cladesi, where they share their culinary secrets in "popular cookery classes."

Cambio de Tercio ◕   23 | 17 | 20 | £43
163 Old Brompton Rd., SW5 (Gloucester Rd./South Kensington),
020-7244 8970; fax 7373 8817; www.cambiodetercio.co.uk
A South Ken "gem not to be missed", this "impressive Spanish oasis" with a "lively" atmosphere offers "authentic", "quality" Iberian fare "with great attention to detail, flavour and presentation" – and a "wine list longer than the Yellow Pages"; if some claim it "has its faults" – "nose bleedingly expensive", service with "too much attitude" – most still label it a "winner"; P.S. try Tendido Cero, their tapas bar across the road, for a "cheaper option."

Camden Brasserie   ▽ 19 | 15 | 19 | £30
9-11 Jamestown Rd., NW1 (Camden Town), 020-7482 2114;
fax 7482 2777; www.camdenbrasserie.co.uk
Nearing its 25th anniversary, this "good Camden choice" has its share of regulars who "wolf down" the "simple

well-executed menu" of midpriced "pub-type" Modern European fare; whilst some claim the unprepossessing premises "lack ambience", the "helpful, family-friendly staff" are appreciated.

Camerino ⊠   ▽ 20 17 23 £41
16 Percy St., W1 (Tottenham Court Rd.), 020-7637 9900; fax 7637 9696; www.camerinorestaurant.com
Expect a "warm welcome", "great service" and a modern Italian menu at this little-known Fitzrovia spot with "decor reminiscent of Matisse drawings"; though some say it "lacks the wow factor for the price", others find "excellent value" in the prix fixe options at lunch and for theatregoers; N.B. it used to be named after owner Paolo Boschi, but now it bears the moniker of his birthplace.

Cantaloupe ⊠   ▽ 17 12 13 £23
35-42 Charlotte Rd., EC2 (Old St.), 020-7729 5566; fax 7613 4111; www.cantaloupe.co.uk
Staffed by "laid-back", "attractive waiters", this "cool", "lively" restaurant/bar is "Hox-ditch to the bone" (as in Hoxton and Shoreditch), and even though its "decor and image have aged" a bit, there's a "solid" Mediterranean-meets-mambo menu that extends to "surprisingly good bar bites"; the main gripe: "horrid when it's overcrowded with locals out drinking"; N.B. DJs hold court Thursday–Sunday.

Canteen   23 18 21 £30
2 Crispin Pl., E1 (Liverpool St.), 0845-686 1122; fax 5686 1144; www.canteen.co.uk
"Funky", "fresh", "what a find!" – the F-words fly in diners' reviews of this "promising newcomer to Spitalfields Market" with a "keenly priced", "down-to-earth" menu whose "simple descriptions don't do justice" to the "well-cooked Traditional British fare"; the only bad F-word is "fellow diners": sitting at long, communal benches "is a pain" that "doesn't encourage lingering."

Cantina del Ponte   16 13 14 £33
Butlers Wharf Bldg., 36C Shad Thames, SE1 (London Bridge/ Tower Hill), 020-7403 5403; fax 7940 1845; www.conran-restaurants.co.uk
Cited by some as the "best value of the Conrans", this "good enough" Butlers Wharf canteen with "great views of Tower Bridge" offers Italian basics (including wood-fired oven pizzas) and a "decent wine list"; yet the "formula is disappointing" to others, who say it's "not cheap" and prefer "better" options that are "only a few yards away."

Cantina Vinopolis   17 18 19 £39
Vinopolis Museum, 1 Bank End, SE1 (London Bridge), 020-7940 8333; fax 7940 8334; www.cantinavinopolis.com
Oenophilia runs rampant among the "knowledgeable-without-being-overbearing" staff at this "good museum

eatery", part of the eponymous 2.5-acre South Bank wine attraction under a Victorian railway viaduct (there's an "interesting thunder of trains overhead"); whilst the "bible-sized" vino list, with "numerous by-the-glass" options, is more interesting than the "generous portions" of Eclectic-Med fare, the place is "fun for groups" and "excellent for entertaining clients" (less so for wooing "the other half").

Canyon

| 17 | 22 | 13 | £37 |

Tow Path, Riverside, near Richmond Bridge, Richmond (Richmond), 020-8948 2944; fax 8948 2945

"On a fine day in summer", "you can't beat" this "lovely" Thames-side perch for "alfresco dining" just "minutes from Richmond Bridge"; still, some say it's a "shame" the "nothing-special" Modern European menu and "poor service" from the "not-well-trained" staff "don't live up" to the "fantastic location."

CAPITAL RESTAURANT, THE

| 26 | 21 | 26 | £78 |

The Capital Hotel, 22-24 Basil St., SW3 (Knightsbridge), 020-7591 1202; fax 7225 0011; www.capitalhotel.co.uk

Chef Eric Chavot's "creative attention to detail" results in "revelatory" New French cuisine that's "in another stratosphere" at this "elegant" Knightsbridge hotel dining room; "polished, professional service" and a "sommelier willing to spend time discussing the wines" add to the "feeling of exclusivity"; on the flip side, some charge that "the bill is Capital punishment", and a few still suggest "the room needs a fresher look" (despite a late-2004 spruce-up).

Caraffini ●🅩

| 21 | 16 | 21 | £40 |

61-63 Lower Sloane St., SW1 (Sloane Sq.), 020-7259 0235; fax 7259 0236; www.caraffini.co.uk

This "comforting", "old-line" Lower Sloane trattoria where "everyone is a local but treated like a king" (and where Signor Caraffini "makes every girl feel like a million dollars") is known for "excellent", "authentic" Northern Italian standards; and whilst critics contend it's "cramped" and it "doesn't live up to the price", defenders insist it's "always busy" and "always accommodating"; P.S. in summer you can "dine alfresco on the expansive terrace."

Caravaggio 🅩

| 17 | 13 | 15 | £42 |

107-112 Leadenhall St., EC3 (Bank/Monument), 020-7626 6206; fax 7626 8108; www.etruscagroup.co.uk

Serving "reliable" and "consistently good Italian" fare this "large", "noisy" City haunt is "suited for most occasions except a romantic night out"; but foes froth that it's "ridiculously expensive for what it is" (even by Square Mile standards) and has the "nothing-special" "decor of a Holiday Inn"; N.B. food is also served at the bar.

CARLUCCIO'S CAFFE 18 | 14 | 15 | £23
3-5 Barrett St., W1 (Bond St.), 020-7935 5927; fax 7487 5436
Fenwick Dept. Store, downstairs, New Bond St., W1 (Bond St.),
020-7629 0699; fax 7493 0069
5-6 The Green, W5 (Ealing Broadway), 020-8566 4458;
fax 8840 8566
8 Market Pl., W1 (Oxford Circus), 020-7636 2228; fax 7636 9650
St. Christopher's Pl., W1 (Bond St.), 020-7935 5927
236 Fulham Rd., SW10 (Fulham Broadway), 020-7376 5960;
fax 7376 3698
Putney Wharf, SW15 (Putney Bridge), 020-8789 0591;
fax 8789 8360
Reuters Plaza, 2 Nash Ct., E14 (Canary Wharf), 020-7719 1749;
fax 7513 1197
12 West Smithfield, EC1 (Farringdon), 020-7329 5904; fax 7248 5981
305-307 Upper St., N1 (Angel/Highbury & Islington),
020-7359 8167; fax 7354 9196
www.carluccios.com
Additional locations throughout London
"Brash, loud" and "ubiquitous", this "love-it-or-hate-it"
chain (26 links at last count) of mogul-chef Antonio
Carluccio's "clean, white" all-day Italian cafes has a "de-
pendably executed" "no-frills" menu, supplemented by
"great prices" and a "good takeaway deli counter"; the
"inconsistent" and "lackadaisical" staff draw ire, but in the
main, this "relaxed", "easy place" lives up to the patron's
"motto of MOF MOF – minimum of fuss, maximum of flavour."

Carpaccio ●☒ 19 | 17 | 18 | £45
4 Sydney St., SW3 (South Kensington), 020-7352 3433;
www.carpaccio.uk.com
This "popular" Chelsea Italian hipster draws a "braying",
"good-looking crowd" with a setting "right out of a Fellini
film", a "sophisticated menu" (featuring, "unsurprisingly, a
great selection of carpaccio") and "solid wine list"; although the omnipresent owner, Guido Campigotta, is a
master at "keeping up the buzz", almost all complain about
bills that are "way too expensive."

Casale Franco ● ▽ 21 | 14 | 18 | £34
134-137 Upper St., N1 (Angel/Highbury & Islington),
020-7226 8994; fax 7359 1114
"A real local institution", this moderately priced, "quirky"
Islington Italian with theatrical decor and "friendly staff"
serves "consistently good", "honest" cooking (pizza is a
house speciality), which is considered "rare on Upper
Street"; P.S. "the alfresco dining is charming."

Cecconi's ● 22 | 20 | 21 | £54
5A Burlington Gardens, W1 (Green Park/Piccadilly Circus),
020-7434 1500; fax 7434 2020; www.cecconis.co.uk
Still "oozing money and power" after being "updated" by
new owner Nick Jones of Soho House fame, this "ele-

gant", "upscale", "outrageously delicious" Mayfair Italian is now open all day; whilst it attracts a "corporate crowd during lunch" and a "trendy pack in the evenings", it remains surprisingly "child-friendly"; P.S. whether it's "too noisy" or pleasantly "buzzy", expect an earful either way.

CHAMPOR-CHAMPOR Ⓩ 23 | 26 | 22 | £40
62-64 Weston St., SE1 (London Bridge), 020-7403 4600;
www.champor-champor.com
Expect a "wake-up call to all the senses" at this "gem" near London Bridge, where the "exceptional" Malay-Asian cuisine runs from the "inventive" (steamed peanut salsa) to the "exotic" (crocodile tail), and the "enticing", "romantic" setting includes "original artefacts" and a balcony loveseat with a "waiter's bell"; N.B. the name translates loosely to 'mix and match' – as diners do with options on the two- and three-course menus.

Chancery, The Ⓩ ▽ 23 | 20 | 23 | £47
9 Cursitor St., EC4 (Chancery Lane), 020-7831 4000;
fax 7831 4002; www.thechancery.co.uk
This unassuming weekday Holborn "hideaway" with floor-to-ceiling windows, a sibling to the Clerkenwell Dining Room, is considered "a treat" in some books for its Modern European menu featuring "strong", "good-quality" choices; a "well-matched" wine list makes up for its brevity with "some comparative bargains."

Chelsea Bun ◑ 20 | 9 | 16 | £14
Limerstone St., SW10 (Sloane Sq./Earl's Court), 020-7352 3635;
fax 7376 5158; www.chelseabun.co.uk
It has "no airs, graces" or "frills", but this "homey" Chelsea cafe is "perfect for those tender mornings" "after the night before" when a huge breakfast "fry up" is a medical necessity; whilst the "decent" Traditional Brit "comfort food" served by "friendly waitresses" is "not too greasy", clearly "if you're after healthy, this is not the place to go!"

Cheyne Walk Brasserie 20 | 19 | 18 | £45
50 Cheyne Walk, SW3 (Sloane Sq./South Kensington),
020-7376 8787; fax 7376 5878; www.cheynewalkbrasserie.com
"There may be a kitchen out back, but all the action" is on a "big BBQ fire in the middle" of this "warm, welcoming" Chelsea Embankment brasserie where "excellent meats and fish" are put to flame; whilst the grub is "pricey", and the "über-French staff may rub some the wrong way", the place attracts a "glam" crowd; N.B. there's also a comfy salon/cigar bar upstairs with a fireplace and river views.

CHEZ BRUCE 27 | 21 | 24 | £54
2 Bellevue Rd., SW17 (Balham/Wandsworth Common B. R.),
020-8672 0114; fax 8767 6648; www.chezbruce.co.uk
"Fight for a table" at Nigel Platts-Martin and Bruce Poole's "perfect place" in, "who would have believed,

Wandsworth" – as in "worth travelling across town for"; the faithful make the pilgrimage for an "extraordinary" Modern British prix fixe menu that "creates nearly religious sensations", plus a "stunning wine list", all overseen by "welcoming", "knowledgeable" staff; nitpickers grouse that it's "overrated" and "not worth the splurge", but the majority rave this "fabulous", "first-rate" spot has "star quality."

CHEZ GÉRARD   18 | 16 | 16 | £33

8 Charlotte St., W1 (Goodge St./Tottenham Court Rd.), 020-7636 4975; fax 7637 4564 ◑
31 Dover St., W1 (Green Park), 020-7499 8171; fax 7491 3818 ◑
119 Chancery Ln., WC2 (Chancery Ln.), 020-7405 0290; fax 7242 2649 ☒
Opera Terrace, The Market, 1st fl., 45 E. Terrace, WC2 (Covent Garden), 020-7379 0666; fax 7497 9060 ◑
Thistle Hotel, 101 Buckingham Palace Rd., SW1 (Victoria), 020-7868 6249; fax 7976 6073
9 Belvedere Rd., SE1 (Waterloo), 020-7202 8470; fax 7202 8474
64 Bishopsgate, EC2 (Bank/Liverpool St.), 020-7588 1200; fax 7588 1122 ☒
14 Trinity Sq., EC3 (Tower Hill), 020-7480 5500; fax 7480 5588 ☒
1 Watling St., EC4 (Mansion House/St. Paul's), 020-7213 0540; fax 7213 0541 ☒
www.santeonline.co.uk

"For a quick steak frites", fans flock to this "bustling" chain noted for its "reliable-rather-than-exciting" but "perfectly seasoned" fare *français*; whilst boohooers bash the "middle-of-the-road" concept as "a tired formula" with "little imagination", supporters say it's a "solid" "standby" for a "good-value" business lunch or "pre-theatre nosh"; P.S. there's an especially "lovely location" within the Covent Garden Opera House.

Chez Kristof ◑   ∇ 22 | 21 | 21 | £35

111 Hammersmith Grove, W6 (Hammersmith), 020-8741 1177; fax 8846 3750; www.chezkristof.co.uk

A "solid place for a date", this "classy" "piece of Paris in Hammersmith" (part of the Wòdka and Baltic family) is "trying hard", with "accommodating, friendly staff" and an "interesting" country French *carte du jour*, "superb value" prix fixe picks, an "easy-to-park" locale and Sunday kids' movies downstairs make it family-friendly too; N.B. the adjacent deli serves an all-day cafe menu, including breakfast until 3 PM.

Chiang Mai   22 | 15 | 18 | £25

48 Frith St., W1 (Leicester Sq./Tottenham Court Rd.), 020-7437 7444; fax 7287 2255

"Your tummy will thank you" for dining at this Soho stalwart as there's a "great variety" of "excellent", "authentic" Thai cuisine, including options that are "good for vegetarians"; whilst stylists snip that the "simple", "bland decor" is in "need of a face-lift", deal-seekers forgive the face of any place that's "inexpensive by local standards."

China Tang ●
19 | 23 | 18 | £67

Dorchester Hotel, 53 Park Ln., W1 (Hyde Park Corner/ Marble Arch), 020-7629 9988; www.dorchesterhotel.com

Global-mogul David Tang's "stunning", "glamourous" new downstairs den – think Shanghai art deco – in Mayfair's Dorchester Hotel is a "see-and-be-seen" scene; the VIP-studded set who grace the space for "fabulous dim sum" and "luxurious Chinese food" at "astronomical prices" seem oh-so-pleased, but those who wonder "what all the hype is about" (or wisecrack that "you can't eat celebrity sightings!") taunt "no Tangk you."

Chinese Experience
19 | 15 | 16 | £21

118-120 Shaftesbury Ave., W1 (Leicester Sq.), 020-7437 0377; fax 7437 0378; www.chineseexperience.com

"Slightly funkier than your average dim sum parlour", this "clean, stark" and "buzzy" "alternative to grotty Chinatown holes" has one of the area's "best-value" selections of "authentic", "inventive" Asian cuisine; fans like the "bargain basement" set menus ("for those who can't decide") and "quick" service, making it a "great location for pre- or post-theatre" dining.

Chor Bizarre
22 | 21 | 19 | £36

16 Albemarle St., W1 (Green Park), 020-7629 9802; fax 7493 7756; www.chorbizarre.com

Although the name translates to 'thieves' market', fans honour this "authentic" Mayfair Indian for its "intriguing, subtle" dishes that can be enjoyed "without taking a second mortgage"; the "exotic", "ethnic decor" (think "funky raj") is crammed with antiques and "amusing" artefacts, many of which "happen to be for sale"; N.B. Chai Bazaar, a tea service, is offered in the afternoons.

Chowki Bar & Restaurant ●
21 | 17 | 18 | £23

2-3 Denman St., W1 (Piccadilly Circus), 020-7439 1330; fax 7287 5919; www.chowki.com

A "properly spicy" salmagundi of "innovative", "excellent-quality" regional Indian dishes makes this "pre- or post-theatre" Piccadilly pick "a joy"; if non-contortionists carp about "awkward" seating and "little sofas without backrests", most diners seem comfortable with how far their pounds stretch at this "unbeatable value."

Christopher's Covent Garden ●
19 | 18 | 18 | £37

18 Wellington St., WC2 (Covent Garden), 020-7240 4222; fax 7240 3357; www.christophersgrill.com

The "grand" marble staircase leads up to this "lively" Covent Garden contender in "stylish" Victorian digs; but whilst admirers say the "well-rounded" menu of "upmarket American" surf 'n' turf fare makes it a "sensible" choice for a "business or pre-theatre meal", detractors dish the "inattentive service" and lament the "common food"; N.B. ratings may not reflect a recent revamp, which included the addition of a martini bar.

Chuen Cheng Ku ◐   20 | 9 | 14 | £23
17 Wardour St., W1 (Leicester Sq./Piccadilly Circus), 020-7437 1398; fax 7434 0533; www.chuenchengku.co.uk
Fans "love" the all-day dim sum and then some ("chicken's feet, anyone?") at this inexpensive "Chinatown institution" where "Hong Kong–style" trolley service is a "great attraction" ("kids love it"); just be prepared for "no-nonsense, no-smiles" waiters, "grim surroundings" and lots of company: the "always-crowded" spot seats 400.

Churchill Arms   22 | 15 | 16 | £14
119 Kensington Church St., W8 (High St. Kensington/ Notting Hill Gate), 020-7727 4242; www.fullers.co.uk
With "proper lagers and ales in front and spicy, delicious food in back", this "always-packed" Notting Hill "bargain" is the proverbial "good place to Thai one on"; whilst "perfunctory" service can annoy, the main gripe is "needing to reserve a week in advance for pub food – who ever heard of that?"; N.B. it's noted for its flowers – and for celebrating its namesake's birthday each year.

Chutney Mary ◐   23 | 23 | 22 | £43
535 King's Rd., SW10 (Fulham Broadway), 020-7351 3113; fax 7351 7694; www.realindianfood.com
Loyalists label this "ab-fab" Punjab near Chelsea Harbour a "feast for the senses", from the "delectable", "innovative", Pan-Indian cuisine that reveals "traces of the British empire" to the "airy", "elegant" interior featuring 19th-century sepia etchings; if trendologists dig that "this vein was mined years ago", defenders contend that their "still great" "favourite" is "definitely worth another visit", especially for the "wonderful jazz brunch" on Sunday.

Chutney's   ∇ 24 | 16 | 19 | £25
124 Drummond St., NW1 (Euston Sq.), 020-7388 0604; fax 7209 0627
After nearly a quarter-century, this unprepossessing yet "still reliable" Indian vegetarian in Euston is "consistent beyond many in the area"; it's particularly valued for its lunch buffet: costing little more than "a one-day bus pass", it just might be "London's best bargain"; N.B. takeaway is only available after 6 PM Monday–Saturday.

Cicada ⌧   18 | 18 | 16 | £30
132-136 St. John St., EC1 (Farringdon), 020-7608 1550; fax 7608 1551; www.cicada.nu
It's no occident that Will Ricker's original Asian fusion joint in London – before e&o or Eight Over Eight – is considered a "funky" "old favourite" that "never goes out of fashion";

with a "still-beautiful" crowd, "stylish" Clerkenwell digs and "tasty" bites, this place packs 'em in, even after a decade; P.S. veterans say "go easy on the cocktails."

Cigala
20 | 17 | 20 | £36

54 Lamb's Conduit St., WC1 (Holborn/Russell Sq.), 020-7405 1717; fax 7242 9949; www.cigala.co.uk

"Wonderful", "hearty, peasant-style Spanish food for non-peasants" is the draw at this "hospitable" spot close to the British Museum; "friendly service", "soothing pale decor" and "a good selection of sherries and port" from an "excellent" Iberian-only wine list are added pluses.

CINNAMON CLUB ☒
24 | 25 | 21 | £52

The Old Westminster Library, 30-32 Great Smith St., SW1 (Westminster), 020-7222 2555; fax 7222 1333; www.cinnamonclub.com

Author/chef-owner Vivek Singh penned the eatery's eponymous cookbook (and has three more on tap), so this "luxurious" former library "in the shadow of Big Ben" is an appropriate setting for his "fantastic" "East-meets-Westminster" Indian that draws "mmms" and ahhs from the gaggle of "local politicos" and "media types" who cram the place; grumblers may bemoan its "steep prices", but believers boom it's "exquisite" and "delivers in all departments."

Cipriani ●
20 | 20 | 18 | £67

25 Davies St., W1 (Bond St.), 020-7399 0500; fax 7399 0501; www.cipriani.com

"Rubberneckers" haunt this *molto famoso* "high-gloss" "high roller" in Mayfair to ogle celebs ("Woody Allen and Elton John on the same evening!") – but some see stars only when the "madly expensive" bill arrives; whilst devotees delight in the "deliciously dependable" menu of Italian classics and "busy and buzzy" international scene, the hoi polloi huff that the "show-offy, clique-y" club is where "the famous get served and the ordinary get ignored."

Circus ●☒
– | – | – | M

1 Upper James St., W1 (Piccadilly Circus), 020-7534 4000; fax 7534 4010; www.egami.co.uk

Good for a "business dinner", "a pre-theatre" hit or even a "fun celebration" (like "hen nights"), this decade-old Soho-er has undergone a post-*Survey* transformation; brasserie-style mirrors and seating now complement the "high ceilings and large windows", whilst French bistro classics (e.g. moules marinière, steak tartare) adorn the menu; the "lovely bar downstairs" remains unchanged.

Citrus
18 | 18 | 19 | £39

Park Lane Hotel, 112 Piccadilly, W1 (Green Park), 020-7290 7364; fax 7499 1965; www.sheraton.com/parklane

"Whilst it's not a destination restaurant", this "bright, light" Piccadilly hotel dining room with "creative", "interesting" Mediterranean cooking "merits a stop" if you're in the area; but the less sanguine say this Park Lane place is "all form, no content", declaring that the "dull food" is best left to hotel guests who are "afraid to venture out to eat."

City Café Westminster ◐
▽ 20 | 16 | 18 | £42

City Inn, 30 John Islip St., SW1 (Pimlico), 020-7932 4600; fax 7932 7575; www.cityinn.com

This little-known brasserie in the "design-led" City Inn hotel offers "lots of choices" on its Modern European menus – including aged Scottish beef that's "out of this world" – and "extremely reasonable special offers" (like kids eating gratis in the school hols); the seasonal terrace seating overlooks art installations and provides football fans a haven for barbecue and beer whilst watching the World Cup on the plasma screens.

Clarke's ⊠
25 | 18 | 24 | £54

124 Kensington Church St., W8 (Notting Hill Gate), 020-7221 9225; fax 7229 4564; www.sallyclarke.com

Sally Clarke's "homely" eatery in Kensington serves "ample portions" of "heartfelt", "unflaggingly spectacular" Modern British fare; "impeccable service" and a "more-than-competent wine list" are further enticements, as is her new policy: after 21 years of no-choice set menu offerings, she now offers four options of each course at dinner; P.S. the '& Clarke's' deli next door is "perfect for quick treats and takeaway."

Clerkenwell Dining Room & Bar
▽ 21 | 17 | 21 | £40

69-73 St. John St., EC1 (Farringdon), 020-7253 9000; fax 7253 3322; www.theclerkenwell.com

Perfect for a "secret rendezvous", this "dimly lit" Clerkenwell two-story hideout with contemporary art on the walls is a "great find" for "excellent", "well-presented" Modern European fare; reviewers still laud the "accommodating", "warm service" – "even if they do top up the glass a tad too frequently."

Cliveden House
▽ 22 | 27 | 26 | £70

Cliveden House Hotel, Taplow, Berkshire, 01628 668 561; fax 01628 661837; www.clivedenhouse.co.uk

"Dine like a duke" – no tiaras, but jacket and tie required – in an "incomparable setting" at this former Astor family estate, now a 375-acre country house hotel in Taplow; "superb" staff preside over both the subterranean Waldo's with an "excellent" Mediterranean menu and the upstairs Terrace room with New French offerings and "amazing views of gardens and the Thames Valley"; however, pound-watchers posit it's "the most expensive dinner in Europe" (not including the National Trust 'donation' added to your bill).

Clos Maggiore ⊠   24 | 24 | 24 | £43
(fka Maggiores)
33 King St., WC2 (Covent Garden/Leicester Sq.), 020-7379 9696;
fax 7379 6767; www.maggiores.uk.com
"With its fireplace and lighted vines", the "setting's extremely romantic" at this "posh but not pretentious" Covent Garden haunt; adding to the ambience is the "creative" combination of Italian and New French flavours, an "amazing wine list that takes hours to read" and "fine service"; and whilst some whine that "prices have risen", this is still "a celebratory sort of restaurant."

CLUB GASCON ⊠   26 | 21 | 22 | £60
57 W. Smithfield, EC1 (Barbican/Farringdon), 020-7796 0600;
fax 7796 0601
For a "foie gras orgy" head to this "quiet, charming corner of Smithfield" where a "mind-blowing" New French small-plates menu reflects the "totally Gallic" obsession for goose liver; whilst "excessive" prices rankle and there's a "limited choice" if you don't go for foie, most applaud this "truly excellent experience" with the added perk of an "unusual" Southwestern French wine list; P.S. next door is the "unpretentious" Cellar Gascon, a "cheaper wine bar" offshoot.

Coach & Horses   ▽ 18 | 13 | 15 | £30
26-28 Ray St., EC1 (Farringdon), 020-7278 8990; fax 7278 1478;
www.thecoachandhorses.com
It looks a bit of a "scruffy boozer", but this "cosy gastropub" in Clerkenwell offers "decently prepared", "hearty" British-Med dishes from an "interesting", "offbeat menu"; it's near Smithfield Market and tends to "fill up fast", so be prepared to "arrive early or book a table"; N.B. there's a garden in back that's heated and covered in winter.

Cocoon ◐⊠   21 | 23 | 17 | £53
65 Regent St., W1 (Piccadilly Circus), 020-7494 7600;
www.cocoon-restaurants.com
A "groovy" "*Austin Powers*" design scheme (e.g. "pod chairs", curtain walls) marries the various areas – including a "quality sushi" bar – of this "pricey" Piccadilly Pan-Asian "treat"; although some say the sometimes-"unreliable" service renders it "more of a drinks-and-snacks" spot, all concede the "trendy, hip vibe", "beautiful people" and "Eurotrash (in the nicest of senses)" make it a "good addition to the London scene", baby.

Collection, The ◐⊠   14 | 20 | 15 | £40
264 Brompton Rd., SW3 (South Kensington), 020-7225 1212;
fax 7225 1050; www.the-collection.co.uk
Kindly reviewers contend this former Katherine Hamnett designer warehouse (hence the name and the "catwalk entrance") in Brompton Cross may have "mediocre" Eclectic food – but at least it's served in an "amazing space";

the less-diplomatic delight in dressing down the "models, movie people" and "trustafarians" who clog this "cavernous" nightspot with "bad cologne" and "attitude galore"; still, after almost a decade in business it's "becoming more of a trendy scene" again.

Como Lario ◐ ⊠
18 | 13 | 19 | £46

18-22 Holbein Pl., SW1 (Sloane Sq.), 020-7730 2954; fax 7730 9046; www.comolario.uk.com
Expect "above-average" Italian fare and "likeable staff" who "treat you as if they've known you for years" at this "reliable", long-standing trattoria "tucked away behind Sloane Square"; if the din police charge it gets "very noisy" with all the tables "jammed together", defenders declare "what comes out of the kitchen" makes it "worth the visit."

Comptoir Gascon ⊠
– | – | – | E

61-63 Charterhouse St., EC1 (Barbican/Farringdon), 020-7608 0851; fax 7608 0871
Francophiles who "long for the French countryside" will revel in this "rustic", "unpretentious" deli-cum-bistro Club Gascon sibling near Smithfield Market, where the "earthy decor" complements the "down-to-earth, hearty" French bistro fare; "well-chosen, affordable wines by the glass" add to the draw, as would "a few more tables – it's often fully booked."

Coq d'Argent
20 | 22 | 18 | £51

1 Poultry, EC2 (Bank), 020-7395 5000; fax 7395 5050; www.conran-restaurants.co.uk
Enjoy "fabulous London views" from the "delightful" lawned roof terrace of Sir Terence Conran's Poultry "power dining venue" – "one of the City's most useful and consistent eateries" – where the "expense-account" crowd gathers for "solid" Classic French preparations; whilst "slow" service can harry hurriers, leisure-lovers insist it's a "must in summer" for "drinks in the sunshine"; P.S. there's a "great Sunday lunch with jazz."

Costas Grill ⊠⊅
– | – | – | M

12-14 Hillgate St., W8 (Notting Hill Gate), 020-7229 3794; www.costasgrill.co.uk
"Don't go dressed up for your anniversary, but do go with friends for a convivial night out" at this "cheerful", unassuming 50-year-old eatery in Notting Hill, where "fresh", "good value" Greek eats ensure "happy customers"; even those who say "it doesn't have much going for it apart from the romantic garden" keep on "forgiving."

Cow Dining Room, The
21 | 15 | 16 | £32

89 Westbourne Park Rd., W2 (Westbourne Park), 020-7221 0021; fax 7727 8687; www.thecowlondon.co.uk
Like something "from another era", the "quirky", "intimate" upstairs dining room of Tom Conran's "laid-back"

gastropub in the heart of "hipster Notting Hill" offers a "simple", "unpretentious" Modern Brit menu brimming with seafood options; regulars also laud the "crowded" ground-floor bar for its "great pub ambience" and all-day dining, but wonder whether it's becoming "a victim of its own success."

Crazy Bear, The 🖾 | 19 | 24 | 17 | £44

26-28 Whitfield St., W1 (Goodge St.), 020-7631 0088; fax 7631 1188; www.crazybeargroup.co.uk

"Amazing decor" abounds at this "cool" Fitzrovian Thai "novelty" where stylists say dark leather banquettes, mod-deco tabletop lamps and a "fabulous" copper-laden downstairs bar with red-leather "crypts" "make you feel special indeed"; but even fans who find the pricey fare "interesting" and "imaginative" seem annoyed by the hideout's "unmarked entrance" and unnecessary game of "try-and-find-the-toilet" ("makes *The Crystal Maze* seem a walk in the park").

Crazy Homies | 20 | 17 | 15 | £21

125 Westbourne Park Rd., W2 (Westbourne Park/Royal Oak), 020-7727 6771; fax 7727 6798

Loco locals say Tom Conran's "hip" Notting Hill Mexican is "pretty legit", from the "crazy good" eats and "margaritas with a kick" down to the "cosy" setting; if some can't take this cantina – "so uncomfortable, you need to see a chiropractor", "clueless service" – the crowd that "packs it to the rafters" upstairs and down don't seem to mind; N.B. it shares an open border (and a phone number) with Lucky 7.

Cru | 18 | 20 | 20 | £29

2-4 Rufus St., N1 (Old St.), 020-7729 5252; fax 7729 1070; www.cru.uk.com

"A pleasant surprise in an area not teeming" with quality eateries, this "warm, friendly" Hoxton venue with a "lazy, gastropub atmosphere" and an "outstanding" small-vineyard vino list serves "reliable", "reasonably priced" Mediterranean cuisine with an organic bent; trump cards include a "wonderful" all-day tapas menu, sharing platters for two and seasonal wine selections.

Dans Le Noir | – | – | – | E

30-31 Clerkenwell Green, EC1 (Farringdon/Chancery Lane), 020-7253 1100; www.danslenoir.com

"Dining in the dark?" – yes, this Clerkenwell "outpost of the Parisian favourite" offers the "surreal experience" of being "taken into a pitch-black dining room" by blind staff and seated at communal tables with "new people whom you'll never see again" (or even now); eating the New French fare is a "mental challenge for the senses", compounded by the fact it's served from a no-choice 'surprise menu'; certainly this is "something to be tried once", especially on a date, "but don't try any hanky-panky, as apparently there are infrared security cameras."

Daphne's ◐
22 | 20 | 20 | £48 |

112 Draycott Ave., SW3 (South Kensington), 020-7589 4257; fax 7581 2232; www.daphnes-restaurant.co.uk

"Whether for a ladies' lunch or a swank dinner", this "fabulously romantic, tranquil" Brompton Cross corner is "still a place to be seen", thanks to "excellent, plain Italian cooking [offering] an oasis from over-elaboration", plus "professional service"; whilst the bill will "burn a hole in your wallet", the delighted declare "they come, they go, but Daphne's is forever."

Daquise
∇ 14 | 12 | 14 | £23 |

20 Thurloe St., SW7 (South Kensington), 020-7589 6117

"Finally reopened after a fire", this "seedy" but "lovable" South Ken sixtysomething has been "restored to look like a WWII cafe right out of John Le Carré"; if you want "wholesome Polish food" and other "Eastern European specialities", "this is the place to go without spending a bundle."

Deep
– | – | – | E |

Imperial Wharf, The Boulevard, SW6 (Fulham Broadway), 020-7736 3337; fax 7736 7578; www.deeplondon.co.uk

The site of the second season of *The F Word*, Gordon Ramsay's TV series, this cream-coloured eatery is "nice enough to impress" even without a show biz pedigree, given its "good" seafood and "great location" in Imperial Wharf; like the floor-to-ceiling windows, however, "prices are sky-high"; N.B. a number of new dishes have been added to the menu post-filming.

Defune
25 | 16 | 20 | £66 |

34 George St., W1 (Baker St./Bond St.), 020-7935 8311; fax 7487 3762

"Awesome" Asian dishes, both raw and cooked, are offered up at this "hidden Japanese" in Marylebone; despite the "entertaining chefs", the "service is slow" and the "decor is not the most inspired, but that doesn't detract" from the "exquisite" eats; just bring a "loaded wallet" because whilst this is some of "the best sushi in London, it's probably the most expensive too."

Deya ⊠
23 | 21 | 21 | £42 |

34 Portman Sq., W1 (Marble Arch), 020-7224 0028; fax 7224 0411; www.deya-restaurant.co.uk

In a "lovely old room with high ceilings and big windows", this "upscale Indian" off Oxford Street prepares "cleverly flavoured", "delightful" dishes, including a "creative vegetarian and seafood" selection; sceptics who say it's "unmemorable" – save for the slightly over-"solicitous service" and "high-end" prices – are outvoted by those who "recommend" "making the effort to go."

dim t
17 | 14 | 14 | £22

32 Charlotte St., W1 (Goodge St.), 020-7637 1122;
fax 7580 1574
1A Hampstead Ln., N6 (Highgate), 020-8340 8800;
fax 8348 1671
3 Heath St., NW3 (Hampstead), 020-7435 0024;
fax 7435 8060

Frequently "full of regulars craving" the "tasty" dim sum and "oodles of noodles", this rapidly "expanding" chain is "good for a quickie" Chinese meal *en famille* ("they welcome kids, even messy ones"); whilst "uneven", the service tries to be "helpful" ("we complained that our fortune cookies had terrible fortunes, and they gave us replacements").

Dine 🗷
– | – | – | E

17-18 Tooks Ct., EC4 (Chancery Lane), 020-7404 1818;
fax 7404 3838; www.dine-restaurant.co.uk

Tricky to find in a maze of narrow Holborn streets, this formerly low-key wine bar has morphed into a homely brasserie with comfy sofas, a table football machine in the bar and artwork on the walls; new chef-patron Thomas Han (ex Roussillon) rustles up Classic French fare – albeit often with regional English ingredients – supported by an all-Gallic wine list; N.B. closed weekends.

Dish Dash
▽ 21 | 21 | 20 | £27

11-13 Bedford Hill, SW12 (Balham B.R.), 020-8673 5555;
fax 8673 7711; www.dish-dash.com

This "stylish" Balham eatery has a "wide-ranging", "definitely different" Iranian-Lebanese menu that "can bewilder" ("if you order the wrong thing, you might want to dash after you get your dish"); but be brave – the "friendly staff provide advice" – and you'll find the food "perfect for sharing (or refusing to share!)"; P.S. break the ice with some "cocktails with a Persian twist."

Diverso ●
20 | 18 | 18 | £39

85 Piccadilly, W1 (Green Park), 020-7491 2222; fax 7495 1977

"A secret best bet with no crowds", this Italian offers cuisine that's "very nice", if "a bit pricey", a "soothing atmosphere that's good for conversation" and "decent service" from "an owner who cares about people"; on the flip side, "this section of Piccadilly near Green Park is quiet (actually, dead) in the evenings."

Don, The 🗷
23 | 20 | 20 | £46

The Courtyard, 20 St. Swithins Ln., EC4 (Bank/Cannon St.),
020-7626 2606; fax 7626 2616; www.thedonrestaurant.co.uk

"Most of the City has now found this place, so you have to fight to get a table" (despite a recent expansion) at this "quirky" "hideaway"; but once inside, the historic (built 1798) premises are most "civilised", whether you opt for the main dining room with its "splendid" Modern European menu or the "intimate" "better-value" bistro downstairs; both earn the ultimate businessman's accolade — "I'd even go back if I were paying myself."

Draper's Arms, The
▽ 21 | 18 | 18 | £27

44 Barnsbury St., N1 (Highbury & Islington), 020-7619 0348; fax 7619 0413; www.thedrapersarms.co.uk

A "favourite for Sunday lunch by the fire", or out "back in the lovely beer garden in summer", this "great local gastropub" in a "quiet Islington neighbourhood" has "come on leaps and bounds" with a "consistently good", often-changing Modern European menu; however, more than a few fret it's "a bit overpriced" for what you get.

Drones
19 | 19 | 19 | £45

1 Pont St., SW1 (Sloane Sq.), 020-7235 9555; fax 7235 9566; www.whitestarline.org.uk

Boasting a "pretty attractive client base", this "civilised, comfortable" Marco Pierre White–owned Belgravia venue offers a "good all-round experience", with "consistent" Modern European cuisine ("nothing innovative or challenging, but sometimes that's just right"); still, antagonistic action-lovers argue it's "aptly named, as the atmosphere will drone you to sleep"; N.B. not to be confused with the Mayfair private club of the same name and ownership.

Duke of Cambridge
▽ 18 | 16 | 13 | £26

30 St. Peter's St., N1 (Angel), 020-7359 3066; fax 7359 1877; www.sloeberry.co.uk

"From its run-of-the-mill interior, it seems to be just another neighbourhood boozer, but there's more than meets the eye" here at this "casual" Islington Modern British whose "unique" "offering of organic" eat and drink is "definitely the upper crust of pub food"; but brickbats are aimed at the "self-congratulatory" staff: "it's only a bloody gastropub — why the attitude?"

Dune ☒
– | – | – | E

11 Haymarket, SW1 (Piccadilly Circus), 020-7839 2424; fax 7839 2626; www.dunerestaurants.com

In the "hidden" Haymarket premises once occupied by Osia, this newcomer has created a "cool chic" dining room, with "high ceilings" and "muted lighting" from quirky chandeliers, where "friendly staff" serve "tasty", upscale North African–influenced Mediterranean fare; the budget-conscious can stick to the bargain pre-theatre menu or tuck into tapas at the "beautiful" bar.

Eagle, The
20 | 14 | 13 | £22

159 Farringdon Rd., EC1 (Farringdon), 020-7837 1353; fax 7689 5882

"A gastropub way before the term became fashionable", this place is "worth a pilgrimage" to Farringdon Road for "hearty, home-cooked" Med fare — indeed, it's a "mad rush" to "order at the bar" the "dishes of the day [once they're listed] on the blackboard"; a few say it's "seriously overrated", given the "grungy" digs and condescending staff, but the fact it's "usually too crowded" to "find a seat" speaks volumes.

e&o

22	20	18	£41

14 Blenheim Crescent, W11 (Ladbroke Grove), 020-7229 5454; fax 7229 5522; www.eando.nu

"The place to hang or dine or both", with "celebs in abundance", this "firm Notting Hill favourite for posing" pleases with "edgy Pan-Asian" fare, plus "cocktails so good you could forget dinner"; foes find its popularity "mystifying", citing a "lack of consistency" in food and service – "extremely efficient" vs. "just plain rude" (especially "when eating early, as they rush you out" for the next seating); still, you better "book early", as "they're always ridiculously busy."

Eat & Two Veg

14	15	15	£25

50 Marylebone High St., W1 (Baker St.), 020-7258 8595; fax 7258 8596; www.eatandtwoveg.com

"Where else can a confirmed veggie get a full English breakfast (craftily adjusted)?" than at this "casual", mod Marylebone diner that serves soy-based products to the "meat-deprived" all day; alas, nearly "all palates" agree that whilst it's "a great concept" and the "price is right, the food is disappointing" – "like cardboard", to quote one comparison.

Ebury Dining Room & Brasserie

▽ 19	18	15	£36

11 Pimlico Rd., SW1 (Sloane Sq./Victoria), 020-7730 6784; fax 7730 6149; www.theebury.co.uk

With a "cool setting" and "hip" crowd, this "bustling" brasserie/bar with "relaxed" dining room above offers "delicious" Modern European fare fans feel; however, the critical call this Pimlico place "young but tired" and "confused – a gastropub with restaurant prices and inconsistent dishes."

Ebury Wine Bar & Restaurant

18	17	18	£31

139 Ebury St., SW1 (Sloane Sq./Victoria), 020-7730 5447; fax 7823 6053; www.eburywinebar.co.uk

This "convivial", "cheery" "haunt of Old Sloanes and Young Belgravia" makes a "fine place to catch a quick bite" or "light Sunday supper" of "interesting" Eclectic fare that "goes well with the wine"; dating back to the '70s, it might be a bit "old-school wine bar" in some minds, but "the local crowd always give the place a buzz."

ECapital ●

▽ 18	13	19	£23

8 Gerrard St., W1 (Leicester Sq./Piccadilly Circus), 020-7434 3838; fax 7434 9991

At this "most unusual Chinatown restaurant", "the employees actually smile" and the menu includes "authentic Shanghaiese food" that puts it a "cut above the general"

area's fare; however, it's definitely "time for a major revamp" of the "tatty interior."

Edera
— | — | — | E

*148 Holland Park Ave., W11 (Holland Park), 020-7221 6090;
fax 7313 9700*

"Much better since it left the A-Z Group" attest *amici* of
this Holland Park Italian that serves "surprising", "exceptional food" and a "good wine selection" that, whilst
costly, are "relatively fairly priced" for the quality; a few
quibblers find the "menu not diverse enough", but often it's
"hard to find a non-Italian in the place."

Ed's Easy Diner
14 | 14 | 14 | £16

*London Trocadero Ctr., 19 Rupert St., W1 (Piccadilly Circus),
020-7287 1951; fax 7287 6998*
*12 Moor St., W1 (Leicester Sq./Tottenham Court Rd.),
020-7439 1955; fax 7494 0173*
*15 Great Newport St., WC2 (Covent Garden), 020-7836 0271;
fax 7836 3230*
*362 King's Rd., SW3 (Sloane Sq.), 020-7352 1956; fax 7352 4660
www.edseasydiner.co.uk*

"Satisfy your unhealthy-food cravings" (burgers, shakes,
etc.) here at this "knock-off diner" chain "bringing '50s
America to London", down to the "small jukeboxes on the
tables"; if detractors dis it as "a dinosaur relic of an inva-
sion that swept the city a decade ago", with "standard,
mostly fried fare" and "tiresome decor", converts confide
it's "cheered me up many a time."

Efes Kebab House ●
14 | 10 | 15 | £21

*175-177 Great Portland St., W1 (Great Portland St.), 020-7436 0600;
fax 7636 6293*
*80-82 Great Titchfield St., W1 (Oxford Circus), 020-7636 1953;
fax 7323 5082* 🅢

"Super-value" "Turkish standards" are served at this veteran Bloomsbury duo, now separately owned; but sagging
scores support reports these "once-excellent eateries are
in decline": whilst "the kebabs are still ok-ish", "the old-
world charm of tightly packed tables and chain-smokers
won't do it anymore", and the staff make you feel "part of
a production line."

1880 🅢
▽ 26 | 21 | 25 | £71

*The Bentley Hotel, 27-33 Harrington Gardens, SW7
(Gloucester Rd.), 020-7244 5361; fax 7259 2121;
www.thebentley-hotel.com*

"In the basement" of a South Ken hotel, this dining room
with opulent "baroque decor" may not be widely known,
but praise rings out for its "out-of-this-world" New French–
Modern European cuisine that includes several "fabulous
grazing menus", "perfectly balanced with wine flights"
and served by "friendly staff"; some sceptics insist the

"overstuffed premises" and "high prices kill any real enjoyment", but most find it a "feel-good" evening from start to finish.

1802 ▽ 14 | 15 | 15 | £26

Museum of Docklands, 1 West India Quay, Hertsmere Rd., E14 (Canary Wharf/West India Quay), 0870-444 3886; fax 7350 1748; www.searcys.co.uk
After a Museum of Docklands visit, "the big, lounge-style space" and "outdoor seating" with a "great view" of Canary Wharf make this venue in an old tea-sorting house an "unexpected delight" during the day, with a mid-division Modern British menu from caterers Searcy's; but by night, it becomes "just a trendy bar", "packed to the rafters with after-work groups swilling lager" (so, no kids allowed after 6 PM).

Eight Over Eight 22 | 21 | 18 | £47

392 King's Rd., SW3 (Sloane Sq.), 020-7349 9934; fax 7351 5157; www.eightovereight.nu
Diners "think outside the box when ordering" from the "imaginative" Pan-Asian menu at this "upscale", "über-cool" Chelsea cousin of e&o; despite the "high expense" of it all, and staff who, whilst "helpful", get "desperate to turn the table" for the next seating, most believe "the buzz is well-deserved" for this "glam" spot.

El Blason ⊠ ▽ 19 | 15 | 20 | £40

8-9 Blacklands Terrace, SW3 (Sloane Sq.), 020-7823 7383; fax 7589 6313
"From the minute you walk in, you are welcomed into the family" at this ash-panelled Spaniard "hidden" in a Chelsea side street; the "fine" fare includes "light, fresh tapas, combined with a rich, rewarding wine list"; a few *enemigos* exclaim it's "overpriced for what you get."

Electric Brasserie, The ● 19 | 18 | 15 | £30

191 Portobello Rd., W11 (Ladbroke Grove/Notting Hill Gate), 020-7908 9696; fax 7908 9595; www.the-electric.co.uk
It's the "smart crowd" that makes this "buzzy Notting Hill choice" such a "cool if noisy scene", with a "chilled front [bar] and more formal back" brasserie serving "robust", if "unimaginative" Eclectic fare (brunch or breakfast "is the best bet"); although service can be "shoddy" – maybe there's "too many people, too few staff" – and "tables could do with more spacing", this all-day locale is "worth the trip", especially if you "see a movie at the adjoining theatre."

Elena's l'Etoile ⊠ 22 | 18 | 22 | £40

30 Charlotte St., W1 (Goodge St.), 020-7636 1496; fax 7637 0122; www.elenasletoile.co.uk
With the "indefatigable Elena Salvoni still holding court", this "old-fashioned" Fitzrovian with "relaxed", "romantic ambience" serves "consistently good" French-Italian fare,

"pretty much like you'd expect in a country house"; it's the sort of spot "to take your parents for lunch."

11 Abingdon Road
21 | 16 | 18 | £43

11 Abingdon Rd., W8 (High St. Kensington), 020-7937 0120; fax 7937 3049

Owned by restaurateur Rebecca Mascarenhas (Sonny's is her flagship), this "understated", art-filled Kensington newcomer "with plenty of space between tables" offers a "clever marriage" of various Modern European cuisines that is a bit "limited" but "by London standards, not dear"; the staff are "more than competent."

El Gaucho
22 | 16 | 17 | £31

Chelsea Farmers Mkt., 125 Sydney St., SW3 (Sloane Sq./ South Kensington), 020-7376 8514; fax 7589 7324
30 Old Brompton Rd., SW7 (South Kensington), 020-7584 8999; fax 7589 7324 ●
www.elgaucho.co.uk

"Not to be confused with Gaucho Grill", this pair of "family-style Argentinean steakhouses" in Chelsea "offer something different" – specifically, "authentic" pampas beef for "when you need to feed the carnivore inside"; although it's "not the best service, you'll still have fun" as the quirky ranch-style decor houses a "jumping", "cheerful vibe" – oh, and it's relatively "cheap" to boot.

Elistano
18 | 13 | 17 | £33

25-27 Elystan St., SW3 (South Kensington), 020-7584 5248; fax 7584 8965

"Fine and fancy free", this "neighbourhood staple" near Chelsea Green is "always full" thanks to "simple Italian" dishes from a "reasonably priced" "menu that never changes – but it works"; maybe "service is a little lacking", but being "kid-friendly", it remains a "gathering place for the local community."

El Pirata ●🗷
20 | 14 | 18 | £28

5-6 Down St., W1J (Green Park/Hyde Park Corner), 020-7491 3810; fax 7491 0853; www.elpirata.co.uk

A "Mayfair oasis for those not running an expense account", this "buzzy" site is "hard to beat" for either "a full-blown Spanish feast or a late-night snack" of tapas (most "wonderful", "some so-so"); even if the "decor is very '70s" and "it gets crowded, the vibe is always friendly", "and copious quantities of Rioja make the evening go with a swing."

Embassy ●🗷
▽ 21 | 18 | 18 | £49

29 Old Burlington St., W1 (Green Park/Piccadilly Circus), 020-7851 0956; fax 7734 3224; www.embassylondon.com

In "swish", glass-fronted premises, this Mayfair "firm favourite" presents an "enjoyable" Modern European menu whose "generous portions are picked over by pretty young things" (or should it be 'pretty young thins'?); but it's the added attraction of the "downstairs club" that makes it a "worthwhile venue": "where else can you get an exquisite meal, fabulous cocktails and dance until the early hours, all under one roof?"

Engineer, The   19 | 15 | 15 | £30
65 Gloucester Ave., NW1 (Chalk Farm), 020-7722 0950;
fax 7483 0592; www.the-engineer.com
There's "always imaginative" dishes on the "hearty", "quality" Modern British menu at this "chilled-out", and "occasionally chic, gastropub" in Primrose Hill; even if it "could do with a decor update" and "service is haphazard", it's still "often hard to get a table", "particularly on a summer evening" in the "great sun-trap of a garden."

ENOTECA TURI ⊠   27 | 21 | 26 | £42
28 Putney High St., SW15 (Putney Bridge), 020-8785 4449;
fax 8780 5409; www.enotecaturi.com
Chef-owner Giuseppe Turi and wife/partner Pamela "keep a close eye on standards" at this "crowded" "little gem" where an "incredibly impressive" Italian menu is matched by a multiregional, "superb wine list" ("describe the type you like, and they'll find the perfect match"), "backed up by knowledgeable service"; now if only this place "in Putney's midst" "weren't so far away from the centre" of town.

Enterprise, The   18 | 19 | 19 | £39
35 Walton St., SW3 (Knightsbridge/South Kensington),
020-7584 3148; fax 7584 2516; www.christophersgrill.com
"Never changing and comfortable", this "gastropub a short walk from Harrods" attracts "lots of posh locals", making it "somewhat more dressy than expected"; "but the service is friendly" and the Eclectic cooking "accomplished"; it's a "good alternative when without a reservation."

Entrecote Café de Paris ◑   15 | 13 | 16 | £30
3a/3b Baker St., W1 (Bond Street/Marble Arch), 020-7935 3030;
fax 7935 3044; www.entrecote.co.uk
You've "no choice but to have a steak" – smothered in a "secret sauce" – plus frites, salad and dessert at this "simple", single-menu French in Baker Street; whilst admitting it's "not going to set the world on fire", *amis* argue it's "good value", but malcontents mutter it's "miles away from the original" concept on the Continent – "they wouldn't get away with it in Paris!"

Esarn Kheaw   – | – | – | I
314 Uxbridge Rd., W12 (Shepherd's Bush), 020-8743 8930;
fax 7243 1250
"Steer clear of the obvious choices, and go for the really rewarding regional specialities" advise aficionados of this "hole-in-the-wall Thai" in a "tough location" in Shepherd's Bush; the "completely authentic" cooking comes at relatively "cheap" prices too.

Essenza ◑

▽ 21 | 14 | 19 | £34

210 Kensington Park Rd., W11 (Ladbroke Grove), 020-7792 1066;
fax 7792 2088; www.essenza.co.uk

Although this Notting Hill trattoria's in a "trendy neighbourhood with plenty more of the same" (including sister Mediterraneo), it "consistently outshines" the others with "dependable" *cucina* that's "tremendous value for money", and served "with a smile" amidst "modern decor"; whilst it's often "full of lively Italians", you "can always get a table."

Eyre Brothers ☒

22 | 21 | 20 | £44

70 Leonard St., EC2 (Old St.), 020-7613 5346; fax 7739 8199;
www.eyrebrothers.co.uk

"Looking like a Clerkenwell architect's office" with its "modern", "clean decor", this Shoreditch venue from David and Robert Eyre gives "good ambience" "for a business lunch", given the "attentive staff" and "slightly pricey" bills; the Portuguese-Spanish cuisine with "strong, rustic flavours" is "interesting", although "too complicated" for some tastes.

Fairuz

21 | 14 | 19 | £28

3 Blandford St., W1 (Baker St./Bond St.), 020-7486 8108;
fax 7935 8581; www.fairuz.uk.com
27 Westbourne Grove, W2 (Bayswater/Queensway),
020-7243 8444; fax 7243 8777 ◑

Whether or not "you are a homesick Middle Easterner", the "warm atmosphere" and "tasty", "authentic" Lebanese "comfort food" will "tempt anyone" to this separately owned, "casual" duo in Bayswater and Marylebone; although they're "a bit crammed" for space, the "prices are not bad" considering that even if you "get the 'small' order, you will be stuffed."

Fakhreldine ◑

22 | 18 | 20 | £39

85 Piccadilly, 1st fl., W1 (Green Park), 020-7493 3424;
fax 7495 1977; www.fakhreldine.co.uk

With a "chichi crowd", "classy ambience" and a "window view over Green Park", this "light, airy" Lebanese offers an "upscale" setting for "super-fresh" fare featuring "fancier traditional dishes"; some nitpick that the lounge "bar has grown to cover most of the place", but in the main, it's considered as "perfect for business lunches" as for "dinner for two."

Farm, The

17 | 20 | 17 | £35

18 Farm Ln., SW6 (Fulham Broadway), 020-7381 3331;
fax 7386 3761; www.thefarmfulham.co.uk

A "hip clientele" frequent what they call the "coolest gastropub in Fulham", with woody, "chic decor" and "better-than-average" Classic French fare; however, it's hard to keep some of 'em down on the farm nowadays, since they feel the "food's been hit-or-miss" of late.

FAT DUCK, THE

| 28 | 21 | 27 | £110 |

High St., Bray, Berkshire, 01628 580333;
www.fatduck.co.uk

It might take "planes, trains and automobiles getting out" to this historic Berkshire cottage, but "genius" chef-owner Heston Blumenthal keeps "diners' taste buds in constant awe" with his "mind-boggling" Modern European menu that's a "journey into molecular cooking" (think "nitro-green tea/lime mousse"); even if foes find it a "fad"-ish, "phenomenally expensive" "silly chemistry show", plaudits ring out for the "flawless service" and "peerless sommelier"; so, "if you can afford to, go for the theatre of it all."

ffiona's

| 23 | 18 | 25 | £36 |

51 Kensington Church St., W8 (High St. Kensington/
Notting Hill Gate), 020-7937 4152; www.ffionas.com

Patron "Ffiona Reid-Owen holds court" in this "cosy" Kensington corner, and "if she decides she likes you, you'll have a fantastic time"; the place is "an oasis of home-cooked" Traditional Brit cuisine ("three words: sticky toffee pudding") in a "simple", homespun atmosphere that's "great for romantic dinners."

Fifteen

| 24 | 20 | 21 | £50 |

15 Westland Pl., N1 (Old St.), 0871-330 1515; fax 7251 2749;
www.fifteenrestaurant.com

"Where else can you dine exquisitely and contribute to society" than at "cool chef" Jamie Oliver's nonprofit school for young restaurateurs in Hoxton, "an interesting concept" that "surprisingly lives up to the hype" (if not always the "expense-account" prices) with an "honest" Med tasting menu in the main room and "hearty Italian" eats in the "more lively trattoria upstairs"; "despite being somewhat green, the staff are charming", so most "are proud to be part of" this endeavour.

Fifth Floor

| 20 | 19 | 18 | £39 |

Harvey Nichols, 109-125 Knightsbridge, SW1 (Knightsbridge),
020-7235 5250; fax 0870-191 6019; www.harveynichols.com

During or "after a hard day of shopping, darling", this "busy" Modern European "at Harvey Nick's" "fulfils the fabulous quotient" with its "futuristic submarinelike setting" ("cool", if "rather spartan"), ample "stargazing" opportunities and "light" cuisine; true, the fare's "pedestrian" for the price and the service ranges from "attentive" to "snooty", but the "way too pretty customer base" usually couldn't care less.

Fifth Floor Cafe

| 18 | 16 | 16 | £30 |

Harvey Nichols, 109-125 Knightsbridge, SW1 (Knightsbridge),
020-7823 1839; fax 7823 2207; www.harveynichols.com

It's "not worth a special trip", really, but "after a spot of retail therapy" in Harvey Nichols, this all-day department store cafe makes a "surprisingly good" "pit stop" for Modern British–Med fare amidst "airy" digs; but it's "so busy", don't be surprised if "sometimes the staff ignore you."

Fino ⌧ — 23 | 20 | 22 | £46

33 Charlotte St., W1 (Goodge St./Tottenham Court Rd.), 020-7813 8010; fax 7813 8011; www.finorestaurant.com

"Exemplary Spanish cuisine" – in the shape of "tapas par excellence" – presented with "elegance, flair and warmth" is the draw at this "delightful, if often crowded" Fitzrovian basement eatery; to some, "nouveau-bland decor lets the side down", and almost all proclaim the prices "a bit steep"; overall, though, it's "worth the inevitable struggle to find the entrance" (it's actually on Rathbone Street).

Fiore — ▽ 24 | 21 | 25 | £48

33 St. James's St., SW1 (Green Park), 020-7930 7100; fax 7930 4070; www.fiore-restaurant.co.uk

Over the years, this St. James's site "has seen some changes, good and bad, but its current incarnation is superb", from the "fresh, imaginative" Italian *cucina* to the "courteous staff" that "seem to care about you and your opinion"; only the grey-toned contemporary space leaves some "slightly cold."

Fire & Stone — 17 | 19 | 15 | £20

31-32 Maiden Ln., WC2 (Covent Garden/Leicester Square), 0845-330 0139; fax 7379 4793; www.fireandstone.com

"Hurrah, another step in the road towards decent pizza in London" has been taken by this "massive", "nicely designed" Covent Garden yearling with an "interesting menu" of "adventurous toppings" (from calamari to yoghurt); however, many versions "sound better than they taste", and "service varies from 'not bad' to 'ok.'"

First Floor — – | – | – | E

186 Portobello Rd., W11 (Ladbroke Grove/Notting Hill Gate), 020-7243 0072; fax 7221 9440; www.firstfloorportobello.co.uk

It's "as if you're in a cool living room" at this "novel", "ideal-for-a-date" eatery with tall windows, loads of candles and Modern British cooking, which, if "not outstanding", is "always a safe bet" – unlike the "moody staff (probably something to do with working in Notting Hill, sweetie)."

fish! — 21 | 16 | 17 | £31

Cathedral St., Borough Mkt., SE1 (London Bridge), 020-7407 3803; fax 7357 8636; www.fishdiner.co.uk

"Big, plate-glass windows make people-watching a breeze" at this "uplifting" Borough Market seafooder, which operates on a "cute multiple-choice system": diners "pick the fish, sauce and a side – simple, but effective"; on the downside, the "cafeteria-style setting" gets "noisy due to the hard surfaces", and whilst it's "still a good catch, it's starting to bite the wallet harder."

Fish Hook
– | – | – | E

6-8 Elliott Rd., W4 (Turnham Green), 020-8742 0766; fax 8742 3374
Its name sounds a lot like Fish Hoek, its South African pre-decessor in this space, but this first solo venture from chef-proprietor Michael Nadra (whose pedigree includes Pétrus and Chez Bruce) has a different way to hook 'em in: sophisticated Modern European seafood dishes that can be ordered as a starter or main; his bright, newly spruced-up Chiswick premises feature simple, tightly packed tables and fish photos adorning the walls.

Fish Shop on St. John St.
▽ 17 | 14 | 14 | £31

360-362 St. John St., EC1 (Angel) 020-7837 1199; fax 7837 3399;
www.thefishshop.net
"They know the best thing to do with fresh, fresh fish is to leave it virtually alone" at this "airy" Modern Brit in Clerkenwell, offering a "broad range of seafood" plus a "few meat and veggie choices too"; however, regulars suggest you "stick to fish 'n' chips – straying upmarket on the menu will only disappoint"; P.S. its Clerkenwell digs make it "an obvious post–Sadler's Wells show venue."

FishWorks
21 | 15 | 16 | £38

89 Marylebone High St., W1 (Baker St.), 020-7935 9796;
fax 7935 8796
6 Turnham Green Terrace, W4 (Turnham Green), 020-8994 0086;
fax 8994 0778
Harvey Nichols, 109-125 Knightsbridge, SW1 (Knightsbridge),
020-7245 6029
54 Northcote Rd., SW1 (Clapham Junction), 020-7228 7893
134 Upper St., N1 (Angel/Highbury & Islington), 020-7354 1279;
fax 7226 8269
57 Regents Park Rd., NW1 (Chalk Farm), 020-7586 9760
13-19 The Square, TW9 (Richmond), 020-8948 5965
www.fishworks.co.uk
"You have to be a real fish lover to enjoy" it at this fast-growing school of seafooders; "the decor is quite basic", the "service needs some energy" and management could use some humility (they "refuse to serve chips!"); but when it comes to fish, "you can't find any fresher" – you "inspect and choose your dinner" as "you walk through their fish-mongers to get to your table" – and that makes all "worth it."

Floridita ●⊠
16 | 21 | 17 | £43

100 Wardour St., W1 (Tottenham Court Rd.), 020-7314 4000;
fax 7314 4040; www.floriditalondon.com
"Named after Hemingway's favourite drinking spot in Havana", this "glammed up", "sizzling" Soho behemoth is a "lively" "all-rounder" that offers "robust" (albeit "under-imaginative") Cuban cuisine, "cigars rolled on-site", an "endless selection of cocktails" and nightly live music that is "sure to pull you off your seat for a dance"; in sum, it's "more of a party zone than a restaurant."

FOLIAGE
26 24 25 £70

Mandarin Oriental Hyde Park, 66 Knightsbridge, SW1 (Knightsbridge), 020-7201 3723; fax 7235 2001; www.mandarinoriental.com

"The food is so dramatic, the setting so serene, you'll swear you are in heaven" at this Mandarin Oriental dining room with "superb views of Hyde Park"; chef Chris Staines creates "unforgettable" French–Modern European dishes with "delicate twists", encouraging "you to be daring", and the staff serving them are "exceptional"; of course it "can be costly", but "for a truly gala evening" (or afternoon), this establishment is "consistently excellent, but never conceitedly so."

Food for Thought ∌
23 7 14 £11

31 Neal St., WC2 (Covent Garden), 020-7836 9072

"As the name implies, this is the thinking gourmet's restaurant" where "brisk counter service" has offered vegetarian "counter-culture food to counter-culture people" for 30 years; the "imaginative", "hearty fare in heavy earthenware bowls" is the Best Buy in London, but given the "cramped" Covent Garden basement digs and "positively Lilliputian tables and chairs", "takeaway is advised."

Food Room, The
– – – M

123 Queenstown Rd., SW8 (Clapham Common), 020-7622 0555; fax 7622 9543; www.thefoodroom.com

"Delicately presented" New French–Med fare is served "without fanfare" (but with an "always warm welcome") in a "relaxed dining room" at this "hidden gem of a neighbourhood restaurant"; those who know it say it "deserves a better location" than "deserted Queenstown Road", though this "unpretentious" address "means prices remain just this side of normal."

Fortnum's Fountain ⌧
18 17 18 £27

Fortnum & Mason, 181 Piccadilly, W1 (Green Park/ Piccadilly Circus), 020-7973 4140; fax 7437 3278; www.fortnumandmason.co.uk

"Step back a few decades" into this "unchanging" ground-floor cafe, favoured as a "fine place to dine with your Aunty Marmalade" – slowly, given the "desultory service" – on "mild" but "surprisingly good" Traditional British "comfort food in the congenial surroundings" of the famed Piccadilly comestibles vendor ("like what you eat? take some home with you"); P.S. the store's fourth-floor St. James's eatery is popular for a "splendid afternoon tea."

Four Seasons Chinese ◐
25 10 13 £22

84 Queensway, W2 (Bayswater), 020-7229 4320; fax 7229 4320

"Smart people" "queue out the door" at "this most venerable institution for roast duck" and other "amazing", "cheap-as-hell" Mandarin dishes; although the "rude service" and "dingy" digs are all part of this Bayswater experience, some would rather "get takeaway and eat in the comfort of home"; P.S. "if you're willing to share a table, it will speed up your waiting time."

1492 ◐

▽ | 18 | 18 | 17 | £33

404 North End Rd., SW6 (Fulham Broadway), 020-7381 3810; fax 7381 1402; www.1492restaurant.com

"Fabulous fusion food in a fashionable setting" is how admirers see this "eclectic" Fulham spot; but "disappointed" discoverers declare the ambitious "combination of Latin American flavours" can be "a bit hit-or-miss."

Franco's ⊠

▽ | 17 | 15 | 19 | £40

61 Jermyn St., SW1 (Green Park), 020-7499 2211; fax 7495 1375; www.francoslondon.com

"Trying very hard" after being taken over by Wilton's, this St. James's eatery (dating back to 1946) offers a "wide-ranging Italian-Med menu" that's "good without being exciting"; recent renovations have given it a "light" 1940s feel, but some still critique the "corporate atmosphere" – perhaps it's all those "people on expense accounts."

Frankie's Italian Bar & Grill

14 | 14 | 14 | £33

The Criterion, 224 Piccadilly, W1 (Piccadilly Circus), 020-7930 0488; fax 7930 8380
68 Chiswick High Rd., W4 (Stafford), 020-8987 9988; fax 8987 9911
263 Putney Bridge Rd., SW15 (Putney Bridge), 020-8780 3366
3 Yeoman's Row, downstairs, SW3 (Knightsbridge),
020-7590 9999; fax 7590 9900
www.frankiesitalianbarandgrill.com

The unusual partnership of chef/entrepreneur Marco Pierre White and top jockey Frankie Dettori, which started in a Yeoman's Row "world of glitter and mirrors", has expanded to three other "over-the-top"-looking Italians; the "huge portions" of the "simple" menu "suit families", but the "food's bland", the "service does not flow" and critics charge the chain's "biggest selling point are its owners."

Frederick's ⊠

23 | 20 | 21 | £52

106 Camden Passage, N1 (Angel), 020-7359 2888; fax 7359 5173; www.fredericks.co.uk

"Want to spoil yourself and others? you can't fail with Frederick's" fawn fans of this "grande dame of the Islington restaurant circuit"; though approaching its 40th birthday, it still attracts 'em with an "atriumlike space that's like a botanical garden" and a "well-worth-the-price", "excellent Modern British–European menu", served by "chirpy staff."

French Horn

25 | 24 | 25 | £60

French Horn Hotel, Sonning-on-Thames, Berkshire, 01189 692204; fax 8944 2210; www.thefrenchhorn.co.uk

"Totally worth the schlep" down to Berkshire, a visit to this "most genteel" inn is like "stepping back into 19th-century

England", where you have "pre-dinner drinks watching ducks roast on the fireplace spit", then proceed to the dining room with a "view through weeping willows down to the Thames"; although the Classic French menu is "not a daring culinary adventure", "they do it so well" – as does the "perfect, unobtrusive service."

French House, The 🖾   ▽ 19 16 16 £32
49 Dean St., W1 (Piccadilly Circus/Tottenham Court Rd.), 020-7437 2477; fax 7287 9109
The "packed pub below belies" this "decent", slightly raffish Soho site that boasts an interesting history – like the fact General "Charles de Gaulle ate here" in WWII – and "simple, dependable" French bistro cooking; with "tables close together", "all private conversations are public", but at least you're "guaranteed to meet an interesting character or two"; N.B. curiously, the pub serves beer only in half pints.

Friends 🌑   ▽ 20 15 19 £27
6 Hollywood Rd., SW10 (Fulham Broadway/South Kensington), 020-7376 3890; fax 7352 6368
"A safe bet if you want for a low-key night out with friends", this "typically Italian" trattoria does "best when sticking to its guns of pizza and pasta rather than the fancier dishes"; it also wins kudos for "kid-friendly service" from Chelsea locals.

Frontline 🖾   ▽ 16 20 16 £35
13 Norfolk Pl., W2 (Paddington), 020-7479 8960; fax 7479 8961; www.thefrontlineclub.com
Co-owned by TV cameraman Vaughn Smith, this "decent" Brit is decorated with "amazing [war] photographs that give it a different atmosphere to your usual bistro"; whilst it's "great to have a place like this near Paddington Station", some reporters reveal it's "not worth a special journey", quipping the menu's "proof that war journalists will eat damn near anything."

Fung Shing 🌑   23 13 16 £29
15 Lisle St., WC2 (Leicester Sq.), 020-7437 1539; fax 7743 0284; www.fungshing.co.uk
"When you want quality" Cantonese, "don't overlook" this unprepossessing 35-year-old Chinatowner for "consistently" "creative" cuisine with "subtle flavours" and "lots of interesting choices"; although "service is mixed", it's "efficient" "before or after the theatre."

Galicia 🌑   ▽ 19 10 17 £29
323 Portobello Rd., W10 (Ladbroke Grove), 020-8969 3539
Although Conservative party leader "David Cameron may have notoriously described it as his 'local spit-and-sawdust'" (making it "hard to get a table"), this Portobello Road haunt has an "authentic rural Spanish feel with faded, stained walls" and pictures of Galicia; expect "au-

thentic" fare from that region, including "great tapas"; despite the onslaught of "too much publicity", the waiters remain "friendly and unintimidating to all comers."

Gallipoli

19 | 17 | 17 | £20

102 Upper St., N1 (Angel), 020-7359 0630; fax 7704 0496
107 Upper St., N1 (Angel), 020-7226 5333
120 Upper St., N1 (Angel), 020-7359 1578; fax 7704 0496
www.gallipolibazaar.com

"Be prepared to dance on the tables to Arabic music" at this "noisy", "lively" Turkish trio, aka the "treasures of Islington", serving "fresh" Middle Eastern fare that "will fill you up" "in three locations along Upper Street"; the "insanely low prices" – "wonderful for groups on a budget" – compensate for "service that's friendly but gets a bit lost if busy" (and it's "always a bit busy").

Galvin at Windows
Restaurant & Bar

– | – | – | VE

London Hilton on Park Ln., 22 Park Ln., W1 (Hyde Park Corner), 020-7208 4021; www.hilton.co.uk

Atop the skyscraping Hilton on Park Lane, an airy, new restaurant/bar has been unveiled after an elegant £1.5 million transformation; the grey-toned, art deco–style premises, with dramatic views across London, hope to offer an equally eye-catching New French menu, designed by executive chef Chris Galvin (of Galvin Bistrot de Luxe) and executed by head chef André Garrett (ex Orrery).

Galvin Bistrot de Luxe

23 | 20 | 19 | £43

66 Baker St., W1 (Baker Street), 020-7935 4007; fax 7486 1735; www.galvinbistrotdeluxe.co.uk

"De luxe is an appropriate phrase" to describe this "dark wood"–adorned debutante with an "upbeat" vibe and "upscale French bistro food" for "surprisingly non-greedy" prices, given its "exciting" quality; a few of the lachrymose "leave underwhelmed, given the hype" it's received, but the majority call it an "impressive addition" to Marylebone.

Garbo's

∇ 17 | 12 | 19 | £24

42 Crawford St., W1 (Baker St./Marylebone), 020-7262 6582; fax 7262 6582

"Still going strong" after 21 years, this "old favourite" in eccentric Marylebone digs (note the elk's head on the wall) is "a place to visit when yearning" for "authentic Swedish fare", and it's "excellent value" too – especially the weekday smorgasbord for under £13; the "nice staff" make it "just like having dinner at home with mom" back in Stockholm.

Gate, The Ⓢ

∇ 26 | 21 | 26 | £32

51 Queen Caroline St., W6 (Hammersmith), 020-8748 6932; www.thegate.tv

Whether or not it "convinces carnivores that meat-free dining is a step upward", this "quirky" vegetarian in an old painter's studio with "changing art on display" is a "place you can really fall in love with", offering an often-organic, "imaginative, compelling" Modern European menu (e.g. aubergine schnitzel) and a "thoughtful wine list"; "the downside is finding it" nestled in an "awful location" behind the Apollo Theatre.

GAUCHO GRILL   22 | 18 | 18 | £38

25 Swallow St., W1 (Piccadilly Circus), 020-7734 4040; fax 7734 1076 ●

125-126 Chancery Ln., WC2 (Chancery Ln.), 020-7242 7727; fax 7242 7723 ⌺

29 Sloane Ave., SW3 (South Kensington), 020-7584 9901; fax 7584 0045

29 Westferry Circus, E14 (Canary Wharf), 020-7987 9494; fax 7987 9292

Bell Inn Yard, EC3 (Bank/Monument), 020-7626 5180; fax 7626 5181 ⌺

5 Finsbury Ave., EC2 (Liverpool St.), 020-7256 6877; fax 7795 2075 ⌺

64 Heath St., NW3 (Hampstead), 020-7431 8222; fax 7431 3714 ●

www.gaucho-grill.com

If you want a serious piece of beef – specifically, "properly hung Argentinean meat" – this "funky", "no-fuss" chophouse chain is "hard to beat for an honest feast", with a "good South American wine list worth browsing for hidden gems"; the "dark" "cow- and zebra-hide decor" strikes some as "hokey", and service tends toward the languorously Latin"; even so, it's "the ideal place to take a warm-blooded male for a manly" meal.

Gay Hussar ⌺   19 | 20 | 19 | £34

2 Greek St., W1 (Tottenham Court Rd.), 020-7437 0973; fax 7437 4631; www.gayhussar.co.uk

"The world moves on", but this Soho "institution" "remains happily in its '50s–'60s time warp", producing "stodgy, yet comforting" "authentically heavy Hungarian food" in "huge portions" that "keep the cold out"; try to "reserve early as they fill up fast", often with "journalists and politicians squeezed in below the array of caricature portraits on the walls."

Geales Fish Restaurant   20 | 9 | 16 | £23

2 Farmer St., W8 (Notting Hill Gate), 020-7727 7528; fax 7229 8632

It's "not much in ambience, decor or service" but "when only comfort food will do", this "mother of all fish 'n' chip shops" in Notting Hill (est. 1939) features "flaky, oh-so-flaky" pieces of cod, mushy peas and puddings; critics knock it's "a cross between neighbourhood joint and tourist stop" now, but to staunch supporters, it's "still real, no matter what they say"; N.B. a summer 2006 revamp may outdate the Decor score.

GEORGE 🖂   22 | 21 | 26 | £56
Private club; inquiries: 020-7491 4433
"Make sure you are invited, at whatever cost" to Mark
Birley's "well-run, welcoming" private club in Mayfair with
a "creative" Modern European menu of "impressive, occasionally dazzling cooking", and "excellent service" that
suits "the suits" and "glamourous" crowd of "young and
not-so-young" alike; there are "outside tables when
weather permits", and a "fantastic downstairs bar" too.

Getti   18 | 13 | 19 | £33
*42 Marylebone High St., W1 (Baker St./Bond St.),
020-7486 3753; fax 7486 7084
16-17 Jermyn St., SW1 (Piccadilly Circus), 020-7734 7334;
fax 7734 7924* 🖂
www.getti.com
"Popular with well-heeled locals", this "neighbourly" duo
in Marylebone and St James's offer a "genuine Italian
nosh in nice surroundings"; there are "no surprises" in the
food or the "modern decor", "but no disappointments, either", and the "attentive staff" make it a "good standby."

Giardinetto 🖂   ▽ 21 | 16 | 23 | £55
*39-40 Albemarle St., W1 (Green Park), 020-7493 7091;
fax 7493 7096; www.giardinetto.co.uk*
Not many surveyors have found this "interesting" Italian
since it moved from Fitzrovia to Mayfair last year, but those
that have esteem it as "excellent for business lunches",
raining praise on the "perfectly presented" platters and a
"wide choice of wines beyond the usual" vinos; a few antagonists attack the "cold atmosphere" of the modern digs
and big prices for "too-small portions."

Gilgamesh ◑🖂   – | – | – | E
*The Stables, Camden Mkt., Chalk Farm Rd., NW1 (Camden Town/
Chalk Farm), 020-7482 5757; www.gilgameshbar.com*
Its namesake Babylonian hero would feel right at home in
these pillared premises – swathed from floor to ceiling in
dramatic wood carvings, and boasting a huge, retractable
saillike roof – which offer a new canvas for respected chef
Ian Pengelley to prepare imaginative Pan-Asian fare that
echoes his e&o days; situated above the chilled-out bou-
tiques of The Stables, Camden Market, the space also
houses a couple of bars (one with a sushi section), a comfy
lounge area and a tearoom.

Ginger   – | – | – | M
*115 Westbourne Grove, W2 (Notting Hill Gate), 020-7908 1990;
fax 7908 1991; www.gingerrestaurant.co.uk*
With "unique dishes" featuring the namesake spice, this
large but little-known Westbourne Grove Bangladeshi is
"more inspirational than your average" Indian, with "excellent prices" and "really friendly staff – although when

they're busy, the kitchen seems to clog up and the only thing that comes out is pappadams."

Giovanni's ● ☒   21 16 20 £33
10 Goodwin's Ct., WC2 (Covent Garden), 020-7240 2877;
www.giovannislondon.com
In "an alley that should be part of a Sherlock Holmes mystery", this "unchanging Theatreland institution" (running since 1951) is a "wonderful secret" that "tourists don't find", serving "good and affordable", if "old-school, Italian" fare, presided over by "warm owner" Pino Ragona; it's "a small space, without being cramped", and ideal "if the destination before/after is in the area."

Giraffe   17 15 18 £20
6-8 Blandford St., W1 (Baker St./Bond St.), 020-7935 2333;
fax 7935 2334
270 Chiswick High Rd., W4 (Turnham Green), 020-8995 2100;
fax 8995 5697
7 Kensington High St., W8 (High St. Kensington), 020-7938 1221;
fax 7938 3330
27 Battersea Rise, SW11 (Clapham Junction/Clapham Common),
020-7223 0933; fax 7223 1037
Royal Festival Hall, Unit 1 & 2, Riverside Level 1, SE1
(Waterloo), 020-7928 2004; fax 7620 1952
Spitalfields Mkt., Unit 1, Crispin Pl., E1 (Liverpoole St.),
020-3116 2000; fax 3116 2001
29-31 Essex Rd., N1 (Angel), 020-7359 5999; fax 7359 6158
348 Muswell Hill Broadway, N10 (Highgate), 020-8883 4463;
fax 8883 1224
46 Rosslyn Hill, NW3 (Hampstead), 020-7435 0343; fax 7431 1317
30 Hill St., Twickenham (Richmond), 020-8332 2646; fax 8332 9171
www.giraffe.net
Additional locations throughout London
"Outfitted with an original animal theme", balloons and drawings, this "relatively cheap and always cheerful" chain can look "more like a children's party destination" than an eatery with a "trustworthy" "Eclectic mix of food" – from Thai curry to Toblerone chocolate cheesecake – and "speedy service"; cynics say "it may be called giraffe, but it doesn't tower enough above others in its class", but proponents praise the "popular formula" – just "don't go here if you're not with kids."

Glas ☒   ▽ 22 15 18 £29
3 Park St., SE1 (London Bridge), 020-7357 6060; fax 7357 6061
"Swedish tapas?" the concept has its sceptics, but they're outvoted by advocates of the "amazingly interesting menu" offered by "helpful staff" at this "relaxed", "intimate" Scandinavian with a "clean Nordic" look near London Bridge; but be aware that "you need to order plenty of dishes", so that "a dinner's worth can come to a quite surprising price."

GLASSHOUSE, THE
26 20 23 £52

14 Station Parade, Kew (Kew Gardens), 020-8940 6777; fax 8940 3833; www.glasshouserestaurant.co.uk

A "grown-up atmosphere" prevails at this "swanky" spot ("sharing ownership with Chez Bruce") "close to Kew Station", where an "outstanding" Modern British menu of "clever combinations" is coupled with a "comprehensive wine list that accommodates most budgets"; looking "a little like a goldfish bowl", it's "a bit cramped" and "the "food does not come flying out of the kitchen", but most remain "impressed" nonetheless.

Globe ⊠
▽ 19 15 19 £24

100 Avenue Rd., NW3 (Swiss Cottage), 020-7722 7200; fax 7722 2772; www.globerestaurant.co.uk

Featuring 'the Globe Girls' drag show, the bi-weekly "cabaret nights are legendary" at this decade-old divas den in purple-toned, "slightly austere" Swiss Cottage surrounds; whilst "it's not worth travelling for", the "light" Modern British fare does well "if you're taking in a play at the Hampstead Theatre" nearby.

Golden Dragon ◐
21 12 15 £24

28-29 Gerrard St., W1 (Leicester Sq./Piccadilly Circus), 020-7734 2763; fax 7734 1073

"Piping hot dim sum" at lunch and "quality Hong Kong–style" dishes keep things "crowded and noisy" at this monster-sized eatery; "a cut above the others" in Chinatown, the "food makes up for the lack of service" and "not hugely cheerful" decor.

Good Earth, The
21 15 18 £30

233 Brompton Rd., SW3 (Knightsbridge/South Kensington), 020-7584 3658; fax 7823 8769 ◐
143-145 The Broadway, NW7 (Mill Hill B.R.), 020-8959 7011; fax 8959 1464

"Still going strong" into its third decade, this earthy Knightsbridge and Hampstead pair "put out a good meal" of "reliable, refreshing" and "reasonable" Mandarin fare with "polite, timely service"; although critics carp the "routine" eats "tend to cost more than expected", the "speedy delivery" service makes them "hands down the best takeaway in the city" (there are several non-dining outposts as well).

Gopal's of Soho ◐⊠
▽ 20 9 16 £25

12 Bateman St., W1 (Leicester Sq./Tottenham Court Rd.), 020-7434 1621; fax 7434 0840

The "menu doesn't try anything too fancy", and the decor doesn't trouble the jury either, but still this Soho site is a "surprise delight" when you're seeking "more than you usual Indian fare"; after nearly 20 years, it's a "good standby" for "lunch or a quick meal" "after the theatre."

GORDON RAMSAY AT CLARIDGE'S

27 26 26 £86

Claridge's Hotel, 45 Brook St., W1 (Bond St.), 020-7499 0099; fax 7499 3099; www.gordonramsay.com

"Even having drinks in the bar is a delight" at Gordon Ramsay's "deliciously decadent" art deco–styled dining room within "venerable" Claridge's Hotel – but why stop there, when "superb white-glove" service "treats you like a VIP", presenting "exquisite" Modern European dishes that "truly tantalise" with a "refusing-to-play-safe mixture of tastes and textures"; it's a bit "pompous", and you best "ask for a defibrillator before the bill comes", but overall, his "class act" "lives up to its billing – and then some."

GORDON RAMSAY AT 68 ROYAL HOSPITAL RD. ⊠

28 25 28 £98

68 Royal Hospital Rd., SW3 (Sloane Sq.), 020-7352 4441; fax 7352 3334; www.gordonramsay.com

"If someone finds faults here, he should look in the mirror" – because "London doesn't get any better" than this "elegant" Chelsea "tour de force", the city's No. 1 for Food and Service; "king of chef"-owners Gordon Ramsay's "culinary artistry" shines in near-"flawless" New French dishes, augmented by a "wine list that resembles a phone directory" and served by "impeccable" "staff acting as gracious gift-bearers"; if you're "lucky enough to secure a coveted reservation", the "eye-wateringly expensive" bill is "worth very penny"; N.B. a post-*Survey* revamp may outdate the Decor score.

Goring Dining Room

22 23 23 £54

The Goring Hotel, 15 Beeston Pl., SW1 (Victoria), 020-7396 9000; fax 7834 4393; www.goringhotel.co.uk

They once quipped "the Goring is boring", but this hotel dining room has "pulled up its socks" of late, beginning with designer David Linley's "beautiful refurb" ("don't crick your neck staring at the unusual chandeliers"); though still "very Traditional and British", the cuisine is "cooked and served well", suiting "a special occasion" or Sunday lunch perfectly; all told, a "classy", "civilised refuge" – just note the "fancy-dressed clientele stopping in after a party at the Palace" (Buckingham, that is) – nearby.

GOURMET BURGER KITCHEN

21 14 14 £15

(aka GBK)

131 Chiswick High Rd., W4 (Turnham Green), 020-8995 4548; fax 8995 4572
50 Westbourne Grove, W2 (Bayswater/Royal Oak), 020-7243 4344; fax 7243 4234
88 The Broadway, Wimbledon, SW19 (Wimbledon), 020-8540 3300; fax 8543 1947
49 Fulham Broadway, SW6 (Fulham Broadway), 020-7381 4242; fax 7381 3222

(continued)

(continued)
GOURMET BURGER KITCHEN
44 Northcote Rd., SW11 (Clapham Junction B.R.),
020-7228 3309
333 Putney Bridge Rd., SW15 (Putney Bridge), 020-8789 1199;
fax 8780 1953
200 Haverstock Hill, Belsize Park, NW3 (Belsize Park),
020-7443 5335; fax 7443 5339
331 West End Ln., NW6 (West Hampstead), 020-7794 5455;
fax 7794 4401
15-17 Hill Rise, Richmond (Richmond), 020-8940 5440;
fax 8940 5772
www.gbkinfo.com

The "name fully reflects" what's on offer at this "growing empire of designer" fast-food joints – "huge, juicy burgers" with "exciting combinations" "for sophisticated adults" (kiwi, anyone?), as well as "superb shakes"; just expect "to stand in line as the joint is so bloody popular."

GRAVETYE MANOR
26 | 26 | 25 | £68
Gravetye Manor, Vowels Ln. near East Grinstead,
West Sussex, 01342 810567; fax 01342 810080;
www.gravetyemanor.co.uk

Surrounded by "great gardens" and a mile-long driveway, this "heavenly" Sussex hotel is "the real thing" as far as "English country manor dining" goes, with "outstanding" Modern British cuisine, "superb wines and port", "civilised" service and "wonderful rooms to bed down" in afterwards; "it's maintained the high standard for 50 years" – and "may it never change."

Great Eastern Dining Room ⊠
19 | 17 | 15 | £36
54-56 Great Eastern St., EC2 (Liverpool St./Old St.), 020-7613 4545;
fax 7613 4137; www.greateasterndining.co.uk

"Balancing good-quality food with an upbeat dining environment", this "Shoreditch standard" is somewhere to "sink in on a Friday night and forget the worries of the week"; if the Pan-Asian fare's "somehow lacking a wow factor" (especially for the price), the "great cocktails" at its two bars more than compensate.

Greenhouse, The ⊠
25 | 23 | 24 | £74
27A Hay's Mews, W1 (Green Park), 020-7499 3331; fax 7499 5368;
www.greenhouserestaurant.co.uk

"Tucked back in a Mayfair mews, a winding wood-plank garden [pathway] sets the stage" for this "veritable haven of serene minimalism" that disciples declare "deserving of its reputation" for "adventurous", "fantastic" New French food and a "wine list that would take a full dinner to read"; some complain that, whilst the "personnel are fawning, it takes forever to bring" the "*petite* portions", but most place this on the "must-visit list", if only for a special occasion ("even my expense account can't afford it much").

Green Olive, The
23 19 18 £40

5 Warwick Pl., W9 (Warwick Ave.), 020-7289 2469;
fax 7289 2463

"Lovely, authentic Italian meals" are the mainstay of this Maida Vale mate to Red Pepper, which manages to be "cosy" despite its "sparse urban surroundings"; "conscientious staff" notwithstanding, the kitchen can be slow, so "leave plenty to time" to dine ("food's worth the wait, though").

Green's
23 20 22 £47

36 Duke St., St. James's, SW1 (Green Park/
Piccadilly Circus), 020-7930 4566; fax 7930 2958;
www.greens.org.uk

"Everything's properly done" at this "clubby" 25-year-old St. James's seafooder – "getting close to being a tradition" – from the "comfortable" setting with "perfect-for-privacy booths" and "old-fashioned service", to the "culinary delights" on an "excellent", if "pricey" Traditional British menu; that said, some wonder whether it's "living on its social reputation" (Simon Parker Bowles owns it) and suggest the "air of faded gentility" "needs an update."

Grenadier, The
17 21 17 £30

18 Wilton Row, SW1 (Hyde Park Corner), 020-7235 3074

"One of the 'must-see' pubs for visitors", this "quaint", "quintessential" "London landmark" (dating back to 1818) was once "the Duke of Wellington's mess" hall ("many locals claim the place is haunted"); "hidden" in a Belgravia mews, it's now more "known for its bloody Marys" than the Traditional British fare that's "maybe a step above basic pub grub."

Greyhound, The
∇ 21 19 19 £37

136 Battersea High St., SW11 (Clapham Junction),
020-7978 7021; fax 7978 0599;
www.thegreyhoundatbattersea.co.uk

It's in a bit of "a dodgy neighbourhood", but this Battersea venue belies its less-than-salubrious address with "inventive" Modern British–European cuisine, an "impressive wine list" and "inviting" ambience; although it's "on the pricey side", the set menu is "perfect value."

GRILL, THE
22 25 25 £52

Brown's Hotel, Albemarle St., W1 (Green Park), 020-7518 4060;
www.brownshotel.com

"Things are happily back to normal" with the reopening of this 170-year-old Mayfair hotel after a £19 million top-to-toe renovation; the "lavish" new dining room has made a "promising" start, offering "Traditional British fare with a stylish twist", and "exemplary service" under "legendary front-of-house Angelo Maresca" (ex Savoy Grill); there's also the Donovan Bar – "very trendy now" – whilst that "wonderful institution", afternoon "tea at Brown's", is taken in an adjacent lounge.

Grill Room, The
23 | 24 | 24 | £68

The Dorchester, 53 Park Ln., W1 (Hyde Park Corner/Marble Arch), 020-7629 8888; fax 7317 6464; www.dorchesterhotel.com

After a "spectacular" revamp – with dramatic, Scottish-themed murals and tartan-clad furniture – this "truly regal" dining room within Mayfair's "venerable" Dorchester is a destination for "delightful dining in the grand manner", courtesy of the "refined" Traditional British menu ("take the daily carving" roast, regulars recommend), along with "staff that's right on"; however, even the "well-heeled" would prefer they "take prices back to a more appropriate level."

Groucho Club, The 🅂
17 | 18 | 20 | £41

Private club; inquiries: 020-7439 4685

From "literary royalty" to "models, actors, wannabes and hangers-on" "you never know who you'll see" at this "informal" private club in Soho, serving Modern British "comfort fayre" in a "formal dining room" or brasserie, "when you can't make it up the stairs" from the "active, friendly bar"; "given all the hype" around it, though, some deem it "disappointing" (well, remember what Groucho said about never belonging to a club that would have him as a member).

Grumbles
20 | 15 | 18 | £29

35 Churton St., SW1 (Pimlico/Victoria), 020-7834 0149; fax 7834 0298; www.grumblesrestaurant.co.uk

A "bit of a Pimlico institution", this "great-value" venue serves "good basic bistro stuff" (both French and Traditional British) that'll soothe any stomach grumbles; though "sometimes seating is rather squished" and "service varies", it remains a "mellow" place, "fantastic for an evening wind-down."

Guinea Grill 🅂
23 | 18 | 23 | £47

30 Bruton Pl., W1 (Bond St.), 020-7499 1210; fax 7491 1442; www.theguinea.co.uk

"Whilst it might be cramped and clubby", this Mayfair "old-timer" "deceptively hidden" next to a pub "hits the spot" with "the best kidney pie" and Traditional British grills in "portions sized more American than European"; malcontents mutter all of it is "more for American tourists" nowadays, but most opine this is "old-school done right."

Gun, The
21 | 19 | 18 | £34

27 Coldharbour, E14 (Canary Wharf), 020-7515 5222; www.thegundocklands.com

Featuring a "fantastic terrace on the Thames" looking "towards the Dome" outside and an "atmosphere fit for Admiral Lord Nelson" (who was a regular) within, this 1750 pub makes a "delightful surprise amongst the office blocks" of Canary Wharf, with "confident" (occasionally "weird") Modern British fare, and "genuinely helpful staff."

Gung-Ho ●   ▽ 22 | 18 | 22 | £29

328-332 West End Ln., NW6 (West Hampstead), 020-7794 1444; fax 7794 5522

The "great choice and unusual dishes" ensure diners are "never bored to eat here" at this "excellent neighbourhood Chinese" in Hampstead; "nice, friendly service" helps make it a "place for the family", although there's "always takeaway" too.

HAKKASAN ●   25 | 25 | 18 | £56

8 Hanway Pl., W1 (Tottenham Court Rd.), 020-7927 7000; fax 7907 1889

Full of "beautiful people posturing", this "über-hip" hot spot off Tottenham Court Road "makes you feel sexy just eating here" with its "subterranean lair of dark wood, subdued lighting" and blue glass, "lethal cocktails" and "sophisticated" Chinese fare "so good" it "dances a bolero on the tongue"; "but don't spend too much time looking at your date – or you'll be moved on to make way for the next reservation" by "ridiculously unaccommodating" staff.

Halepi ●   21 | 16 | 22 | £26

18 Leinster Terrace, W2 (Lancaster Gate/Queensway), 020-7262 1070; fax 7262 2630

"A "familylike feeling" suffuses this "old-fashioned Greek" in Bayswater, "with a warm welcome" from "loud patrons" very much part of the "experience"; the menu offers a "wide choice" of "deliciously well-seasoned", if "predictable", offerings; N.B. they sold the Belsize Park branch.

Harbour City ●   ▽ 21 | 14 | 13 | £27

46 Gerrard St., W1 (Leicester Sq./Piccadilly Circus), 020-7439 7859; fax 7734 7745

"Probably tops the Chinatown Chinese stakes" believe boosters of this bustling bi-level haunt best known for "great dim sum", along with "good" Cantonese mains, at a "reasonable price"; decor and service, though, are "nothing special"; P.S. "sit downstairs, period."

Hard Rock Cafe ●   14 | 19 | 16 | £23

150 Old Park Ln., W1 (Green Park/Hyde Park Corner), 020-7629 0382; fax 7629 8702; www.hardrock.com

"Rockin' since '71", this "loud" "landmark" off Hyde Park Corner was the first of the chain now "known to more tourists than a Holiday Inn" – so "it might be worth seeing where it all started": the rock 'n' roll ambience, the "amazing" music memorabilia, the "usual mementoes to collect"; of course, the Yankee "food is just a side note" and the "service minimal", so unless you're a kid or an "unadventuresome American", "skip the meal and just buy a T-shirt."

Harlem ◐
▽ 14 | 16 | 14 | £25

78 Westbourne Grove, W2 (Bayswater/Queensway),
020-7985 0900; fax 7985 0901; www.harlemsoulfood.com
The downstairs bar with its "moody lighting" and "great music is the place to be seen" at this "trendy" Westbourne Grove American serving "Southern comfort food" three meals a day; but whilst "the menu has such promise, the fare itself is a disappointment" several say, and the "service is apathetic."

Harry's Bar ◐ ⊠
23 | 24 | 25 | £61

Private club; inquiries: 020-7408 0844
"Deliciously decadent", Mark Birley's members-only Mayfair address feels "like a scene out of the movies" with "beautiful", "elegantly dressed people" enjoying some of "the most expensive Northern Italian food in the world, but some of the best too" – because "they'll make you anything you want, and I mean anything"; simultaneously "sharp and personable service" shines also, so whilst this is "truly a place to spend pounds by the buckets", to believers it's "the best", "bar none."

Haz ◐
– | – | – | M

9 Cutler St., E1 7DJ (Liverpool St.), 020-7929 7923; fax 7623 5132;
www.hazrestaurant.com
"Crowded with City types" (it's "inevitably rammed by midday"), this large "lunchtime favourite" knows how "to balance taste requirements with time restraints" in serving its "light", "delicious" Turkish fare; the "staff do a tremendous job treading the tightrope between those dining and those waiting", but if you want to dodge the hordes, regulars recommend that you "go at dinner or on the weekend" (it's open every day).

Home House ◐
▽ 19 | 23 | 22 | £49

Private club; inquiries: 020-7670 2100
Attracting "a vibrant, less stuffy membership" ("quite unlike other London clubs"), this imposing Portman Square Heritage building boasts a "very nice garden at the rear" and a "beautiful", high-ceilinged dining room; "if the kitchen could match the glorious look and feel of the place – wow!" but alas, the Modern British–European fare is "good but not great."

Hosteria del Pesce ⊠
– | – | – | E

84-86 Lillie Rd., SW6 (West Brompton/West Kensington),
020-7610 0037
This new homey, wood-fronted seafooder on the border between Fulham and Earl's Court is sister to an established namesake in Rome, from which chef Paolo Petruccelli receives a daily delivery of fish (much of it displayed on ice) to prepare his upscale Italian fare; reservations are already advised.

Hoxton Apprentice
▽ 18 | 20 | 19 | £30

16 Hoxton Sq., N1 (Old St.), 020-7749 2828; fax 7749 2829;
www.hoxtonapprentice.com

As this "socially responsible restaurant" doubles "as a training school for young [disadvantaged] people", everyone is "eager to please" – and for the most part they do, with a "surprisingly good" Eclectic menu ("your favourite basics plus a few innovations") and "down-to-earth" service; definitely "worth a visit" to the "grand yet quirky" digs on Hoxton Square.

HUNAN 🗷
27 | 12 | 21 | £45

51 Pimlico Rd., SW1 (Sloane Sq.), 020-7730 5712; fax 7730 8265

"Don't let the unassuming location and plain decor fool you" – this "offbeat" Pimlico Green Chinese offers an "amazing procession of flavours" from a "truly special" procession of "bite-sized servings"; "based on your likes and dislikes", chef-owner Michael Peng "brings what he thinks you should have", making it "hard to keep tabs on the tab"; but most say, "don't argue – just enjoy."

Hush 🗷
17 | 18 | 15 | £42

8 Lancashire Ct., W1 (Bond St.), 020-7659 1500; fax 7659 1501;
www.hush.co.uk

"Tucked away off Bond Street", the atmosphere "is definitely not hushed" at this "happening place" ("started by Roger Moore's son"), which boasts a Modern British brasserie, a Classic French eatery and a "posh pickup scene" at the bar; dining- and servicewise, the first two are "not bad, but not memorable either"; however, "in the summer, alfresco eating" in the courtyard "makes up for" much.

Ikeda 🗷
▽ 24 | 15 | 23 | £46

30 Brook St., W1 (Bond St.), 020-7629 2730; fax 7490 5992

"Unspoilt by the recent surge in quasi-Japanese" fusion fare, this "tiny" Mayfair spot "can be relied upon to deliver" "terrific upscale" sushi, plus "a host of robatayaki and other cosy, warm dishes"; "best go at lunch", when the specials ease the squeeze of "expensive" bills.

Ikkyu
▽ 22 | 8 | 15 | £22

67A Tottenham Court Rd., W1 (Goodge St.),
020-7636 9280

"A true, no-frills sushi joint", this Tottenham Court Road "treasure" is "filled with Japanese people" enjoying "authentic", "freshly prepared" victuals, both cooked and raw; the "affordable prices" "make up for the erratic service."

Il Bordello
23 | 17 | 20 | £28

81 Wapping High St., E1 (Wapping), 020-7481 9950

"They certainly pack the punters" into the "tight tables" at this "amazingly popular", "family-run" Wapping trattoria in an exposed-brick converted warehouse where an "energetic crowd" eat "enormous portions" of "consistently good" traditional Italian fare from a "vast menu"; N.B. there's a small offshoot, La Figa, in nearby Limehouse.

Il Convivio ⊠   23 | 21 | 22 | £47

143 Ebury St., SW1 (Sloane Sq./Victoria), 020-7730 4099; fax 7730 4103; www.etruscarestaurants.com

There's a "touch of flair" to the "modern Italian food", along with an "impressive wine list", at this "expensive" but "convivial (as one might expect)" townhouse on the Belgravia-Pimlico border; always a "safe bet for a business dinner", it's especially "great in summer when the roof opens."

Il Falconiere ●⊠   – | – | – | M

84 Old Brompton Rd., SW7 (Gloucester Rd./ South Kensington), 020-7589 2401; fax 7589 9158; www.ilfalconiere.co.uk

"Seating is fairly cramped" at this South Ken trattoria, but the "decent" Italian menu "is worth keeping arms close to the body" for, especially as "efficient service" does not prolong the agony; other plus points of this "good neighbourhood" place are the "reasonable" prices and the way they "open their doors onto the street in summer, for an alfresco dining" effect.

Il Portico ●⊠   23 | 17 | 25 | £32

277 Kensington High St., W8 (High St. Kensington), 020-7602 6262

It "feels like a cosy evening in the heart of an Italian family" at this "comfy" Kensington trattoria ("two feet away from the Odeon" cinema), which attracts "an attractive, upscale crowd of regulars" – plus "a few dedicated celebrities" – with its "carefully prepared" cuisine; the staff "do an exceptional job of warmly welcoming customers."

Imli   – | – | – | M

167-169 Wardour St., W1 (Tottenham Court Rd.), 020-7287 4243; fax 7287 4245; www.imli.co.uk

"Stylish in a pleasant, casual way", this "unique" Soho newcomer from the Tamarind team offers a "great concept" – namely, Indian small plates; but "if you want to do tapas, make dishes people can share, not just portions for one" scold sceptics, who "leave feeling disappointed" (not to mention hungry).

Imperial China ●   18 | 20 | 16 | £23

25A Lisle St., WC2 (Leicester Sq./Piccadilly Circus), 020-7734 3388; fax 7734 3833; www.imperial-china.co.uk

"Smarter than your average Chinatown restaurant", with "well-spaced tables" too, this "huge, open" venue serves "reliable" Cantonese fare, and even "better dim sum"; less than imperial, however, is the "patchy service" – especially if you "end up on the top floor."

Imperial City ⊠
▽ 19 | 19 | 15 | £41

Royal Exchange, Cornhill, EC3 (Bank), 020-7626 3437; fax 7338 0125; www.orientalrestaurantgroup.co.uk
"Relying on" its "interesting, if not uplifting" berth "in the basement of the Royal Exchange", this venue wins over some as "ideal for business banqueting" with cuisine that's "a step above your average Chinese", but loses others who find the fare "overpriced" and "boring."

Inaho ⊠
▽ 21 | 9 | 13 | £30

4 Hereford Rd., W2 (Westbourne Park), 020-7221 8495
"Like finding a spot off the philosopher's trail in Kyoto", this "tiny" "treat" off Westbourne Park is all about "very, very authentic" Japanese cooking from a chef who "pays attention to detail"; "points to criticise" include tables "squashed together" in "Swiss chalet–like" surrounds "and slow service."

Incognico ⊠
19 | 19 | 18 | £40

117 Shaftesbury Ave., WC2 (Leicester Sq./Tottenham Court Rd.), 020-7836 8866; fax 7240 9525; www.incognico.com
With a "hallmark of straightforward, elegantly presented" innovative and "classic brasserie food served to well-spaced tables" by "informed staff", this French citizen near Cambridge Circus is a "good choice pre- or post-theatre"; a "management change" has given it a light face-lift.

Indigo ●
23 | 20 | 21 | £44

One Aldwych Hotel, 1 Aldwych, WC2 (Charing Cross/ Covent Garden), 020-7300 0400; fax 7300 1001; www.onealdwych.com
"Above the madding crowds" of the One Aldwych Hotel's "trendy bar", this all-day mezzanine dining room is a "relaxed", "efficient spot for a business lunch or dinner", as well as "after the theatre"; the "pleasant, reliable" Modern European menu "pitches to the health conscious" (lots of organic produce), and although the bill can be "annoyingly high", "eager staff" and "comfortable chairs" compensate.

Inn The Park
19 | 19 | 16 | £31

St. James's Park, SW1 (St. James's Park), 020-7451 9999; fax 7451 9998; www.innthepark.com
This Traditional Brit benefits from its "beautiful location in St. James's Park", as "wonderful in the height of summer as on a crisp winter's day"; but the "perfect" premises are "belied by the food" ("straightforward" but "so-so") and "confused staff", whilst "the conflict between the take-out and dining-in" areas makes the room "loud and unfriendly."

Isarn ⊠
▽ 18 | 22 | 18 | £28

119 Upper St., N1 (Angel), 020-7424 5153
As it's co-owned by the sister of top restaurateur Alan Yau (Hakkasan, Busaba Eathai), perhaps it's no surprise that

this young Asian makes a "brilliant date spot", with "wonderfully designed", "sleek decor" and "flavoursome Thai cooking"; the "ambience outshines the fare", however, and whilst the bill isn't bad, some aren't sure it should be "higher than what Busaba charges for similar food."

Ishbilia   23 | 12 | 17 | £32
Harrods, 2nd fl., 87-135 Brompton Rd., SW1 (Knightsbridge), 020-7893 8598
9 William St., SW1 (Knightsbridge), 020-7235 7788; fax 7235 7771; www.ishbilia.com ⏺

The "crowded" space "lacks originality" (not to mention comfort) and the service can be "brusque", but "probably the best Lebanese fare in town" is served by this Belgravia bastion claim converts who "get really nervous if we don't go at least once a month"; P.S. the younger Harrods' branch is "convenient", but doesn't take reservations.

Ishtar ⏺   – | – | – | M
10-12 Crawford St., W1 (Baker St.), 020-7224 2446; www.ishtarrestaurant.com

"Not your typical Turkish restaurant", this wood-panelled Marylebone debutante "departs from the usual" with "succulent spiced meats and exotic vegetables" cooked on a charcoal grill and complemented by "commendable service"; "the bar downstairs gets very lively at weekends, with live music and belly dancers."

Island Restaurant & Bar   – | – | – | M
Royal Lancaster Hotel, Lancaster Terrace, W2 (Lancaster Gate), 020-7551 6070; fax 7551 6071; www.islandrestaurant.co.uk

A "chic modern" look and an "imaginative" Modern British menu make this low-profile hotel eatery a discreet "spot for duo dining", especially on the early evening "excellent fixed-price menu"; its name derives from its location – a large traffic island above the Lancaster Gate tube station.

I-Thai   – | – | – | VE
Hempel Hotel, 31-35 Craven Hill Gardens, W2 (Lancaster Gate), 020-7298 9000; fax 7402 4666; www.the-hempel.co.uk

"New owners and a new chef have made a big difference" to the serene, supremely minimalist dining room of this Bayswater hotel, introducing a "nouveau-style Thai" menu whose dishes "look like works of art", albeit "small" ones; one aspect hasn't changed: "the place seems a little too expensive."

itsu   19 | 16 | 15 | £25
167 Piccadilly, W1 (Green Park), 020-7495 4048
Vogue House, 1 Hanover Sq., W1 (Bond St./Oxford Circus), 020-7491 9799; fax 7491 7193 ⌨
103 Wardour St., W1 (Piccadilly Circus/Oxford Circus), 020-7479 4794; fax 7479 4795

88   **subscribe to zagat.com**

(continued)
itsu
*118 Draycott Ave., SW3 (South Kensington), 020-7590 2400;
fax 7590 2403
Cabot Pl. E., level 2, E14 (Canary Wharf), 020-7512 5790;
fax 7512 5791* 🅯
*Jubilee Pl. Mall, 28A Bank St., E14 (Canary Wharf), 020-7512 9650
www.itsu.co.uk*
"What you get is what you see" at this "hip, simple" "sushi
'merry-go-round'" chain that features conveyor belts of
"surprisingly competent" Japanese fare – with some
Western and "Pan-Asian influences to keep things interesting"; even if they "feel like a glorified cafeteria" and the
"prices do add up", this "well-thought-out" concept is "a
must for kids or quick lunch"; P.S. veterans advise "sit near
the kitchen so you can snaffle the fresh plates."

IVY, THE ●   23 | 21 | 22 | £53
*1 West St., WC2 (Leicester Sq.), 020-7836 4751; fax 7240 9333;
www.the-ivy.co.uk*
"In a league of its own" lies this Theatreland "institution"
that, "for such a hot place" ("celebrity sightings guaranteed"), "has a laid-back feel"; perhaps it's the "remarkably
consistent" menu, a "mix of traditional and Modern" British–
Euro fare, or the "simple" "dark wood/white tablecloths"
decor, or the "courteous staff"; dissenters "don't know
why people flock" here (it's "only slightly easier to get
into than Fort Knox"), but to admirers "it's like an adult
security blanket – a home away from home."

Iznik ●   _ | _ | _ | M
*19 Highbury Park, N5 (Highbury & Islington), 020-7704 8099;
fax 7354 5697*
Expect "an authentic atmosphere", from the "funky
decor" – Ottomanesque antiques, lanterns, etc. – to the
"fantastic" food at this family-run, candlelit Turk that's
"worth the time it takes to get" to Islington; "service is
friendly" to boot.

Jade Garden ●   19 | 14 | 16 | £21
*15 Wardour St., W1 (Leicester Sq./Piccadilly Circus),
020-7437 5065; fax 7429 7851; www.londonjadegarden.co.uk*
"Delicious" dim sum and Mandarin mains ("lots of choices
if you like seafood)" "make it worthwhile" to check out this
Chinatowner, "despite its lacklustre decor" and the "efficient" staff's tendency "to throw plates on the table";
"they stay open late" too.

Jenny Lo's Tea House 🅯⇄   20 | 9 | 17 | £15
14 Eccleston St., SW1 (Victoria), 020-7259 0399
Owned by Ken Lo's daughter, this "cheery", "casual" noodle
house near Victoria Station is a "safe bet for an excellent-
value Chinese" meal, "delivered promptly by friendly staff",

and if sitting at "communal, bare tables" is not to your liking, try the "good takeaway" service.

Jim Thompson's
17 | 18 | 16 | £25

141 The Broadway, SW19 (Wimbledon), 020-8540 5540; fax 8540 8728
617 King's Rd., SW6 (Fulham Broadway), 020-7731 0999; fax 7731 2835
408 Upper Richmond Rd., SW15 (East Putney), 020-8788 3737; fax 8788 3738
889 Green Lanes, N21 (Southgate/Wood Green), 020-8360 0005; fax 8364 3006

The "exotic decor – all of which is for sale if you like it that much" – adds to the "tacky, touristy fun" of this Thai quartet serving "spicy fare that'll blow your socks off" supporters say; but authentic-minded antagonists argue against the "ersatz" eats and "tired"-acting servers.

JIN KICHI
25 | 10 | 17 | £33

73 Heath St., NW3 (Hampstead), 020-7794 6158; fax 7794 6158; www.jinkichi.com

It's "tiny" and "cramped", but this "bustling" Hampstead "hangout" defies its "sparse" surrounds by offering "virtually every [aspect of] Japanese cuisine" – from "fresh-tasting sushi to great yakitori" – on a menu that's "not Westernised at all"; just remember "not to get there late, as things run out."

Joe Allen ●
17 | 17 | 18 | £32

13 Exeter St., WC2 (Covent Garden), 020-7836 0651; fax 7497 2148

After 30 years, this Theatreland "Yankee-Doodle hangout for burgers and stateside fare" (based on the "NYC original") is "still going strong"; some sniff it's "a silly place", and "you definitely go for the American speakeasy atmosphere rather than the food", but it remains a "low-key", "late-night refuge" for thespians and tourists alike.

Joe's
▽ 16 | 15 | 17 | £35

126 Draycott Ave., SW3 (South Kensington), 020-7225 2217; fax 7584 1133

A "great lunch spot for a shopping break" – it just happens to be located across the street from the fashion store Joseph (which owns it) – is this Brompton Cross bistro with "wavy, coloured walls"; however, the fact that the "ok, but not very exciting" Modern British fare comes in "portions for models" suggests it's more "a place to be seen than be fed."

Joe's Restaurant Bar
20 | 20 | 16 | £29

Joseph, 16 Sloane St., SW1 (Knightsbridge), 020-7235 9869; fax 7235 3218

"Perfect for a little stop-by on a shopping day", the "chic" Joseph store's cafe features "fresh, light" Modern British fare (especially "great salads"); true, it appeals to "a particular clientele" – "think thin rich women eating well" –

but it's surprisingly "reasonably priced", and there's "fab people-watching (check out the hair extensions)."

Joy King Lau ●

21 | 9 | 15 | £22

3 Leicester St., WC2 (Leicester Sq./Piccadilly Circus), 020-7437 1133; fax 7437 2629

"It's nothing to look at", but this eatery "just north of Leicester Square" spreads joy across four "huge" floors with its "excellent dim sum" and other "exceptional-value" Cantonese dishes; the presence of a "Chinese clientele tells you that this is as good as it comes" – even though it comes with a "frown" from the "efficient" staff.

J. SHEEKEY ●

26 | 21 | 23 | £51

28-32 St. Martin's Ct., WC2 (Leicester Sq.), 020-7240 2565; fax 7497 0891; www.j-sheekey.co.uk

They'll "treat you royally" at this "chic", "clubby" Theatreland seafooder – the "highly popular" "little sister of The Ivy" – offering "brilliant", "classic" dishes (plus their "'must-try' mushy peas") and "close-up celebrity watching" throughout a "series of wood-panelled rooms"; although "it's not cheap", this "bubbly spot" (complete with "top-hatted doorman") manages to be both "date- and parent-friendly."

Julie's ●

19 | 24 | 19 | £39

135 Portland Rd., W11 (Holland Park), 020-7229 8331; fax 7229 4050; www.juliesrestaurant.com

"Survey the place before bringing your paramour to ensure you have the best nook" at this Holland Park "hideaway", which "lives up to its reputation" for romance with "different decor" in each room (some swear there's no true London love story that "doesn't have a Julie's milestone"); whilst the Modern British "food is not up to the cosy atmosphere, it's not bad either"; same goes for the "reasonable service."

Just St. James's ☒

17 | 20 | 15 | £41

12 St. James's St., SW1 (Green Park), 020-7976 2222; fax 7976 2020; www.juststjames.com

An old "bank building, elegantly restored", provides a "posh" if sometimes "noisy" setting for this St. James's "mecca for the fund manager/broker" set; but since the Modern British "food is unreliable – fine one visit, bland the next" – and the "staff erratic (in a sweet way)", many have "stopped playing this lottery"; P.S. "the words 'bargain basement' were invented for the lunch set menu" at the downstairs eatery, Just Oriental.

Kai Mayfair

25 | 21 | 22 | £51

65 S. Audley St., W1 (Bond St./Marble Arch), 020-7493 8988; fax 7493 1456; www.kaimayfair.co.uk

"The chef makes even the simplest dish exotic" at this "subdued" yet "swish" Mayfair venue where a "sophisticated" multiregional menu (featuring "liberal interpretations of traditional" dishes) is "as gourmet as Chinese can get"; although there's only "a modest service charge", it's still "no bargain", but with service "to the nines", and "a harpist on some days", few are carping.

Kandoo ◑   – | – | – | I
458 Edgware Rd., W2 (Edgware Rd.), 020-7724 2428; fax 7724 6769
Despite opening in 2000, this "charming", family-run "neighbourhood" spot on Edgware Road is "still not very well known, so it's easy to get a last minute table" – just "don't go if you like fancy places"; the "simple, fresh" Persian dishes clock in at "great value", and there's a beehive-shaped clay oven producing "bread to die for"; P.S. "bring your own wine as there is no license."

Kensington Place ◑   19 | 15 | 18 | £41
201-209 Kensington Church St., W8 (Notting Hill Gate), 020-7727 3184; fax 7229 2025; www.egami.co.uk
"Like an old suit – classic and dependable", this "humming" Kensington haunt "may not be as happening as a few years ago" (it turns 20 in 2007), but it still "oozes the confidence" that comes when the Modern British "food is good, the drinks are wet and the service efficient" (despite some "uncharacteristically slooow" lapses); the main gripe, as ever, is the "unconscionably loud setting."

Kettners ◑   15 | 19 | 17 | £26
29 Romilly St., W1 (Leicester Sq.), 020-7734 6112; fax 7287 6499; www.pizzaexpress.com/kettners
"Most odd", this 1867 "beautiful old building" once owned by Napoleon III's chef, now by a fast-food conglomerate: there's "a posh champagne bar" with 100 types of bubbly, several "ritzy" rooms "and then Pizza Express food, plus some extras" on the Eclectic menu; cynics sneer it's just "a tarted-up [chainster] with jazz music", but it remains a "Soho tradition" for theatregoers – not to mention "the most elegant pizza-eating experience ever."

Kew Grill   – | – | – | E
10B Kew Green, Kew (Kew Gardens), 020-8948 4433; fax 8605 3532; www.awtonline.co.uk
Celebrity chef Antony Worrall Thompson and his wife, Jay, are the team behind this "fabulous neighbourhood" Traditional Brit in rustic, casual quarters close to Kew Gardens; though long on organic ingredients, the "menu's limited, but all's very tasty" (savants suggest "you go for the steak").

Khan's ◑   20 | 10 | 14 | £18
13-15 Westbourne Grove, W2 (Bayswater/Queensway), 020-7727 5420; fax 7229 1835; www.khansrestaurant.com
In 30 years, "not much has changed" at this "barnlike" Bayswater "institution": it's "well-known" for its "excit-

ing", "flavourful" Indian fare at "budget" prices – and equally renowned for its "careless" staff who seem mainly "to be trying to get you in and out"; but if they're "testy", the food's "tasty" – so the crowds continue to form.

Khan's of Kensington ●
20 | 13 | 17 | £25
3 Harrington Rd., SW7 (South Kensington), 020-7584 4114; fax 7581 2900
This "small" South Ken Indian satisfies supporters who say you "can't go wrong" with its "straightforward" "favourites" at "great-value" prices, but foes fume "the food isn't worth" the often-"surly service" and "average" decor; P.S. "don't confuse this with the Khan's" in Bayswater (no relation).

Kiku
∇ 24 | 14 | 21 | £48
17 Half Moon St., W1 (Green Park), 020-7499 4208; fax 7409 3359; www.kikurestaurant.co.uk
"When that craving for real Japanese cuisine hits you", this "lively", "loud" Mayfair venue hits the mark, with "sushi to die for" and other "reliable, quality" eats; yes, it's "pricey", but there are "cheap set lunches" for those who wish they "could afford it more often"; just "don't come here for glam" decor.

Koi
21 | 18 | 20 | £47
1E Palace Gate, W8 (Gloucester Rd./High St. Kensington), 020-7581 8778; fax 7589 2788
Kensington citizens claim they're "always able to get a reservation" at this "reliably good local" for sushi and cooked Japanese fare; but "order carefully, as the price of [all] the dishes soon mounts – I have seen people go pale on getting the bill."

Kulu Kulu Sushi ⌧
19 | 9 | 16 | £19
76 Brewer St., W1 (Piccadilly Circus), 020-7734 7316; fax 7734 6507
51-53 Shelton St., WC2 (Covent Garden), 020-7240 5687; fax 7240 5687
39 Thurloe Pl., SW7 (South Kensington), 020-7589 2225; fax 7589 2225
"When you don't feel like dropping 30 quid on an expensive sit-down" place, or you're too "hungry to wait to be served", this "drab"-looking chain of "conveyor-belt sushi" spots "focus on getting you fresh" fish fast, and "for a reasonable price"; however, their "maximum seating time" limit – "rigidly enforced by staff" – is "annoying."

La Bouchée
20 | 15 | 18 | £36
56 Old Brompton Rd., SW7 (South Kensington), 020-7589 1929; fax 7584 8625
"Like being in a Parisian railway carriage" (ok, it's considerably "cramped"), this "candlelit" South Ken "bistro *du quartier*" is "full of ooh-la-la and rustic ambience" – even the "rather abrupt" waiters add to the "authentic" feel; the

Classic French dishes are quite "competently executed", and whilst it's "not as cheap as it used to be", it's still "good value" for a "romantic" eve.

La Brasserie
17 | 15 | 13 | £32

272 Brompton Rd., SW3 (South Kensington), 020-7581 3089; fax 7581 1435

In a "fabulous location at Brompton Cross", this "typically bustling brasserie" – with "tin ceilings, mirrors and the smell and sound of Paris" – serves "perfectly fine" "French basics"; "nothing special, nothing terrible", but at age 35, it does make a "great neighbourhood stalwart."

Ladbroke Arms
20 | 18 | 17 | £27

54 Ladbroke Rd., W11 (Notting Hill Gate), 020-7727 6648; www.capitalpubcompany.co.uk

This "laid-back" "atmospheric gastropub in Notting Hill" is just "how a gastropub should be", providing quite "good Modern European food at good prices in a friendly atmosphere"; you "should not trek across town" for it, but locals are "very happy indeed to have it around the corner", with the "lovely patio" an extra plus.

Ladurée
23 | 23 | 19 | £30

Harrods, ground fl., 87-135 Brompton Rd., SW1 (Knightsbridge), 020-7893 8293; fax 3155 0112; www.laduree.com

"At last it's here" proclaim proponents of the legendary Paris *patisserie,* which recently opened a "pretty tearoom/sexy restaurant" "in the shopper's paradise" of Harrods; it's a faithful "import", from the "frothy", chandelier-and-marble decor to those "luscious macaroons in a variety of flavours and fashionable colours", and if "service is brusque and prices outrageous", it's cheaper "than hopping the Eurostar", *n'est-ce pas?*

La Famiglia ●
21 | 14 | 20 | £42

7 Langton St., SW10 (Fulham Broadway/Sloane Sq.), 020-7351 0761; fax 7351 2409; www.lafamiglialondon.com

"Sunday lunch is like a day in the Tuscan countryside" at this "family-run" and family-friendly World's End trattoria (now into its fifth decade) boasting a "homely feel" and "extensive menu" of "gutsy" Italian dishes; with "no egos – how refreshing" – amongst the "army of waiters", and an "awesome outdoor" terrace (open all year round), it's little surprise the place is "always packed."

La Fromagerie Café
24 | 16 | 15 | £23

2-4 Moxon St., W1 (Baker St.), 020-7935 0341; fax 7935 0341; www.lafromagerie.co.uk

They "love to educate about fabulous boutique cheeses" at this Marylebone "secret" cafe in a "divine" deli, whose "cramped seating" area (basically, a communal table) "belies a luxurious menu" of "wholesome, interesting" Modern European fare; although it's "always crowded and impossible to get the attention" of "sometimes befuddled staff", "there should be more places like this."

La Genova ☒
23 | 19 | 26 | £38

32 N. Audley St., W1 (Bond St.), 020-7629 5916; www.lagenovarestaurant.com

The "charming owner watches everything like a benevolent hawk", so "you can count on" "comfortable", "classic Northern Italian food", a "pleasant setting" and staff who "make you feel welcome" ("they must have thought we were regulars") at this "jovial" veteran; the menu "doesn't change that much, but this place is all about the familiar" – and you "can't beat the location", "near the U.S. Embassy."

Lanes
23 | 24 | 24 | £54

Four Seasons Hotel, Hamilton Pl., W1 (Green Park/ Hyde Park Corner), 020-7499 0888; fax 7493 6629; www.fourseasons.com/london

Since it's not on the ground floor, "it often gets overlooked", but this dining room offers a leisurely, "lovely experience", from the "real Four Seasons service to the "terrific" Eclectic cuisine to the surroundings, dominated by glass works of art and "Hyde Park views."

LANESBOROUGH CONSERVATORY
22 | 26 | 24 | £52

The Lanesborough, 1 Lanesborough Pl., SW1 (Hyde Park Corner), 020-7333 7254; fax 7259 5606; www.lanesborough.co.uk

Like an "exotic Regency garden", this "elegant", "old-fashioned" conservatory-style dining room on Hyde Park Corner makes a "gorgeous venue" for "a business lunch to impress" or "truly stellar" afternoon tea; perhaps the Eclectic menu "could be more creative", but the staff are "sweet" – they "wished my mother a happy 40th birthday on her 50th; safe to say she'll be going back."

Langan's Bistro ☒
19 | 18 | 21 | £42

26 Devonshire St., W1 (Baker St.), 020-7935 4531; fax 7493 8309; www.langansrestaurants.co.uk

"A little haven of happiness" for those who like "safe choices", this fortysomething Marylebone venue makes a "great retreat from the bustle of everyday life", with "nice staff" and "pleasant" decor featuring David Hockney art; the Traditional British–French comfort food is, well, "comfortable."

Langan's Brasserie ●☒
18 | 18 | 18 | £46

Stratton House, Stratton St., W1 (Green Park), 020-7491 8822; fax 7493 8309; www.langansrestaurants.co.uk

"Big, bustling and very British", this Mayfair "real character" with a rep for the "odd celeb-spotting" is the kind of place where "nothing's changed for 30 years" – "same Anglo-French menu, same decor, same staff" (who "better know you, or you're a toe rag"); many find that "most comforting", and even sceptics who call it "touristy and trite" say it's "somehow still fun."

La Noisette ☒ — — — VE
Jumeirah Carlton Tower Hotel, 164 Sloane St., SW1 (Knightsbridge), 020-7750 5000; fax 7750 5001
Restaurateur Gordon Ramsay's backing yet another establishment, on the site of the shuttered Pengelley's in Knightsbridge; slated to open as this guide goes to press, the elegant slate-and-wood, modern art–decorated venture is in collaboration with chef Bjorn van der Horst (ex Greenhouse), who's doing a Classic French menu with innovative touches, such as watermelon carpaccio and trout with asparagus marmalade; there's also a £65 'culinary adventure' that lets diners design their dinner in tandem with the toque.

Lansdowne, The 19 15 14 £27
90 Gloucester Ave., NW1 (Chalk Farm), 020-7483 0409; fax 7586 1723
"Jam-packed, and for good reason", this Primrose Hill "neighbourhood gastropub" "remains ahead of the game" in terms of its "good vibe/set of people" – "frequent thespian sightings help" – and "stylish" Eclectic–Modern European fare; but those downe on it snap the fare's "sturdy rather than inspired", and scold "staff who figure the place is only there for them to strut around in."

La Piragua — — — M
176 Upper St., N1 (Highbury & Islington), 020-7354 2843; fax 7354 2843; www.lapiragua.co.uk
"For big meat eaters on a budget", this "delightfully cheery" Islingtonian is "the place for a juicy Argentinean steak" and other "hearty", "home-cooked South American" fare; equally flavourful are the "fat, naked lady portraits on the walls."

La Porchetta Pizzeria 20 12 17 £17
33 Boswell St., WC1 (Holborn), 020-7242 2434 ☒
84-86 Rosebury Ave., EC1 (Angel), 020-7837-6060; fax 7837 6200
265 Muswell Hill Broadway, N10 (Highgate), 020-8883 1500 ◗
147 Stroud Green Rd., N4 (Finsbury Park), 020-7281 2892; fax 7837 6200 ◗
141-142 Upper St., N1 (Angel/Highbury & Islington), 020-7288 2488 ◗
It "feels like a train station waiting room, but it's worth the wait" for the "man-hole–sized pizzas" and other "fantastically priced" fare at this perpetually "packed-to-the-hilt" Italian chain; "the house wine is decent – another plus" – and "staff are friendly, if rushed" dealing with the "exuberant", ubiquitous party groups ("judging by the number of times 'Happy Birthday' is blared out each night").

La Porte des Indes ◗   22 | 25 | 20 | £43

32 Bryanston St., W1 (Marble Arch), 020-7224 0055;
fax 7224 1144; www.laportedesindes.com

The setting's "a bit bonkers" ("impressive waterfalls" et al.)
at this "delightful", "Disney exhibition–like" "giant" in
Marylebone – but at least this is "one place where over-
whelming decor doesn't mask underwhelming food",
since most find the "French-style Indian fare" "spicy and
highly varied" and "service most attentive"; still, some
malcontents mutter it's all "way too pricey" for an adventure that's "strictly tourist-time."

La Poule au Pot   21 | 22 | 18 | £42

231 Ebury St., SW1 (Sloane Sq.), 020-7730 7763; fax 7259 9651

Despite – or due to – its "idiosyncratic", "rustic" decor
(is that "chicken wire next to my seat"?), this "little piece
of France" in Pimlico remains a "romantic benchmark"
after 35 years; "though not earth-shattering", the "generous portions" of "French country classics" satisfy, and
the servers have "just the right amount of attitude";
even those who find it "overpriced" are seduced by the
"terrific alfresco dining."

La Rueda ◗   16 | 12 | 16 | £28

102 Wigmore St., W1 (Bond St.), 020-7486 1718; fax 7486 1718
66-68 Clapham High St., SW4 (Clapham Common/Clapham North),
020-7627 2173; fax 7627 2173
642 King's Rd., SW6 (Fulham Broadway), 020-7384 2684;
fax 7384 2684
www.larueda.co.uk

"Drink, dine and dance all under one roof" at this "still
sassy salsa" trio, which "keep on rolling" as a "good place
to have fun"; whilst "authentic", the Spanish fare "could
definitely be better", so many just "go for tapas" and
the "great sangria."

Latium 🖺   22 | 17 | 20 | £40

21 Berners St., W1 (Goodge St.), 020-7323 9123; fax 7323 3205;
www.latiumrestaurant.com

Fans flip for the "*fanissimo*" "Italian fare in Bloomsbury"
backed by "friendly service" and "decent wine list" at this
small venue; "they pack them in" (especially at lunch),
but "that's to be expected", given the "reasonable prices"
for the area.

LA TROMPETTE   27 | 22 | 22 | £49

5-7 Devonshire Rd., W4 (Turnham Green), 020-8747 1836;
fax 8995 8097; www.latrompette.co.uk

It may be "tricky to find" in Turnham Green, but this "luxu-
riously restrained" "sister to The Glasshouse" and Chez
Bruce "is everything you'd expect from a top-class restaurant", with "exemplary" New French–Modern European
cooking from "technically excellent" new chef James

Bennington; "service is on occasion a little slow, but nothing to spoil a wonderful night out" – especially since you're getting "Mayfair quality at Chiswick prices."

La Trouvaille | 19 | 18 | 18 | £38 |
12A Newburgh St., W1 (Oxford Circus), 020-7287 8488;
fax 7434 4170 🅂
353 Upper St., N1 (Angel), 020-7704 8323; fax 7359 6671
www.latrouvaille.co.uk

"Reflecting the buzz from Carnaby Street and musical venues nearby", this "sweet little" Soho spot, with an Islington brasserie-style branch, "is like a little theatre itself", starring almost "comically French waiters" and both Classic and New Gallic dishes; but whilst it was "recently refurbished", many reviewers regret it "lacks the panache that used to be there."

Launceston Place | 22 | 20 | 23 | £45 |
1A Launceston Pl., W8 (Gloucester Rd.), 020-7937 6912;
fax 7938 2412; www.egami.co.uk

It's like dining "at home in the country with some very civilised folks" (the staff "look after you so well") at this "spacious" Kensington "townhouse with several rooms"; both the "simple", "consistent" "modern cuisine" – "insist on the goat cheese soufflé" – and the decor have a "quintessentially English" feel, though the latter "needs updating, like a comfy shirt with frayed cuffs" some say.

L'Aventure 🅂 | 20 | 16 | 17 | £46 |
3 Blenheim Terrace, NW8 (St. John's Wood), 020-7624 6232;
fax 7625 5548

"You never know who might wander in after a [recording] session at nearby Abbey Road Studios" to this "typical romantic Classic French" "hidden in St. John's Wood"; although it's "not the most comfortable of places to sit" and the service can have "off days", regulars reassure us the cuisine "stays as consistent as ever."

Le Boudin Blanc | 22 | 18 | 19 | £38 |
Shepherd's Mkt, 5 Trebeck St., W1 (Green Park), 020-7499 3292;
fax 7495 6973; www.boudinblanc.co.uk

"They squeeze you in like sardines" to this "snug" Shepherd's Market "boîte" where "scrumptious", "homey" Classic French cuisine is served to "candlelit tables" by "cheery staff" (who "can fray under pressure", however); still, it's so authentically "atmospheric" and "so romantic" you may "have to keep checking to see if you are in London."

Le Café du Jardin ● | 18 | 16 | 17 | £35 |
28 Wellington St., WC2 (Covent Garden), 020-7836 8769;
fax 7836 4123; www.lecafedujardin.com

With "a view of passers-by" from the glass-fronted dining room (a better option than the "dark basement"), this Modern European brings a "breath of fresh air" to "crowded" Covent Garden; "reliable, if unexciting" eats and "considerate service" make it a "bustling pre-/post-theatre" pit stop.

Le Café du Marché Ⓔ
20 | 18 | 20 | £42

22 Charterhouse Sq., EC1 (Barbican), 020-7608 1609; fax 7251 8575

There's a "warm glow" to this "wonderful piece of France" near Smithfield Marché that offers an "authentic" "Parisian bistro"–style prix fixe, plus "pleasant staff" and "atmosphere that's all creaky wood, cosy candle flames" and exposed bricks; "no complaints, but not worth going out of your way" some say.

LE CAPRICE ●
24 | 20 | 23 | £54

Arlington House, Arlington St., SW1 (Green Park), 020-7629 2239; fax 7493 9040; www.le-caprice.co.uk

"Fizzy and fun, like living in a glass of champagne", this "sister to The Ivy" in "art deco–infused" premises just "off the main drag" of Piccadilly is "still hot after a long run"; "nothing's capricious here" – neither the Modern British–European menu that "never misses" nor the "smart service" overseen by director "Jesus Adorno, who walks on water"; when you leave, "you'll be broke, but happy"; P.S. whilst getting a booking takes "a heroic effort", "you can often squeeze in at the bar" at the last minute.

Le Cercle Ⓔ
24 | 20 | 18 | £48

1 Wilbraham Pl., SW1 (Sloane Sq.), 020-7901 9999; fax 7901 9111

"The concept of tapas-style French cuisine works" at this high-ceilinged Sloane Square basement that features an "inventive" menu of "great foie gras and other artery-clogging wonders" backed up by a "satisfying Gallic wine list"; but beware – the "small plates" formula "does add up fast", pricewise, and staff "refusals to turn down the music" don't help the "noisy" digs.

Le Colombier
20 | 19 | 20 | £44

145 Dovehouse St., SW3 (South Kensington), 020-7351 1155; fax 7351 5124

"In an age when trendy trumps tradition", this "charming hideaway" off Fulham Road fights back with "well-cooked, old-fashioned Classic French food" served in a "very Paris bistro" setting, plus "glorious terrace"; although the "correct service" can "show real gaps when it gets busy", this "popular" haunt "must be doing most things right."

LEDBURY, THE
26 | 22 | 25 | £66

127 Ledbury Rd., W11 (Westbourne Park), 020-7792 9090; www.theledbury.com

"Run by the same folks as The Square", this "sophisticated" yearling in "what was until recently a so-so fringe of Notting Hill" is the "kind of place to propose" in – since your intended will be impressed by the "sublime New French creations" from a "young Australian chef", "adorable staff" and "comfortably spaced tables" in the "stylish" room (it could use "some colour", though); true, the "shockingly expensive" tabs restrict it to "a treat" – but it's a "triumph" nonetheless.

Le Deuxième ●   21 | 16 | 20 | £34

65A Long Acre, WC2 (Covent Garden), 020-7379 0033; fax 7379 0066; www.ledeuxieme.com
Set in a "great spot" along Long Acre, this "quieter, more intimate sister to Le Café du Jardin" (the owners' *'deux-ième'* venture) makes a "good value hangout" for "delectable" Modern European cuisine with "a steal of a pre-/post-theatre prix fixe", and "pleasant service"; it's the kind of "bright", unassuming place "that would be your local if you lived in Paris."

Lee Ho Fook ●   18 | 12 | 13 | £23

15-16 Gerrard St., W1 (Leicester Sq./Piccadilly Circus), 020-7494 1200; fax 7494 1700
Mixed views greet this "busy" Chinatown "stalwart" that's dished the dim sum for over 45 years: some say it's still a "must-stop" for "authentic" Cantonese fare; but critics claim they "can no longer rely on this former 'always-rely-on'" cavern, citing "routine" eats and "inattentive staff."

LE GAVROCHE ⌧   28 | 25 | 26 | £89

43 Upper Brook St., W1 (Marble Arch), 020-7408 0881; fax 7491 4387; www.le-gavroche.co.uk
"Old-fashioned, but never out of fashion" profess patrons who make the "pilgrimage to this shrine" of Classic French cuisine in Mayfair; chef-owner Michel Roux Jr.'s "wizards in the kitchen" produce "intricately prepared", "mind-bending" meals in "overstuffed" surrounds; naturally, some "nitpick" that it's "lacking novelty", but they're out-voted by those who want to be "spoiled" by the "perfectly orchestrated" staff; P.S. prices are as "ultrarich" as the food, but "lunch is great value" (relatively speaking).

LE MANOIR AUX QUAT'SAISONS   28 | 26 | 26 | £88

Le Manoir aux Quat'Saisons, Church Rd., Great Milton, Oxfordshire, 01844 278881; fax 01844 278847; www.manoir.com
It's "a bit of a drive from London", but for a taste of "what life is about", few surpass this "culinary heaven" in the Cotswolds; "everything is brilliantly done", from the "gracious" setting – a 15th-century manor house featuring "sumptuous lounges for pre- and post-dinner drinks" – to the "refined", "exquisite" New French cuisine displaying "chef Raymond Blanc's passion for perfection" to the "standard-setting", "solicitous service"; P.S. an after-meal stroll in the "beautiful" gardens "is both a necessity and a pleasure."

Le Mercury ◐
19 17 20 £22
140A Upper St., N1 (Angel/Highbury & Islington), 020-7354 4088;
fax 7359 7186

"If romance is in the air", this Islington bistro will seal the deal with its "fireplace, candlelight" and "tables on several levels", creating quite a "cosy" ambience; the New French menu is something of "a culinary marvel" – "well-prepared" at relatively "cheap" prices; however, it "never changes, so repeat visits can be boring."

Lemonia ◐
19 15 20 £29
89 Regent's Park Rd., NW1 (Chalk Farm), 020-7586 7454;
fax 7483 2630

"People from miles around return with regularity" – often "in large groups and parties" – to Primrose Hill's "never-less-than-packed" "Greek legend"; even if "it's not ground-breaking", its "huge portions" of "almost home-cooked", "good-value" fare are "served with gusto and efficiency" "under the watchful eyes of the owner."

Leon
21 14 16 £13
35 Great Marlborough St., W1 (Oxford Circus), 020-7437 5280
136 Brompton Rd., SW3 (Knightsbridge), 020-7589 7330;
fax 7589 7346
3 Crispin Pl., E1 (Liverpool St.), 020-7247 4369; fax 7377 1653
12 Ludgate Circus, EC4 (Blackfriars), 020-7489 1580 ⊠
www.leonrestaurants.co.uk

"Proving that takeaway can be inventive and good for you", this "super-busy" self-service quartet "in the middle of Soho" (where "you're guaranteed to queue with pretty people") and elsewhere have got hold of a "fabulous idea" – "fresh Med" fast food "for modest prices"; they're "disappointing for dinner – just not designed for it" – but suit most other meals "in your daily grind."

Le Palais du Jardin ◐
20 19 17 £39
136 Long Acre, WC2 (Leicester Sq.), 020-7379 5353; fax 7379 1846

Big and "bustling", this brasserie is "always a safe bet" for relatively "reasonable", "genuine old-fashioned" Classic French dishes; "it's a factory", with "close tables" and "indifferent service to match", but a "convenient" "lifesaver" when combating the "Covent Garden crowds."

Le Pont de la Tour ◐
22 24 20 £55
Butlers Wharf Bldg., 36D Shad Thames, SE1 (London Bridge/
Tower Hill), 020-7403 8403; fax 7403 0267;
www.conran-restaurants.co.uk

It's so close, "Tower Bridge [seems] next to your table" at this "beautiful" "true room with a view" in a "converted warehouse" at Shad Thames; "the location sells it" but the Classic French "food does not let it down", with a "memorable" focus on "fresh" fish; pretty "good service" "helps you get over the shock of the prices."

Le Relais de Venise
23 | 18 | 22 | £31

120 Marylebone Ln., W1 (Bond Street/Marylebone),
020-7486 0878; www.relaisdevenise.com
"Finally, this Paris institution arrives in London" with the
Marylebone opening of this official branch (there have
been unofficial clones) and their "tried-and-tested" "one-
menu-only" featuring entrecôte in a secret green sauce;
it's "heaven for the steak-frites crowd, hell for local veg-
gies", but the "authentic brasserie look" and "motherly
Gallic service (as many helpings as you wish)" make it a
"reliable outpost" of the original.

L'Escargot ⚫🅱
22 | 22 | 20 | £46

48 Greek St., W1 (Leicester Sq./Tottenham Court Rd.),
020-7437 6828; fax 7437 0790; www.whitestarline.org.uk
"For a friendly meal with fellow French-food lovers", this
"classy", "comfortable" Soho-ite is "a sure thing", with
Classic cuisine that "sees no need to reinvent the wheel";
it's "a bit corporate" to some, but most agree this "buzzing" spot "puts you in a good mood"; P.S. whilst the "mirrored ground floor" is "ok", "try to book the Picasso Room"
upstairs, with its "amazing" artwork.

L'Estaminet 🅱
19 | 18 | 19 | £37

14 Garrick St., WC2 (Covent Garden/Leicester Sq.), 020-7379 1432;
fax 7379 1530
"A welcome bit of calm in the hubbub of Theatreland", this
"comfy" bistro "does what it says, and does it well", serving "dependable" Classic French fare with a "remarkable
bargain of a prix fixe" pre-theatre; *hélas,* the "service
doesn't seem so coordinated" nowadays, and dissenters
deem it all "disappointingly ordinary."

LES TROIS GARÇONS 🅱
20 | 28 | 20 | £48

1 Club Row, E1 (Liverpool St.), 020-7613 1924; fax 7012 1236;
www.lestroisgarcons.com
The "outlandish", "completely OTT" decor of antiques and
animal heads – "like the Victoria & Albert Museum on
acid" – overshadows the Classic French menu at this "off-
the-beaten-track" Shoreditch site, voted No. 1 for Decor;
still, the service is always "attentive", making this "ab-
surd, yet fabulous" venue a "favourite."

Le Suquet ⚫
22 | 16 | 19 | £40

104 Draycott Ave., SW3 (South Kensington), 020-7581 1785;
fax 7225 0838
"It's like being in a small French port" – right down to the
"old-fashioned, scruffy" setting – at this "stalwart" seafooder, "one of the better kept secrets" of Brompton Cross;
it's the place for "perfectly prepared", "swimmingly fresh
fish", including a "literal mountain of a seafood platter"
amid the "warm ambience" of southern France (in fact, it's
named after an old part of Cannes).

L'ETRANGER 🖾
26 | 21 | 22 | £52

36 Gloucester Rd., SW7 (Gloucester Rd.), 020-7584 1118;
fax 7584 8886; www.etranger.co.uk
"Sleek, streamlined and sophisticated", this South
Kensingtonian seduces with a "surprising", "great fusion
of Asian and New French" flavours; it's also blessed with
a "well-researched, adventurous wine list" and "professional service", causing many to wonder "why don't I
come here more often"; P.S. before or after dinner, "de-
scend into the Opal bar below for a relaxed good time."

Le Vacherin
∇ 25 | 15 | 22 | £43

76-77 South Parade, W4 (Chiswick Park), 020-8742 2121;
fax 8742 0799; www.levacherin.co.uk
"Expertly cooked" Classic French cuisine, including a "fabulous rib-sticking cassoulet" in winter, and "great wine (and
sommelier)" are the main attractions at this "perfect place
for bistro dining" in Chiswick; but the "uninspiring atmosphere" makes it seem "overpriced" to opponents.

LEVANT ●
21 | 25 | 17 | £37

Jason Ct., 76 Wigmore St., W1 (Bond St.), 020-7224 1111;
fax 7486 1216; www.levant.co.uk
There's "no such thing as a quiet corner" at this "party
Lebanese" in Marylebone, featuring "fabulous" Moroccan
decor and "fetching belly dancers most nights"; whilst
it's "good for big groups", the "abrupt service" and noise
may alienate tables for two ("don't bring anyone you want
to talk to").

Levantine ●
∇ 20 | 19 | 20 | £31

26 London St., W2 (Paddington), 020-7262 1111; fax 7402 4039;
www.levant.co.uk
Brought by "knowledgeable servers", the "authentic,
well-executed" fare "goes down pretty well" at this atmospheric Lebanese (Levant's sibling) in Paddington; still,
some "like the place more for its ambience than its food" –
"dark" digs, loud music and "entertaining belly dancer
(more so for the men obviously)"; "prices are reasonable,
provided you don't go wacky on the wine list."

Light House
∇ 17 | 18 | 17 | £36

75-77 Ridgeway, SW19 (Wimbledon), 020-8944 6338; fax 8946 4440
"Paradoxical food combinations consistently please" at
this bright Eclectic "jewel in the crown of Wimbledon dining"; but despite it "doing well in the area", darker minds
mutter it's "not good enough to charge these prices."

Lilly's
– | – | – | M

75 Wapping High St., E1 (Wapping), 020-7702 2040; fax 7702 4828;
www.lillysrestaurant.co.uk
"After a day at the office, the menu has all the items you
want" – "well-cooked burgers", grills and other "basics" –

at this brasserielike Modern Brit; whilst it's a wow in Wapping, "don't travel across London to visit it", though.

L'Incontro ●☒   19 | 20 | 16 | £51
87 Pimlico Rd., SW1 (Sloane Sq.), 020-7730 3663; fax 7730 5062;
www.lincontro-restaurant.com
"Traditional Venetian food" "in uncomplicated recipes" is the culinary formula at this "smart", "quiet" Pimlico Northern Italian; however, it's "highly priced for what you get" – causing lachrymose linguists to say they "misread the name to mean 'the bill' (*conto*) rather than 'the meeting'" (*incontro*).

Little Bay   22 | 17 | 21 | £18
140 Wandsworth Bridge Rd., SW6 (Fulham Broadway),
020-7751 3133; fax 7223 6131
228 York Rd., SW11 (Clapham Junction), 020-7223 4080;
fax 7223 6131 ●
171 Farringdon Rd., EC1 (Farringdon), 020-7278 1234;
fax 7278 5368 ●
228 Belsize Rd., NW6 (Kilburn Park), 020-7372 4699;
fax 7223 6131 ●♊
www.little-bay.co.uk
"Filled with interesting nooks and crannies", these "amazing little neighbourhood hangouts" promote "a sense of fun", from the "friendly staff" to the often "outrageous decor" to the Modern European–Med menu that's "not brilliant, but well cooked" and "reliable"; but what really has diners baying in delight are the "dirt-cheap" bills – "how do they do it?"

Little Italy ●   ▽ 18 | 11 | 15 | £29
21 Frith St., W1 (Leicester Sq./Tottenham Court Rd.),
020-7734 4737; fax 7734 1777
"So good to have the joint open again after a refurb" carol the "nocturnal crowds" who come to this family-run Soho site; whilst the fare's "standard Italian", it comes in "big portions", and there's no doubt it's "a great place to kick off your shoes" "post-dinner, when the music, singing and dancing begins."

Livebait   17 | 13 | 15 | £32
21 Wellington St., WC2 (Covent Garden), 020-7836 7161;
fax 7836 7141 ☒
43 The Cut, SE1 (Waterloo), 020-7928 7211;
fax 7928 2279
www.santeonline.co.uk
There's "lots of hustle and bustle" at both the Covent Garden and Waterloo sites of these two "staple" seafooders, who bait clients with "(almost) live fish", "simply prepared"; but you "go for the freshness, not the decor" – whose white tiles are "especially cold" – or the staff, who tend to "flap about."

Living Room, The   18 | 19 | 15 | £34

3-9 Heddon St., W1 (Oxford Circus/Piccadilly Circus),
0870-1662 225; fax 0870-1662 226; www.thelivingroomW1.co.uk
It "gets a little crowded and rowdy after work (had beer
spilled on my head!)", but life's still "good" at this yearling in
a former post office off Regent Street that "spreads over two
floors"; downstairs includes a meandering menu of brasserie classics, while the "fine-dining" Modern European option
upstairs includes "blinds to separate tables for more intimacy"; given the "great" 17-metre-long bar, though, some
wonder "why would you go for the food" at all.

LMNT   – | – | – | M

316 Queensbridge Rd., E8 (Dalston Kingsland B.R.),
020-7249 6727; fax 7249 6538; www.lmnt.co.uk
The "strange pseudo-Egyptian pharaoh-and-mummy decor" makes this converted Hackney pub one of "the more
bizarre and beautiful restaurants in London"; but it's "an
eatery remembered for its pyramids, rather than food", as
surveyors are as silent as the tomb when it comes to the
Modern Euro–New French cooking; P.S. do "check out the
porno-tiled loos."

LOCANDA LOCATELLI   25 | 23 | 23 | £59

Hyatt Regency London – The Churchill, 8 Seymour St., W1
(Marble Arch), 020-7935 9088; fax 7935 1149;
www.locandalocatelli.com
Go with a foodie willing to experiment and share" chef-
owner Giorgio Locatelli's "inventive" "take on traditional
Northern Italian" *cucina* at this "epitome of epicurean elegance" in Marylebone – an "unpretentious special treat
place" in "charmingly modern" digs; true, the "reservation
process is a pain" and the "expensive" bills put it "in dan-
ger of becoming a business canteen" some fret, but at
least "you don't need to be a rock star to get great service"
(although "Madonna often shows up").

Locanda Ottoemezzo 🏴   23 | 17 | 21 | £42

2-4 Thackeray St., W8 (High St. Kensington), 020-7937 2200;
fax 7937 9871; www.locandaottoemezzo.co.uk
With movie posters on the walls ("Sophia Loren rules!")
and an "unfailingly good", albeit "short menu" of "home-
style classic Italian dishes"("don't miss the risotto in a
Parmesan rind"), this "cute" trattoria just "off Kensington
Square" is "the best place after the Royal Albert Hall";
"friendly staff" complete the rosy picture, which rocks after 9 PM (when the local "crowd pushes up the decibels").

Lola's   ▽ 22 | 19 | 23 | £41

The Mall Bldg., 359 Upper St., N1 (Angel), 020-7359 1932;
fax 7359 2209; www.lolas.co.uk
The frequent change of chefs at least means it never gets
boring" at this Islington venue where the "newest" arrival is

considered "a big improvement (not so obsessed with expensive ingredients)", preparing Modern European cuisine that's "classy in every way"; the "very good service" includes a "wine waiter who knows what he is talking about."

Lonsdale, The   ▽ 14 | 23 | 13 | £35

48 Lonsdale Rd., W11 (Ladbroke Grove/Notting Hill Gate), 020-7727 4080; fax 7727 6030; www.thelonsdale.co.uk

The "main attraction" of this "beautiful Notting Hill playground" is to "schmooze with sexy, sassy young things" over "dangerously good cocktails"; and even though it's "much better for drinks" than eats, the "new Pan-Asian menu" is fine for "finger food" – "not if you are hungry, unless you are into super-model portions."

L'ORANGER ☒   27 | 24 | 25 | £63

5 St. James's St., SW1 (Green Park), 020-7839 3774; fax 7839 4330

"Elegant" and "exceptionally discreet", this "St. James's gem" may seem "stilted" to some, but it earns plaudits for "grown-up", "sublime" Classic French cooking that, "although expensive, is worth the price"; the "accommodative" service "delivers without seeming to try too hard" and all told, this "posh" place is "perfect for clinching a big deal over a civilised lunch" ("with the extra advantage of a private room downstairs").

Lou Pescadou ●   ▽ 20 | 13 | 20 | £35

241 Old Brompton Rd., SW5 (Earl's Ct.), 020-7370 1057; fax 7244 7545

"Nothing fishy about this place" pun patrons of the daily-changing seafood cooked with "Classic French flair" at this "friendly neighbourhood bistro" in Earl's Court; the "service is charming", if "quirky", but the decor is "so outdated, it should be a museum."

L-Restaurant & Bar ●   – | – | – | E

2 Abingdon Rd., W8 (High St. Kensington), 020-7795 6969; www.l-restaurant.co.uk

Restaurateur Eddy Lim is the force behind this new spot just off Kensington High Street – a narrow but airy two-tiered room with a dramatic glass roof and stone floor; it specialises in sophisticated Iberian fare in plates large and small; you can also nibble at the snug bar in front.

Luciano ●☒   20 | 17 | 12 | £50

72-73 St. James's St., SW1 (Green Park), 020-7408 1440; fax 7439 6670; www.lucianorestaurant.co.uk

Designed by David Collins, this St. James's "newcomer" from owner Marco Pierre White has a "glamourous bar" up front, leading to a "spacious" dining room with "many tables"; the Italian fare is "simple" and "well prepared" but "one hopes the service will catch up" – as with many debutantes, it's currently a little "chaotic."

Lucio
25 | 23 | 23 | £47

257-259 Fulham Rd., SW3 (South Kensington), 020-7823 3007; fax 7823 3009

"When you eat here, you want to book the next day – it's that good" declare devotees of this "glamorous" venue "conveniently located" in Chelsea, with a "balanced menu" of "classical" Italian fare; the "slick service" is supervised by namesake owner Lucio Altana, "a wonderful man who cares about his clientele."

Lucky 7
20 | 18 | 16 | £16

127 Westbourne Park Rd., W2 (Royal Oak/Westbourne Park), 020-7727 6771; fax 7727 6798

"Even if you're cheek-by-jowl with your neighbour", it's "always a cool, relaxing" scene at owner Tom Conran's "funky" "little" Notting Hill "American diner" that's "perfect when you're craving a real burger" "transformed into something fresh and exciting"; the "real drag is waiting a while for a table", and service can be "such a disappointment."

Luigi's of Covent Garden ◑ ⌧
18 | 15 | 19 | £33

15 Tavistock St., WC2 (Covent Garden), 020-7240 1789; fax 7497 0075

"Luigi, you make my heart sing" warble worshippers of this "festive" Covent Garden trattoria, a "standby" since 1964 for "solid Italian fare", "reasonably priced"; staff can be "brusque on busy nights", but at least it gets you "in and out" "when going to the theatre."

Lundum's
23 | 23 | 24 | £46

117-119 Old Brompton Rd., SW7 (Gloucester Rd./ South Kensington), 020-7373 7774; fax 7373 4472; www.lundums.com

Though "not very well known", this "family-run" South Ken Scandinavian "does a surprisingly exciting job" in its "elegant", "civilised surroundings", serving "flavoursome", "authentic Danish food" with "attentive-to-detail" service; in sum, an "interesting" "alternative to the ubiquitous Italians and Indians over town."

Made in Italy ◑
20 | 14 | 14 | £25

249 King's Rd., SW3 (Sloane Sq./South Kensington), 020-7352 1880

"It's usually full of Italians, so they must be doing something right" at this "cheap", "cramped" Chelsea trattoria known for "great, long" Neapolitan pizzas "cooked in a brick oven"; but the "food might be more enjoyable if the service" was less "sloppy."

Maggie Jones's
20 | 22 | 19 | £37

6 Old Court Pl., W8 (High St. Kensington), 020-7937 6462; fax 7376 0510

"A bolt-hole away from the hustle and bustle of Kensington High Street", this "whimsical", "rustic" eatery ("none of

the tables and chairs match, adding to the country charm")
is "outstanding for getting an atmosphere fix"; the "solid"
Traditional British menu of "heavy, winter food" ensures
"you'll never go home hungry" and comes courtesy of
"well-run" staff; P.S. insider's tip: "sit upstairs where
there's more room."

Ma Goa
21 | 17 | 18 | £26

194 Wandsworth Bridge Rd., SW6 (Fulham), 020-7384 2122
242-244 Upper Richmond Rd., SW15 (East Putney), 020-8780 1767
www.ma-goa.com

It's "not your average curry house", but most find "pleasure" at this Putney purveyor of "unusual" "authentic",
"home-cooked Goan food" that comes at "a reasonable
price" and with "friendly" service; there are numerous
"specials" – both early-bird dinner and an all-you-can-eat
lunch buffet, so despite the "tight space", you "can't really
fault this place"; N.B. the new Fulham branch is unrated.

Malabar ●
21 | 16 | 17 | £29

27 Uxbridge St., W8 (Notting Hill Gate), 020-7727 8800;
www.malabar-restaurant.co.uk

"Not just curry and beer, but serious cooking" is to be
found at this "unadorned" Indian in a "convenient location"
behind Notting Hill's Coronet cinema; but despite "innovative" touches, "like the fact they serve Indian champagne", a few feel this veteran "needs a bit of zap" now.

Malabar Junction ●
20 | 15 | 19 | £25

107 Great Russell St., WC1 (Tottenham Court Rd.), 020-7580 5230;
fax 7436 9942

"Seconds away from Tottenham Court Road" (and the
British Museum) stands this "overdecorated but airy" conservatory space, serving "good, reliable" Keralan food
that's "different to the normal Indian" fare; "if you show an
interest in the [southern regional] cuisine", "they'll cook
you food off the menu" too.

Malmaison Hotel Bar & Brasserie
▽ 15 | 14 | 17 | £35

Malmaison Hotel, 18-21 Charterhouse Sq., EC1 (Barbican/
Farringdon), 020-7012 3700; fax 7012 3702;
www.malmaison.com

It's "a little obscure", "tucked away" in a Smithfield boutique
hotel basement, but this "useful bistro" with secluded
booths makes a "reliable standby" for French brasserie
fare; it's "nothing fancy", though.

Mandalay 🚫
25 | 10 | 24 | £20

444 Edgware Rd., W2 (Edgware Rd.), 020-7258 3696; fax 7258 3696

The "super-friendly" "brothers who own the place come
by and share stories with diners" at this "no-frills" Edgware
Road eatery that's "out of the way", but "worth finding"
for its "authentic Burmese fare" that's "superb – and great
value on top of it."

Mandarin Kitchen ❶
24 | 11 | 16 | £30

14-16 Queensway, W2 (Bayswater/Queensway), 020-7727 9012; fax 7727 9468

Whilst it's "not as flashy" as other "Queensway options" (the "decor's getting tired", actually), "some of the best Chinese seafood" in town is on hand at this "hectic but heavenly" site; the crustacean-oriented cuisine causes converts to cry "this restaurant is the reason God created lobster."

Mango Tree
21 | 22 | 19 | £42

46 Grosvenor Pl., SW1 (Victoria), 020-7823 1888; fax 7838 9275; www.mangotree.org.uk

"A contemporary Asian setting" – "upmarket", if possessing something of the "noisy, echoey" "railway-platform ambience" of nearby Victoria Station – attracts "lots of suits at lunch", "after-work groups enjoying cocktails" and "Saturday night clubbers" to this Thai "with a European twist"; however, the hostile huff it's "expensive for a stir-fry" and cringe from the "cold service."

Manicomio
21 | 17 | 16 | £39

85 Duke of York Sq., SW3 (Sloane Sq.), 020-7730 3366; fax 7730 3377; www.manicomio.co.uk

It's "wonderful outside in summer" at this Italian in the redeveloped Duke of York barracks, filled with local "Sloane Square sales and PR types"; whilst the "fabulous" forecourt is "the real reason to go", the "simple Italian food" is "always delicious" and "worth waiting for" from staff who "struggle to get the orders right" when "it's busy."

Manzi's ⊠
21 | 15 | 19 | £34

Manzi's Hotel, 1-2 Leicester St., WC2 (Leicester Sq./Piccadilly Circus), 020-7734 0224; fax 7437 4864; www.manzis.co.uk

"If you don't want Chinese in Chinatown", this "old-fashioned" 1928 seafooder is still serving "straightforward fish" dishes that, "whilst not grand gourmet", are "reliable" for a "relaxed meal", and "perfect pre- or post-theatre."

Mao Tai ❶
∇ 19 | 16 | 16 | £31

58 New King's Rd., SW6 (Parsons Green), 020-7731 2520; fax 7471 8992; www.maotai.co.uk

It comes "at a price", but this "long-established", plant-bedecked Parsons Green Chinese "does serve consistently good", "well-presented" cuisine that "gives the impression of trying hard to be healthy"; P.S. "the Chelsea branch has cashed in on its location" and closed.

MARK'S CLUB ⊠
25 | 25 | 27 | £76

Private club; inquiries: 020-7499 2936

One is made to feel *très* important" at this "endearingly old-fashioned" Mayfair private club – and not just because there's "absolutely no admittance to the general public"; rather, it's the "really grown-up" experience of "very personal service", "marvellous" Classic French–British cooking and "understatedly elegant" decor, all of which "suits the captains of industry who eat there" and their "seriously wealthy and titled" friends; "if you can get in", it's "like going to a private dinner party."

Maroush ●
22 | 12 | 17 | £26

1-3 Connaught St., W2 (Marble Arch), 020-7262 0222
21 Edgware Rd., W2 (Marble Arch), 020-7723 0773; fax 7723 3161
68 Edgware Rd., W2 (Marble Arch), 020-7224 9339; fax 7723 3161
62 Seymour St., W1 (Marble Arch), 020-7724 5024; fax 7723 3161
4 Vere St., W1 (Bond St.), 020-7493 5050; fax 7723 3161
38 Beauchamp Pl., SW3 (Knightsbridge), 020-7581 5434;
fax 7723 3161
www.maroush.com

Londoners never tire of the "tasty morsels that transport you to the Jaffa Gate" offered by this "all-time classic", if somewhat "chaotic", Lebanese chain; whilst "you can't go wrong" using them "for casual eating, more formal dining or takeaway", they're really "heaven on the way home at 2 AM" (there's "always a queue", even then).

Masala Zone
19 | 14 | 16 | £19

9 Marshall St., W1 (Oxford Circus/Piccadilly Circus),
020-7287 9966; fax 7287 8555
147 Earl's Court Rd., SW5 (Earl's Court), 020-7373 0220;
fax 7373 0990
80 Upper St., N1 (Angel), 020-7359 3399; fax 7359 6560
www.realindianfood.com

"Funky" and "festive" (a nice word for "loud"), this "perpetually busy" trio "offer an updated take on Indian food" with "inventive", "piping hot" "street food"–style dishes at "very down-to-earth prices"; "the fastest service ever encountered" ensures you won't stay in this zone for long.

Mash 🚫
17 | 16 | 16 | £28

19-21 Great Portland St., W1 (Oxford Circus), 020-7637 5555;
www.mashbarandrestaurant.co.uk

A "smartly dressed, twenty-to-thirtysomething crowd" mingles at this Modern European with a "buzzing bar" stocked with the house microbrews, and a '70s retro-themed eatery "one floor above" that's "good for a quick bite"; but the "bright" Bloomsbury digs make for "a better drinking than eating spot" snap sceptics, squirming "if uncomfortable is the 'in' thing, this place is a winner."

Matsuri
22 | 17 | 20 | £46

71 High Holborn, WC1 (Holborn), 020-7430 1970; fax 7430 1971 🚫
15 Bury St., SW1 (Green Park), 020-7839 1101; fax 7930 7010
www.matsuri-restaurant.com

"Covering many different types of Japanese cuisine", from tempura to teppanyaki, this "pleasant, dependable" duo are "hard to fault", except perhaps for the "so-so decor" (at the St. James's site, anyway – the Holborn branch is "unusually soothing"); whilst often "filled with Asian business-men", they're "foreigner-friendly" as well, and so "worth the expense for an experience" of "quality" fare.

MAZE
24 20 21 £63

10-13 Grosvenor Sq., W1 (Bond St.), 020-7107 0000;
fax 7107 0001; www.gordonramsay.com

"Fabulous little works of art, one after the other" march across the table at this "pricey" "new concept" from Gordon Ramsay, which presents Asian-accented New French takes on tapas-sized fare in "cool", mod (some say "odd") Mayfair digs; antagonists argue it's "appropriately named", as sometimes "the service and food lose their way", but they're outnumbered by disciples of the "dazzling kaleidoscope of tastes", who marvel at the "multiple orgasmic experiences" to be had here.

Medcalf
▽ 20 15 19 £31

40 Exmouth Mkt., EC1 (Angel), 020-7833 3533; fax 7833 1321;
www.medcalfbar.co.uk

"The chef does know how to cook meat" at this Exmouth Market ex–butcher's shop, making this Brit a "great destination" "for carnivores"; be advised, though, that the "low-key", "funky" scene gets "more frenetic come night-time", particularly at the "popular bar."

Mediterraneo ⚫
20 15 17 £35

37 Kensington Park Rd., W11 (Ladbroke Grove), 020-7792 3131;
fax 7243 3630

Boosters yell "bravo" for this "homely Italian" near Portobello Market, where the "dependable" kitchen "keeps cooking standards up" – and "prices fair" too; but *enemici* grumble about staff who "don't seem to like customers after 9:45 PM", carping this is "just a copy of Osteria Basilico [its nearby sibling] – but not as nice."

Mela ⚫
23 15 20 £25

152-156 Shaftesbury Ave., WC2 (Leicester Sq.), 020-7836 8635;
fax 7379 0527; www.melarestaurant.co.uk

"Generous portions" of Indian fare "with a difference" (like "unusual" "country dishes") draw 'em in to this "unaffected" venue, "conveniently located" for Theatreland visits; although it gets "very noisy when full", it "can't be surpassed for value" – or speed ("the food came almost instantly").

Memories of China
22 17 18 £39

353 Kensington High St., W8 (High St. Kensington), 020-7603 6951;
fax 7603 0848
65-69 Ebury St., SW1 (Victoria), 020-7730 7734;
fax 7730 2992 ⚫

"Nice to have an elegant, old-fashioned Chinese still around" say those with fond memories of this "traditional" duo in Belgravia and Kensington; despite being "over-shadowed by newer entrants", the cooking is "done in a refined way", and so it remains a "welcoming" option where "old favourites are served with young enthusiasm."

Meson Don Felipe ⧄   19 | 17 | 16 | £23
53 The Cut, SE1 (Southwark/Waterloo), 020-7928 3237; fax 7736 9857
"It's buzzing most nights, so arrive early for a table" at this "cramped, crowded" Spaniard near Waterloo – "un-changing, but all the better for it" – that makes a "safe bet" for an "atmospheric" night out, with "authentic tapas", "a great wine selection" ("fine finos") and "good live music" from a nightly guitarist.

Mestizo   – | – | – | M
103 Hampstead Rd., NW1 (Warren St.), 020-7387 4064; www.mestizomx.com
"Located in a dead zone near Euston Station", this "new-ish" bright red–ceilinged premises offers highly "credible Mexican" fare, along with staff who "willingly help those who can't tell their quesadillas from their enchiladas"; "and if that isn't enough, downstairs is a tequila bar where you can practice your salsa moves."

Metrogusto   ∇ 25 | 21 | 23 | £50
11-13 Theberton St., N1 (Angel/Highbury & Islington), 020-7226 9400; fax 7226 9400; www.metrogusto.co.uk
"Any tough critic" would melt after the ministrations of the "magical owner" and the "modern", "brilliant" fare at this "magical Islington Italian"; add in "interesting" artwork and a "top wine list", and you've got a special place" that "feels like home."

Meza ◑⧄   19 | 21 | 17 | £38
100 Wardour St., W1 (Tottenham Court Rd.), 020-7314 4002; fax 7314 4040; www.conran-restaurants.co.uk
"A cool place to watch" the "beautiful people", this "mas-sive" "modern" Soho site offers an "interesting", tapas-style menu, and even if the "food is not its best feature" (has only "a distant touch of Spain"), the "lively" atmo-sphere ensures it gets "crowded", "especially on a week-end" when the DJs play "loud" music.

Michael Moore ⧄   24 | 16 | 23 | £43
19 Blandford St., W1 (Baker St./Bond St.), 020-7224 1898; fax 7224 0970; www.michaelmoorerestaurant.com
Well-travelled chef-owner "Michael Moore often says hi" to diners – and enters into "entertaining philosophical discussions" – at this "unpretentious" eatery in Marylebone, whose "exquisite" Eclectic dishes are "beautifully presented"; the "minimalist decor borders on cold" critics carp, but the "professional service" "from start to finish" makes amends.

Mildreds ⊠⊅ ▽ 23 | 14 | 14 | £17

45 Lexington St., W1 (Oxford Circus/Piccadilly Circus),
020-7439 2392; fax 7439 2392; www.mildreds.co.uk

"If you're a vegetarian and in Soho", this "sweet little hideaway" offers "both standard comfort fare and more adventurous dishes" that "even avid carnivores" can love; "it's not full of crustys in woolly jumpers" but caters to "a mostly twentysomething female crowd" – or at least the "harried staff" try to.

Mimmo d'Ischia ◑⊠ 21 | 16 | 21 | £45

61 Elizabeth St., SW1 (Sloane Sq./Victoria), 020-7730 5406;
fax 7730 9439; www.mimmodischia.co.uk

"This family-owned and -run Belgravia staple" is "one of the old greats" for sitting amongst a "star-studded" clientele enjoying "the biggest bowls of pasta" and other Southern Italian delights; founded over 35 years ago, it's "still very '70s in decor", and some newcomers grouse you get "better service if you're known."

Mint Leaf ◑ 19 | 22 | 16 | £45

Corner of Haymarket & Suffolk Pl., SW1 (Piccadilly Circus),
020-7930 9020; fax 7930 6205;
www.mintleafrestaurant.com

"Bombay techno-pop is the way to describe" the sound and the scene at this "incredibly dark" ("bring your flashlight"), "high-end" Indian with a "huge bar" in Haymarket; the "sleek" setting is more impressive than the food and the service"; however, it all "can be enjoyable – if someone else is paying."

Mirabelle ◑ 23 | 23 | 23 | £61

56 Curzon St., W1 (Green Park), 020-7499 4636; fax 7499 5449;
www.whitestarline.org.uk

Within its "glitzy-glam" "subterranean" interior, owner Marco Pierre White's "well-known", "quite pricey" Mayfair address serves Classic French fare "unfazed by modern culinary developments"; doubters declare it all "feels a little dated" now, but steady scores support enthusiasts who exclaim the experience is still "excellent", from the "sleek" (if slightly "snooty") staff to the "fine food."

Mitsukoshi ▽ 22 | 17 | 22 | £38

Mitsukoshi Department Store, 14-20 Lower Regent St., SW1
(Piccadilly Circus), 020-7930 0317; fax 7839 1167;
www.mitsukoshi-restaurant.co.uk

The Japanese clientele "who frequent this establishment" attest to the "authenticity of the sushi" and "classic" cooked dishes at this "undiscovered basement" eatery in a Piccadilly department store; "elegant presentation" compensates for the fact that the rather spare decor offers "no atmosphere."

Miyama
▽ | 23 | 9 | 20 | £42

38 Clarges St., W1 (Green Park), 020-7499 2443; fax 7493 1573
"Frequented mostly by Japanese", this 25-year-old "quiet retreat" "has not rested on its laurels", but continues to serve a "wonderful cooked menu" ("addicted to their sukiyaki") and "the best sashimi in town", all "at a very agreeable price for Mayfair"; the "jaded interior" "could do with a cosmetic upgrade", however.

Mju
21 | 18 | 19 | £52

Millennium Knightsbridge Hotel, 17 Sloane St., SW1 (Knightsbridge), 020-7201 6330; fax 7201 6353; www.mju-restaurant.co.uk
In the little-known Millennium Knightsbridge, this "expense-account", "elegant" eatery (pronounced 'mew') offers up "inventive" "Asian-French fusion cuisine" with "wonderful" wine pairings – leading enthusiasts to extol it as "a repeat-able experience"; but catty critics shrug it's "still hotel food", adding a "quarter-full dining room leads to little ambience."

MOMO
20 | 25 | 17 | £44

25 Heddon St., W1 (Piccadilly Circus), 020-7434 4040; fax 7287 0404
"A sexy setting suitable for a sultan" is the selling point of this Piccadilly Moroccan populated with a "glamourous" crowd and "drop-dead gorgeous staff" (who are some-times "slow"); the North African food usually "holds its own", but it's not the point" – "the real joy is the atmo-sphere" with everyone "dancing in the aisles" and imbibing "amazing cocktails"; be aware, though, "the bill can leave you with a hangover."

Mon Plaisir ●🗷
18 | 17 | 17 | £37

21 Monmouth St., WC2 (Covent Garden/Leicester Sq.), 020-7836 7243; fax 7240 4774; www.monplaisir.co.uk
"Still going strong with young and old alike", this "quaint" 65-year-old Covent Garden "institution" offers plenty of *plaisir* to playgoers, with its "rabbit warren" of "com-pletely different rooms" and "trad, not rad" French bistro fare; "offhand service" and a drop in the Food score sug-gest it may be "resting on its reputation", but "at these prices, you can't complain" too much.

Montpeliano ●
18 | 17 | 19 | £43

13 Montpelier St., SW7 (Knightsbridge), 020-7589 0032; fax 7838 0268
"Tucked away in Knightsbridge", this "Italian old-timer" is often "packed", given its "good location to the shops"; but what fans find "fabulously old-fashioned", naysayers say "needs a shot in the arm", citing "run-of-the-mill" eats, service that ranges from "lengthy to exceptional, depend-ing on their mood" and "dingy" decor (despite "all the framed pictures of Marilyn Monroe").

Monza
| 19 | 14 | 18 | £37 |

6 Yeoman's Row, SW3 (Knightsbridge/South Kensington), 020-7591 0210; fax 7591 0210

Adorned with "Formula One photos on the wall" (a "petrol head's paradise!"), Knightsbridge's "archetypical neighbourhood" Italian is "still racing along", serving "dependable", "if uneventful", fare; "don't miss the after-dinner peach drink they offer – it'll have you dancing on the tables."

Morel
| – | – | – | M |

14 Clapham Park Rd., SW4 (Clapham Common), 020-7627 2468; www.morelrestaurant.co.uk

Don't be put off by the down-at-heel facade around the corner from Clapham Common tube station – this cosy, wood-floored cream-and-red-coloured bistro belies its environs with chef-owner Jean Chaib's confident Classic French–Med menu – incorporating liberal use of the namesake fungi, naturally – at commendable prices.

MORGAN M
| 26 | 16 | 20 | £54 |

489 Liverpool Rd., N7 (Highbury & Islington), 020-7609 3560; fax 8292 5699

"In a most unlikely location – the wrong end of Liverpool Road" – resides this "top-notch" New French, whose "exquisite" cuisine includes "innovative" vegetarian dishes; the decor's a bit "bright", the staff a bit "snooty" and it's "not cheap, but you're paying for something special" – as owner Morgan Meunier is "sure to be among the next generation of celebrity chefs."

Moro ⊠
| 25 | 17 | 21 | £38 |

34-36 Exmouth Mkt., EC1 (Angel/Farringdon), 020-7833 8336; fax 7833 9338; www.moro.co.uk

"Enter a world of tantalising delights" when you traipse into this "aromatic" Med in "buzzy Exmouth Market"; although "the noise level is deafening" within the "industrial decor, it does not detract" from the "exciting", "exotic" "Spanish-Moorish food"; the "warm and welcoming" service also inspires love for this "lively, hip" place.

MORTON'S ●⊠
| 25 | 24 | 27 | £59 |

Private club; inquiries: 020-7518 2982

If "the membership fee is a problem", "find somebody to take you" to this "beautiful", art-adorned private club overlooking Berkeley Square – and "go hungry", because the New French fare is pretty "fabulous" and the wine list "first class"; there's also a "great bar downstairs" with a wall that changes colour as the day progresses.

Moshi Moshi Sushi
| 21 | 12 | 15 | £22 |

Canary Wharf Waitrose, Canada Pl., E14 (Canary Wharf), 020-7512 9201; fax 7512 9685

(continued)

(continued)

Moshi Moshi Sushi
*24 Upper Level, Liverpool St. Station, Broadgate, EC2
(Liverpool St.), 020-7247 3227; fax 7247 3227* 🖄
www.moshimoshi.co.uk
They won't win any ambience awards, but these sushi
spots – one located "very obviously in a supermarket" in
Canary Wharf, the other "overlooking the Liverpool Street
train station" – are "always a sure bet" to make "taste buds
happy", with their "fresh" fish delivered via "high-speed"
conveyor belt; the "sensible prices" are equally satisfying.

MOSIMANN'S 🖄   27 | 25 | 26 | £64
Private club; inquiries: 020-7235 9625
"Perfection", "outstanding", "absolutely first-rate" – the
compliments keep on coming for "master chef Anton
Mosimann's" members' club in Belgravia; its setting, a
19th-century converted church, provides an "intimate, elegant environment" for eating "refined" Eclectic cuisine
with "dignitaries and movie stars", overseen by "awesome service"; "although it's not as exciting or innovative
as some places", "if you can get an invite – take it."

Motcombs   17 | 17 | 19 | £37
*26 Motcomb St., SW1 (Knightsbridge/Sloane Sq.),
020-7235 6382; fax 7245 6351; www.motcombs.co.uk*
There's a "reassuring consistency" to the "simple, but
more than adequate" Eclectic fare at this bi-level
Belgravia venue with "lots of character", a "well-priced
wine list" and outside tables "to be enjoyed on balmy
days"; sure, some feel it "hasn't kept up with the times",
but that seems to matter little to its "faithful clientele" of
locals and "glamourous grannies."

Moti Mahal ●🕒🖄   ▽ 17 | 14 | 17 | £27
*45 Great Queen St., WC2 (Covent Garden/Holborn), 020-7240 9329;
fax 7836 0790; www.motimahal-uk.com*
The first London outpost of a Delhi-based chain, this "upmarket", fashionably white-hued Indian newcomer off Drury
Lane offers a midpriced menu focusing on "tasty" tandoor
clay-oven cooking; of its two floors, the upstairs features a
view of the glass-walled open kitchen, whilst the basement
space is more intimate and features a champagne bar.

Mr. Chow ●   22 | 20 | 21 | £50
*151 Knightsbridge, SW1 (Knightsbridge), 020-7589 7347;
fax 7584 5780; www.mrchow.com*
"Feel a celebrity going here" to this "fashionable", fortysomething Knightsbridge "institution", world-renowned
for its "Chinese food for the elite" (and at pretty elitist
prices as well – do "they pick the numbers out of a hat"?);
surveyors disagree as to whether its approach is "tried-
and-true" or "tired", but in a way, it's irrelevant – "when

you're on London's 'must list'", "why even think you should play a different hand?" P.S. you must "order the special noodles, for the theatrical presentation" alone.

Mr. Kong ●
22 | 7 | 16 | £24

21 Lisle St., WC2 (Leicester Sq.), 020-7437 7341
"The decor may be shockingly stark" and the "service variable", but reviewers make "regular stops" to this "reasonably priced" "Chinatown standby" 'cos "Mr. Kong knows his stuff"; it's "not gourmet cuisine, but everything works", and with last orders at 2:45 AM, it's "great for a late-night pig-out."

Nahm
23 | 20 | 23 | £58

Halkin Hotel, 5 Halkin St., SW1 (Hyde Park Corner), 020-7333 1234; fax 7333 1100; www.halkin.co.uk
"Crossing authenticity with creativity" ("the flavours are traditional, but the combinations are not") is the specialty of this "tranquil" Thai in Belgravia, where "polite servers" operate amidst "modern" (some say "sterile") decor; but whilst mavens relish "mouth-watering memories" of the menu, those reeling from "sticker-shock" snap "the price is remembered long after the cuisine is savoured."

Naked Turtle ●
– | – | – | E

505 Upper Richmond Rd. W., SW14 (Richmond), 020-8878 1995; fax 8392 1388; www.naked-turtle.com
At this "quaint, homey" spot in "sleepy East Sheen", a "creative" Eclectic menu ("go for the platter with crocodile and kangaroo – it won't disappoint") co-stars with "singing waitresses" and "live jazz" – all of which "makes for a nice evening if you don't feel like talking"; perhaps it's "slightly overpriced" for what it is.

Nam Long-Le Shaker ●⊠
16 | 16 | 14 | £37

159 Old Brompton Rd., SW5 (Gloucester Rd./South Kensington), 020-7373 1926; fax 7373 6043
"A restaurant that wants to be a bar" quip surveyors of this "relaxed" South Kensingtonian beloved of bankers and such; true, it's probably "better for its legendary cocktails"– its "Flaming Ferraris will get you racing", alright – than for its food, though the Vietnamese fare's "reliable" enough; just bear in mind "service can be slow at times", not to mention "rude."

National Dining Rooms, The
– | – | – | E

The National Gallery, Sainsbury Wing, WC2 (Charing Cross), 020-7747 2525; www.thenationaldiningrooms.co.uk
Another venture overseen by the ever-active Oliver Peyton, this bustling eatery in the National Gallery's Sainsbury Wing stands ready to refresh weary museum-goers throughout the day, either in a casual cafe with communal tables or in a spacious, beige-and-black dining

room with a homestyle Modern British menu; N.B. open for dinner (until 8:30 PM) on Wednesdays only.

Nautilus Fish ▽ | 19 | 4 | 18 | £14

27-29 Fortune Green Rd., NW6 (West Hampstead), 020-7435 2532

"For decent fish 'n' chips" – "no more, no less" – this "traditional" West Hampstead seafooder is "quick and easy" say those who've "been using it for 30 years"; it "remains consistently good" for takeaway too.

Neal Street Restaurant ☒ | 22 | 16 | 18 | £44

26 Neal St., WC2 (Covent Garden), 020-7836 8368; fax 7240 3964; www.carluccios.com

Restaurateur/cookbook author "Antonio Carluccio's launch pad" eatery in Covent Garden 36 years ago, this "temple of Italian cuisine" is "the place to go for exotic mushroom" and truffle dishes, plus other "lovingly cooked, adoringly consumed" fare; a few feel it "could do with a revamp" ("don't expect ambience"), and flinch at "excessive prices", but most rate it worth a try for "a true fungi experience."

New Culture Revolution | 16 | 10 | 14 | £16

157-159 Notting Hill Gate, W11 (Notting Hill Gate), 020-7313 9688
75 Southampton Row, WC1 (Holborn), 020-7436 9706
305 King's Rd., SW3 (Sloane Sq.), 020-7352 9281
42 Duncan St., N1 (Angel), 020-7833 9083
43 Parkway, NW1 (Camden Town), 020-7267 2700
www.newculturerevolution.co.uk

It won't start a culinary revolution, but this "decent enough" Chinese chain offers "fresh" "comfort food" (dumplings, noodles, etc.) that works "pre-cinema" or "for a quick lunch that won't break the bank"; given the "cafeteria"-like decor, however, many prefer the "efficient" "takeaway option."

New World ◗ | 19 | 13 | 14 | £20

1 Gerrard Pl., W1 (Leicester Sq.), 020-7434 2508; fax 7287 8994

"Take somebody for their first dim sum experience" to this "tatty" "barn of a place" in Chinatown, where the "huge selection of goodies" is "wheeled around on trolleys" 11 AM–6 PM daily (there are regular Chinese dishes too, although they "don't knock the socks off"); it's "an excellent deal, if you're willing to bear" the "depressed staff."

Nicole's ☒ | 19 | 19 | 18 | £43

Nicole Farhi, 158 New Bond St., W1 (Bond St./Green Park), 020-7499 8408; fax 7409 0381

"A hot spot for the ladies who lunch and shop Bond Street", this airy dining room "tucked away in the basement" of Nicole Farhi offers an "especially good" Med–Modern European menu in a "light, friendly" – and, of course, "trendy" – atmosphere.

NOBU BERKELEY ◑
26 | 21 | 20 | £63

*15 Berkeley St., W1 (Green Park), 020-7290 9222; fax 7290 9223;
www.noburestaurants.com*

This Mayfair "über-cool" "addition to the Nobu group" offers all the usual Japanese-Peruvian "mesmerising" "multi-orgasmic taste sensations", plus "wood-fired-oven dishes"; if it "doesn't top the Park Lane" sib foodwise, it "has a better scene going on", thanks to the "vibrant" "people-watching bar"; there's some debate over decor ("stunning" vs. "sparse") and service ("helpful" vs. "lacking"), but most "will be back as much as my wallet can afford it"; P.S. "they now take reservations."

NOBU LONDON
27 | 21 | 21 | £71

*Metropolitan Hotel, 19 Old Park Ln., W1 (Hyde Park Corner),
020-7447 4747; fax 7447 4749; www.noburestaurants.com*

"Spot the latest A-listers in town" at chef-restaurateur Nobu Matsuhisa's "ultramodern", "ultraswank" address, offering an "awesome" Japanese menu "with a wonderful Peruvian twist" that's "easiest to afford if you run a hedge fund or two"; a few fret it's now "too formulated to be a favourite", especially given the "bland" decor and "uneven service" if "you are not 'known'"; nevertheless, almost "no restaurant in Mayfair can top a night at Nobu."

Noor Jahan ◑
20 | 14 | 17 | £30

*26 Sussex Pl., W2 (Lancaster Gate), 020-7402 2332; fax 7402 5885
2A Bina Gardens, SW5 (South Kensington), 020-7373 6522*

"Steps up from the usual curry house", this "casual" duo in Notting Hill and South Ken serve "consistent" Indian fare that's "not too expensive" either; even though they're "always busy", the scene is "possibly a little, er, boring" – so, maybe try their takeaway.

North Sea ☒
23 | 12 | 18 | £19

7-8 Leigh St., WC1 (Kings Cross), 020-7387 5892; fax 7388 9770

"Killer" "fish 'n' chips for the connoisseur" – with "many different kinds" on offer – dominate the menu at this 30-year-old Traditional British seafooder in a large room in Bloomsbury; the decor is straight out of 1970 and the staff and customers like something from a "TV comedy set" ("lots of local colour"), but "you can't beat the prices" for the flakiest fish around.

Noto
20 | 12 | 18 | £22

*Harrods, ground fl., 87-135 Brompton Rd., SW1 (Knightsbridge),
no phone
2-3 Bassishaw Highwalk, EC2 (Bank/Moorgate), 020-7256 9433;
fax 7588 5656 ☒
www.noto.co.uk*

Even if "totally predictable", this "simple"-looking pair are "perfect" for "quick", "cheap" meals from a "decent", "flavourful" Japanese menu that "covers all bases (sushi, noodle soups, grilled stuff)"; whether in Harrods or near the Barbican, they're "just the spot for a quick lunch" or dinner; N.B. no cooked food at the store branch.

Notting Grill
22 | 17 | 18 | £39

123A Clarendon Rd., W11 (Holland Park/Ladbroke Grove), 020-7229 1500; fax 7229 8889; www.awtonline.co.uk
"Vegetarians beware, it's strictly for meat lovers" here at "celeb chef" Antony Worrall Thompson's "perfectly rustic", "cleverly named" Notting Hill chophouse serving "flavoursome" "burgers, steaks and all the filling sides to go with them"; "service is friendly, but begins to wane when it gets crowded – which it invariably does"; P.S. "upstairs is quieter", but "downstairs is more fun."

Notting Hill Brasserie
25 | 24 | 24 | £48

92 Kensington Park Rd., W11 (Notting Hill Gate), 020-7229 4481; fax 7221 1246
"Perfect for a date" or "civilised night out", this "intimate" Notting Hill eatery "is not trying to be anything it isn't": "just a calm, warm" setting with "soothing jazz", "proper", "relaxed service" and chef Mark Jankel's "imaginative" Modern European menu that "goes from strength to strength"; although the place is a "wallet weakener", "they do everything right."

Noura ●
22 | 19 | 19 | £36

16 Curzon St., W1 (Green Park), 020-7495 1050; fax 7495 1055
16 Hobart Pl., SW1 (Victoria), 020-7235 9444; fax 7235 9244
22 Lower Regent St., SW1 (Piccadilly Circus), 020-7839 2020; fax 7839 7700
www.noura.co.uk
"Filled with Lebanese families who know the real thing", these "relaxed" Middle Eastern "haunts" have "maintained sophisticated standards" as they've spread, with an "extensive menu" of healthy fare cooked "with flair", plus "efficient service"; a few sceptics warn "sharing small dishes" means "the bill quickly adds up", but in the main, they make a "lively, satisfying place to graze."

Nozomi ● ⊠
15 | 19 | 14 | £51

15 Beauchamp Pl., SW3 (Knightsbridge), 020-7838 0181; www.nozomi.co.uk
It's still early days for this "expensive Japanese" in skylit, "sexy" Knightsbridge digs, and whilst some believe the "booming bar buzz" makes it "perfect for pre-club dinner and drinks", detractors decry the "dizzy service" and "confused", "limited" menu.

Nyonya
▽ 21 | 13 | 17 | £19

2A Kensington Park Rd., W11 (Notting Hill Gate), 020-7243 1800; fax 7243 2006; www.nyonya.co.uk
"For die-hard foodies who miss the real deal, this is it" claim fans of this "interesting", "inexpensive" Malaysian

"in the heart of Notting Hill"; however, the "canteen-style" digs make it best for a "quick" bite – "it's a bit too casual for an evening meal."

Obika

_ _ _ M

Selfridges, 2nd fl., 400 Oxford St., W1 (Bond St.), 020-7318 3620

"Nestling amongst the haute couture" on Selfridges' second floor is London's purportedly first "mozzarella bar – a great idea" for *fromage* fans, as it celebrates the cheese in various forms, along with "delicious" light Italian fare; service is "excellent", and you get "good portions", which adds up to "good value."

OCCO ◑

_ _ _ M

58 Crawford St., W14 (Edgware Road/Marylebone), 020-7724 4991; fax 7724 4500; www.occo.co.uk

"Bringing a fresh attitude to Moroccan cuisine" – "some dishes are delicious, some curious" – this "converted pub" on a Marylebone street corner makes "a perfect place to hideaway or hang out with friends" in a "tardis-like" space comprising various "cosy" dining areas and a "thronged bar."

Odette's

∇ 21 21 20 £43

130 Regent's Park Rd., NW1 (Chalk Farm), 020-7586 5486; fax 7722 5388

"Back to its old self" say those who feel this "discreet", "romantic" 29-year-old Primrose Hill "hangout" is "much improved in the last year"; it's "perfect for a quiet soirée surrounded by the charming decoration" of antique mirrors and green chairs, consuming "upscale", "uncomplicated" Modern British–New French fare and "great, albeit expensive, wines"; N.B. it acquired a new owner post-*Survey*.

Odin's 🏛

21 21 22 £44

27 Devonshire St., W1 (Baker St.), 020-7935 7296; fax 7493 8309; www.langansrestaurants.co.uk

"Still going strong" after 40 years, this Marylebone "old favourite" is like "dining in a gracious home, surrounded by fine art"; if "not really a gastronomic experience", the Classic French–Traditional British cuisine is "excellent", and comes courtesy of "pleasant" service, making this "good for business" or "older couples on a date."

Oliveto

20 13 16 £33

49 Elizabeth St., SW1 (Sloane Sq./Victoria), 020-7730 0074; fax 7823 5377

A "simple", yet "original" Sardinian menu – featuring "excellent thin-crust pizzas" with "creative" toppings – makes this Belgravia "local" a "refreshingly atypical Italian"; despite the "cramped" setting, the place is "always buzzing" with a "stylish clientele" – which can make the room "very loud" and "service erratic" at busy times.

Olivo   23 16 21 £37
21 Eccleston St., SW1 (Victoria), 020-7730 2505
Those craving "something different" ("like sea urchin sauce
on the pasta") find this Italian behind Victoria Station "keeps
dragging them back" thanks to "genuine", "unfussy cooking" and staff who "give good attention and advice" –
"why else would you sit in" those "cramped" surrounds?

1 Lombard Street ☒   22 19 20 £59
1 Lombard St., EC3 (Bank), 020-7929 6611; fax 7929 6622;
www.1lombardstreet.com
"If you're not here on business, you must be lost", as this
"prestigious" site slap bang in the middle of the Square
Mile makes an "all-round safe place for client" entertaining, with a "classy", "expense-account-only" New French
menu and "grand", slightly "clinical decor"; whilst the
"noise from the Brasserie" alongside puts off some, others
are happy to "go for lunch and stay all afternoon."

1 Lombard Street Brasserie ☒   20 19 16 £41
1 Lombard St., EC3 (Bank), 020-7929 6611; fax 7929 6622;
www.1lombardstreet.com
Considered "more relaxed (and fun) than the restaurant" behind it, this "stylish former banking hall" is a place City folk
"bank on" for "reliably good" Modern European fare during "breakfast and luncheon client meetings" and "see-
and-be-seen" drinks; but a "disgruntled" few find it "way
too noisy to accomplish anything", and object to "waiters
getting on-the-job training."

One-O-One   24 18 20 £54
Sheraton Park Tower, 101 William St., SW1 (Knightsbridge),
020-7290 7101; fax 7201 7884
An "imaginative" New French menu – specialising in "fish
so fresh they swim to the table" – is the main draw of this
Knightsbridge hotel dining room, handy for "an after-meal
walk in Hyde Park"; even if it looks "a little sterile" and
costs "over what it should do", many profess surprise it's
"still not been discovered."

Oriel   12 15 12 £28
51 Sloane Sq., SW1 (Sloane Sq.), 020-7730 2804; fax 7730 7966
This "Chelsea staple" with a "Continental cafe atmosphere" serves a "simple menu" of brasserie fare; "thanks
to the location" in Sloane Square, it has "a real buzz", "although the food's absolutely average and overpriced", and
the "service poor."

Origin ☒   25 20 20 £49
The Hospital, 24 Endell St., WC2 (Covent Garden), 020-7170 9200;
www.origin-restaurant.com
In place of the late Thyme, this Modern European makes
"a highly welcome addition to the Covent Garden area";

"Adam Byatt's (one of the previous place's chef-owners) innovative cooking" is "exquisitely crafted", "with everything available in small portions" – "almost tiny" some sigh – "to create your own tasting menu"; whilst the "food does the shouting, rather than the wallpaper", the decor's quite nice, adorned with "beautiful artwork"; "staff take pains to explain the different dishes" too.

ORIGINAL LAHORE KEBAB HOUSE ☻
26 | 6 | 17 | £14

2-10 Umberston St., E1 (Aldgate East/Whitechapel), 020-7481 9737; fax 7488 1300
148-150 Brent St., NW4 (Hendon Central), 020-8203 6904
"Ignore the surroundings", however "shabby" they may be, as this Wapping stalwart (which expanded next door in 2005 "without any change in decor") and younger Finchley sibling are "the purest example of substance over form", "offering an endless stream of well-spiced", "succulent" Pakistani dishes "dirt-cheap" – and "BYO booze keeps the prices extra low"; plus, "now they're not nearly as rude as they used to be."

Original Tagine 🖭
▽ 22 | 17 | 20 | £24

7A Dorset St., W1 (Baker St.), 020-7935 1545
"Better keep it a secret" plead those who appreciate this "modest establishment" near Baker Street for its "cosy atmosphere", "interesting", "authentic" North African cuisine and "charming waitresses" – "all at prices that beat anything in the area for value."

ORRERY
26 | 24 | 24 | £62

55 Marylebone High St., W1 (Baker St./Regent's Park), 020-7616 8000; fax 7616 8080; www.orrery.co.uk
"Proof that Sir Terence [Conran's group] can produce a 'top of the pile' restaurant", this "elegant, understated" venue "with a Saint Marylebone Church view" is a "very grown-up affair" "where sophisticated New French food is presented with pomp" by "accomplished service"; there's particular praise for the "paired wine tastings" and "cheese trolley to die for", and if antagonists ask "isn't it all a bit stiff?", converts cry it's "well worth splurging on"; N.B. the Food score doesn't reflect a chef change post-*Survey*.

Orso ☻
21 | 17 | 20 | £39

27 Wellington St., WC2 (Covent Garden), 020-7240 5269; fax 7497 2148
"In an area chockabloc with restaurants", this "below-street-level" place "provides a lively, yet romantic ambience" for "decent", "homely Italian dishes"; although those "indifferent" indicate it's "showing its age" (22 years and counting), there's a sense "you can't go wrong" here especially when needing to make a Covent Garden "curtain with no time to spare."

Oslo Court ⌧
24 | 15 | 25 | £46

*Charlbert St., Prince Albert Rd., NW8 (St. John's Wood),
020-7722 8795; fax 7586 7695*

"A well-oiled machine" that "just goes on and on", this 35-year-old St. John's Wood "gem" offers a "dizzying choice" of "sumptuous", "rich" Classic French "standbys served by friendly, efficient staff"; "decorated like an '80s cruise ship (with a clientele to match)", this "throwback to olden times" is "not everybody's cup of tea", but the fact "one can rarely get a table here" suggests swarms still support it.

Osteria Antica Bologna
∇ 22 | 15 | 15 | £28

*23 Northcote Rd., SW11 (Clapham Junction B.R.), 020-7978 4771;
fax 7978 4771; www.osteria.co.uk*

An "unpretentious", dark-wood-and-wrought-iron setting belies the "out-of-the-ordinary menu" of regional Italian dishes at this Battersea Bolognese; it's "always popular" with the locals, making it "a little noisy" at times.

Osteria Basilico ●
23 | 18 | 19 | £33

*29 Kensington Park Rd., W11 (Ladbroke Grove/Notting Hill Gate),
020-7727 9957; fax 7229 7980; www.osteriabasilico.co.uk*

This Italian is constantly hailed for the "hearty", "home-style food" that makes it "a perennial favourite" amongst Notting Hill noteworthies; the "rustic" setting can feel a bit "claustrophobic", as it's "always buzzing", and some wonder if "popularity has gone to their heads" (though "once you are known by the staff", "they make you feel right at home"); just don't get a spontaneous craving for the "*bellissimo*" fare, "because you won't get in at short notice."

Osteria dell'Arancio
∇ 23 | 22 | 23 | £39

*383 King's Rd., SW10 (Sloane Sq./South Kensington),
020-7349 8111; fax 7349 8123; www.osteriadellarancio.co.uk*

"Set in a quirky townhouse" (the artwork includes a portrait of Queen Elizabeth with a salami crown) on a busy King's Road junction, this Northern Italian features "distinctive" fare and "good, little-known wines" "from the Marche region"; the service is a bit "in your face" – but in a "pleasant" way; P.S. they've dropped the "limited set menu" format.

Ottolenghi
23 | 17 | 16 | £24

*63 Ledbury Rd., W11 (Notting Hill Gate), 020-7727 1121
287 Upper St., N1 (Angel), 020-7288 1454; fax 7704 1456
www.ottolenghi.co.uk*

"Half-canteen, half-shop", this "white, bright" all-day duo in Notting Hill and Islington "pull in the hipsters" with its "intense, interesting", ever-changing variety of Med prepared foods in "tapas-type portions"; "service is efficient if charmless", but the real "complaint is the rather crowded setting" – "you have to be quick to get a seat at the [communal] table" (so many opt for takeaway).

OXO TOWER
22 25 21 £57

*Oxo Tower Wharf, Barge House St., SE1 (Blackfriars/
Waterloo), 020-7803 3888; fax 7803 3838;
www.harveynichols.com*

"If you can snag a table by the river, this is one of the best
places to eat", especially if you've got "out-of-town guests
to impress" agree advocates of this "formal" South Bank
landmark with "stunning views" across London; otherwise,
opponents opine it's "overpriced" for Modern European
fare that's "a bit hit-and-miss (though usually very good)"
and "trained", if "attitudy service"; of course, you can always just "come in for a pre-dinner cocktail and watch the
city lights change."

Oxo Tower Brasserie
19 22 19 £42

*Oxo Tower Wharf, Barge House St., SE1 (Blackfriars/Waterloo),
020-7803 3888; fax 7803 3838; www.harveynichols.com*

"Still packing them in (literally)", this "noisy brasserie"
shares the same Thames "view to kill for" as sister Oxo
Tower, but attracts a younger "hip" crowd with nightly live
jazz (it gets "shoulder to shoulder" some nights); the
Modern European menu with "Asian influences" is "decent, but should really be better for the price" – as should
the "amusingly confused service" – but the South Bank
setting makes it "perfect pre- or post–Tate Modern" or "if
you're going to the National Theatre."

Ozer Restaurant & Bar ●
▽ 16 16 13 £30

*5 Langham Pl., W1 (Oxford Circus), 020-7323 0505; fax 7323 0111;
www.sofra.co.uk*

"Satisfying" Turkish food ("mostly kebabs and the like")
keeps the scene "always buzzing" at this Marylebone
Middle Easterner from the Sofra team; still, some think it a
"shame" about the ambience (or lack thereof) of the red-
and-gold "modern space."

Pacific Bar & Grill ●
– – – M

*320 Goldhawk Rd., W6 (Stamford Brook), 020-8741 1994;
fax 8741 9980*

On a busy roundabout in Chiswick, this ex–Cafe Med has
been transformed by its owners into an "appealing"
American with an open kitchen, fireplace and large-walled
terrace that catches the sun; the wide-ranging, family-
friendly menu "with a Californian/Southwestern twist" is
"good" and comes with "efficient service."

Pacific Oriental ⌧
▽ 17 18 17 £33

*1 Bishopsgate, EC2 (Bank), 020-7621 9988; fax 7929 7227;
www.orientalrestaurantgroup.co.uk*

Boasting a six-metre-high waterfall, this spacious bi-level
eatery offers "a nice change of pace" for City dining, serving "fairly good" "Pan-Asian-style dishes" in either the
"lively downstairs" or quieter upstairs; but cynics, snap-

ping it's "more of a bar that happens to serve food", stick to the "great bento boxes for a fast lunch."

Painted Heron, The
23 20 19 £43

112 Cheyne Walk, SW10 (Sloane Sq.), 020-7351 5232; fax 7351 5213
205-209 Kennington Ln., SE11 (Kennington), 020-7793 8313;
fax 7793 8323
www.thepaintedheron.com

The "refined", "fresh-tasting" cuisine "clearly shows the kitchen is confident" at this "posh" pair of Indians on Chelsea Embankment and in Kennington; although some grumble about "offhand service", most "can't wait to return" for their "beautiful curries – the kind you actually want nice wine with."

Palmerston, The
∇ 21 15 20 £29

91 Lordship Ln., SE22 (East Dulwich B.R.), 020-8693 1629;
fax 8693 9662; www.thepalmerston.co.uk

Ex-Bibendum chef and co-owner "Jamie Younger excels" at creating "lovely" Modern British meals at this "lively", librarylike (wood panelling, etc.) East Dulwich "neighbourhood gastropub"; it's an especially "good" "stop after visiting the Dulwich picture gallery" (about a 15-minute walk away).

Papillon ●
– – – E

96 Draycott Ave., SW3 (South Kensington), 020-7225 2555;
www.papillonchelsea.co.uk

Near Brompton Cross, the latest venture from restaurateur Soren Jessen (1 Lombard Street) is a swish, mirrored brasserie that's drawing an equally flashy crowd of social butterflies; it's open every day from 8 AM (10 AM on Sundays), serving a polished French menu that mixes Classic, gutsy Gallic dishes with lighter creations and a long, meandering wine list.

Pappagallo
– – – E

54-55 Curzon St., W1 (Green Park), 020-7629 2742

A revamped version of the veteran Ristorante Italiano, this "comfortable" Mayfair eatery makes an "attractive" option "for business lunches and neighbourhood denizens" when "a casual meal" is called for; the "delicious" Italian fare is "right on the mark", and not terribly expensive, considering the area.

Park, The
– 24 23 £55

Mandarin Oriental Hyde Park, 66 Knightsbridge, SW1 (Knightsbridge), 020-7201 3722; fax 7235 2001;
www.mandarinoriental.com

Everything tastes "top-notch" at this "creative" eatery in the Mandarin Oriental, which changed its menu to an all-Asian shared-plate format post-*Survey*; but with "a wonderful view" of the namesake Park (Hyde, that is) and "excellent service", it's still sure to be a most "enjoyable" spot – especially for an early dinner, when the "set menu includes unlimited wine" (pre–8 PM).

Pasha ●
∇ | 19 | 18 | 16 | £33

301 Upper St., N1 (Angel/Highbury & Islington), 020-7226 1454; fax 7226 1617

An "upmarket" "standout on Upper Street", this "busy" family-run haunt is "a great place to spoil yourself" on "value-for-money" Turkish fare with "authentic spicing", presented by "waiters who know what they are serving"; P.S. "ask for a table at the front for good people-watching."

Pasha ●
– | – | – | M

1 Gloucester Rd., SW7 (Gloucester Rd.), 020-7589 7969; fax 7581 9996; www.pasha-restaurant.co.uk

After being bought by Tony Kitous, the man behind Levant and Levantine, this bi-level South Ken spot retains its North African identity – but a major revamp has decked it out with new artefacts and evocative design touches, including an eye-catching, ochre-hued front; the new Moroccan menu is well-pitched pricewise, and includes light snacks for those preferring the comfy lounge to the downstairs restaurant.

Passione ⊠
23 | 15 | 20 | £46

10 Charlotte St., W1 (Goodge St.), 020-7636 2833; fax 7636 2889; www.passione.co.uk

"Find time to drop by" and "smell the Amalfi coast wafting from the kitchen" at this "cramped" Charlotte Street Italian where "every dish is prepared with total passion"; all's overseen by "co-owner Gennaro D'Urso, who's got to be the nicest man in the business."

Patara
24 | 20 | 20 | £37

15 Greek St., W1 (Leicester Sq./Tottenham Court Rd.), 020-7437 1071; fax 7437 1089
3-7 Maddox St., W1 (Oxford Circus), 020-7499 6008; fax 7499 6007
9 Beauchamp Pl., SW3 (Knightsbridge/South Kensington), 020-7581 8820; fax 7581 2155
181 Fulham Rd., SW3 (South Kensington), 020-7351 5692; fax 7351 5692
www.patarathailand.com

"A boutique chain that retains its roots", this "sumptuous", "upscale" Southeastern Asian quartet offers a menu that's "quite modern" and "more unusual than your standard Thai fare"; naturally, service varies given the locale, but most hail the "helpful" staff ("their recommendations can be respected").

Paternoster Chop House
17 | 15 | 14 | £43

Warwick Ct., Paternoster Sq., EC4 (St. Paul's), 020-7029 9400; fax 7029 9409; www.conran-restaurants.co.uk

"Designed to help London's financial movers and shakers eat well, without too much fuss", this "stark" City Conran Group eatery serves up a "basic" British menu (plus "some wild" items) that has "much to please the carnivores"; even they, though, say both the fare and "service could use some help"; best bet is to sit outside, as it's "situated in a breathtakingly beautiful square alongside St. Paul's Cathedral."

Patisserie Valerie
19 | 14 | 15 | £17

27 Kensington Church St., W8 (High St. Kensington), 020-7937 9574; fax 7937 9574
105 Marylebone High St., W1 (Baker St./Bond St.), 020-7935 6240; fax 7935 6543
44 Old Compton St., W1 (Leicester Sq.), 020-7437 3466; fax 7734 6133
162 Piccadilly, W1 (Green Park), 020-7491 1717
8 Russell St., WC2 (Covent Garden), 020-7240 0064; fax 7240 0064
215 Brompton Rd., SW3 (Knightsbridge), 020-7823 9971; fax 7589 4993
81 Duke of York Sq., King's Rd., SW3 (Sloane Sq.), 020-7730 7094; fax 7730 7094
34 Hans Crescent, SW1 (Knightsbridge), 020-7590 0905
17 Motcomb St., SW1 (Knightsbridge), 020-7245 6161; fax 7245 6161
The Pavillion Bldg., Bishops Sq., 37 Brushfield St., E1 (Liverpool St.), 020-7247 4906
www.patisserie-valerie.co.uk
Additional locations throughout London
"Famous for its delicious *patisserie*" parisienne, this "cute" chain of all-day French bistros is a "firm favourite with young and old" and "yummy mummies *not* watching their waistlines"; even though "service is mediocre at best", and the decor looks "tired" at some branches, this "London institution's" "magnetism" means it "remains the place to meet" to hit that "sweet spot."

Patterson's ☒
22 | 18 | 19 | £51

4 Mill St., W1 (Oxford Circus), 020-7499 1308; fax 7491 2122; www.pattersonsrestaurant.com
"Slightly hidden away" in Mayfair, this "family-run" New French is "well worth seeking out" for "beautifully presented food that tastes pretty good too", served by "relaxed" staff in a "calm, soothing" space of marble walls and small trees; although it's a "bustling business lunch place", evenings are considerably quieter.

Pearl
▽ 26 | 24 | 22 | £66

Renaissance Chancery Court Hotel, 252 High Holborn, WC1 (Holborn), 020-7829 7000; fax 7829 9889; www.pearl-restaurant.com
Chef Jun Tanaka "produces interesting flavour combinations (nearly all of which work)" on an "adventurous" New French menu at this "huge" Holborn hotel dining room, with "highly responsive servers" circulating amid "stunning" modern decor; however, the "elaborate" environment

makes some proclaim this pearl "perfect for business, less so for personal dining."

Pellicano
18 | 17 | 18 | £36

19-21 Elystan St., SW3 (South Kensington), 020-7589 3718; fax 7584 1789

"You can be assured of a home-cooked", "honest Italian" meal and "helpful staff" at this "comfortable" Chelsea trattoria; but declines in the Food and Service scores suggest that whilst "an ideal neighbourhood" place, it's not worth venturing far for.

Pepper Tree
20 | 12 | 16 | £17

19 Clapham Common Southside, SW4 (Clapham Common), 020-7622 1758; fax 7720 7531; www.thepeppertree.co.uk

"It's not meant to be a lingering romantic restaurant", but this "cramped", "cheerful" Clapham Common corner with "canteen-y", "communal seating" is "perfect for a quick, tasty" "bite with mates" from a "healthy", "not-too-pricey" Thai menu; beware, though, it "can get busy later in the night."

Pescatori 🖂
20 | 16 | 19 | £39

57 Charlotte St., W1 (Goodge St.), 020-7580 3289; fax 7580 0539
11 Dover St., W1 (Green Park), 020-7493 2652; fax 7499 3180
www.pescatori.co.uk

"An old favourite" in Fitzrovia, with a younger Mayfair sister, this family-run duo serve up a "tasty " ("not a foodie's dream, but still pretty good") Mediterranean menu of "mainly fish" dishes, although the "smart staff" "can cope with [meat] eaters too"; the bill "can be quite reasonable for the area", but "do watch what you order, as the price can go up" fast.

Petersham, The
∇ 22 | 20 | 25 | £41

The Petersham Hotel, Nightingale Ln. (Richmond), 020-8940 7471; fax 8939 1002; www.petershamhotel.co.uk

"For special family occasions", this 1865 "romantic", riverside Richmond hotel makes a "wonderful respite from London"; the "well-prepared" Modern British menu, which comes courtesy of "old-school" service, "almost matches the stunning" setting; just make "sure your seat has a view of the Thames."

Petersham Nurseries Café
- | - | - | E

Petersham Nurseries, off Petersham Rd., Richmond, 020-8605 3627

"Under a canopy of sumptuous greenery", this "delightful" greenhouse cafe in a Richmond plant nursery (a "rather nontraditional location!") offers a "locally produced", daily changing Modern British menu, featuring "superb" "organic" options; sure, it's "expensive", "the wine list needs work" and "they never have enough staff", but most rate this one of "London's best-kept culinary secrets."

PÉTRUS ⬛   27 | 25 | 26 | £88

Berkeley Hotel, Wilton Pl., SW1 (Hyde Park Corner), 020-7235 1200; www.petrus-restaurant.com

"Prepare to indulge" at this "intimately proportioned, elegantly decorated" Belgravia hotel dining room where chef/co-owner Marcus Wareing "defines class" with his "refined" New French fare that's "nothing short of phenomenal", and "topped" off by "meticulous, thoughtful service"; even though the "sky-high prices" make it "almost as dear as the wine whose name it takes" – note the 40 different varieties on the "intense list" – fans find it's "worth every pound"; P.S. the £30 "lunch is a great deal."

Phoenix Palace ⬤   ▽ 23 | 17 | 16 | £29

3-5 Glentworth St., NW1 (Baker St.), 020-7486 3515

It "feels like the middle of Hong Kong, not the middle of Marylebone" at this "spacious" Cantonese, which attracts "a melting pot of nationalities" with its "fascinating menu" featuring "reasonably priced dim sum"; it's "worth the trip", even if "staff are not really up-to-speed."

PIED À TERRE ⬛   27 | 23 | 25 | £73

34 Charlotte St., W1 (Goodge St.), 020-7636 1178; www.pied-a-terre.co.uk

"Thank the gods, it's back and better than ever" sigh supporters of this "sophisticated" Fitzrovian townhouse that's "risen from the ashes" after a fire, and now boasts an "elegant" "Zen-minimalist" interior; chef Shane Osborn once again mans the stove, preparing "tantalising", "ambrosial" New French cuisine – "a foody fireworks display!" – enhanced by "service that purrs"; true, the already "posh" "prices have moved up in tandem with the makeover", "but you get what you pay for."

Pigalle Club, The ⬛   – | – | – | E

215 Piccadilly, W1 (Piccadilly Circus), 020-7734 8142; fax 7494 2022; www.thepigalleclub.com

In a former cinema on the edge of Piccadilly Circus comes this hip newcomer from music entrepreneur Vince Power, a retro-themed dinner-only venue named after Al Burnett's famous club from the 1940s; spread over two softly lit floors, its cosy dining tables face a stage where an in-house band plays nightly (followed by DJs mixing into the wee hours); the prix fixe menu mixes Modern European and Classic French fare to good effect.

Pig's Ear   ▽ 21 | 21 | 19 | £30

35 Old Church St., SW3 (Sloane Sq.), 020-7352 2908; fax 7352 9321; www.thepigsear.co.uk

"Whenever you don't feel like cooking, drop by" this "cosy Chelsea secret", a "great gastropub" comprising a "top" ground-floor bar ("get the table next to the fireplace") and "charming restaurant" upstairs with a "decent" New

French–Traditional British menu; "personal service" adds to its "intimate" appeal.

Ping Pong ●

20 | 21 | 16 | £23

45 Great Marlborough St., W1 (Oxford Circus), 020-7851 6969
10 Paddington St., W1 (Baker St.), 020-7009 9600
74-76 Westbourne Grove, W2 (Notting Hill Gate), 020-7313 9832; fax 7313 9849
www.pingpongdimsum.com

"Finally, you can have dim sum at dinner in this town" cheer converts of this "sleek", "black-lacquered Chinese" trio dishing the "delicious" little bites, along with "exotic drinks" and teas ("ask for the jasmine, you're in for a surprise") at quite "affordable" prices; on the downside, the "service needs serious help", no reservations equals "inevitable queues", and some say that, for dim-sum specialists, "their selection seems limited."

PIZZA EXPRESS

16 | 13 | 15 | £17

35 Earl's Court Rd., W8 (Earl's Ct.), 020-7937 0761 ●
137 Notting Hill Gate, W11 (Notting Hill Gate), 020-7229 6000 ●
29 Wardour St., W10 (Leicester Sq./Piccadilly Circus), 020-7437 7215; fax 7494 2582 ●
9-12 Bow St., WC2 (Covent Garden), 020-7240 3443; fax 7497 0131 ●
46-54 Battersea Bridge Rd., SW11 (Earl's Ct./Sloane Sq.), 020-7924 2774
7 Beauchamp Pl., SW3 (Knightsbridge), 020-7589 2355; fax 7589 5159 ●
363 Fulham Rd., SW10 (Fulham Broadway/South Kensington), 020-7352 5300 ●
895-896 Fulham Rd., SW6 (Parsons Green), 020-7731 3117; fax 7371 7884 ●
The Pheasantry, 152-154 King's Rd., SW3 (Sloane Sq.), 020-7351 5031; fax 7349 9844 ●
125 Alban Gate, London Wall, EC2 (Moorgate/St. Paul's), 020-7600 8880; fax 7600 8128
www.pizzaexpress.com
Additional locations throughout London

Surveyors express mostly kind words about this "surprisingly effective chain" specialising in "smoky, light pizzas" with "quite a bit of variety" (from margarita to niçoise versions), plus "inexpensive" Italian pastas; whilst the service and "decor vary greatly" from branch to branch, it's "always good, whichever one you visit."

Pizza Metro

∇ 21 | 16 | 20 | £24

64 Battersea Rise, SW11 (Clapham Common/ Clapham Junction B.R.), 020-7228 3812; fax 7738 0987; www.pizzametropizza.com

"Still one of the better pizzerias in town" – "certainly one of the most original", with its pizza-served-by-the-metre system – this bubbly Battersea spot also features "freshly made pastas", proffered by staff who "bring all their Italian charm to your table."

Pizza on the Park
16 | 16 | 15 | £23
11 Knightsbridge, SW1 (Hyde Park Corner), 020-7235 5273; fax 7235 6853; www.pizzaonthepark.co.uk
After 30-odd years, "very little has changed" at this "informal" haunt near Hyde Park Corner – neither the decor that is "reminiscent of a '70s American pizzeria", nor the "not-bad" namesake dish, nor the nightly "live jazz music – the icing on the pizza", so to speak; of course, the "staff could be slicker", and cynics say "go for the music, not the chow" – but "the punters still roll in" to this "everlasting" place.

Pizza Pomodoro ◗
16 | 14 | 15 | £21
51 Beauchamp Pl., SW3 (Knightsbridge), 020-7589 1278; fax 7247 4001
7-8 Bishopsgate Churchyard, EC2 (Liverpool St.), 020-7920 9207; fax 7920 9206 🖥
www.pomodoro.co.uk
"You'll come out grinning from ear to ear" – maybe even after "dancing on the tables" to the live bands – from these "entertaining pizza places" in Knightsbridge and the City, which get "crowded" ("sometimes too crowded") with "glam models, soccer stars" and "past-expired-date celebs"; the "decent-priced" Italian fare is "solid, if unspectacular", but "be ready to order when a waiter approaches – it may be awhile before you see him again."

PJ's Bar & Grill ◗
15 | 17 | 16 | £30
30 Wellington St., WC2 (Covent Garden), 020-7240 7529; fax 7836 3426; www.pjsgrill.net
52 Fulham Rd., SW3 (South Kensington), 020-7581 0025; fax 7584 0820
Separately owned but similarly themed, these "easy"-going places in Covent Garden ("reasonable pre- or post-theatre") and Chelsea (with "polo scene" decor) serve American "staples"; although "a little tired" now, they're a "useful, if unadventurous" option for "a shopping pick-me-up" or weekend brunch.

Planet Hollywood ◗
11 | 16 | 13 | £22
13 Coventry St., W1 (Leicester Sq./Piccadilly Circus), 020-7437 7639; fax 7734 0835;
www.planethollywoodlondon.com
"If what you want is themed", then this "cheery" Piccadilly chainster is "great", stuffed with "cool movie props" and memorabilia; foodwise, there's the "typical" "boring" American-style burger menu, brought by staff "wandering everywhere, but accomplishing nothing", and as for the clientele – "can you spell t-o-u-r-i-s-t?"

Plateau
21 | 25 | 20 | £49

Canada Pl., 4th fl., E14 (Canary Wharf), 020-7715 7100;
www.conran-restaurants.co.uk

"The style is sleek, and the welcome warm" at the Conran Group's "eastern-most outpost" – an airy Canary Wharf aerie with a "beautiful summer terrace"; the "very palatable", "unfussy" New French fare is "a safe bet to please all", and even if the service "spoils" things for a few ("easier to catch bird flu than the waiter's eye" sometimes), most "corporate cats" rate it a "terrific place to take clients."

Poissonnerie de L'Avenue ●ಠ
22 | 18 | 20 | £52

82 Sloane Ave., SW3 (South Kensington), 020-7589 2457;
fax 7581 3360; www.poissonnerie.co.uk

"Still going strong" after 43 years, this "correct, elegant" eatery at Brompton Cross serves "excellent seafood" in an "old-school type, Classic" French cuisine style; however, hipsters say the combination of "old-fashioned fish in an old-fashioned setting" ("like a library in an aristocratic manor house") limits its "appeal to the older set" of the "upper classes."

Portal ಠ
– | – | – | E

88 St. John St., EC1 (Barbican/Farringdon), 020-7253 6950;
www.portalrestaurant.com

"In a luscious setting" with an "ideal-for-summer conservatory at the back", this "great-looking" Clerkenwell yearling opens the door to "sophisticated dining"; its "zesty", "modern approach to Portuguese" and other Med cuisines is complemented by "zealous service"; P.S. for more exclusive occasions, "check out the private wine-cellar room."

Porters ●
17 | 13 | 18 | £23

17 Henrietta St., WC2 (Covent Garden), 020-7836 6466;
fax 7379 4296; www.porters.uk.com

"With a no-frills attitude" and "quaint, cosy" look, Lord Bradford's "Covent Garden favourite" is a "comforting" "place to go when you need to be warmed" by "simple", "very Traditional English" fare ("I was back in the nursery with my pudding for dessert"); the less-enamoured say this near-30-year-old is "tired" and more "for the tourist crowd", but all concede it gives you "a good deal at the price."

Portrait
∇ 14 | 24 | 13 | £31

The National Portrait Gallery, 3rd fl., 2 St. Martin's Pl., WC2
(Charing Cross/Leicester Sq.), 020-7312 2490;
fax 7925 0244; www.searcys.co.uk

"The sun streams in through the large windows" of the National Portrait Gallery top-floor eatery, affording "fab views" across the roofs around Trafalgar Square; respondents paint a less pretty picture of the Modern British fare (just "decent") and "harried staff" ("slow, occasionally rude"), but the panorama "makes up for everything."

Prince Bonaparte

▽ 15 | 18 | 12 | £19

80 Chepstow Rd., W2 (Bayswater/Notting Hill Gate), 020-7313 9491; fax 7792 0911

Now under new management, this "fine gastropub" in Notting Hill attracts a "great crowd" with its "cosy", "living-room standard" decor ("big leather couches by the fireplace", etc.); the "hearty" Modern British grub comes at "good value", making "getting a table painful sometimes (no reservations allowed.")

Princess Garden ●

22 | 16 | 20 | £47

8-10 N. Audley St., W1 (Bond St.), 020-7493 3223; fax 7629 3130; www.princessgardenofmayfair.com

This Chinese-art-filled Mandarin in Mayfair offers "tasty", "upscale" fare "for the Western palate" that's "elegantly served" profess the princes and princesses who patronise it; but some rebels roar the place has "seen better days" – and it's "not cheap", either; N.B. a recent revamp may affect the Decor score.

Prism ⌾

▽ 19 | 21 | 19 | £48

147 Leadenhall St., EC3 (Bank/Monument), 020-7256 3888; fax 7191 6025; www.harveynichols.com

Making "cool" "use of an old banking hall" full of "fantastically high ceilings", this "classy" Harvey Nichols–owned City eatery seems "always packed with insurance types and their lawyers", who appreciate having "sufficient privacy and attentive service" as they consume the Modern British fare; it "can be noisy if very busy, though"; P.S. whilst there's no code, "power dressing" is preferred.

Providores, The/Tapa Room

22 | 17 | 18 | £39

109 Marylebone High St., W1 (Baker St./Bond St.), 020-7935 6175; fax 7935 6877; www.theprovidores.co.uk

"Innovative" fare cooked "with Down Under flair" and "fantastic" New Zealand wines rule at this "king of fusion"; there's the "cramped" but "buzzing" Tapa Room, offering an "excellent small plates selection" (but "don't mistake this for Spanish tapas – 'tapa' refers to fabric created out of tree" bark), and the "relaxed" Providores, which lets you "avoid the communal-table chaos downstairs"; "service can be spotty" and the food too "trendoid" for some, but most cheer this truly "creative" Marylebone Eclectic.

Quadrato

24 | 22 | 25 | £52

Four Seasons Hotel Canary Wharf, 46 Westferry Circus, E14 (Canary Wharf), 020-7510 1999; fax 7510 1998; www.fourseasons.com

A "quality business" venue, this "elegant" dining room of the Four Seasons Canary Wharf offers a "varied menu" of "consistent", "lush Italian food" with a "decent amount of creativity" (cooked in plain "entertaining" view from the open kitchen); staff are equipped with "impeccable manners", leaving the main "downside being that you are aware you're in a hotel lobby."

Quaglino's ◐
18 | 21 | 17 | £50

16 Bury St., SW1 (Green Park), 020-7930 6767; fax 7839 2866; www.quaglinos.co.uk

It's "not the hippest place in town" anymore, but this "long-established" "giant Conran Group food hall" in St. James's "still attracts a crowd" (and "impresses the girls") with its "dramatic" decor – from the "breathtaking staircase" to the raw bar's "fountain of seafood"; alas, aside from the "amazing crustaceans", the Modern European menu's "a bit hit-and-miss", "service can be tardy at times" and the "busloads of tourists" do nothing for the "loud atmosphere."

Quality Chop House ◐
20 | 19 | 17 | £34

92-94 Farringdon Rd., EC1 (Farringdon), 020-7837 5093; fax 7833 8748; www.qualitychophouse.co.uk

The "super-quirky" wooden benches from its "earlier incarnation as a [Victorian] workingman's" restaurant create a "special experience" – also an "uncomfortable" one, but that's "part of the charm, I guess" – at this characterful Farringdon haunt, which does have a comfy, modern dining room for less-padded rears; as the name says, quality chophouse fare is featured on the "real" Traditional British menu, but some still find it most "memorable" for the ambience.

Quilon ⌧
▽ 25 | 19 | 22 | £43

Crowne Plaza London St. James Hotel, 41 Buckingham Gate, SW1 (St. James's Park/Victoria), 020-7821 1899; fax 7828 5802; www.quilon.co.uk

"Not your mainstream Indian", this "big secret" near Buckingham Palace proffers "light" Keralan fare ("spicy, but European-style") brought by "deferential service"; decor featuring paintings of the subcontinent's southwest coast doesn't quite dispel the "hotel atmosphere."

QUIRINALE ⌧
26 | 20 | 25 | £46

1 Great Peter St., SW1 (Westminster), 020-7222 7080; fax 7233 3080; www.Quirinale.co.uk

"Watch journalists lunch with politicians at this Westminster haunt" where a "constantly changing" Italian menu of "splendid", "inventive" dishes receives "nothing but praise", as does the vino list "with obscure wines we should all drink" and the staff's "attention to detail"; only downsides: the "stark" basement setting and the fact it can be "dead on weekends" (and after the Commons Division Bell).

Quo Vadis ⌧
21 | 21 | 20 | £42

26-29 Dean St., W1 (Leicester Sq./Tottenham Court Rd.), 020-7437 9585; fax 7736 7593; www.whitestarline.org.uk

Surveyors are split on this "well-established" Soho Italian under the aegis of Marco Pierre White; whilst supporters salute the "old-style graciousness in the decor, service and surprisingly interesting food", cynics shrug over the "outdated, stuffy" experience; "it's still there, but getting a little tired" perhaps sums it up best.

Racine
24 | 19 | 22 | £44

239 Brompton Rd., SW3 (South Kensington), 020-7584 4477; fax 7584 4900
"Just what a French bistro ought to be", this Knightsbridge venue is "as good as it gets for rustic" Gallic eats – "reasonably priced", "considering the standard" of the food – supported by "seamless service"; throw in the "quintessentially bustling atmosphere", and a visit here is like being "back in Paris" – but "without all that nasty Eurostar business."

Rainforest Cafe
11 | 20 | 14 | £24

20-24 Shaftesbury Ave., W1 (Piccadilly Circus), 020-7434 3111; fax 7434 3222; www.rainforestcafe.com
The "ridiculously over-the-top rainforest decor", complete with animatronic "giant gorillas banging their chests, parrots flying and elephants" trumpeting, make this Piccadilly franchise of the global chain "good for kids" (especially "cranky" ones); as for the "Disneyfied" American eats and "slow" staff – well, suffice to say food and service are "not why you go here."

Randall & Aubin
20 | 18 | 18 | £33

14-16 Brewer St., W1 (Piccadilly Circus), 020-7287 4447; fax 7287 4488
329-331 Fulham Rd., SW10 (Fulham Broadway/South Kensington), 020-7823 3515; fax 7823 3991 ◗
"Fab for people-watching" a "young attractive crowd", this "funky", "loud" Modern Brit in a former Soho butcher's shop (converted into "extreme campiness [with] a glitter ball on the ceiling") "gets crowded" "serving up a superb range of fresh fish as well as other fare"; its "quieter" sibling on "busy Fulham Road" offers "decent" delectables with a more Modern European bent.

Ransome's Dock
∇ 19 | 15 | 21 | £41

35-37 Park Gate Rd., SW11 (Sloane Sq./South Kensington), 020-7223 1611; fax 7924 2614; www.ransomesdock.co.uk
Chef-owner "Martin Lam and his team are attentive, without being too obsequious" at this Modern British–Eclectic beside a Battersea dock (its "outdoor seating is great in summer"); organic, "fresh ingredients mean tasty basics, plus some more adventurous" dishes, and "a killer wine list."

Raoul's
17 | 14 | 13 | £23

13 Clifton Rd., W9 (Warwick Ave.), 020-7289 7313; fax 7266 4752
105-107 Talbot Rd., W11 (Westbourne Park), 020-7229 2400; fax 7243 8070
"Popular with locals", this Maida Vale cafe ("with great deli across the street") and its new Notting Hill '60s "modish" –

style sibling offer a Med menu that's rather "basic" – except for the "superior brunch" on weekends that features "amazing yellow eggs specially flown in from Italy"; but "very inconveniently", reservations aren't taken for brunch, and even the "wonderful dishes can't compensate for the inattentive, often rude service" sceptics snap.

Rasa
23 | 15 | 20 | £29

5 Charlotte St., W1 (Tottenham Court Rd.), 020-7637 0222; fax 7637 0224
6 Dering St., W1 (Bond St./Oxford Circus), 020-7629 1346; fax 7637 0224 Ⓢ
Kings Cross Holiday Inn, 1 Kings Cross Rd., WC1 (Leicester Sq./Farringdon), 020-7833 9787
55 Stoke Newington Church St., N16 (Stoke Newington B.R.), 020-7249 0344; fax 7637 0224
56 Stoke Newington Church St., N16 (Stoke Newington B.R.), 020-7249 1340; fax 7637 0224
www.rasarestaurants.com

"Exquisite Keralan cuisine" "leaves the usual sludgy curries far behind" at this "inventive" South Indian string that stretches from the West End to Stoke Newington; even if "the pink-themed decor" is a love-it-or-hate-it thing, and the "helpful staff" can be "slow", these eateries are "immensely popular", "especially for vegetarians in search of flavour at a reasonable cost."

RASOI VINEET BHATIA Ⓢ
26 | 22 | 24 | £63

10 Lincoln St., SW3 (Sloane Sq.), 020-7225 1881; fax 7581 0220; www.vineetbhatia.com

"If food was a method of communication, this would solve the world's problems" profess pundits of the "unforgettable", "high-end Indian" cuisine created by chef-owner Vineet Bhatia at his "cosy" Chelsea townhouse; add in "attentive-without-being-overbearing staff" and "well-thought-out wine pairings", and "even the sky-high prices are justified"; P.S. "portions can be large, so be careful not to over-indulge."

Real Greek & Mezedopolio, The Ⓢ
16 | 15 | 15 | £27

15 Hoxton Mkt., N1 (Old St.), 020-7739 8212; fax 7739 4910

Real Greek Souvlaki & Bar, The

56 Paddington St., W1 (Baker St.), 020-7486 0466
31-33 Putney High St., SW15 (Putney Bridge), 020-8788 3270
Units 1 & 2, Riverside House, 2A Southwark Bridge Rd., SE1 (London Bridge/Southwark), 020-7620 0162
140-142 St. John St., EC1 (Farringdon), 020-7253 7234; fax 7253 7235 Ⓢ
www.therealgreek.co.uk

"Simple, fresh" "Greek fast food" offers a real deal at this fast-growing chain that's "a favourite with big groups" looking "to throw back a few ouzos" or "surprisingly good"

Hellenic wines; but a Food score drop suggests that the new branches "spawned from the excellent Hoxton [original] have let the side down", with "functional decor" and "disinterested staff"; P.S. the Mezedopolio wine bar, next to the Hoxton parent, specialises in "mezzes that are better than the mains" many maintain.

Red Fort
24 | 21 | 21 | £41

77 Dean St., W1 (Oxford Circus/Tottenham Court Rd.), 020-7437 2525; fax 7434 0721; www.redfort.co.uk
"London knows curry, and this is up there with the best" assert admirers of this "regional Indian stalwart" in Soho; "old favourites as well as new delights" are "elegantly served" amid "swish", "almost Zen-like atmosphere"; some protest the "posh" prices, but "if you want to impress someone, this is the place to do it."

Red Pepper
19 | 11 | 14 | £27

8 Formosa St., W9 (Warwick Ave.), 020-7266 2708; fax 7266 5522
"What they lack in size" – "stretch and you'll smack the bloke at the next table" – "they make up for in food" find fans of the "fresh pastas" and "good value" pizzas at this Maida Vale Italian; be aware, the "fairly scuzzy" surrounds get "horribly noisy" on busy nights (when staff can be "annoyingly unfriendly"), so "better to sit upstairs if you can."

Refettorio ⊠
20 | 18 | 20 | £45

Crowne Plaza, 19 New Bridge St., EC4 (Blackfriars), 020-7438 8052; www.london-city.crowneplaza.com
A large antipasti display that's "a cheese-and-prosciutto-lovers' haven" is only the beginning of an "excellent" meal at this upscale Italian in a low-profile Blackfriars hotel; the airy, casual L-shaped dining room is dominated by a communal table with "bench seating that gets uncomfortable after a while" – which, along with the City locale, may explain why it's unjustly "deserted some evenings."

Reubens
18 | 10 | 11 | £26

79 Baker St., W1 (Baker St.), 020-7486 0035; fax 7486 7079; www.reubensrestaurant.com
For those "unwilling to travel to Golders Green", this "busy" deli/"old-world" dining room in Marylebone is the "real deal" for "classic, dependable" Jewish food, like "rib-sticking latkes or fantastic salt beef"; "but the service leaves everything to be desired, unless you are a regular" – then "everything is kosher" (literally).

Rhodes Twenty Four ⊠
24 | 23 | 23 | £57

Tower 42, 24th fl., 25 Old Broad St., EC2 (Bank St./Liverpool St.), 020-7877 7703; fax 7877 7788; www.rhodes24.co.uk
"Very much a City dining experience (lots of suits)", this Traditional Brit offers "great views over London" from its

spacious digs on the 24th floor of the town's tallest building; executive chef Gary Rhodes "keeps an eye on the kitchen" as it turns out slightly "heavy, but elegant" offerings from a "short menu (helps cut down decision time)"; "excellent service" also ensures "an unforgettable evening" – just remember to allow time to clear the ground-level security.

Rhodes W1

| – | – | – | E |

The Cumberland Hotel, Great Cumberland Pl., W1 (Marble Arch), 020-7479 3838; www.garyrhodes.com

Almost a year after the Cumberland Hotel underwent a transformational overhaul, energetic chef-restaurateur Gary Rhodes took over the smart, spacious basement brasserie and jazzed up the victuals, introducing a hearty, upscale Modern British menu that reflects his penchant for puddings ("order the sticky toffee" version), and "good" gutsy grills and game.

Rib Room & Oyster Bar

| 24 | 21 | 24 | £57 |

Jumeirah Carlton Tower Hotel, 2 Cadogan Pl., SW1 (Knightsbridge/Sloane Sq.), 020-7858 7053; fax 7823 1708; www.carltontower.com

"Classy and classic", this "dark", "masculine" dining room in Belgravia's Carlton Tower Hotel – "an anchor establishment for the neighbourhood" – is a "carnivore's heaven" thanks to a Traditional British menu that's strong on "succulent" chophouse fare; the "waiters watch out for" you, and there's also a smart "bar for quiet business conversations."

Riccardo's

| ▽ | 16 | 10 | 14 | £33 |

126 Fulham Rd., SW3 (Gloucester Rd./South Kensington), 020-7370 6656; fax 7373 0604

"Fall in anytime you're a little lazy and a little hungry" to this "casual" Fulham Road trattoria where the "Italian tapas"-style fare is "surprisingly good for its price"; count on being "greeted like long-lost family" – though, given the way they pack them in here, they must have lots of family members"; N.B. there's also a popular front patio, covered in winter.

Richard Corrigan at Lindsay House ⊠

| 25 | 20 | 22 | £67 |

1 Romilly St., W1 (Leicester Sq./Piccadilly Circus), 020-7439 0450; fax 7437 7349; www.lindsayhouse.co.uk

An "oasis of calm in Soho", this "quaint" "cosy townhouse" creates an "unpretentious" canvas for chef-owner Richard Corrigan to "remind us that Modern British food can be amazing" with an "Irish-inspired" "inventive" menu – "the man loves his produce and it shows on the plate"; although the "charming service" can be "slow"("they take not rushing to a new level"), consolation comes via "a wine list that will satiate the most sophisticated" interests.

Richoux
15 | 14 | 14 | £23

172 Piccadilly, W1 (Green Park/Piccadilly Circus), 020-7493 2204,
fax 7495 6658
41A S. Audley St., W1 (Bond St.), 020-7629 5228;
fax 7491 0825
86 Brompton Rd., SW3 (Knightsbridge), 020-7584 8300;
fax 7589 8547
3 Circus Rd., NW8 (St. John's Wood), 020-7483 4001;
fax 7483 3810
www.richoux.co.uk

"Good any time of the day", this "old standby" chain of "conveniently located" Traditional British tearooms makes a "cosy place" for "satisfactory" fare, spanning "light plates, pastries and an abundance of chocolate" even though some branches look "very tired" and the "service ranges from good to terrible", at least they "always let you linger."

RITZ, THE
23 | 27 | 26 | £67

Ritz Hotel, 150 Piccadilly, W1 (Green Park), 020-7300 2370;
fax 7300 2375; www.theritzlondon.com

"Step back into 18th-century France" when you enter this frescoed, gold-leaf "paean to glamour and extravagance" aka the Ritz dining room, where "white-glove service" will teach you "what being waited on hand and foot really means"; if the "outrageously expensive" Classic French-Traditional British food is not "up to the decor" or staff, it's still rather "delightful"; oh, and let's not forget afternoon tea in the adjacent Palm Court – "getting touristy", it's true but still "the marker by which all others are judged."

Riva
▽ 24 | 13 | 20 | £45

169 Church Rd., SW13 (Hammersmith), 020-8748 0434;
fax 8748 0434

Within a low-key parade of shops in Barnes, owner Andrea Riva's 17-year-old Italian offers "brilliant food with a bit of celeb spotting" for extra spice; there's "not much table space", and some grumble that the staff's "scraping and fawning" seems to be reserved for "what one supposes are regulars."

RIVER CAFÉ
26 | 21 | 24 | £60

Thames Wharf, Rainville Rd., W6 (Hammersmith), 020-7386 4200;
fax 7386 4201; www.rivercafe.co.uk

"Everything is very laid-back, except the cooking" – "inspired" "tastes of Italy" "bursting with flavour" – at this "vibrant" venue beside the Thames in Hammersmith; whilst the interior's a "little utilitarian", "you get the most beautiful sunsets through the big glass windows" and on the "fab alfresco" terrace; naysayers note it's "getting unreasonably expensive" nowadays ("divine food, diabolical prices"), but after 20 years, it remains one of the "best Italians in town."

Rivington Grill Bar Deli   21 16 20 £35

Greenwich Picturehouse Cinema, 178 Greenwich High Rd.,
SE10 (Greenwich), 020-8293 9270 ⊠
28-30 Rivington St., EC2 (Old St.), 020-7729 7053; fax 7729 7086;
www.rivingtongrill.co.uk

It's "a little out of place in the wilds of Shoreditch", but this
"relaxed" spot (from the owners of The Ivy and Le Caprice)
attracts "a sophisticated arty crowd" with "wholesome",
"hearty" Traditional British fare that's "not cheap, but does
make you feel you've been out" for a meal; many "recommend a light meal at the bar" as well; N.B. the new
Greenwich sibling is unrated.

Roast   22 23 17 £48

Borough Mkt., The Floral Hall, Stoney St., SE1 (London Bridge),
020-7940 1300; fax 7015 1866; www.roast-restaurant.com

With "a great view over the craziness of Borough Market",
this "light, elegant" "glass-enclosed" dining room is off to
a "busy, buzzy" start; although the "trendy, farmery" (as in
"fresh" regional produce) Modern British cooking "has
the right idea, it's not always bang on with execution" and
staff can be "variable" too; but overall, it's "nice to have an
upscale place" serving three meals a day; P.S. to avoid
noise, "sit on the second level, away from the kitchen."

Rocket   17 18 14 £30

4 Lancashire Ct., W1 (Bond St.), 020-7629 2889; fax 7629 2881 ⊠
Putney Wharf, Brewhouse St., SW15 (East Putney),
020-8789 7875; fax 8789 7876
www.rocketrestaurants.co.uk

"If you don't mind the noise volume" and "slow service", this
"cool" duo in a "cosy" Mayfair courtyard ("a standout in
summer") and in Putney with a "gorgeous Thames view"
and "super-sexy bar" are "perfect for catching up with
friends"; there's a "lengthy" list of Med munchies (special
mention to the "enormous" wood-fired-oven pizzas).

Rodizio Rico ◐   ∇ 18 15 20 £24

111 Westbourne Grove, W2 (Bayswater), 020-7792 4035;
fax 7243 1401
77-78 Upper St., N1 (Angel), 020-7354 1076; fax 7359 8052

"Prepare to be stuffed" with "big chunks of meat carved at
table" at this "friendly Brazilian" churrascaria couple in
Westbourne Grove and Islington; "good service" ensures
the prix fixe parade of Portuguese barbecue keeps coming, but carnivorous connoisseurs advise "don't fall for the
chicken wings or sausages – hold out for the filet."

Roka ◐   22 20 17 £49

37 Charlotte St., W1 (Goodge St./Tottenham Court Rd.),
020-7580 6464; fax 7153 4502; www.rokarestaurant.com

An "excellent alternative to the usual Japanese suspects", this "modern", bright Fitzrovian "sister of Zuma" is

"always full of happy people" enjoying the "great vibe" and "stylish", "highly original" dishes from the open robata grill where "you can usually get a seat without a reservation"; staff get mixed marks, though: some find them "fawning", others say "they should stick to trying to be models"; P.S. don't miss the downstairs Shochu, "a trendy cocktail lounge" with the "coolest drinks ever."

Rosmarino
20 | 18 | 17 | £44

1 Blenheim Terrace, NW8 (St. John's Wood), 020-7328 5014; fax 7625 2639

"Prices are high – but it *is* in St. John's Wood" say surveyors of this "sophisticated" Italian that attracts "a bit of an older crowd"; several swear it's "still a delightful place" with "an appealing menu" and "pleasant" terrace; but sliding Food and Service scores support critics' contention it "could do with a bit of lift to the standard it was a couple of years ago."

ROUSSILLON ☒
27 | 21 | 26 | £71

16 St. Barnabas St., SW1 (Sloane Sq./Victoria), 020-7730 5550; fax 7824 8617; www.roussillon.co.uk

"A combination of some of the best New French food in London and warm, congenial" service (plus a "sommelier who relishes a challenge") makes this decade-old yet relatively "undiscovered" Pimlico place "perfect for confidential business lunches and romantic evenings" alike; chef/co-owner Alexis Gauthier's "imaginative" cuisine, with an "accent on vegetarian items", "has hit new heights" of late and it's backed by "a brilliant wine list" starring labels from the namesake region.

Rowley's
18 | 19 | 18 | £36

113 Jermyn St., SW1 (Piccadilly Circus), 020-7930 2707; fax 7839 4240; www.rowleys.co.uk

It resides in "the fashionable men's clothing street", but this "small, quaint" St. James's stalwart stays impervious to trends; whilst offering some Modern Euro entrees "they're proud of the steak" with herb-butter sauce and unlimited chips, served in a "historical room" dating back to the 1790s; and if the "reliable" fare can be "rather bland", that's all part of the Traditional British charm.

ROYAL CHINA
23 | 15 | 16 | £30

24-26 Baker St., W1 (Baker St.), 020-7487 4688; fax 7935 7893
13 Queensway, W2 (Queensway), 020-7221 2535; fax 7792 5752
30 Westferry Circus, E14 (Canary Wharf), 020-7719 0888; fax 7719 0889
68 Queen's Grove, NW8 (St. John's Wood), 020-7586 4280; fax 7722 4750
www.royalchinagroup.co.uk

"The queues can be horrendous, but they are testament" to the "high-quality" Chinese fare – "both homestyle dishes and elaborate gourmet ones", plus "legendary", "yum yum dim sum" – at this ever-crowded quartet; be prepared to suffer "strip-club decor"(except at the "lovely Canary Wharf location") and "service like an old boiler – sometimes it works, other times not."

Royal China Club
22 | 17 | 18 | £38

40-42 Baker St., W1 (Baker Street), 020-7486 3898; www.royalchinagroup.co.uk

From the company behind the Royal China chain comes this dark-hued venture with "a new feel" for the group: it's smaller, smarter and the Chinese menu includes both "consistently good dim sum" and some "yummy surprises" – such as seafood so fresh it's swimming up until you order it; of course, it's "more expensive" than its cousins too; N.B. as the name suggests, there are plans to introduce a membership option.

Royal Exchange
Grand Café & Bar ☒
▽ 15 | 21 | 16 | £35

The Royal Exchange, The Courtyard, EC3 (Bank), 020-7618 2480; fax 7618 2490; www.conran-restaurants.co.uk

"Surrounded by history" in the "beautifully restored" Royal Exchange courtyard, this "civilised" Conran Group all-day cafe is a place that City folk find "convenient for a light" bite of cold Modern Euro fare (e.g. the "delicious lobster sandwich"); given the "limited menu", however, critics carp there's "nothing special other than the setting" here; P.S. those who prefer hot meals might head for the mezzanine level, where the new, weekday-only Sauterelle offers a "fine Classic French" menu.

R.S.J. ☒
20 | 12 | 20 | £37

33 Coin St., SE1 (Waterloo), 020-7928 4554; fax 7401 2455; www.rsj.uk.com

"An oasis in the South Bank desert", this "unpretentious" spot is all about "imaginative", "accomplished" Modern British cooking and an impressive "Loire-heavy wine list at light prices"; it's "a good bet" "before or after a performance" at the National Theatre over the road, despite the "airport lounge–like decor."

Rudland & Stubbs ☒
– | – | – | E

35-37 Greenhill Rents, EC1 (Farringdon), 020-7253 0148; www.rudlandstubbs.co.uk

In a cul-de-sac around the corner from Smithfield Market, this veteran seafooder has reopened after a spruce-up from new owners (the team behind Cafe Med and Pacific Bar & Grill); a chef from the defunct Osia continues the fishy tradition, with options ranging from lobster pot-au-feu to miso-glazed tuna, complemented by an international wine list with 20 offerings by the glass; the simply attired premises boasts marble tables and original white tiling from the '50s.

RULES ◐   23 | 24 | 23 | £48
35 Maiden Ln., WC2 (Covent Garden), 020-7836 5314;
fax 7497 1081; www.rules.co.uk

It "feels like dining in the pages of a Jane Austen novel" at this "splendid" Covent Gardener ("going strong since 1798"), whose "whiff-of-a-gentlemen's-club" ambience is like a "breath of fresh air amongst all the minimalist restaurants around"; its "old-world menu" of "classically British food, beautifully done" specialises in "succulent", "perfectly matured game", and is matched by "genial", "verrry English service"; of course, don't be surprised if "you find more tourists than natives here."

Sabor   – | – | – | M
108 Essex Rd., N1 (Angel), 020-7226 5551; fax 7288 0880;
www.sabor.co.uk

The "inventive" Colombian cuisine will "set your taste buds singing" ("the black bean soup converted me") at this "interesting" Islingtonian also boasting "excellent-value" drinks and "enthusiastic service"; "beautiful" carnival masks enliven the simple, white-walled decor.

Saigon ◐ ▨   ∇ 19 | 13 | 17 | £29
45 Frith St., W1 (Leicester Sq./Piccadilly Circus), 020-7437 7109;
fax 7734 1668

"Just next to Ronnie Scott's" in Soho, this "much-overlooked" Vietnamese is fine "for a quick bite" before hitting that jazz joint or a show; but some suggest "a trip back to the homeland to rejuvenate their cuisine" – and perhaps, attitude: "service is fast but unfriendly."

Saki Bar & Food Emporium ▨   – | – | – | M
4 W. Smithfield, EC1 (Barbican/Farringdon), 020-7489 7033;
www.saki-food.com

With authentic Japanese touches in abundance, this imaginative Smithfield newcomer features a hard-edged, black-and-red basement dining room with both a communal table and a sushi counter; the well-priced menu offers tapas-style kobachi dishes and separate sections for protein- and carb-laden fare; as the name suggests, there's also a well-stocked bar and a ground-floor store stocked with imported Asian foods and cooking paraphernalia.

Sakura   24 | 11 | 14 | £25
9 Hanover St., W1 (Oxford Circus), 020-7629 2961

It's "nothing to look at" (except for "sumo wrestling on the TVs"), but this "unpretentious Japanese near Oxford Circus" is "an absolute lifesaver when out shopping", with its "authentic food", including "abundant sushi", at "moderate prices"; it's worth "the stress of their fierce, 10-minute-window reservation policy."

Sale e Pepe ●☒   23 | 17 | 22 | £39 |
9-15 Pavilion Rd., SW1 (Knightsbridge), 020-7235 0098;
fax 7225 1210; www.saleepepe.co.uk
"If you are in a boisterous mood and prepared to shout
at your neighbours", you "cannot go wrong" with this
"rowdy" Knightsbridge Italian where the "amazing antics"
from "clownish", "singing waiters" make for "a lot of
fun"; the "consistent", "old-school-all-the-way" cooking,
"whilst not fancy, is satisfying"; P.S. "lunch is a better
bet: less crowded."

Salloos ●☒   24 | 17 | 19 | £39 |
62-64 Kinnerton St., SW1 (Hyde Park Corner/Knightsbridge),
020-7235 4444
"Buy a compass to find this hidden gem" down a discreet
Belgravia street; "it will be worth it" for "excellent", "traditional Pakistani and North Indian food" – indeed, even
the thought of the "hot", "spicy dishes" sets some surveyors "salivating"; it's "family-run, and feels that way."

Salt Yard ☒   22 | 14 | 20 | £33 |
54 Goodge St., W1 (Goodge Street), 020-7637 0657; fax 7580 7435;
www.saltyard.co.uk
"London needs more places like this" profess fans of this
Fitzrovian spread over two floors where "attentive",
"pretty waitresses" offer a "great choice" of Modern
European fare – majoring on "interesting" Spanish tapas –
that "keeps budgets low without missing too much on
quality"; the downside: you have "to deal with the noise"
enhanced by the minimalist decor.

Salusbury Pub & Dining Room   – | – | – | E |
50-52 Salusbury Rd., NW6 (Queen's Park), 020-7328 3286
"Popular" with a "local crowd" of "trendy thirtysomethings", this Queen's Park place proffers "interesting"
Italian-Med "food that surpasses pub fare"; even if it is
"overpriced for the area", that doesn't stop the place being "full almost every night."

Sam's Brasserie & Bar ●   21 | 21 | 17 | £33 |
Barley Mow Ctr., 11 Barley Mow Passage, W4 (Chiswick Park),
020-8987 0555; www.samsbrasserie.com
"Chiswick loves it so much you can't get in" to this yearling
that "has hit its stride" with "straightforward, well-
prepared" Modern European fare, "funky", former paper
factory digs and "casual", "baby-friendly" attitude; it's
"only marred by" being "slightly overpriced" for gastropub
grub grumble some.

San Lorenzo ●☒≠   20 | 18 | 18 | £52 |
22 Beauchamp Pl., SW3 (Knightsbridge), 020-7584 1074;
fax 7584 1142

(continued)

(continued)
San Lorenzo Fuoriporta
38 Wimbledon Hill Rd., SW19 (Wimbledon), 020-8946 8463;
fax 8947 9810
www.sanlorenzo.com
"You have to be good at air-kissing or you won't fit in" to
this "great see-and-be-seen", 44-year-old Knightsbridge
legend run by Lorenzo and the "still very sociable Mara"
Berni – an "open", bright space, serving "consistently
good" Italian edibles; but sceptics say they're "so over
it", and wonder "what is it with not taking credit cards" –
especially given the "pricey" bills; P.S. the "friendly,
smart neighbourhood" Wimbledon sibling is run by
the Bernis' sons.

Santa Lucia | – | – | – | M |
2 Hollywood Rd., SW10 (South Kensington), 020-7352 8484;
fax 7351 2390
The "less-frantic sister of Made in Italy", this "unpretentious trattoria" in Chelsea churns out some of "London's
best pizza and parmigiana" ("don't waste your time on
anything else" on the menu); but some think this "once-
great neighbourhood place has gone downhill", citing
"real service issues" with staff.

Santini | 24 | 19 | 22 | £52 |
29 Ebury St., SW1 (Victoria), 020-7730 4094; fax 7730 0544;
www.santini-restaurant.com
Works "without fail each time" avow *amici* of this "stylish"
spot where "helpful staff" serve up "fantastic" Italian fare
and "wonderful wines" from all over The Boot; it's "not the
best value" going, but what in Belgravia is?

Saran Rom ● | – | – | – | VE |
The Boulevard, Townmead Rd., Imperial Wharf, SW6
(Fulham Broadway), 020-7751 3111; www.saranrom.com
Located in the new Imperial Wharf development, this
wood-panelled tri-level Thai offers "great views across
the water to Battersea" – especially if you snag one of the
daybeds on the heated terrace; the refined menu aims
high, with traditional haute cuisine from a Bangkok chef
and a globe-trotting wine list; N.B. don't miss the loos –
Japanese-style cubicles with heated automated seats and
piped-in music.

Sardo ⊠ | 21 | 14 | 19 | £38 |
45 Grafton Way, W1 (Warren St.), 020-7387 2521; fax 7387 2559;
www.sardo-restaurant.com
"Authentically Sardinian in both food and wine", this intimate Italian is "one of Fitzrovia's best-kept secrets" for
"lovely food" – "even the bread is gorgeous" – and "warm
service"; true, the "menu doesn't change much and it's a
bit cramped – but well worth a visit."

Sardo Canale
19 | 21 | 18 | £40

42 Gloucester Ave., NW1 (Chalk Farm), 020-7722 2800;
www.sardocanale.com

"Stylish yet welcoming", this Primrose Hill "Italian with a Sardinian twist" is "almost as good as its Sardo" sibling, but with a "much nicer" ambience – thanks to the "canal-side setting" complete with 300-year-old olive tree in the "perfect summer courtyard"; however, "it's a bit more pricey too", "disappointing" those who "were hoping for more" – literally ("portions are small").

Sarkhel's
▽ 21 | 15 | 20 | £30

197-199 Replingham Rd., SW18 (Southfields), 020-8870 1483;
fax 8871 0808
199 Upper Richmond Rd. W., SW14 (Mortlake B.R.), 020-8876 6220
www.sarkhels.com

"High-class Indian" cuisine "with a twist on everything" was the original claim to fame of this unassuming Southfields site with a "Sheen branch"; the fact that the menu "is still the same" makes it seem "more mainstream" now – but you still get "above-average food" at "reasonable prices", and they do delivery and "takeaway as well."

Sartoria ⌧
20 | 21 | 19 | £47

20 Savile Row, W1 (Oxford Circus/Piccadilly Circus),
020-7534 7000; fax 7534 7070; www.conran-restaurants.co.uk

"Swish" and "sumptuous", this "spacious" Savile Row site with a sartorial theme suits for "discreet business" meals; the "upmarket" "Italian comfort food" is "pricey" (also "unremarkable" in some eyes), but that's to be expected given the "chic, sophisticated atmosphere."

Satsuma
21 | 15 | 16 | £22

56 Wardour St., W1 (Leicester Sq./Piccadilly Circus),
020-7437 8338; fax 7437 3389

"An oasis amongst the hustle and bustle" of Soho, this bi-level Japanese "packs the pub crawlers into communal tables" ("not suitable for a first date, but you'll always meet someone to talk to"); it's "good for a quick meal" – "the bento boxes offer everything the body needs" – just be cautious around the "crazy-assed staff."

SAVOY GRILL
24 | 24 | 24 | £61

Savoy Hotel, The Strand, WC2 (Covent Garden/Embankment),
020-7592 1600; fax 7592 1601; www.gordonramsay.com

"One of Gordon Ramsay's flock", this "classic" on the Strand "has been brought into this century" with chef Marcus Wareing's "expertly cooked", contemporary takes on the "old English standards", a "brighter" (but still woody) "modern-chic decor" and "gracious service"; naturally, nostalgists sigh it's "not like the old days" – "you could be anywhere in London" now – but to most, this "unpretentious but upscale" site is "still a place everyone should eat at once."

Scalini ◑
20 | 15 | 18 | £50

1-3 Walton St., SW3 (Knightsbridge/South Kensington), 020-7225 2301; fax 7225 3953

It's always a "loud, jolly" scene at this "Chelsea footballers' favourite", a "crowded" Italian "sister to Signor Sassi"; but if the "large portions" of "dependable" dishes "never fail", the "prompt" staff sometimes do ("unless you are a star").

Seashell ⊠
20 | 8 | 14 | £20

49-51 Lisson Grove, NW1 (Marylebone), 020-7224 9000; fax 7724 9071; www.seashellrestaurant.co.uk

"Proper fish 'n' chips" is the hook at this somewhat "surly" seafooder "a bit off the beaten track" in Marylebone; and even if some feel fame has made it "lose much of its previous lustre", loyalists maintain "tourist traps have never tasted so good"; P.S. "takeaway is a great option", given the "traditionally" "basic" decor.

SHANGHAI BLUES ◑
21 | 25 | 20 | £39

193-197 High Holborn, WC1 (Holborn), 020-7404 1668; www.shanghaiblues.co.uk

"Beautifully decorated with giant hanging lamps", this "serene, elegant" eatery is "one of the more handsome Chinese restaurants in London" – not to mention something of a "best-kept secret for dim sum" in the daytime and "appealing", "upmarket" fare at night, served by generally "charming staff"; given this Holborn haunt's high-class nature, however, perhaps it works better as a "business-orientated experience than a family-friendly" one.

Shepherd's ⊠
21 | 22 | 23 | £34

Marsham Ct., Marsham St., SW1 (Pimlico), 020-7834 9552; fax 7233 6047; www.langansrestaurants.co.uk

"See politicians at work" (as well as the odd "ex-general") at this "steady, doesn't-let-you-down" Westminster stalwart; from the gentlemen's club–like premises decorated with cartoons and posters to the "wholesome", "old-fashioned" menu ("nothing here to scare the horses"), it's a "very English" experience – specifically, one of "upmarket school diners" cynics smirk.

Signor Sassi ◑⊠
23 | 18 | 23 | £41

14 Knightsbridge Green, SW1 (Knightsbridge), 020-7584 2277; fax 7225 3953

Some say it gets "really grating", but most "love" the "loud, festive" atmosphere at this ever-"popular", "very Italian" trattoria that's served "great hunks" of "delicious food" for over 20 years (as evidenced by the "dated decor"); the "old-school waiters" seem "happy to see you" and there's "no rushing" you out either – the reason "the clientele always goes back", despite it being "a bit expensive even for Knightsbridge."

Silks & Spice

▽ 18 | 13 | 15 | £23

95 Chiswick High Rd., W4 (Turnham Green), 020-8995 7991;
fax 8994 7773
Temple Ct., 11 Queen Victoria St., EC4 (Bank/Mansion House),
020-7248 7878; fax 7248 9595 ⊠
www.silksandspice.net

"Reliable", but "no surprises" sums up this "standard"
Southeast Asian duo in the City and Chiswick; being "inexpensive" means they can get "overcrowded" at key hours,
but most call them "nice enough, in a TGI Thai kind of way."

Simpson's-in-The-Strand

20 | 22 | 23 | £48

100 The Strand, WC2 (Charing Cross), 020-7836 9112;
fax 7836 1381; www.fairmont.com/savoy

"Feel like you are stepping back in time" at this "splendidly
panelled" Strand "institution" (founded circa 1828), boasting
"lots of atmosphere" of the "imperial-British-tradition"
kind and a corresponding menu of "never extraordinary,
just reliable" joints, roasts, etc., "carved from a silver trolley" and "served with flair" by "old-world" staff ("worth it
just to see a proper carver"); sure, it's all "a little stodgy for
some tastes", but "everyone should go – at least once."

Singapore Garden

21 | 13 | 17 | £28

83/83A Fairfax Rd., NW6 (Swiss Cottage), 020-7328 5314;
fax 7624 0656

"Lots of good Singaporean" and Malay "authentic dishes",
plus "all the usual Chinese classics", are on hand at this
"popular local" in Swiss Cottage; "fast service" makes it
"fine for families", and whilst it won't win any design
awards, "the new setup [eliminating a wall to create one
big room] is a massive improvement."

Singapura ⊠

▽ 17 | 15 | 19 | £32

31 Broadgate Circle, EC2 (Liverpool St.), 020-7256 5045
78-79 Leadenhall St., EC3 (Aldgate/Tower Hill), 020-7929 0089;
fax 7621 0366
1-2 Limeburner Ln., EC4 (Blackfriars/St. Paul's), 020-7329 1133;
fax 7236 1805
www.singapuras.co.uk

Supporters sing the praises of this City string of Southeast
Asians as "standbys" for swift "social or business"
lunches – "reliable" if "unexciting"; the "courteous" staff
are always "efficient", and there's "tasty takeaway" too.

Six-13 ⊠

▽ 16 | 13 | 14 | £54

19 Wigmore St., W1 (Bond St./Oxford Circus), 020-7629 6133;
fax 7629 6135; www.six13.com

"One of the few kosher places to eat in town" is this art
deco–styled eatery in Wigmore Street, offering a "diverse"
Modern European menu that's definitely "not your grandma's
cooking"; but antagonists argue the fare's "average, pricey"
and "only worth eating if you're strictly" observant.

SKETCH – THE GALLERY ⑤   18 | 26 | 18 | £59

9 Conduit St., W1 (Oxford Circus), 0870-777 4488;
fax 7629 1698; www.sketch.uk.com

Join the "size-six fashion crowd" at this "wacky" Mayfair
venue, a brasserie/club with futuristic decor "so cool people
rave about the WCs" ("after all, it isn't often you have an egg-
shaped loo to yourself"); pity that the "happening scene is
more exciting than the food", "ridiculously expensive",
"experimental" Modern European morsels from chef
Pierre Gagnaire, or the "way-too-fussy service"; P.S. for
daytime dining, venture into The Glade, the new adjacent
lunch venue whose "imaginative setting" evokes a forest.

SKETCH – THE LECTURE   22 | 25 | 23 | £90
ROOM & LIBRARY ⑤

9 Conduit St., W1 (Oxford Circus), 0870-777 4488; fax 7629 1684;
www.sketch.uk.com

"Flamboyant", "French boudoir" decor (an "eclectic" mix
of warm-toned upholstery, leather-studded walls and plas-
terwork) sets the stage for "elaborate dining" on a "Pierre
Gagnaire–supervised" Modern European menu; the leisurely procession of courses strikes some as "superb",
others as "incoherent", but all agree the staff are "absolutely delightful"; "of course it is expensive", "but you see
where the money's going" – and "what a place for a date!"

Smiths of Smithfield –   20 | 17 | 17 | £36
Dining Room ⑤

67-77 Charterhouse St., 2nd fl., EC1 (Barbican/Farringdon),
020-7251 7950; fax 7236 0488; www.smithsofsmithfield.co.uk

"There's the usual cacophony of noise" coming from a
"buzzing, trendy twentysomething crowd" at this "casual"
bi-level bistro next to Smithfield Market; "famous for its pork
bellies", the "meat-centric" Modern British menu is "a bit
pricey" but "reliable"; "service is indifferent", but "quick."

Smiths of Smithfield – Top Floor   22 | 21 | 20 | £49

67-77 Charterhouse St., EC1 (Barbican/Farringdon),
020-7251 7950; fax 7236 0488; www.smithsofsmithfield.co.uk

"Sophisticated, but casual" at the same time, this "nicely
spaced" Smithfield dining room with "great people-
watching" and "fantastic views of St Paul's, especially
from the terrace", makes a "classy place for business"
dining; but "go elsewhere if you don't like red meat" as the
Traditional British menu specialises in "solid steakhouse"
fare – and bear in mind "top floor means top prices."

Smollensky's   16 | 15 | 16 | £31
American Bar & Grill

Bradmore House, Queen Caroline St., W6 (Hammersmith),
020-8741 8124; fax 8741 5695 ⑤
105 The Strand, WC2 (Charing Cross/Covent Garden),
020-7497 2101; fax 7836 3270

(continued)

Smollensky's American Bar & Grill
*Hermitage Wharf, 22 Wapping High St., E1 (Tower Bridge/
Wapping High St.), 020-7680 1818; fax 7680 1787*
*1 Reuters Plaza, E14 (Canary Wharf), 020-7719 0101;
fax 7719 0060* 🚫
62 Carter Ln., EC4 (St. Paul's), 020-7248 4220; fax 7248 4221 🚫
"Nothing complicated – just simple" American eats (burgers, peanut butter cheesecake) is the deal at this "lively"
chain with "buzzy" bars; but "unless you've got kids with
you" or office mates needing to "unwind", foes say "skip it."

Snows on the Green 🚫 ▽ | 18 | 17 | 19 | £34 |
*166 Shepherd's Bush Rd., W6 (Hammersmith), 020-7603 2142;
fax 7602 7553; www.snowsonthegreen.co.uk*
"In a bit of a no-man's-land location" by Brook Green, this
Modern Brit hits the mark "for that midweek night out",
when all an "upmarket Londoner" wants is some "reliable,
reasonably priced" Modern British fare and "warm service."

Sofra | 18 | 13 | 16 | £25 |
*18 Shepherd St., W1 (Green Park), 020-7493 3320;
fax 7499 8282* ☻
*1 St. Christopher's Pl., W1 (Bond St.), 020-7224 4080;
fax 7224 0022* ☻
*36 Tavistock St., WC2 (Covent Garden), 020-7240 3773;
fax 7836 6633*
19-21 Exmouth Mkt., EC1 (Angel), 020-7833 1111
*11 Circus Rd., NW8 (St. John's Wood), 020-7586 9889;
fax 7586 8778*
www.sofra.co.uk
This "casual", constantly "crowded" chain "churns out"
"copious portions" of "value-packed food hot from Turkey"
and the Mediterranean, "at manageable prices" too; even
though the dining experience is "none too exciting" it's a
dependable "default" – especially "for something quick."

Soho House ☻🚫 | 20 | 20 | 19 | £42 |
Private club; inquiries: 020-7734 5188
"Stiff drinks and comfort food in a room full of beautiful
people" – no wonder it's "well worth the trouble to cajole
a member's invitation" to this Soho "private club with traditional townhouse atmosphere", "which caters mainly to
the film and TV industry"; "although it's still very much a
see-and-be-seen scene", the Modern British "food seems
to have improved over the past year", and service is
"obliging", "no matter how (not) famous you are."

Soho Spice ☻ | 20 | 15 | 16 | £27 |
*124-126 Wardour St., W1 (Tottenham Court Rd.), 020-7434 0808;
fax 7434 0799; www.sohospice.co.uk*
"For something slightly different than your regular curry
house", try this "vibrant, trendy" Soho site, which offers an

"unusual, extensive menu" of "Indian food with a good kick" ("get lots of water"), and at "cheapish" prices too; however, the "hipster decor" may not be to everyone's taste.

Solly's
▽ 19 | 12 | 14 | £25
148A Golders Green Rd., NW11 (Golders Green), 020-8455 2121
"A great bustling atmosphere, reminiscent of Tel Aviv", greets diners at "Golders Green's best option for kosher Israeli food"; the "huge portions" of "succulent grilled meats and fresh pitta bread" are appreciated more than the "tired" setting and staff, though the latter are at least "kid-friendly."

Song Que Café
▽ 23 | 7 | 15 | £23
134 Kingsland Rd., E2 (Old St.), 020-7613 3222
"You do not come here for the decor" (whose "shocking" appearance is further "marred by the crowds trying to get tables") nor for the "spotty service"; rather, you venture to this Shoreditch Southeast Asian for "fabulously cheap", "fantastic food", including the "best selection of pho around"; whilst there are Chinese dishes on the menu too, most voters vet the Vietnamese fare alone.

Sonny's
▽ 25 | 18 | 19 | £39
94 Church Rd., SW13 (Barnes Bridge B.R.), 020-8748 0393; fax 8748 2698; www.sonnys.co.uk
Though it's "been around for years", this "Barnes standard for fine dining" "doesn't rest on its laurels", but still dishes up "consistently great" Modern British fare; "light and airy even in the depths of winter", it's always "bustling with local genteel folk" ("yummy mummies and delicious daddies"); service that supporters call "never hurried" strikes sceptics as "slow", "but the meals are so nice, it's ok."

Sophie's Steakhouse & Bar ●
21 | 16 | 16 | £33
311-313 Fulham Rd., SW10 (South Kensington), 020-7352 0088; fax 7349 9776; www.sophiessteakhouse.com
"If you don't mind waiting for a table" – beware, their no-booking policy makes it "seem like an eternity", especially "when Chelsea FC is at home" – you may find contentment at this "perpetually packed" Chelsea chophouse that "seems very American", from the "convivial" vibe to the "superb steaks"; hostiles huff about the noise and the non-beef dishes that are "nothing special", but admit it's "good for a first date – not expensive, yet hip enough to impress."

Sotheby's Cafe Ⓢ
18 | 15 | 16 | £31
Sotheby's Auction House, 34 New Bond St., W1 (Bond St./ Oxford Circus), 020-7293 5077; fax 7293 6993; www.sothebys.com
"View art movers and shakers" and "hear news of the hottest bargains" at this "casual" cafe in Bond Street's famous auctioneers; whilst "not exactly fine art", the Modern British menu is "reliable", and though they need to "improve the service to have a winning bid", it's "always a

pleasure having lunch", a "coffee or bite between sales" here (it's closed for dinner).

Souk ◐
▽ | 22 | 23 | 13 | £25

27 Litchfield St., WC2 (Leicester Sq.), 020-7240 1796; fax 7240 3382

Souk Medina ◐

1A Short's Gardens, WC2 (Covent Garden), 020-7240 1796
www.soukrestaurant.co.uk

"The floor pillows, belly dancer" on weekends and "genie's lamp"–like lighting decor are all part of the "Aladdin's cave" experience at this "atmospheric" North African near Leicester Square with a Covent Garden cousin; the "gorgeous" Moroccan cooking, with many "veggie dishes", makes "a refreshing change"; the only "downside" is the "disorganised service."

Spago ◐
▽ | 21 | 13 | 18 | £37

6 Glendower Pl., SW7 (South Kensington), 020-7225 2407

"For [just] 'another Italian' in London, it is a cut above" claim advocates of this "relaxed" South Ken veteran "concentrating on wood-fired-oven pizza" that's decent "value for money"; live guitar music on Saturdays adds ambience to the traditional decor, and late hours make it an option after a concert at Royal Albert Hall nearby.

Spiga ◐
17 | 13 | 14 | £27

84-86 Wardour St., W1 (Leicester Sq./Piccadilly Circus),
020-7734 3444; fax 7734 3332; www.vpmg.net

A "decent alternative" to the chains, this "easy-going, contemporary Italian" "positively bustles with local Soho professionals", thanks to "hearty pastas" and "big pizzas" ("don't bother with a starter, you won't have room"); if the "reliable, but unspectacular" menu offers "no surprises", neither does the bill.

Spighetta
▽ | 17 | 10 | 17 | £24

43 Blandford St., W1 (Baker St.), 020-7486 7340; fax 7486 7340;
www.spighetta.co.uk

It's in "an odd basement setup" with "not much atmosphere", but this "unpretentious" Marylebone Italian is "reliable" for "thin-crust, wood-oven-fired pizzas" and other "Sardinian-accented" fare at "reasonable prices"; "friendly service" is appreciated as well.

Spoon at Sanderson
20 | 22 | 18 | £55

Sanderson Hotel, 50 Berners St., W1 (Goodge St./Oxford Circus),
020-7300 1444; fax 7300 5540; www.chinagrillmgt.com/spoon

From the decor to the portion size, "minimalist is where it is at, and they make no bones about it" at this Fitzrovian "place for the beautiful people to adore each other"; executive chef "Alain Ducasse impresses as usual" with a "quirky" Eclectic menu from which you choose "across a grid" of choices, from "imaginative peppered foie gras" to mojito ice cream; that said, some snap "this is yesterday's scene" ("kind of '90s") and "would expect better at the price."

SQUARE, THE   27 | 22 | 26 | £82

6-10 Bruton St., W1 (Bond St./Green Park), 020-7495 7100; fax 7495 7150; www.squarerestaurant.com

"Nothing square about this place" maintain mavens of this "memorable" "modern" Mayfair address where you'll be "blown away" by the "fabulous, light New French cuisine" and "assured" yet "flexible" service ("'no' is not in their vocabulary"); a few critics complain of getting a "cold" feeling from the "metal-and-glass" decor (though it's been softened post-*Survey*) and "strictly business" staff, but they're outnumbered by enthusiasts who insist even the high prices here represent "good value for a special-occasion meal in London."

Sri Nam ⊠   14 | 12 | 14 | £28

10 Cabot Sq., E14 (Canary Wharf), 020-7715 9515; www.orientalrestaurantgroup.co.uk

"Not a bad call if you fancy something different – and haven't booked anywhere" in advance, this "comfy", bi-level Canary Wharf Thai "does the job for a quick" meal at a "reasonable price" – though habitués hiss there's too "little variation in the menu"; table-arrangement tips: "stay downstairs for lunch – it's more cheerful", but "make sure you're seated upstairs" at dinner, unless you like mingling with the bar's "after-work drinks and big-screen football crowd."

Sri Siam City ⊠   18 | 13 | 16 | £36

85 London Wall, EC2 (Liverpool St.), 020-7628 5772; fax 7628 3395; www.orientalrestaurantgroup.co.uk

Whilst it's "not cheap", "its City location means it's a trusted fallback" the suits say of this "solid Thai"; "the food's unadventurous, but it satisfies" – and they do make it "very spicy on request"; some report being "always a little rushed" by staff.

Sri Thai Soho   ∇ 20 | 15 | 14 | £24

16 Old Compton St., W1 (Leicester Sq.), 020-7434 3544; fax 7287 1311; www.orientalrestaurantgroup.co.uk

It's "not Bangkok, but it's not bad" is the prognosis on this minimalist "Soho spot", sister to Sri Nan and Sri Siam City; the digs can be "noisy and staff inattentive, but the food is worth the wait" – especially the "great green chicken curry."

Star of India ●   22 | 14 | 18 | £33

154 Old Brompton Rd., SW5 (Gloucester Rd./South Kensington), 020-7373 2901; fax 7373 5664

"Try all the new, fashionable Indian spots, then return" to this "cosy" 55-year-old South Kensington for "fresh, fragrant dishes" from an "upscale", "authentic" menu; even though the "interior's looking a little tired" ("dingy" even), the "hospitable staff" ensure this "old reliable" is "still fun after all the years."

Sticky Fingers

13 | 16 | 15 | £25

1A Phillimore Gardens, W8 (High St. Kensington), 020-7938 5338; fax 7937 0145; www.stickyfingers.co.uk

Jammed with "interesting Rolling Stones memorabilia" – and enjoying the occasional visit from founder Bill Wyman – this "super-loud" site just off Kensington High Street is best for fare that gets your fingers sticky, like "big bad burgers" and ribs; it's clearly "one for the kids" – otherwise, adults avoid the "average" American eats.

ST. JOHN 🔁

26 | 18 | 22 | £47

26 St. John St., EC1 (Farringdon), 020-7251 0848; fax 7251 4090; www.stjohnrestaurant.com

"It's not offal, it's quite good" grin punsters of this Smithfield specialist in "nose-to-tail Modern British cooking" that does "brilliantly original" things with all the "deliciously nasty bits" of creatures ("the crunchiness of the fried-ear soup was sublime"); so what if the "clangourous" "setting resembles a prison dining hall" and you pay "exorbitant prices for entrails" – just "pick the right bits of the pig and you'll go home happy."

St. John Bread & Wine

24 | 17 | 20 | £32

94-96 Commercial St., E1 (Liverpool St.), 020-7251 0848; fax 7247 8924; www.stjohnbreadandwine.com

"Adventurous diners only" need visit this all-day, "spartan" Spitalfields "baby brother of St. John", where "large communal tables" are served "interesting, uncommon" starter-size Modern British dishes (pig's cheek with dandelion, anyone?), plus "exceptional baked goods" made on-site, by "perky" staff; the daily changing, "random menu can leave you in a bind" sometimes, but most find compensation in it being "cheaper" than its sibling.

Strada

18 | 14 | 16 | £21

9-10 Market Pl., W1 (Oxford Circus), 020-7580 4644; fax 7580 7877

15-16 New Burlington St., W1 (Oxford Circus), 020-7287 5967; fax 7287 6074

6 Great Queen St., WC2 (Holborn), 020-7405 6293; fax 7405 6284

11-13 Battersea Rise, SW11 (Clapham Junction), 020-7801 0794; fax 7801 0754

102-104 Clapham High St., SW4 (Clapham North), 020-7627 4847; fax 7720 2153

237 Earl's Court Rd., SW5 (Earl's Court), 020-7835 1180; fax 7835 2093

175 New King's Rd., SW6 (Parsons Green), 020-7731 6404; fax 7731 1431

91 Wimbledon High St., SW19 (Wimbledon), 020-8946 4363

(continued)

(continued)
Strada
8-10 Exmouth Mkt., EC1 (Farringdon), 020-7278 0800;
fax 7278 6901
105-106 Upper St., N1 (Angel), 020-7226 9742; fax 7226 9187
www.strada.co.uk
Additional locations throughout London
"Unpretentious" and "ultrareliable", these trattorias
around town "have upped the stakes when it comes to
Italian chain restaurants", with their "swish takes on standards like pizza and pasta"; they're "often irritatingly
busy" – especially "at weekends due to the big buggy
brigade" – and "service can be so-so", but they're "extremely well priced", and the "complimentary filtered water is a nice touch."

Stratford's   ▽ 22 | 18 | 22 | £38
7 Stratford Rd., W8 (High St. Kensington), 020-7937 6388;
fax 7938 3435
Perhaps it "won't impress a girlfriend, but you'll do well
with your aunt and uncle" at this "old-school" Kensington
Classic French that "specialises in seafood" ("try the fish
stew"); the "pleasant" decor is blessed "with lots of natu-
ral light", and all's overseen by "charming hosts."

Sugar Hut ●   ▽ 14 | 26 | 16 | £42
374 North End Rd., SW6 (Fulham Broadway), 020-7386 8950;
fax 7386 8428; www.sugarhutfulham.com
The "lacklustre" Thai "food is very much secondary to the
great drinking, talking" and overall "buzz" of this "expensive", youth-favouring Fulham venue; it's "a favourite for
secret dinner dates" due to "fantastic", "romantic" Asian-
Moroccan decor – "book a bed" to dine on if you can.

Sugar Reef ●▨   ▽ 15 | 19 | 15 | £37
42-44 Great Windmill St., W1 (Piccadilly Circus), 020-7851 0800;
fax 7851 0807; www.sugarreef.net
Expect "twentysomething businessmen" at lunch and
"trendy groups" by night at this "way big" Piccadilly place;
if you're seeking serious cuisine, "don't get shipwrecked
here" – the Modern European menu is no better than
"decent" – but if you just need sustenance as it "morphs
into a nightclub", you'll find it quite "cool to visit."

Sumosan ●   24 | 18 | 17 | £55
26 Albemarle St., W1 (Green Park), 020-7495 5999;
fax 7355 1247
In a former Mayfair Volvo showroom, this "formal", "low
profile" Japanese is "populated by ladies who lunch and
men who watch" them; though it "lacks the buzz of a
Nobu" or Zuma, the "sushi-plus" "food oozes quality as
well as flavour", and whilst it's "best if you're on an expense account", the "set lunch is almost a bargain."

Sweetings 🅢   23 | 15 | 18 | £39
39 Queen Victoria St., EC4 (Mansion House),
020-7248 3062

It's "scruffy, but who cares?" – this "anachronistic" lunch-only "City institution" (founded 1889) is "an absolute treat" for "awesome fish" from a "quality" Traditional British "all-seafood menu" expect "pin-striped bankers galore" ("everyone from Lloyds is there"), but as "no bookings" are taken, you may need to "pull up a stool" and "dine at the counter"; N.B. closed weekends.

TAMAN GANG ●🅢   21 | 25 | 17 | £55
141 Park Ln., W1 (Marble Arch), 020-7518 3160; fax 7518 3161;
www.tamangang.co.uk

Follow the "super-trendy designer crowd" to this "swanky" Southeast Asian, whose "fantastic", "dramatic" stone-and-mahogany decor offers "oasis from the grime of Oxford Street" nearby; friends find the "surprisingly good", albeit pricey, Pan-Asian food "bursting with flavour", but even they gang up on the "disorganised" "staff with limited culinary or wine knowledge"; a "lounge DJ" spins tunes after 9 PM most nights.

TAMARIND ●   25 | 22 | 24 | £49
20 Queen St., W1 (Green Park), 020-7629 3561; fax 7499 5034;
www.tamarindrestaurant.com

"A jewel in the crown of Mayfair", this "lovely" Indian offers "creative", "hypnotic dishes" "spiced just right for most palates" (and if you're in doubt, "polite" staff are "willing to decipher and advise" on the menu); even if the "high-end" prices ruffle a few feathers, this "stellar cellar" is considered "one of the best of the genre" – "even to those who don't like curry."

Tamesa@oxo   – | – | – | M
Oxo Tower Wharf, 2nd fl., Barge House St., SE1 (Blackfriars/
Waterloo), 020-7633 0088; www.coinstreet.org

With an impressive full-length view of the Thames along one side, this bright and breezy newcomer on the second floor of South Bank's landmark Oxo Tower makes full use of its attractive location, offering the twin options of a brasserie serving simple Modern European fare, and a casual, comfy lounge with circular bar for light bites, which can be accessed directly from the river walk.

Tapas Brindisa 🅢   21 | 15 | 16 | £28
Borough Mkt., 18-20 Southwark St., SE1 (London Bridge),
020-7357 8880

"Raising the stakes for the city's tapas bars" is this "packed" Borough Market yearling where the combo of "well-executed" "small plates of Spanish tasties" and no reservations means it's "almost impossible to get a table unless you're there early"; even though "a little soundproofing to cut the noise wouldn't go amiss", most feel it's "worth the wait for a wonderful" time.

Taqueria
16 | 10 | 12 | £22

139-143 Westbourne Grove, W11 (Notting Hill Gate/Bayswater), 020-7229 4734; www.coolchile.co.uk

"Authentic Mexican fare with no frills, not the usual gloopy Tex-Mex out of a jar", is the "ambitious" aim of this Notting Hill newcomer from a Latino food importer (whose wares are sold on the premises); devotees are delighted by the "dainty, exotic taco combinations", but hostile hombres find them "expensive for the small portions" and lament the "long waits for confused service."

Tartine
19 | 15 | 15 | £32

114 Draycott Ave., SW3 (South Kensington), 020-7589 4981; fax 7589 5048; www.tartine.co.uk

"Succulent, delicious tartines" and other "simple" French brasserie fare is the focus of this "Draycott Avenue hideaway" ideally suited "for Sunday brunches" – "sit in front and you get to see everyone in Chelsea pass by"; but more tart tongues say tasting "tiny bites at gigantic prices" gets "boring after a while."

Tas ◐
20 | 15 | 17 | £23

72 Borough High St., SE1 (London Bridge), 020-7403 7200; fax 7403 7022
33 The Cut, SE1 (Southwark), 020-7928 1444; fax 7633 9686
20 New Globe Walk, SE1 (London Bridge), 020-7928 3300; fax 7261 1166
www.tasrestaurant.com

"Nothing beats the atmosphere" at this "tasty Turkish" trio around town, "serving unusual dishes alongside the standards" at "bargain basement prices"; but with "decor that's a bit bland" and "staff that can be abrupt", it's "not a fine-dining" experience here.

Tate Britain Restaurant
19 | 22 | 17 | £29

Tate Britain, Millbank, SW1 (Pimlico), 020-7887 8825; fax 7887 8902; www.tate.org.uk

Often the words "'good museum restaurant' are an oxymoron", but this Modern Brit in the Tate is an exception; the "unhurried, clubby" ambience is dominated by a "special" Rex Whistler mural, whilst the "dependable" fare makes a "perfectly acceptable" "finish to the great gallery" of art; tour-minded reviewers recommend "lunch here, then onto the museum's boat to the Tate Modern."

Tate Modern
18 | 21 | 16 | £27

Tate Modern, Bankside, SE1 (Blackfriars/London Bridge), 020-7401 5020; www.tate.org.uk/modern

"Even if you don't like contemporary art", the Tate Modern's seventh-floor cafe is "impossible to pass up for the sweet location alone", which affords "fabulous views of St. Paul's and the river"; "for a canteen, they provide decent grub" of a Modern European sort; but the "service is slow", and many find the fare "overpriced" ("but then, most museum food is").

Tatsuso 🖂   ▽ 25 | 17 | 21 | £64

32 Broadgate Circle, EC2 (Liverpool St.), 020-7638 5863; fax 7638 5864

"Typically occupied by bankers and brokers", this bi-level Broadgate Circle Japanese has you go "upstairs for the best teppanyaki" and downstairs for "traditional" sushi and other "quality" dishes; regulars swear they've "never been disappointed" here, even if "the prices are verging on the shocking" – and "even more expensive if you add the dry cleaning to remove the [smoky] smell off your clothes."

TECA 🖂   22 | 20 | 20 | £47

54 Brooks Mews, W1 (Bond St.), 020-7495 4774; fax 7491 3545

"Tucked away in Mayfair" – it's "great whilst shopping in Bond Street" – this "sleek establishment" serves "seriously good" "Italian staples" and wines with "more hits than misses"; however, it's best "if you aren't in too much of a hurry", as the "warm service" can "deteriorate once it gets busy."

Tentazioni 🖂   ▽ 25 | 16 | 23 | £44

Lloyd's Wharf, 2 Mill St., SE1 (London Bridge/Tower Hill), 020-7237 1100; fax 7237 1100; www.tentazioni.co.uk

With "so many temptations" on the Italian menu and "the enthusiasm of chef/co-owner" Ricardo Giacomini, this "first-rate" eatery is "worth the trek", even if it is "tucked away in the middle of nowhere" (actually, Shad Thames); adorned with modern paintings, the Pop Art–toned decor is slightly "weird" but "stylish", and whilst the place is "not cheap, it's good value."

Terminus   15 | 14 | 15 | £32

Great Eastern Hotel, 40 Liverpool St., EC2 (Liverpool St.), 020-7618 7400; fax 7618 7401; www.great-eastern-hotel.co.uk

It "works for us City folk" profess patrons of this "busy", all-day Modern Brit by Liverpool Street Station (which makes it a "perfect breakfast spot" for commuters); but it's the end of the line for opponents who say "if you want to eat in a station this is what it feels like – noisy, slow service" and an "unappealing" menu.

Texas Embassy Cantina   14 | 16 | 16 | £22

1 Cockspur St., SW1 (Charing Cross/Piccadilly Circus), 020-7925 0077; fax 7925 0444; www.texasembassy.com

For all you "Tex-Mex lovers out there looking for a good ol' place to enjoy yore beans and stuff", this huge site "right there in the middle of Trafalgar Square" will "hit the spot"; yup, the fare's kinda bland – like "Brit-Mex" maybe – and the pseudo-saloon decor goes "a little overboard"; "but sometimes you just gotta get yerself a fajita" (however "fake" it is) and a "toxic margarita" – so "step up to the trough, cowboy."

T.G.I. Friday's ◐   11   12   13   £21

96-98 Bishop's Bridge Rd., W2 (Bayswater/Queensway), 020-7229 8600; fax 7727 4150
25-29 Coventry St., W1 (Piccadilly Circus), 020-7839 6262; fax 7839 6296
6 Bedford St., WC2 (Charing Cross/Covent Garden), 020-7379 0585; fax 7240 3239
Fulham Broadway Ctr., Fulham Rd., SW6 (Fulham Broadway), 020-7385 0470
www.tgifridays.com

"For those dying for American comfort food" – or families with kids – these West End outposts of the "quintessential" Yankee chain "tirelessly churn out formulaic dishes"; you "won't leave hungry", given the "huge portions" and "free soda refills" on hand; but antagonists argue "with all the excellent restaurants in London, why bother with this tired step above fast food?"

Thai Pavilion   –   –   –   M

42 Rupert St., W1 (Leicester Sq./Piccadilly Circus), 020-7287 6333; fax 7587 0484; www.thaipavilion.com ◐
82 Kennington Rd., SE11 (Lambeth North), 020-7587 0455; fax 7587 0484; www.pavilioneast.com

A "serene atmosphere" prevails at this pair of "friendly" Thais in Soho and Kennington (the latter most "welcome for those who live nearby"); both specialise in "light", "vibrant" fare, "full of fresh herbs and seeds rather than the usual pastes", brought by "helpful staff" as you sit at either regular tables or *sans* shoes at authentically low ones (Rupert Street only).

Thai Square   17   16   16   £27

5 Princes St., W1 (Oxford Circus), 020-7499 3333 ⌧
27-28 St. Anne's Ct., W1 (Tottenham Court Rd.), 020-7287 2000 ◐⌧
148 The Strand, WC2 (Covent Garden), 020-7497 0904 ◐⌧
21-24 Cockspur St., SW1 (Charing Cross/Piccadilly Circus), 020-7839 4000; fax 7839 0839 ◐
19 Exhibition Rd., SW7 (South Kensington), 020-7584 8359
2-4 Lower Richmond Rd., SW15 (Putney/Putney Bridge), 020-8780 1811; fax 8780 1211 ◐
1 Great St. Thomas Apostle, EC4 (Mansion House), 020-7329 0001 ◐⌧
136-138 Minories, EC3 (Tower Hill), 020-7680 1111; fax 7680 1112 ◐⌧
347-349 Upper St., N1 (Angel), 020-7704 2000; fax 7704 2277 ◐
www.thaisq.com

Maybe it's a "mass-market Thai", but "the curries are light and fragrant" and the artefact-laden "decor looks the part too"; it's "nothing special", but a "solid performer in a crowded field" and a good place to be "on a date (as pretty much everyone is.")

Thomas Cubitt, The
∇ 21 | 22 | 21 | £41

44 Elizabeth St., SW1 (Victoria), 020-7730 6060; fax 7730 6055; www.thethomascubitt.co.uk

Named after a 19th-century architect who worked on Buckingham Palace nearby, this "atmospheric" Belgravia boozer has been given a smart gastropub revamp, and now boasts a wood-panelled bar with "a nice vibe" and cosy, L-shaped dining room upstairs; early surveyors are "impressed" by the Modern British menu and "foxy waiters", though some scold the "not-ready-for-prime-time service."

Tiger Lil's
17 | 13 | 16 | £21

270 Upper St., N1 (Highbury & Islington), 020-7226 1118; fax 7288 1108; www.tigerlils.com

"Choosing your ingredients, and then seeing them flipped and fried in front of you", Mongolian BBQ–style, is the "fun" part of this "novel" Islington Asian eatery, an especially "cheap way out" for groups or kids; "the food could be better, though."

Timo
∇ 23 | 16 | 22 | £43

343 Kensington High St., W8 (High St. Kensington), 020-7603 3888; fax 7603 8111

"Don't expect a scene, but do expect great food" at this low-key, bi-level Kensington Northern Italian specialising in seafood and housemade pastas; devotees are "never disappointed by the food" or the "friendly" service, but the contemporary setting is "cold."

Tokyo Diner ◑
∇ 14 | 9 | 15 | £17

2 Newport Pl., WC2 (Leicester Sq.), 020-7287 8777; fax 7434 1415; www.tokyodiner.com

"It's not much in terms of decor" (in fact, it's "looking pretty tired"), but the "authentic Japanese food" "really hits the spot" at this eatery "on the fringe of Chinatown"; it's "cheap" and "they don't accept tips", which makes it a "student/budget classic", but some cynics sniff "you get what you pay for."

Tom Aikens ⊠
25 | 22 | 23 | £82

43 Elystan St., SW3 (South Kensington), 020-7584 2003; fax 7584 2001; www.tomaikens.co.uk

This "sleek" Chelsea "treat" "never fails to sparkle" for culinary adventurers who adore "golden boy"/"mad genius" Tom Aikens' "unique, daring combinations", along with the "world's greatest cheese board", served by "casually professional staff" who "don't rush the patrons"; opponents opine "prices are obscene" for "overcomplicated New French fare", "but there are signs the chef is calming down" now – and besides, it's all "so unique" you should try it, "even if you don't recognise what you're eating."

Tom's Delicatessen   ▽ 17 14 14 £19

226 Westbourne Grove, W11 (Notting Hill Gate), 020-7221 8818;
fax 7221 7717

"Not worth travelling to, but nice to have in the neighbourhood'" of Westbourne Grove, Tom Conran's "cute", all-day
cafe is "good for a snack" or sandwich from a "pricey, but
tasty" Eclectic deli menu; the "small space is always busy"
so expect to "wait" for a table (pass the time by "spotting
beautiful people and the occasional celebrity").

Tootsies   16 13 14 £20

148 Chiswick High Rd., W4 (Turnham Green), 020-8747 1869;
fax 8987 0686
35 James St., W1 (Bond St.), 020-7486 1611;
fax 7935 4957
120 Holland Park Ave., W11 (Holland Park),
020-7229 8567
35 Haven Green, W5 (Ealing Broadway), 020-8566 8200;
fax 8991 1491
36-38 Abbeville Rd., SW4 (Clapham South), 020-8772 6646;
fax 8772 0672
1 Battersea Rise, SW11 (Clapham Junction),
020-7924 4935
48 High St., SW19 (Wimbledon), 020-8946 4135
107 Old Brompton Rd., SW7 (South Kensington), 020-7581 8942;
fax 7590 0979
196-198 Haverstock Hill, NW3 (Belsize Park), 020-7431 3812;
fax 7794 8478
www.tootsiesrestaurants.co.uk
Additional locations throughout London

A "chain, but a good chain", these long-established
American diners are "dependable" for "good-sized" burgers, "wicked milkshakes" and the like – plus "the staff are
cheerful and friendly even when your children aren't"; still,
some think it's "time to up its game" lest it be "left behind by
the new-style burger bars" springing up around town.

Toto's   23 20 23 £51

Walton House, Walton St. at Lennox Garden Mews, SW3
(Knightsbridge), 020-7589 2062; fax 7581 9668

"Be whisked away from the bustling city" by this "romantic hideaway" – complete with "wonderful Murano glass
chandelier" – in a discreet Chelsea mews ("all the more fun
finding it"); the Northern Italian fare is "on the expensive
side", but "heaven for the senses", and it's complemented
by a "very comprehensive wine list"; "smooth-as-silk"
service rounds out the scene.

Troubadour, The ●   13 20 14 £20

265 Old Brompton Rd., SW5 (Earl's Court), 020-7370 1434;
fax 7341 6329; www.troubadour.co.uk

"Don't go for the food – go for the mood" at this "Earl's Court
haunt where poets, philosophers and idlers play chess,

drink herbal tea" and listen to live music and readings amidst the "dark corners and candles" or in the "lovely garden in back"; the Eclectic eats harken back to "comfort food from the '70s", and "the attitude factor is, worryingly, increasing" amongst the staff; still, it's the "atmospheric" ambience that attracts folks, as it's done for some 50 years.

Truc Vert

20	15	13	£25

42 N. Audley St., W1 (Bond St.), 020-7491 9988;
fax 7491 7717

"If you like rustic France", this Mayfair bistro "gets the basics right", from breakfast (starring "scrambled eggs like a soufflé") to dinner; despite "laughably misguided service", the ambience manages to be "relaxing" – especially "in the evening after the shoppers have gone and only the locals turn up."

Tsunami

24	18	18	£43

5-7 Voltaire Rd., SW4 (Clapham North), 020-7978 1610;
fax 7978 1591

The "Nobu-style" "menu teems with delicate, creative dishes" – but at nearly "half the price" claim converts of this Clapham "neighbourhood Japanese"; the "rather sad"-looking "decor could use a step up", however, and it's a "shame about the prima donna staff."

Tugga

–	–	–	E

312-314 King's Rd., SW3 (Sloane Square), 020-7351 0101;
www.tugga.com

A "great addition to the King's Road" say fans of this vibrantly coloured yearling serving "different" Portuguese fare in "small"-plate sizes, supported by an Iberian "wine list of surprising quality"; the less-excited excoriate the "bland" fare and "variable" service, but they do admit that even if much is "disappointing, the bar scene is hopping" with DJs most nights.

Tuttons Brasserie ◑

15	15	16	£29

11-12 Russell St., WC2 (Covent Garden), 020-7836 4141;
fax 7379 9979

"For what seems to be a touristy place, the food is surprisingly good" at this French brasserie with Modern Brit overtones in Covent Garden ("good to go after the theatre"); and if the "service is streaky", most forgive because the "prices don't put pressure on the plastic."

Two Brothers Fish ⊠

25	13	18	£22

297-303 Regent's Park Rd., N3 (Finchley Central), 020-8346 0469;
fax 8343 1978

"Really owned by two brothers", this "brightly lit", frills-free Finchley stalwart will "bring you a feast" of "fantastic fresh fish" "done any way you like" (their "fish 'n' chips are some of the best") "at reasonable prices" to boot; it's often "packed with regulars", but there's "also takeaway."

202
17 | 18 | 15 | £25

Nicole Farhi, 202 Westbourne Grove, W11 (Notting Hill Gate), 020-7727 2722; fax 7792 9217

This "combined shopping-and-eating" concept in Notting Hill's Nicole Farhi offers a "simple" Modern European menu that's "excellent for brunch" or "a girlie lunch" spiced with prime "people-watching"; it gets "crowded on weekends", so head for the "great back patio" or "go at off-hours."

Ubon by Nobu ☒
25 | 21 | 19 | £58

34 Westferry Circus, E14 (Canary Wharf), 020-7719 7800; fax 7719 7801; www.noburestaurants.com

"Convenient when you're stuck in Canary Wharf", this "Nobu offshoot" is "more corporate, less scene-y than the original"; you still have the "absolutely fab" Japanese-Peruvian cuisine, plus "spectacular views" that "alone are worth the trip"; "service has a few issues" ("hard to get [their] attention"), and overall "it's not as good" or "as cool" as the big N, perhaps; but it is "marginally cheaper" and you can get in "without the long wait for a reservation."

Uli
▽ 22 | 15 | 22 | £33

16 All Saints Rd., W11 (Ladbroke Grove), 020-7727 7511

"Always ready to explain and make suggestions", "the owners look after you like you are one of their own" at this "best-kept secret in Notting Hill"; a "cosy", modest place, it "draws a fairly chic crowd" for its "delicious" menu that "offers a bit of all Far Eastern cuisines."

UMU ☒
26 | 25 | 24 | £85

14-16 Bruton Pl., W1 (Bond St.), 020-7499 8881

"Not a sushi place, but an experience" enthuse surveyors abut this "stylish", ornate Asian in Mayfair, specialising in "Kyoto-style cuisine" that's "as authentic as it can be out-side of Japan"; however, given the "exorbitant prices" and "endless" procession of kaiseki-menu courses, some say it "suits special occasions only."

Union Cafe
18 | 15 | 17 | £31

96 Marylebone Ln., W1 (Bond St.), 020-7486 4860; fax 7486 4860; www.brinkleys.com

Brinkley's "bright", "buzzy" sibling in Marylebone Lane ("tucked away so you aren't dealing with tourists") offers "good, straightforward" Med–Modern British fare; there's some dissension over service – "friendly" vs. "indifferent" – but union is restored over the "fantastic-value wine list", whose "markups are much lower than average."

Upstairs Bar & Restaurant
– | – | – | E

89B Acre Ln., SW2 (Clapham North/Brixton), 020-7733 8855; www.upstairslondon.com

A trio of French owners are behind this quirky Brixton new-comer in a space that has lain vacant since the 1960s; it now comprises a simple first-floor bar and cosy upstairs restaurant with an open fire, where a former chef from La Trompette offers a varied, fortnightly changing Modern European menu alongside a short, modestly priced wine list.

Vama ●   25 20 22 £42
438 King's Rd., SW10 (Sloane Sq.), 020-7565 8500; fax 7565 8501; www.vama.co.uk
"They somehow take Indian dishes you know and transform them to the next level" at this "exciting" eatery far down King's Road ("allow for a stroll from the Sloane Square tube"); the menu offers both "a veritable vegetarians' paradise" and plenty of "zesty" meat dishes, served in recently modernised, "dressed-up digs" by "experienced staff"; though they're not low, most "don't mind the prices" – especially if they spot "a famous face seated somewhere."

Vasco & Piero's Pavilion ☒   ▽ 24 16 22 £37
15 Poland St., W1 (Oxford Circus), 020-7437 8774; fax 7437 0467; www.vascosfood.com
This "fabulous, retro Italian" ("Austin Powers would love it") makes a "surprising find on the northern edges of Soho"; its "simple, unfussy" Umbrian dishes "are cooked to perfection", and the service is "friendly, without being over-familiar"; perhaps the digs are a bit "squashed."

Veeraswamy ●   23 22 23 £39
Victory House, 99-101 Regent St., W1 (Piccadilly Circus), 020-7734 1401; fax 7439 8434; www.realindianfood.com
Now "looking great" (e.g. the higher Decor score) after a "revamp to 1920s maharajah style", from gold-speckled granite floor to silver ceiling, this "elegant" eightysomething earns plaudits for Indian classics – now "with a modern interpretation" that makes them quite "exciting"; "service is crisp and precise", and whilst it's a bit "expensive" "visiting this old friend", he still offers a respite one floor up "from the hustle and bustle of Regent Street."

Verbanella ●   19 16 21 £40
30 Beauchamp Pl., SW3 (Knightsbridge), 020-7584 1107; fax 7589 9662
"Like an old shoe – comfortable, if a bit scruffy" – this "quiet" Knightsbridge trattoria is "one of the less expensive places in the West End" for a "dependable" Italian meal; what really gives it "favourite" status, though, is the "helpful staff" who "make you feel you are sitting in their home kitchen."

Viet Hoa ●   22 8 12 £20
70-72 Kingsland Rd., E2 (Old St.), 020-7729 8293; fax 7729 8293
It looks "like a trusty work canteen", but get past the "neon-lit surroundings" and you'll find "wonderful, interesting" Vietnamese fare for a "bargain price"; the "ado-

lescent" "service is friendly but inefficient – the arrival of [everyone's] food is likely to be staggered" – but that doesn't stop this Shoreditch spot from being "full of locals."

Villandry

18 | 14 | 16 | £35

170 Great Portland St., W1 (Great Portland St.), 020-7631 3131; fax 7631 3030; www.villandry.com

Mixed reactions greet this "functional" Marylebone eatery with a "fancy deli up front": some say it's a "relaxing" place serving "decent", even "quite inventive" Modern European fare, with "competent service", but others detect an "identity crisis here – is it a takeaway or restaurant?", with "bare decor", "limited menu" and "understaffing" not boding well for the latter; it's probably "best for breakfast."

Vineyard at Stockcross

▽ 25 | 22 | 25 | £63

Vineyard at Stockcross, Stockcross, Newbury, Berkshire, 01635 528770; fax 01635 528398; www.the-vineyard.co.uk

In a "good setting" amongst "horse country", this handsome Berkshire hotel is "worth the journey", fans find, for "beautifully prepared" Classic French–Modern British dishes, supported by a "stunning", 2,000-label-strong wine list; cynics get cross at the "small portions with big prices" – though the combined "accommodation and dinner packages are good value."

Vingt-Quatre ●

14 | 12 | 14 | £24

325 Fulham Rd., SW10 (South Kensington), 020-7376 7224; fax 7352 2643

"Show up any time" – "it's open 24 hours a day" – at this "people-watching place" on Fulham Road; the "diverse" Eclectic fare is "not stellar" and probably "overpriced for what you get", but it fits the bill for "hangover cures" or when "you have a burger urge at 5 AM" after "spilling in from a club."

Vivat Bacchus ☒

_ | _ | _ | E

47 Farringdon St., EC4 (Chancery Ln./Farringdon), 020-7353 2648; www.vivatbacchus.co.uk

"A most prepossessing exterior hides" this "tricky-to-find", rustic Farringdon basement eatery most appreciated for its "phenomenal" "walk-in wine cellars and cheese room" with a "surprising selection of 80" *fromages*; the "South African owners have put together" a "good" Modern European menu, supported by "friendly staff" and (of course) "knowledgeable sommeliers."

Volt ☒

▽ 17 | 20 | 15 | £44

17 Hobart Pl., SW1 (Victoria), 020-7235 9696; www.voltlounge.com

"Is it a club or a restaurant?" query customers of this "hip, energetic" novice behind Buckingham Palace that "has found a niche with the jet set"; there's a "really cool lounge

scene" and "amazing" futuristic, monochromatic decor;
but the Italian fare, whilst "innovative", is "not consistent"
and the "amateurish service" "needs more polishing."

Vrisaki ● ☒   – | – | – | M
73 Myddelton Rd., N22 (Bounds Green/Wood Green),
020-8889 8760; fax 8889 0103
From grilled fish to "the best souvlaki in town", "you have
never experienced so much food" as you do at this
"friendly", highly "authentic" Muswell Hill Greek, which has
been stuffing stomachs for over a quarter-century; the ambience is "not sophisticated", however, so for some "takeaway is the better option, if you can bear the queues."

WAGAMAMA   20 | 14 | 17 | £17
26A Kensington High St., W8 (High St. Kensington),
020-7376 1717
10A Lexington St., W1 (Oxford Circus/Piccadilly Circus),
020-7292 0990
101A Wigmore St., W1 (Bond St./Oxford Circus),
020-7409 0111
4A Streatham St., WC1 (Holborn/Tottenham Court Rd.),
020-7323 9223; fax 7323 9224
1 Tavistock St., WC2 (Covent Garden), 020-7836 3330;
fax 7240 8846
Harvey Nichols, 109-125 Knightsbridge, SW1 (Knightsbridge),
020-7201 8000; fax 7201 8080
109 Fleet St., EC4 (Blackfriars/St. Paul's),
020-7583 7889 ☒
1A Ropemaker St., EC2 (Moorgate), 020-7588 2688 ☒
40 Parkfield St., N1 (Angel), 020-7226 2664
11 Jamestown Rd., NW1 (Camden Town), 020-7428 0800;
fax 7482 4887
www.wagamama.com
Additional locations throughout London
"It's easy to believe the 'positive eating + positive living'
mantra" of these high-energy Japanese "noodle can-
teens" offering a "no-frills, no-fuss, efficient" experience
that "doesn't leave you strapped for cash at the end of a
wholesome", "postmodern comfort-food" meal; even if the
"cafeteria-style seating" means sitting "shoulder to shoulder" with strangers and "not lingering", the "fantastic formula" is "hard to beat" – and again London's Most Popular;
P.S. go ahead – "let down your inhibitions, and slurp."

Wapping Food   ▽ 19 | 22 | 18 | £40
*Wapping Hydraulic Power Station, Wapping Wall, E1
(Wapping), 020-7680 2080; www.thewappingproject.com*
A "most unique setting" – a converted hydraulic power station, with "old industrial machinery and retro furniture" – is
"worth the trip" to this way-out Wapping venue; and even
if the "good", "regularly changing" Modern European
menu "doesn't match the interest of the surroundings", the

fact that "they also host different [art] exhibitions", concerts and film screenings makes it a "destination."

WATERSIDE INN
28 | 26 | 27 | £94

Waterside Inn, Ferry Rd., Bray-on-Thames, Berkshire,
01628 620691; fax 01628 784710;
www.waterside-inn.co.uk

"Oozing with English countryside charm" – thanks to a "stunning" site "overlooking the Thames" – this "beautiful" Berkshire venue has "few equals" for "a splurge to remember"; run by Roux *père et fils,* it's surprisingly "not at all formal or stuffy", but just offers "outstanding" "old-school Classic French cooking" melded with "sophisticated new-world culinary styles" and "flawlessly served" ("nothing is too much trouble" for the staff); "you get more than you pay for – but be sure to have a big budget", anyway.

Wells, The
18 | 18 | 17 | £34

30 Well Walk, NW3 (Hampstead), 020-7794 3785;
www.thewellshampstead.co.uk

Like "a lovely country pub that happens to have landed in London", this Georgian spot "on the way to Hampstead Heath" is "ideal for the proverbial Sunday brunch with kids"; amongst the dining options, many prefer the "unpretentious" but "inviting" ground-floor area ("upstairs is more of a restaurant"); some malcontents mutter the "stylish" Modern European fare "has declined from a year ago", but their views (and the Food score) may not reflect the arrival of a new "chef from Villandry" mid-*Survey.*

Westbourne, The
18 | 16 | 8 | £24

101 Westbourne Park Villas, W2 (Royal Oak/Westbourne Park),
020-7221 1332; fax 7243 8081

"If you don't live in Notting Hill and want to pretend you do – come on down" to this gastropub, the area's "ultimate hangout" that's always "packed solid" with a "studied casual crowd" (plus "poseurs looking to be spotted by a casting agent"); though it's more for "socialising and a drink" ("the terrace is specially cool"), the Eclectic–Modern European food is "good"; but virtually every reviewer roars about the "rudeness and arrogance" of the "preening" staff, whose service "takes an eternity."

White Hart, The
– | – | – | M

185 Kennington Ln., SE11 (Kennington), 020-7735 1061;
www.thewhitehartpub.co.uk

"The replacement for La Finca", the longtime occupant of this Kennington address, is a "not-bad gastropub" "specialising in Argentinean steaks" and other Modern European grub from rock singer Bryan Adams' ex chef; decked out with exposed brick and leather furniture, it's already getting "busy", even if it's "going through some growing pains with regards to service."

White Swan Pub & Dining Room ⑧

19 | 18 | 18 | £32

*108 Fetter Ln., EC4 (Chancery Ln./Farringdon), 020-7242 9696;
www.thewhiteswanlondon.com*

This high-ceilinged, "quirky restaurant over a pub" is an "excellent addition to the EC4/EC1 dining scene", offering "good, standard" British fare of the fish-and-chips or steak-and-kidney-pudding variety; they've given "great attention to the wine menu", but of course, most just pant for "pints, pints and pints."

Whit's ⑧

_ | _ | _ | E

*21 Abingdon Rd., W8 (High St. Kensington), 020-7938 1122;
www.whits.co.uk*

"The thing that stands out are the friendly owners" (one of whom is also the chef) at this low-key brasserie, known for "imaginative", "filling" Classic French–Traditional British cuisine, matched by "good service"; alas, some are not a whit for all that, noting "it has a lot of competition here" in Kensington.

Wilton's ⑧

25 | 22 | 25 | £63

*55 Jermyn St., SW1 (Green Park/Piccadilly Circus),
020-7629 9955; fax 7495 6233; www.wiltons.co.uk*

After 265 years, this "venerable, venerated" venue is "still going strong" in St. James's, and it's "like taking a trip back to yesteryear" to sit amidst the "clubby", "civilised" digs "heavy hitters and grandees get the [sought-after] booths") and dine on dishes that are "dull-sounding" but "delicious", including "outstanding" oysters and fish "Wilton's is the main reason God gave us oceans"); service is "wonderfully old-school", and whilst "prices are outrageous", this is "old England at its formal best."

Wizzy ●⑧

▽ 26 | 10 | 17 | £32

616 Fulham Rd., SW6 (Parsons Green), 020-7736 9171

"Deserves to be discovered for delicious food" exclaim enthusiasts for this "excellent Korean" yearling in Fulham; the namesake "chef-proprietor is extremely nice", "often coming out of the kitchen to say hello and serve" her "succulent" bulgoki or chocolate fondant – all "reasonably priced"; only the "austere" decor "needs to be improved."

Wòdka ●

19 | 13 | 19 | £37

*12 St. Albans Grove, W8 (High St. Kensington), 020-7937 6513;
fax 7937 8621; www.wodka.co.uk*

Known as much for its "comprehensive vodka list" as its "beautiful, pouting" waitresses ("hotties with an attitude"), this "buzzing, lively" Kensington bistro with "tables jammed together" makes a "great venue for groups in need of a big night out"; the "hearty" "Polish food" is "surprisingly tasty", even if it plays second fiddle to the "party-at" atmosphere and "fantastic shots."

WOLSELEY, THE ●
21 | 26 | 20 | £45

160 Piccadilly, W1 (Green Park), 020-7499 6996; fax 7499 6888,
www.thewolseley.com

Full of "noise, energy and great snob appeal", this "pricey" Piccadilly brasserie is simply "a stunner"; everyone adores the art deco–era digs, a "mélange of Asian aristocratic with Paris chic" "that still manages to feel intimate", whilst the Modern European menu (available from 7 AM on) has "something to suit all but the quirkiest palates"; staff have a tendency to "ignore normal punters to crawl over celebs", but still, most wonder "what did we ever do without it?"

Wong Kei ●⌷
16 | 5 | 8 | £12

41-43 Wardour St., W1 (Leicester Sq./Piccadilly Circus), 020-7437 8408

"Don't expect much finesse from the staff", and "don't pay attention to the decor" either, at this Chinatowner that's achieved "institution" status for just one thing: being a "reliable, cheap source" for Cantonese "food on the hoof"; also be advised that, whilst the service is "not as rude as it used to be", "obligatory surliness" is still on the menu.

W'Sens ⊠
▽ 21 | 23 | 16 | £53

12 Waterloo Pl., SW1 (Piccadilly Circus), 020-7484 1355; fax 7484 1366; www.wsens.co.uk

The combination of an "imaginative" Eclectic–New French menu, "fab French regional wines" and "fantastic", red-toned contemporary decor creates "a completely novel experience" at this "trendy" offering from the Gallic restaurant group La Compagnie des Comptoirs; and if some feel the "food does not match the exquisite surroundings" and point to problematic service ("long time between plates"), most think the place "worthy of repeat custom."

Yakitoria ⊠
– | – | – | E

25 Sheldon St., W2 (Paddington), 020-3214 3000; fax 3214 3001; www.yakitoria.co.uk

Within the Paddington Central development near Little Venice (it's next to a canal), this "über-modern" Japanese offers an "extensive menu" of both "fresh, well-presented" sushi and, as the name suggests, "innovative" grilled fare; early reports say all's "decently" done, but the "finished result somehow lacks soul."

YAUATCHA
25 | 23 | 17 | £39

15 Broadwick St., W1 (Oxford Circus), 020-7494 8888; fax 7494 8889

"A class act from start to finish", owner Alan Yau's "moody", "sleek" Soho hot spot offers a "daunting variety" of "delectable" dim sum that's "better than sex", along with "imaginative" Chinese mains – oh, and "make sure you save space for cakes from the tearoom" upstairs; true, the

170

"knowledgeable" staff "could do with some cheering up"
and the "strict time limit on meals is a pain"; but in general,
this "expensive" Asian is "worth every pence."

Ye Olde Cheshire Cheese   16 | 23 | 16 | £22

*145 Fleet St., EC4 (Blackfriars), 020-7353 6170;
fax 7353 0845*

"For historic pub fanatics", this "quaint", "characterful
inn" (circa 1667) off Fleet Street is an "awesome place
to explore, with lots of nooks and crannies" and interesting literary connections from Samuel Pepys to Charles
Dickens; though the "no-fuss, no-frills" Traditional British
fare is "better than you might think", plenty prefer to "just
stick with a pint."

YO! Sushi   15 | 14 | 14 | £22

*52 Poland St., W1 (Oxford Circus), 020-7287 0443; fax 7439 3660
Selfridges, 400 Oxford St., W1 (Bond St.), 020-7318 3944;
fax 7318 3885
Unit R07, Paddington Station, W2 (Paddington), 020-7706 9550
Whiteley's, Unit 218, 151 Queensway, W2 (Bayswater),
020-7727 9392; fax 7727 9390
11-13 Bayley St., WC1 (Tottenham Court Rd.); 020-7636 0076;
fax 7439 3663
Fulham Broadway Ctr., 1st fl., Fulham Rd., SW6
(Fulham Broadway), 020-7385 6077; fax 7385 9584
Harrods 102, 102 Brompton Rd., SW1 (Knightsbridge),
020-7730 1234* ☒
*Harvey Nichols, 5th fl., Knightsbridge, SW1 (Knightsbridge),
020-7235 5000; fax 7318 3885
County Hall, Unit 3B, Belvedere Rd., SE1 (Westminster),
020-7928 8871; fax 7928 5619
95 Farringdon Rd., EC1 (Farringdon), 020-7841 0785; fax 7841 0798
www.yosushi.com
Additional locations throughout London*

Want "a cool spot to pop while you grab some
sushi"? then this "techie-chic" chain – with "rotating conveyor belts", "server-paging buttons" and "robots delivering
drinks" – is a "quick, easy place" for Japanese "staples",
plus some Western variations; but foes just say No! Sushi,
warning the food's as "plastic" as the decor and those "little plates add up to big bills" – oh, and "don't expect a hu-
man to show up when you need one."

Yoshino ☒   23 | 16 | 19 | £33

*3 Piccadilly Pl., W1 (Piccadilly Circus), 020-7287 6622;
fax 7287 1733; www.yoshino.net*

"Shhh, it's a great secret" whisper those "who want to
keep to themselves" this "jewel" of a Japanese "just off
Piccadilly Circus"; an "amazing value for the area", it offers "exceptional" "traditional cuisine" and "sushi prepared to Tokyo standards" – all of which "makes up for"
the "basic" setting.

ZAFFERANO
25 20 23 £56

15 Lowndes St., SW1 (Knightsbridge), 020-7235 5800;
fax 7235 1971

"Lively and vibe-y", this "pricey" Belgravia Italian makes "a
good choice for a special occasion that doesn't go over the
top", with "refined", "divine" dishes ("try the truffle-based
menu"), served by "unfailingly friendly" "staff who don't
take themselves too seriously"; a few feel the place has
"lost its lustre with the expansion" last autumn, but steady
scores support those who maintain it's "*magnifico*" here.

Zaika
25 24 22 £48

1 Kensington High St., W8 (High St. Kensington), 020-7795 6533;
fax 7937 8854; www.zaika-restaurant.co.uk

"Inventive" Indian dishes with "haunting flavours" "take
taste buds to exotic locales they didn't even know existed"
at this "classy" Kensingtonian; some warn it's an "expensive affair" with "professional, if somewhat cool staff",
to which fans retort "stop the naysaying" – "this is a
top-notch" place.

Zen Central ◑
22 16 22 £45

20 Queen St., W1 (Green Park), 020-7629 8089; fax 7493 6181;
www.zencentralrestaurant.com

"The food still pleases" at this slightly "Europeanised"
Mandarin in Mayfair, and staff have "improved" (as reflected in a Service score rise); "but the decor leaves
much to be desired" and it all seems "a bit pricey (which
is unsurprising, given the location.")

ZeNW3 ◑
16 15 16 £36

83-84 Hampstead High St., NW3 (Hampstead), 020-7794 7863,
fax 7794 6956; www.zenw3.com

This large, veteran Asian can still be "a fun spot" say
Hampsteaders happy with its "varied" offerings; but a
drop in the Food rating supports those "disappointed"
by a menu that "has lost some great options" of late, so
that it now seems "not much more than an overpriced
version of a standard Chinese local"; furthermore, the
glass-fronted "decor looks like a worn-out set from an
'80s yuppie movie."

Zetter Restaurant & Rooms
18 20 18 £41

The Zetter, 86-88 Clerkenwell Rd., EC1 (Farringdon),
020-7324 4455; fax 7324 4445; www.thezetter.com

"Bit of an 'in' place at the moment", this "relaxed"
Clerkenwell corner (in the old Zetter Football Pools warehouse) offers "food with a twist" that's "better" than "the
usual bland hotel fare" fans find; however, hostiles hiss its
"inconsistent quality doesn't live up to the groovy decor"
which includes "tables far enough apart so that you don't
have to listen to the Hoxton types discuss their new
iPods"; N.B. ratings don't reflect a new chef's Med menu.

Ziani ◐

45 Radnor Walk, SW3 (Sloane Sq.), 020-7351 5297; fax 7244 8387
Think of it "like having dinner with a family of 60", all "squished" into the "tightly packed" tables, at this "crazy" Italian "hidden on a side street off King's Road"; most feel the "food never fails to satisfy", but whilst the waiters are "very warm", they "really rush you" – not nice, when you're paying "above-average prices."

Zilli Fish ☒

36-40 Brewer St., W1 (Piccadilly Circus), 020-7734 8649;
www.zillialdo.com
There's "fresh fish in abundance" on the "pricey" menu at celebrity chef Aldo Zilli's ever-"crowded" Soho Italian that's "good for pre-theatre" and "open late for a bite after" as well; but "they pack you in" as tightly as sardines, which doesn't improve the "impersonal atmosphere."

Zimzun

Retail Ctr., Fulham Rd., SW6 (Fulham Broadway), 020-7385 4555;
fax 7386 8555; www.zimzun.co.uk
Its modern Asian digs decorated with wood benches and tables (the latter adorned with square glass bowls of floating flowers), this shopping-complex Thai is "good for a bite before or after the cinema" in the Fulham Broadway Retail Centre; the "lightly cooked" food's just "ok quality, but for the price, you can't complain."

Zinc Bar & Grill

21 Heddon St., W1 (Oxford Circus/Piccadilly Circus),
020-7255 8899; fax 7255 8888
11 Jerdan Pl., SW6 (Fulham Broadway), 020-7386 2250;
fax 7386 2260
"It's lovely to sit outside in the summertime" at these "modern-looking" premises in Piccadilly and Fulham, which offer "staples" for "ok", if "not overly memorable" Modern British–Euro fare "at a reasonable price"; that said, service can be mixed and both "would be better with more buzz."

Zizzi

33-41 Charlotte St., W1 (Goodge St.), 020-7436 9440
231 Chiswick High Rd., W4 (Chiswick), 020-8747 9400
35-38 Paddington St., W1 (Baker St.), 020-7224 1450
110-116 Wigmore St., W1 (Bond St.), 020-7935 2336
20 Bow St., WC2 (Holborn), 020-7836 6101
73-75 The Strand, WC2 (Charing Cross), 020-7240 1717;
fax 7379 9753
194-196 Earl's Court Rd., SW5 (Earl's Court),
020-7370 1999
202-208 Regents Park Rd., N3 (Finchley Central),
020-8371 6777

(continued)

(continued)

Zizzi

1-3 Hampstead Ln., N6 (Highgate), 020-8347 0090
87 Allitsen Rd., NW8 (St. John's Wood), 020-7722 7296
www.zizzi.co.uk
Additional locations throughout London

With decor that's "slightly more refined than its competitors", this much-"talked-about chain" around town features well-priced Italian fare – primarily, pizzas with "creative [toppings] to keep your mouth happy"; sure, there's plenty to carp about, from "clueless service" to a certain "pre-fab" feeling to "kids, kids everywhere"; still, it's a "solid" choice "for low-key dates, large groups" or "when one is faced with surprise visitors."

ZUMA   26 | 23 | 20 | £61

5 Raphael St., SW7 (Knightsbridge), 020-7584 1010;
fax 7584 5005; www.zumarestaurant.com

"Where the beautiful people go" (some "surgically enhanced"), this Knightsbridge Japanese is "achingly trendy" – "but unlike many such, it also delivers superlative cuisine" in everything from "amazing sushi" to "stunning robata grill" dishes amidst minimalist granite decor that "oozes contemporary class"; "ranging from remarkably attentive to totally unacceptable", "service remains the main drawback" and it's "very hard to get a table", but those who can, do – "and hope someone else pays the bill."

Indexes

CUISINES
LOCATIONS
SPECIAL FEATURES

CUISINES

American
All Star Lanes (WC1)
Arkansas Cafe (E1)
Astor Bar & Grill (W1)
Automat (W1)
Big Easy (SW3)
Bodeans (multi. loc.)
Christopher's (WC2)
Ed's Easy Diner (multi. loc.)
Hard Rock Cafe (W1)
Harlem (W2)
Joe Allen (WC2)
Lucky 7 (W2)
Pacific Bar & Grill (W6)
PJ's B&G (multi. loc.)
Planet Hollywood (W1)
Rainforest Cafe (W1)
Smollensky's (multi. loc.)
Sophie's Steak (SW10)
Sticky Fingers (W8)
T.G.I. Friday's (multi. loc.)
Tootsies (multi. loc.)

Argentinean
El Gaucho (multi. loc.)
Gaucho Grill (multi. loc.)

Asian
Asia de Cuba (WC2)
Blakes (SW7)
Cicada (EC1)
Cocoon (W1)
e&o (W11)
Eight Over Eight (SW3)
Gilgamesh (NW1)
Great Eastern (EC2)
L'Etranger (SW7)
Lonsdale (W11)
Mju (SW1)
Pacific Oriental (EC2)
Park, The (SW1)
Singapura (EC3)
Tiger Lil's (N1)
Uli (W11)

Bangladeshi
Ginger (W2)

Belgian
Abbaye (EC1)
Belgo (multi. loc.)
Bierodrome (multi. loc.)

Brazilian
Rodizio Rico (multi. loc.)

British (Modern)
Admiral Codrington (SW3)
Admiralty (WC2)
Alastair Little (W1)
Anchor & Hope (SE1)
Anglesea Arms (W6)
Annie's (multi. loc.)
Aurora (EC2)
Axis (WC2)
Balans (multi. loc.)
Balham Kitchen (SW12)
Bankside (multi. loc.)
Barnsbury (N1)
Belvedere (W8)
Blandford St. (W1)
Bluebird Brass. (SW3)
Boxwood Café (SW1)
Bradley's (NW3)
Brinkley's (SW10)
Chez Bruce (SW17)
Clarke's (W8)
Cow Din. Rm. (W2)
Duke of Cambridge (N1)
1802 (E14)
Engineer (NW1)
Fifth Floor Cafe (SW1)
First Floor (W11)
Fish Shop on St. John (EC1)
Frederick's (N1)
Glasshouse (Kew)
Globe (NW3)
Gravetye Manor (W. Sus)
Greyhound (SW11)
Groucho Club (W1)
Gun (E14)
Home House (W1)
Hush (W1)
Island Rest. (W2)
Ivy (WC2)
Joe's (SW3)
Joe's Rest./Bar (SW1)
Julie's (W11)
Just St. James's (SW1)
Kensington Pl. (W8)
Launceston Place (W8)
Le Caprice (SW1)

Lilly's (E1)
Livebait (multi. loc.)
Medcalf (EC1)
National Dining Rooms (WC2)
Odette's (NW1)
Palmerston (SE22)
Paternoster Chop (EC4)
Petersham (Richmond)
Petersham Nurseries
  (Richmond)
Portrait (WC2)
Prince Bonaparte (W2)
Prism (EC3)
Randall & Aubin (multi. loc.)
Ransome's Dock (SW11)
Rhodes W1 (W1)
Richard Corrigan (W1)
Roast (SE1)
S.J. (SE1)
Savoy Grill (WC2)
Smiths/Dining Rm. (EC1)
Snows on Green (W6)
Soho House (W1)
Sonny's (SW13)
Sotheby's Cafe (W1)
St. John (EC1)
St. John Bread/Wine (E1)
Tate Britain Restaurant (SW1)
Terminus (EC2)
Thomas Cubitt (SW1)
Suttons Brasserie (WC2)
Union Cafe (W1)
Vineyard/Stockcross (Berks)
Vinc B&G (multi. loc.)

British (Traditional)
Abbeville (SW4)
Annabel's (W1)
Bentley's (W1)
Bistrot 190 (SW7)
Bluebird Club (SW3)
Boisdale (multi. loc.)
Brian Turner (W1)
Browns (multi. loc.)
Builders Arms (SW3)
Butlers Wharf (SE1)
Café Fish (W1)
Canteen (E1)
Chelsea Bun (SW10)
Coach & Horses (EC1)
Mona's (W8)
Fish! (SE1)

Fortnum's Fountain (W1)
Frontline (W2)
Goring Din. Rm. (SW1)
Green's (SW1)
Grenadier (SW1)
Grill, The (W1)
Grill Room, The (W1)
Grumbles (SW1)
Guinea Grill (W1)
Inn The Park (SW1)
Kew Grill (Kew)
Langan's Bistro (W1)
Langan's Brasserie (W1)
Maggie Jones's (W8)
Mark's Club (W1)
Medcalf (EC1)
North Sea (WC1)
Notting Grill (W11)
Odin's (W1)
Paternoster Chop (EC4)
Pig's Ear (SW3)
Porters (WC2)
Quality Chop Hse. (EC1)
Rhodes 24 (EC2)
Rib Room (SW1)
Richoux (multi. loc.)
Ritz (W1)
Rivington Grill (multi. loc.)
Rowley's (SW1)
Rules (WC2)
Shepherd's (SW1)
Simpson's (WC2)
Smiths/Top Floor (EC1)
Sweetings (EC4)
White Swan (EC4)
Whit's (W8)
Wilton's (SW1)
Ye Olde Cheshire (EC4)

Burmese
Mandalay (W2)

Chinese
(* dim sum specialist)
Bar Shu (W1)
China Tang (W1)*
Chinese Exp. (W1)*
Chuen Cheng Ku (W1)*
dim t (multi. loc.)*
ECapital (W1)
Four Seasons (W2)
Fung Shing (WC2)
Golden Dragon (W1)*

Good Earth (multi. loc.)
Gung-Ho (NW6)
Hakkasan (W1)*
Harbour City (W1)*
Hunan (SW1)
Imperial China (WC2)*
Imperial City (EC3)
Jade Garden (W1)*
Jenny Lo's Tea Hse. (SW1)
Joy King Lau (WC2)*
Kai Mayfair (W1)
Lee Ho Fook (W1)*
Mandarin Kitchen (W2)
Mao Tai (SW6)*
Memories/China (multi. loc.)
Mr. Chow (SW1)
Mr. Kong (WC2)
New Culture Rev. (multi. loc.)
New World (W1)*
Phoenix Palace (NW1)*
Ping Pong (multi. loc.)*
Princess Garden (W1)*
Royal China (multi. loc.)*
Royal China Club (W1)*
Shanghai Blues (WC1)*
Song Que Café (E2)
Wong Kei (W1)
Yauatcha (W1)*
Zen Central (W1)
ZeNW3 (NW3)

Chophouse
Astor Bar & Grill (W1)
Black & Blue (multi. loc.)
Butlers Wharf (SE1)
Christopher's (WC2)
El Gaucho (multi. loc.)
Gaucho Grill (multi. loc.)
Guinea Grill (W1)
Kew Grill (Kew)
Le Relais de Venise (W1)
Notting Grill (W11)
Paternoster Chop (EC4)
Quality Chop Hse. (EC1)
Rib Room (SW1)
Rules (WC2)
Smiths/Top Floor (EC1)
Smollensky's (multi. loc.)
Sophie's Steak (SW10)

Cuban
Asia de Cuba (WC2)
Floridita (W1)

Danish
Lundum's (SW7)

Eclectic
Annex 3 (W1)
Archipelago (W1)
Axis (WC2)
Babalou (SW2)
Banquette (WC2)
Blakes (SW7)
Books for Cooks (W11)
Brunello (SW7)
Cafe Med (multi. loc.)
Cantina Vinopolis (SE1)
Collection (SW3)
Ebury Wine Bar (SW1)
Electric Brasserie (W11)
Enterprise (SW3)
Giraffe (multi. loc.)
Hoxton Apprentice (N1)
Kettners (W1)
Lanes (W1)
Lanesborough (SW1)
Lansdowne (NW1)
Light House (SW19)
Michael Moore (W1)
Mosimann's (SW1)
Motcombs (SW1)
Naked Turtle (SW14)
PJ's B&G (SW3)
Providores/Tapa (W1)
Ransome's Dock (SW11)
Spoon (W1)
Tom's Deli (W11)
Troubadour (SW5)
Vingt-Quatre (SW10)
Wapping Food (E1)
Westbourne (W2)
W'Sens (SW1)

European (Modern)
Abbeville (SW4)
Abingdon (W8)
Addendum (EC3)
Admiral Codrington (SW3)
Albannach (WC2)
Andrew Edmunds (W1)
Angela Hartnett's (W1)
Arbutus (W1)
Avenue (SW1)
Babylon (W8)
Bank Aldwych (WC2)

Bank Westminster (SW1)
Blandford St. (W1)
Bluebird Club (SW3)
Blueprint Café (SE1)
Bountiful Cow (WC1)
Brackenbury (W6)
Bull, The (N6)
Camden Brasserie (NW1)
Canyon (Richmond)
Chancery (EC4)
City Café (SW1)
Clerkenwell (EC1)
Don (EC4)
Draper's Arms (N1)
Drones (SW1)
Ebury Din. Rm. (SW1)
1880 (SW7)
Embassy (W1)
Fat Duck (Berks)
Fifth Floor (SW1)
Fish Hook (W4)
Foliage (SW1)
Frederick's (N1)
Gate (W6)
George (W1)
Gordon Ramsay/Claridge's (W1)
Greyhound (SW11)
Home House (W1)
Indigo (WC2)
Ivy (WC2)
Ladbroke Arms (W11)
La Fromagerie (W1)
Lansdowne (NW1)
La Trompette (W4)
Le Café du Jardin (WC2)
Le Caprice (SW1)
Le Deuxième (WC2)
Little Bay (multi. loc.)
Living Room, The (W1)
LMNT (E8)
Lola's (N1)
Mash (W1)
Nicole's (W1)
Notting Hill Brass. (W11)
1 Lombard Brass. (EC3)
Oriel (SW1)
Origin (WC2)
Oxo Tower (SE1)
Oxo Tower Brass. (SE1)
Pigalle Club (W1)
Quaglino's (SW1)

Randall & Aubin (SW10)
Roundhouse Café (NW1)
Rowley's (SW1)
Royal Exchange (EC3)
Salt Yard (W1)
Sam's Brass. (W4)
Six-13 (W1)
Sketch/Gallery (W1)
Sketch/Lecture Rm. (W1)
Sugar Reef (W1)
Tamesa@oxo (SE1)
Tate Modern (SE1)
202 (W1)
Union Cafe (W1)
Upstairs Bar/Rest. (SW2)
Villandry (W1)
Vivat Bacchus (EC4)
Wapping Food (E1)
Wells (NW3)
Westbourne (W2)
White Hart (SE11)
Wolseley (W1)
Zinc B&G (multi. loc.)

Fish 'n' Chips
fish! (SE1)
Fish Shop on St. John (EC1)
Geales Fish (W8)
Livebait (multi. loc.)
Nautilus Fish (NW6)
North Sea (WC1)
Seashell (NW1)
Sweetings (EC4)
Two Bros. Fish (N3)

French (Bistro)
Aubaine (SW3)
Bibendum Oyster (SW3)
Bistrotheque (E2)
Café des Amis (WC2)
Café Rouge (multi. loc.)
Circus (W1)
Comptoir Gascon (EC1)
French House (W1)
Galvin Bistrot (W1)
Grumbles (SW1)
La Bouchée (SW7)
La Poule au Pot (SW1)
Le Café du Marché (EC1)
Le Colombier (SW3)
Mon Plaisir (WC2)
Pat. Valerie (multi. loc.)

Racine (SW3)
Truc Vert (W1)

French (Brasserie)
Bellamy's (W1)
Brasserie Roux (SW1)
Brass. St. Quentin (SW3)
Café Boheme (W1)
Cheyne Walk (SW3)
Chez Gérard (multi. loc.)
Incognico (WC2)
La Brasserie (SW3)
Langan's Brasserie (W1)
La Trouvaille (N1)
Le Palais du Jardin (WC2)
Malmaison Hotel (EC1)
Oriel (SW1)
Papillon (SW3)
Tartine (SW3)
Tuttons Brasserie (WC2)

French (Classic)
Almeida (N1)
Annabel's (W1)
Aurora (EC2)
Bradley's (NW3)
Brass. St. Quentin (SW3)
Chez Gérard (multi. loc.)
Chez Kristof (W6)
Coq d'Argent (EC2)
Dine (EC4)
Ebury Wine Bar (SW1)
Elena's l'Etoile (W1)
Entrecote Café (W1)
Farm (SW6)
Foliage (SW1)
French Horn (Berks)
Hush (W1)
La Bouchée (SW7)
La Brasserie (SW3)
Ladurée (SW1)
Langan's Bistro (W1)
Langan's Brasserie (W1)
La Noisette (SW1)
La Poule au Pot (SW1)
La Trouvaille (multi. loc.)
L'Aventure (NW8)
Le Boudin Blanc (W1)
Le Café du Marché (EC1)
Le Colombier (SW3)
Le Gavroche (W1)
Le Palais du Jardin (WC2)

Le Pont de la Tour (SE1)
Le Relais de Venise (W1)
L'Escargot (W1)
L'Estaminet (WC2)
Les Trois Garçons (E1)
Le Suquet (SW3)
Le Vacherin (W4)
L'Oranger (SW1)
Lou Pescadou (SW5)
Mirabelle (W1)
Mon Plaisir (WC2)
Morel (SW4)
Odin's (W1)
Oslo Court (NW8)
Papillon (SW3)
Pigalle Club (W1)
Poissonnerie (SW3)
Racine (SW3)
Ritz (W1)
Stratford's (W8)
Vineyard/Stockcross (Berks)
Waterside Inn (Berks)
Whit's (W8)

French (New)
Aubergine (SW10)
Beauberry House (SE21)
Belvedere (W8)
Berkeley Square (W1)
Bibendum (SW3)
Bleeding Heart (EC1)
Bonds (EC2)
Café des Amis (WC2)
Capital (SW3)
Cliveden House (Berks)
Clos Maggiore (WC2)
Club Gascon (EC1)
Dans Le Noir (EC1)
1880 (SW7)
Food Room (SW8)
Galvin/Windows (W1)
Gordon Ramsay/68 Royal (SW3)
Greenhouse (W1)
Incognico (WC2)
La Noisette (SW1)
La Trompette (W4)
La Trouvaille (W1)
Le Cercle (SW1)
Ledbury (W11)
Le Manoir/Quat (Oxon)
Le Mercury (N1)

L'Etranger (SW7)
LMNT (E8)
Maze (W1)
Mju (SW1)
Morgan M (N7)
Morton's (W1)
Odette's (NW1)
1 Lombard St. (EC3)
One-O-One (SW1)
Orrery (W1)
Patterson's (W1)
Pearl (WC1)
Pétrus (SW1)
Pied à Terre (W1)
Pig's Ear (SW3)
Plateau (E14)
Roussillon (SW1)
Square (W1)
Tom Aikens (SW3)
Waterside Inn (Berks)
W'Sens (SW1)

Greek
Costas Grill (W8)
Halepi (W2)
Lemonia (NW1)
Real Greek (multi. loc.)
Vrisaki (N22)

Hamburgers
Arkansas Cafe (E1)
Ed's Easy Diner (multi. loc.)
Gourmet Burger (multi. loc.)
Hard Rock Cafe (W1)
Joe Allen (WC2)
Kettners (W1)
Lucky 7 (W2)
Planet Hollywood (W1)
Smollensky's (multi. loc.)
Sophie's Steak (SW10)
Sticky Fingers (W8)
T.G.I. Friday's (multi. loc.)
Tootsies (multi. loc.)
Vingt-Quatre (SW10)

Hungarian
Gay Hussar (W1)

Indian
Agni (W6)
Amaya (SW1)
Anakana (EC1)
Benares (W1)

Bengal Clipper (SE1)
Bombay Bicycle (multi. loc.)
Bombay Brasserie (SW7)
Café Lazeez (multi. loc.)
Café Spice Namasté (E1)
Chor Bizarre (W1)
Chowki Bar (W1)
Chutney Mary (SW10)
Chutney's (NW1)
Cinnamon Club (SW1)
Deya (W1)
Gopal's (W1)
Imli (W1)
Khan's (W2)
Khan's/Kensington (SW7)
La Porte des Indes (W1)
Ma Goa (multi. loc.)
Malabar (W8)
Malabar Junction (WC1)
Masala Zone (multi. loc.)
Mela (WC2)
Mint Leaf (SW1)
Moti Mahal (WC2)
Noor Jahan (multi. loc.)
Painted Heron (multi. loc.)
Quilon (SW1)
Rasa (multi. loc.)
Rasoi Vineet Bhatia (SW3)
Red Fort (W1)
Sarkhel's (multi. loc.)
Soho Spice (W1)
Star of India (SW5)
Tamarind (W1)
Vama (SW10)
Veeraswamy (W1)
Zaika (W8)

Irish
Richard Corrigan (W1)

Italian
Aglio e Olio (SW10)
Al Duca (SW1)
Alloro (W1)
Amici/Italian Kitchen (SW17)
Aperitivo (W1)
Ark (W8)
Artigiano (NW3)
Ask Pizza (multi. loc.)
Assaggi (W2)
Bertorelli (multi. loc.)
Brunello (SW7)

Cuisines

Buona Sera (multi. loc.)
Caldesi (W1)
Camerino (W1)
Cantina del Ponte (SE1)
Caraffini (SW1)
Caravaggio (EC3)
Carluccio's (multi. loc.)
Carpaccio (SW3)
Casale Franco (N1)
Cecconi's (W1)
Cipriani (W1)
Clos Maggiore (WC2)
Como Lario (SW1)
Daphne's (SW3)
Diverso (W1)
Edera (W11)
Elena's l'Etoile (W1)
Elistano (SW3)
Enoteca Turi (SW15)
Essenza (W11)
Fiore (SW1)
Franco's (SW1)
Frankie's Italian (multi. loc.)
Friends (SW10)
Getti (multi. loc.)
Giardinetto (W1)
Giovanni's (WC2)
Green Olive (W9)
Harry's Bar (W1)
Hosteria del Pesce (SW6)
Il Bordello (E1)
Il Convivio (SW1)
Il Falconiere (SW7)
Il Portico (W8)
La Famiglia (SW10)
La Genova (W1)
La Porchetta (multi. loc.)
Latium (W1)
L'Incontro (SW1)
Little Italy (W1)
Locanda Locatelli (W1)
Locanda Ottoemezzo (W8)
Luciano (SW1)
Lucio (SW3)
Luigi's Covent Gdn. (WC2)
Made in Italy (SW3)
Manicomio (SW3)
Mediterraneo (W11)
Metrogusto (N1)
Mimmo d'Ischia (SW1)
Montpeliano (SW7)

Monza (SW3)
Neal Street (WC2)
Obika (W1)
Oliveto (SW1)
Olivo (SW1)
Orso (WC2)
Osteria Antica (SW11)
Osteria Basilico (W11)
Osteria dell'Arancio (SW10)
Pappagallo (W1)
Passione (W1)
Pellicano (SW3)
Pizza Express (multi. loc.)
Pizza Metro (SW11)
Pizza on Park (SW1)
Pizza Pomodoro (multi. loc.)
Quadrato (E14)
Quirinale (SW1)
Quo Vadis (W1)
Red Pepper (W9)
Refettorio (EC4)
Riccardo's (SW3)
Riva (SW13)
River Café (W6)
Rosmarino (NW8)
Sale e Pepe (SW1)
Salusbury Pub (NW6)
San Lorenzo (multi. loc.)
Santa Lucia (SW10)
Santini (SW1)
Sardo (W1)
Sardo Canale (NW1)
Sartoria (W1)
Scalini (SW3)
Signor Sassi (SW1)
Spago (SW7)
Spiga (W1)
Spighetta (W1)
Strada (multi. loc.)
TECA (W1)
Tentazioni (SE1)
Timo (W8)
Toto's (SW3)
Vasco & Piero's (W1)
Verbanella (SW3)
Volt (SW1)
Zafferano (SW1)
Ziani (SW3)
Zilli Fish (W1)
Zizzi (multi. loc.)

Japanese
(* sushi specialist)
Abeno (multi. loc.)
Beauberry House (SE21)
Benihana (multi. loc.)
Café Japan (NW11)*
Defune (W1)*
Ikeda (W1)*
Ikkyu (W1)
Inaho (W2)*
Itsu (multi. loc.)*
Jin Kichi (NW3)*
Kiku (W1)*
Koi (W8)*
Kulu Kulu Sushi (multi. loc.)*
Matsuri (multi. loc.)*
Mitsukoshi (SW1)*
Miyama (W1)*
Moshi Moshi (multi. loc.)*
Nobu Berkeley (W1)*
Nobu London (W1)*
Noto (multi. loc.)*
Nozomi (SW3)*
Roka (W1)*
Saki Bar/Food (EC1)*
Sakura (W1)*
Satsuma (W1)
Sumosan (W1)
Tatsuso (EC2)*
Tokyo Diner (WC2)
Tsunami (SW4)
Ubon by Nobu (E14)*
Umu (W1)*
Wagamama (multi. loc.)
Yakitoria (W2)*
YO! Sushi (multi. loc.)*
Yoshino (W1)*
Zuma (SW7)*

Jewish
Bloom's (NW11)
Reubens (W1)

Korean
(* barbecue specialist)
Wizzy (SW6)*

Kosher
Bloom's (NW11)
Reubens (W1)
Six-13 (W1)
Solly's (NW11)

Lebanese
Al Bustan (SW7)
Al Hamra (W1)
Al Sultan (W1)
Al Waha (W2)
Beiteddine (SW1)
Dish Dash (SW12)
Fairuz (multi. loc.)
Fakhreldine (W1)
Ishbilia (SW1)
Levant (W1)
Levantine (W2)
Maroush (multi. loc.)
Noura (multi. loc.)

Malaysian
Awana (SW3)
Champor (SE1)
Nyonya (W11)
Silks & Spice (multi. loc.)

Mediterranean
Baker & Spice (multi. loc.)
Bistrot 190 (SW7)
Cafe Med (multi. loc.)
Cantaloupe (EC2)
Cantina Vinopolis (SE1)
Citrus (W1)
Cliveden House (Berks)
Coach & Horses (EC1)
Cru (N1)
Dune (SW1)
Eagle (EC1)
Fifteen (N1)
Fifth Floor Cafe (SW1)
Food Room (SW8)
Franco's (SW1)
Leon (multi. loc.)
Little Bay (multi. loc.)
Morel (SW4)
Moro (EC1)
Nicole's (W1)
Ottolenghi (multi. loc.)
Pescatori (W1)
Portal (EC1)
Raoul's (multi. loc.)
Rocket (multi. loc.)
Salusbury Pub (NW6)
Union Cafe (W1)
Zetter (EC1)

Mexican
Cafe Pacifico (WC2)
Crazy Homies (W2)
Mestizo (NW1)
Taqueria (W11)
Texas Embassy (SW1)

Moroccan
Aziz (SW6)
OCCO (W14)
Pasha (SW7)

North African
Dune (SW1)
Momo (W1)
Moro (EC1)
Original Tagine (W1)
Souk (WC2)

Pacific Rim
Pacific Oriental (EC2)

Pakistani
Original Lah. Kebab (multi. loc.)
Salloos (SW1)

Persian/Iranian
Alounak (multi. loc.)
Dish Dash (SW12)
Kandoo (W2)

Pizza
Ask Pizza (multi. loc.)
Buona Sera (multi. loc.)
Cantina del Ponte (SE1)
Casale Franco (N1)
Fire & Stone (WC2)
Friends (SW10)
Il Bordello (E1)
Kettners (W1)
La Porchetta (multi. loc.)
Made in Italy (SW3)
Oliveto (SW1)
Orso (WC2)
Osteria Basilico (W11)
Pizza Express (multi. loc.)
Pizza Metro (SW11)
Pizza on Park (SW1)
Pizza Pomodoro (multi. loc.)
Red Pepper (W9)
Rocket (multi. loc.)
Spago (SW7)
Spiga (W1)
Spighetta (W1)

Strada (multi. loc.)
Zizzi (multi. loc.)

Polish
Baltic (SE1)
Daquise (SW7)
Wòdka (W8)

Portuguese
Eyre Brothers (EC2)
Portal (EC1)
Tugga (SW3)

Scottish
Albannach (WC2)
Boisdale (multi. loc.)

Seafood
Belgo (multi. loc.)
Bentley's (W1)
Bibendum Oyster (SW3)
Big Easy (SW3)
Bluebird Brass. (SW3)
Café Fish (W1)
Christopher's (WC2)
Cow Din. Rm. (W2)
Deep (SW6)
fish! (SE1)
Fish Hook (W4)
Fish Shop on St. John (EC1)
FishWorks (multi. loc.)
Geales Fish (W8)
Green's (SW1)
Hosteria del Pesce (SW6)
J. Sheekey (WC2)
Le Suquet (SW3)
Livebait (multi. loc.)
Lou Pescadou (SW5)
Manzi's (WC2)
Nautilus Fish (NW6)
North Sea (WC1)
One-O-One (SW1)
Pescatori (W1)
Poissonnerie (SW3)
Randall & Aubin (multi. loc.)
Rudland & Stubbs (EC1)
Seashell (NW1)
Stratford's (W8)
Sweetings (EC4)
Two Bros. Fish (N3)
Wilton's (SW1)
Zilli Fish (W1)

Small Plates

(See also Spanish tapas specialist)
Amaya (SW1) (Indian)
Aperitivo (W1) (Italian)
Club Gascon (EC1) (French)
Glas (SE1) (Swedish)
Hunan (SW1) (Chinese)
Il Convivio (SW1) (Italian)
Le Cercle (SW1) (French)
Lonsdale (W11) (Pan-Asian)
Maze (W1) (French)
Moro (EC1) (Mediterranean)
Origin (WC2) (Mod. European)
Providores/Tapa (W1) (Eclectic)
Tugga (SW3) (Portuguese)

South American

Cantaloupe (EC2)
1492 (SW6)
La Piragua (N1)
Sabor (N1)

Southeast Asian

Bam-Bou (W1)
Singapore Garden (NW6)
Singapura (multi. loc.)
Song Que Café (E2)
Taman gang (W1)

Spanish

(* tapas specialist)
Cambio de Tercio (SW5)
Cigala (WC1)*
El Blason (SW3)*
El Pirata (W1J)*
Eyre Brothers (EC2)
Fino (W1)*
Galicia (W10)*
La Rueda (multi. loc.)*
L-Restaurant (W8)
Meson Don Felipe (SE1)*
Meza (W1)*
Moro (EC1)
Salt Yard (W1)*
Tapas Brindisa (SE1)*

Swedish

Garbo's (W1)
Glas (SE1)

Thai

Ben's Thai (W9)
Blue Elephant (SW6)
Busaba Eathai (multi. loc.)
Chiang Mai (W1)
Churchill Arms (W8)
Crazy Bear (W1)
Esarn Kheaw (W12)
Isarn (N1)
I-Thai (W2)
Jim Thompson's (multi. loc.)
Mango Tree (SW1)
Nahm (SW1)
Patara (multi. loc.)
Pepper Tree (SW4)
Saran Rom (SW6)
Silks & Spice (multi. loc.)
Sri Nam (E14)
Sri Siam City (EC2)
Sri Thai Soho (W1)
Sugar Hut (SW6)
Thai Pavilion (multi. loc.)
Thai Square (multi. loc.)
Zimzun (SW6)

Turkish

Efes Kebab (W1)
Gallipoli (N1)
Haz (E1)
Ishtar (W1)
Iznik (N5)
Ozer (W1)
Pasha (N1)
Sofra (multi. loc.)
Tas (SE1)

Vegetarian

Blah! Blah! Blah! (W12)
Chutney's (NW1)
Eat & Two Veg (W1)
Food for Thought (WC2)
Gate (W6)
Lanesborough (SW1)
Mildreds (W1)
Morgan M (N7)
Rasa (multi. loc.)
Roussillon (SW1)

Vietnamese

Bam-Bou (W1)
Nam Long-Le Shaker (SW5)
Saigon (W1)
Song Que Café (E2)
Viet Hoa (E2)

LOCATIONS

CENTRAL LONDON

Belgravia
Amaya
Baker & Spice
Beiteddine
Boxwood Café
Drones
Ebury Wine Bar
Grenadier
Il Convivio
Ishbilia
Jenny Lo's Tea Hse.
Lanesborough
La Noisette
Memories/China
Mimmo d'Ischia
Mosimann's
Motcombs
Nahm
Oliveto
Pat. Valerie
Pétrus
Pizza on Park
Rib Room
Salloos
Santini
Thomas Cubitt
Volt
Zafferano

Bloomsbury/Fitzrovia
Abeno
All Star Lanes
Annex 3
Archipelago
Ask Pizza
Bam-Bou
Bertorelli
Busaba Eathai
Camerino
Carluccio's
Chez Gérard
Cigala
Crazy Bear
dim t
Efes Kebab
Elena's l'Etoile
Fino

Hakkasan
Ikkyu
Latium
Malabar Junction
Mash
North Sea
Passione
Pescatori
Pied à Terre
Rasa
Roka
Salt Yard
Sardo
Spoon
Villandry
Wagamama
YO! Sushi
Zizzi

Chinatown
Chinese Exp.
Chuen Cheng Ku
ECapital
Fung Shing
Golden Dragon
Harbour City
Imperial China
Jade Garden
Joy King Lau
Lee Ho Fook
Manzi's
Mr. Kong
New World
Tokyo Diner
Wong Kei

Covent Garden/Holborn
Admiralty
Asia de Cuba
Axis
Bank Aldwych
Banquette
Belgo
Bertorelli
Bierodrome
Bleeding Heart
Bountiful Cow
Browns

Café des Amis
Cafe Pacifico
Café Rouge
Chancery
Chez Gérard
Christopher's
Clos Maggiore
Dine
Ed's Easy Diner
Fire & Stone
Food for Thought
Gaucho Grill
Giovanni's
Indigo
Ivy
Joe Allen
J. Sheekey
Kulu Kulu Sushi
La Porchetta
Le Café du Jardin
Le Deuxième
Le Palais du Jardin
L'Estaminet
Livebait
Luigi's Covent Gdn.
Matsuri
Mon Plaisir
Moti Mahal
Neal Street
New Culture Rev.
Origin
Orso
Pat. Valerie
Pearl
Pizza Express
PJ's B&G
Porters
Rules
Savoy Grill
Shanghai Blues
Simpson's
Smollensky's
Sofra
Souk
Strada
T.G.I. Friday's
Thai Square
Tuttons Brasserie
Wagamama
White Swan
Zizzi

Knightsbridge

Brass. St. Quentin
Café Rouge
Capital
Fifth Floor
Fifth Floor Cafe
FishWorks
Foliage
Frankie's Italian
Good Earth
Ishbilia
Joe's Rest./Bar
Ladurée
Leon
Maroush
Mju
Montpeliano
Monza
Mr. Chow
Noto
Nozomi
One-O-One
Park, The
Patara
Pat. Valerie
Pizza Express
Pizza Pomodoro
Racine
Richoux
Sale e Pepe
San Lorenzo
Signor Sassi
Verbanella
Wagamama
YO! Sushi
Zuma

Marylebone

Black & Blue
Blandford St.
Caldesi
Carluccio's
Chutney's
Defune
Deya
Eat & Two Veg
Entrecote Café
Fairuz
FishWorks
Galvin Bistrot
Garbo's
Getti

Giraffe
Home House
Ishtar
Kandoo
La Fromagerie
Langan's Bistro
La Porte des Indes
La Rueda
Le Relais de Venise
Levant
Locanda Locatelli
Mandalay
Maroush
Michael Moore
Obika
OCCO
Odin's
Original Tagine
Orrery
Ozer
Pat. Valerie
Phoenix Palace
Ping Pong
Providores/Tapa
Real Greek
Reubens
Rhodes W1
Royal China
Royal China Club
Seashell
Six-13
Sofra
Spighetta
Strada
Tootsies
Union Cafe
Wagamama
YO! Sushi
Zizzi

Mayfair

Al Hamra
Alloro
Al Sultan
Angela Hartnett's
Annabel's
Ask Pizza
Automat
Bellamy's
Benares
Benihana
Berkeley Square

Brian Turner
Browns
Carluccio's
Cecconi's
Chez Gérard
China Tang
Chor Bizarre
Cipriani
El Pirata
Embassy
Galvin/Windows
George
Giardinetto
Gordon Ramsay/Claridge's
Greenhouse
Grill, The
Grill Room, The
Guinea Grill
Harry's Bar
Hush
Ikeda
itsu
Kai Mayfair
Kiku
La Genova
Lanes
Langan's Brasserie
Le Boudin Blanc
Le Gavroche
Mark's Club
Masala Zone
Maze
Mirabelle
Miyama
Morton's
Nicole's
Nobu Berkeley
Nobu London
Noura
Pappagallo
Patara
Patterson's
Pescatori
Princess Garden
Rasa
Richoux
Rocket
Sakura
Sartoria
Sketch/Gallery
Sketch/Lecture Rm.

Sofra
Sotheby's Cafe
Square
Strada
Sumosan
Taman gang
Tamarind
TECA
Thai Square
Truc Vert
Umu
Veeraswamy
Zen Central

Piccadilly

Astor Bar & Grill
Bentley's
Chowki Bar
Citrus
Cocoon
Diverso
Dune
Ed's Easy Diner
Fakhreldine
Frankie's Italian
Gaucho Grill
Hard Rock Cafe
itsu
Living Room, The
Mitsukoshi
Momo
Pat. Valerie
Pigalle Club
Planet Hollywood
Rainforest Cafe
Richoux
Sugar Reef
Wolseley
W'Sens
Yoshino
Zinc B&G

Soho

Abeno
Alastair Little
Albannach
Andrew Edmunds
Aperitivo
Arbutus
Balans
Bar Shu
Bertorelli

Bodeans
Busaba Eathai
Café Boheme
Café Fish
Café Lazeez
Café Rouge
Chiang Mai
Circus
Ed's Easy Diner
Floridita
French House
Gay Hussar
Gopal's
Groucho Club
Imli
Incognico
itsu
Kettners
Kulu Kulu Sushi
La Trouvaille
Leon
L'Escargot
Little Italy
Mela
Meza
Mildreds
National Dining Rooms
Patara
Pat. Valerie
Ping Pong
Pizza Express
Portrait
Quo Vadis
Randall & Aubin
Red Fort
Richard Corrigan
Saigon
Satsuma
Soho House
Soho Spice
Souk
Spiga
Sri Thai Soho
Thai Pavilion
Thai Square
Vasco & Piero's
Wagamama
Yauatcha
YO! Sushi
Zilli Fish
Zizzi

St. James's

Al Duca
Avenue
Brasserie Roux
Fiore
Fortnum's Fountain
Franco's
Getti
Green's
Inn The Park
Just St. James's
Le Caprice
L'Oranger
Luciano
Matsuri
Mint Leaf
Noura
Quaglino's
Quilon
Ritz
Rowley's

Texas Embassy
Thai Square
Wilton's

Victoria

Ask Pizza
Bank Westminster
Boisdale
Chez Gérard
Goring Din. Rm.
Mango Tree
Noura
Olivo

Westminster

Cinnamon Club
City Café
Quirinale
Shepherd's
Tate Britain Restaurant
YO! Sushi

EAST/SOUTH EAST LONDON

Blackfriars/City

Aurora
Bankside
Bertorelli
Boisdale
Bonds
Browns
Café Spice Namasté
Caravaggio
Chez Gérard
Coq d'Argent
Don
Gaucho Grill
Haz
Imperial City
Leon
Little Bay
Moshi Moshi
Noto
1 Lombard St.
1 Lombard Brass.
Pacific Oriental
Paternoster Chop
Pat. Valerie
Pizza Express
Pizza Pomodoro
Prism
Refettorio

Rhodes 24
Royal Exchange
Silks & Spice
Singapura
Smollensky's
Sri Siam City
Sweetings
Tatsuso
Terminus
Thai Square
Vivat Bacchus
Wagamama
Ye Olde Cheshire

Bow/Mile End/Hackney/ Bethnal Green

Bistrotheque
LMNT

Canary Wharf/Docklands

Browns
Café Rouge
Carluccio's
1802
Gaucho Grill
Gun
itsu
Moshi Moshi

subscribe to zagat.com

Plateau
Quadrato
Royal China
Smollensky's
Sri Nam
Ubon by Nobu
Wapping Food

Clerkenwell/Smithfield/ Farringdon

Abbaye
Carluccio's
Cicada
Clerkenwell
Club Gascon
Coach & Horses
Comptoir Gascon
Dans Le Noir
Eagle
Fish Shop on St. John
La Porchetta
Le Café du Marché
Malmaison Hotel
Medcalf
Moro
Portal
Quality Chop Hse.
Real Greek
Rudland & Stubbs
Saki Bar/Food
Smiths/Dining Rm.
Smiths/Top Floor
Sofra
St. John
Strada
YO! Sushi
Zetter

Greenwich/Blackheath

Rivington Grill

Shoreditch/Spitalfields/ Hoxton/Whitechapel

Anakana
Arkansas Cafe
Cantaloupe
Canteen
Cru
Eyre Brothers
Fifteen
Giraffe
Great Eastern

Hoxton Apprentice
Leon
Les Trois Garçons
Real Greek
Rivington Grill
Song Que Café
St. John Bread/Wine
Viet Hoa

South Bank/Borough

Cantina Vinopolis
fish!
Glas
Oxo Tower
Oxo Tower Brass.
Real Greek
Roast
Tamesa@oxo
Tapas Brindisa
Tas
Tate Modern

Tower Bridge/Limehouse/ Wapping

Addendum
Bengal Clipper
Blueprint Café
Browns
Butlers Wharf
Cantina del Ponte
Champor
Il Bordello
Le Pont de la Tour
Lilly's
Original Lah. Kebab
Smollensky's
Tentazioni

Waterloo/Southwark/ Kennington

Anchor & Hope
Baltic
Bankside
Chez Gérard
Giraffe
Livebait
Meson Don Felipe
Painted Heron
R.S.J.
Tas
Thai Pavilion
White Hart

NORTH/NORTH WEST LONDON

Camden Town/Chalk Farm/Kentish Town/Primrose Hill
Belgo
Camden Brasserie
Engineer
FishWorks
Gilgamesh
Lansdowne
Lemonia
New Culture Rev.
Odette's
Roundhouse Café
Sardo Canale
Wagamama

Golders Green/Finchley
Bloom's
Café Japan
Jim Thompson's
Original Lah. Kebab
Solly's
Two Bros. Fish
Zizzi

Hampstead/Kilburn/Swiss Cottage
Artigiano
Ask Pizza
Baker & Spice
Black & Blue
Bombay Bicycle
Bradley's
dim t
Gaucho Grill
Giraffe
Globe
Good Earth
Gourmet Burger
Gung-Ho
Jin Kichi
Little Bay
Mestizo
Nautilus Fish
Salusbury Pub
Singapore Garden
Tootsies
Wells
ZeNW3

Highgate/Muswell Hill/Crouch End/Tufnell Park
Bull, The
Café Rouge
dim t
Giraffe
La Porchetta
Vrisaki
Zizzi

Islington
Almeida
Barnsbury
Bierodrome
Browns
Cafe Med
Carluccio's
Casale Franco
Draper's Arms
Duke of Cambridge
FishWorks
Frederick's
Gallipoli
Giraffe
Isarn
Iznik
La Piragua
La Porchetta
La Trouvaille
Le Mercury
Lola's
Masala Zone
Metrogusto
Morgan M
New Culture Rev.
Ottolenghi
Pasha
Rasa
Rodizio Rico
Sabor
Strada
Thai Square
Tiger Lil's
Wagamama

St. John's Wood
Benihana
Ben's Thai
Cafe Med
Café Rouge

Green Olive
L'Aventure
Oslo Court
Raoul's
Red Pepper
Richoux
Rosmarino

Royal China
Sofra
Zizzi

Stoke Newington
La Porchetta
Rasa

SOUTH/SOUTH WEST LONDON

Barnes
Annie's
Riva
Sonny's

Battersea
Buona Sera
FishWorks
Food Room
Giraffe
Greyhound
Osteria Antica
Pizza Express
Pizza Metro
Ransome's Dock
Tootsies

Brixton/Clapham
Abbeville
Babalou
Bierodrome
Bodeans
Bombay Bicycle
Café Rouge
Gourmet Burger
La Rueda
Little Bay
Morel
Pepper Tree
Strada
Tootsies
Tsunami
Upstairs Bar/Rest.

Camberwell/Dulwich/ Herne Hill
Beauberry House
Palmerston

Chelsea
Admiral Codrington
Aglio e Olio
Ask Pizza

Aubergine
Awana
Baker & Spice
Benihana
Big Easy
Bluebird Brass.
Bluebird Club
Brinkley's
Builders Arms
Buona Sera
Caraffini
Carpaccio
Chelsea Bun
Cheyne Walk
Chutney Mary
Daphne's
Ed's Easy Diner
Eight Over Eight
El Blason
El Gaucho
Elistano
Enterprise
Friends
Gaucho Grill
Gordon Ramsay/68 Royal
itsu
La Famiglia
Le Cercle
Le Colombier
Le Suquet
Lucio
Made in Italy
Manicomio
New Culture Rev.
Oriel
Osteria dell'Arancio
Painted Heron
Pat. Valerie
Pellicano
Pig's Ear
Pizza Express
PJ's B&G

Poissonnerie
Randall & Aubin
Rasoi Vineet Bhatia
Riccardo's
Santa Lucia
Scalini
Sophie's Steak
Tartine
Tom Aikens
Toto's
Tugga
Vama
Vingt-Quatre
Ziani

Earl's Court
Balans
Lou Pescadou
Masala Zone
Strada
Troubadour
Zizzi

Fulham
Aziz
Blue Elephant
Bodeans
Carluccio's
Deep
Farm
1492
Gourmet Burger
Hosteria del Pesce
Jim Thompson's
La Rueda
Little Bay
Ma Goa
Mao Tai
Pizza Express
Saran Rom
Strada
Sugar Hut
T.G.I. Friday's
Wizzy
YO! Sushi
Zimzun
Zinc B&G

Pimlico
Como Lario
Ebury Din. Rm.
Grumbles
Hunan

La Poule au Pot
L'Incontro
Roussillon

Putney/Richmond
Ask Pizza
Café Rouge
Canyon
Carluccio's
Enoteca Turi
FishWorks
Frankie's Italian
Giraffe
Glasshouse
Gourmet Burger
Jim Thompson's
Kew Grill
Ma Goa
Naked Turtle
Petersham
Petersham Nurseries
Real Greek
Rocket
Sarkhel's
Thai Square

South Kensington
Al Bustan
Ask Pizza
Aubaine
Bibendum
Bibendum Oyster
Bistrot 190
Black & Blue
Blakes
Bombay Brasserie
Café Lazeez
Cambio de Tercio
Collection
Daquise
1880
El Gaucho
Il Falconiere
Joe's
Khan's/Kensington
Kulu Kulu Sushi
La Bouchée
La Brasserie
L'Etranger
Lundum's
Nam Long-Le Shaker
Noor Jahan
Papillon

Pasha
Patara
Spago
Star of India
Thai Square
Tootsies

Wandsworth/Balham/Wimbledon
Amici/Italian Kitchen
Balham Kitchen

Chez Bruce
Dish Dash
Gourmet Burger
Jim Thompson's
Light House
San Lorenzo
Sarkhel's
Strada
Tootsies

WEST LONDON

Bayswater
Al Waha
Fairuz
Four Seasons
Ginger
Gourmet Burger
Halepi
Island Rest.
I-Thai
Khan's
Mandarin Kitchen
Rodizio Rico
Royal China
T.G.I. Friday's
YO! Sushi

Chiswick
Annie's
Ask Pizza
Balans
Café Rouge
Fish Hook
FishWorks
Frankie's Italian
Giraffe
Gourmet Burger
La Trompette
Le Vacherin
Pacific Bar & Grill
Sam's Brass.
Silks & Spice
Tootsies
Zizzi

Hammersmith
Agni
Brackenbury
Carluccio's
Chez Kristof

Gate
River Café
Smollensky's

Kensington
Abingdon
Ask Pizza
Babylon
Balans
Black & Blue
Brunello
Clarke's
Edera
11 Abingdon Rd.
ffiona's
Giraffe
Il Portico
Kensington Pl.
Koi
Launceston Place
Locanda Ottoemezzo
L-Restaurant
Maggie Jones's
Memories/China
Pat. Valerie
Pizza Express
Sticky Fingers
Stratford's
Timo
Wagamama
Whit's
Wòdka
Zaika

Notting Hill/Holland Park/Westbourne Grove
Alounak
Ark
Ask Pizza

Assaggi
Belvedere
Bombay Bicycle
Books for Cooks
Churchill Arms
Costas Grill
Cow Din. Rm.
Crazy Homies
e&o
Electric Brasserie
Essenza
First Floor
Galicia
Geales Fish
Harlem
Inaho
Julie's
Ladbroke Arms
Ledbury
Lonsdale
Lucky 7
Malabar
Mediterraneo
New Culture Rev.
Noor Jahan
Notting Grill
Notting Hill Brass.

Nyonya
Osteria Basilico
Ottolenghi
Ping Pong
Pizza Express
Prince Bonaparte
Raoul's
Taqueria
Tom's Deli
Tootsies
202
Uli
Westbourne

Olympia
Alounak

Paddington
Frontline
Levantine
Yakitoria

Shepherd's Bush
Anglesea Arms
Blah! Blah! Blah!
Café Rouge
Esarn Kheaw
Snows on Green

IN THE COUNTRY

Cliveden House
Fat Duck
French Horn
Gravetye Manor

Le Manoir/Quat
Vineyard/Stockcross
Waterside Inn

SPECIAL FEATURES

(Indexes list the best in each category. Multi-location restaurants' features may vary by branch.)

All-Day Dining
Abeno (multi. loc.)
Albannach (WC2)
Anakana (EC1)
Annie's (SW13)
Aperitivo (W1)
Ask Pizza (multi. loc.)
Aubaine (SW3)
Automat (W1)
Baker & Spice (multi. loc.)
Balans (multi. loc.)
Balham Kitchen (SW12)
Baltic (SE1)
Banquette (WC2)
Belgo (WC2)
Bibendum Oyster (SW3)
Big Easy (SW3)
Black & Blue (multi. loc.)
Bloom's (NW11)
Browns (multi. loc.)
Busaba Eathai (multi. loc.)
Café Boheme (W1)
Café Fish (W1)
Cafe Pacifico (WC2)
Café Rouge (multi. loc.)
Canteen (E1)
Carluccio's (multi. loc.)
Cecconi's (W1)
Chelsea Bun (SW10)
Chez Gérard (multi. loc.)
Chowki Bar (W1)
Chuen Cheng Ku (W1)
Cipriani (W1)
Crazy Homies (W2)
ECapital (W1)
Ed's Easy Diner (multi. loc.)
Efes Kebab (W1)
Electric Brasserie (W11)
Fifth Floor Cafe (SW1)
Fire & Stone (WC2)
fish! (SE1)
FishWorks (SW1)
Food for Thought (WC2)
Four Seasons (W2)

Gaucho Grill (multi. loc.)
Giraffe (multi. loc.)
Great Eastern (EC2)
Grenadier (SW1)
Gun (E14)
Halepi (W2)
Harbour City (W1)
Hard Rock Cafe (W1)
Harlem (W2)
Haz (E1)
Hoxton Apprentice (N1)
Hush (W1)
Ishbilia (SW1)
Ishtar (W1)
itsu (multi. loc.)
Joe Allen (WC2)
Joe's (SW3)
Julie's (W11)
Kettners (W1)
La Brasserie (SW3)
Ladurée (SW1)
La Fromagerie (W1)
Leon (multi. loc.)
Levant (W1)
Levantine (W2)
Lilly's (E1)
Livebait (multi. loc.)
Living Room, The (W1)
Lucky 7 (W2)
Meson Don Felipe (SE1)
Noto (W1)
Noura (multi. loc.)
Obika (W1)
1 Lombard Brass. (EC3)
Oriel (SW1)
Orso (WC2)
Ottolenghi (multi. loc.)
Pat. Valerie (multi. loc.)
Ping Pong (multi. loc.)
Pizza Express (multi. loc.)
Pizza Metro (SW11)
Pizza on Park (SW1)
PJ's B&G (multi. loc.)
Planet Hollywood (W1)
Porters (WC2)

Portrait (WC2)
Prince Bonaparte (W2)
Rainforest Cafe (W1)
Randall & Aubin (multi. loc.)
Ransome's Dock (SW11)
Real Greek (multi. loc.)
Riccardo's (SW3)
Richoux (multi. loc.)
Royal China (multi. loc.)
Royal China Club (W1)
Royal Exchange (EC3)
Rules (WC2)
Salt Yard (W1)
Sam's Brass. (W4)
Satsuma (W1)
Sofra (multi. loc.)
Soho Spice (W1)
Solly's (NW11)
Sophie's Steak (SW10)
Sotheby's Cafe (W1)
Souk (WC2)
Spago (SW7)
Sticky Fingers (W8)
St. John Bread/Wine (E1)
Tas (SE1)
Texas Embassy (SW1)
T.G.I. Friday's (W1)
Tom's Deli (W11)
Tootsies (multi. loc.)
Troubadour (SW5)
Truc Vert (W1)
Tuttons Brasserie (WC2)
202 (W11)
Villandry (W1)
Vingt-Quatre (SW10)
Wagamama (multi. loc.)
Wolseley (W1)
Ye Olde Cheshire (EC4)
YO! Sushi (multi. loc.)
Zinc B&G (multi. loc.)
Zizzi (multi. loc.)

Breakfast

(See also Hotel Dining)
Annie's (multi. loc.)
Aubaine (SW3)
Automat (W1)
Baker & Spice (multi. loc.)
Balans (multi. loc.)
Balham Kitchen (SW12)
Bank Aldwych (WC2)

Books for Cooks (W11)
Café Boheme (W1)
Café Rouge (multi. loc.)
Carluccio's (multi. loc.)
Cecconi's (W1)
Cinnamon Club (SW1)
Coq d'Argent (EC2)
Eat & Two Veg (W1)
Electric Brasserie (W11)
Engineer (NW1)
Fifth Floor Cafe (SW1)
Fortnum's Fountain (W1)
Giraffe (multi. loc.)
Harlem (W2)
Hush (W1)
Inn The Park (SW1)
Joe's (SW3)
Joe's Rest./Bar (SW1)
Julie's (W11)
La Brasserie (SW3)
Ladurée (SW1)
La Fromagerie (W1)
Le Pont de la Tour (SE1)
Lucky 7 (W2)
Lundum's (SW7)
Nicole's (W1)
1 Lombard Brass. (EC3)
Oriel (SW1)
Ottolenghi (multi. loc.)
Papillon (SW3)
Pat. Valerie (multi. loc.)
Pizza on Park (SW1)
Portrait (WC2)
Providores/Tapa (W1)
Quality Chop Hse. (EC1)
Raoul's (W9)
Richoux (multi. loc.)
Rivington Grill (multi. loc.)
Roast (SE1)
Royal Exchange (EC3)
Simpson's (WC2)
Sotheby's Cafe (W1)
St. John Bread/Wine (E1)
Tate Britain Restaurant (SW1)
Tom's Deli (W11)
Tootsies (multi. loc.)
Troubadour (SW5)
Truc Vert (W1)
Tuttons Brasserie (WC2)
202 (W11)

Villandry (W1)
Vingt-Quatre (SW10)
Wolseley (W1)

Brunch
Abingdon (W8)
Admiral Codrington (SW3)
Annie's (multi. loc.)
Aubaine (SW3)
Automat (W1)
Aziz (SW6)
Balham Kitchen (SW12)
Bank Aldwych (WC2)
Big Easy (SW3)
Bistrot 190 (SW7)
Bluebird Brass. (SW3)
Bluebird Club (SW3)
Blue Elephant (SW6)
Butlers Wharf (SE1)
Canyon (Richmond)
Cecconi's (W1)
Christopher's (WC2)
Chutney Mary (SW10)
Clarke's (W8)
Cru (N1)
1802 (E14)
Fakhreldine (W1)
Fifth Floor Cafe (SW1)
Fish Shop on St. John (EC1)
Garbo's (W1)
Giraffe (multi. loc.)
Harlem (W2)
Joe Allen (WC2)
Joe's Rest./Bar (SW1)
La Brasserie (SW3)
Lanesborough (SW1)
Le Caprice (SW1)
Lucky 7 (W2)
Lundum's (SW7)
Malmaison Hotel (EC1)
Motcombs (SW1)
Nicole's (W1)
PJ's B&G (multi. loc.)
Portrait (WC2)
Providores/Tapa (W1)
Quadrato (E14)
Ransome's Dock (SW11)
Sam's Brass. (W4)
Sophie's Steak (SW10)
Tom's Deli (W11)
Troubadour (SW5)

Truc Vert (W1)
202 (W11)
Vama (SW10)
Villandry (W1)
Vingt-Quatre (SW10)
Wapping Food (E1)
Zetter (EC1)

Business Dining
Addendum (EC3)
Al Duca (SW1)
Alloro (W1)
Almeida (N1)
Amaya (SW1)
Angela Hartnett's (W1)
Arbutus (W1)
Astor Bar & Grill (W1)
Aubergine (SW10)
Aurora (EC2)
Avenue (SW1)
Awana (SW3)
Axis (WC2)
Bank Aldwych (WC2)
Bank Westminster (SW1)
Beauberry House (SE21)
Bellamy's (W1)
Belvedere (W8)
Benares (W1)
Bentley's (W1)
Berkeley Square (W1)
Bibendum (SW3)
Blakes (SW7)
Bleeding Heart (EC1)
Bluebird Club (SW3)
Blueprint Café (SE1)
Bodeans (W1)
Bonds (EC2)
Boxwood Café (SW1)
Brian Turner (W1)
Brunello (SW7)
Capital (SW3)
Caravaggio (EC3)
Cecconi's (W1)
Chancery (EC4)
Chez Gérard (multi. loc.)
China Tang (W1)
Christopher's (WC2)
Cinnamon Club (SW1)
Cipriani (W1)
Circus (W1)
Clarke's (W8)

Club Gascon (EC1)
Deya (W1)
Drones (SW1)
Edera (W11)
1880 (SW7)
Elena's l'Etoile (W1)
Embassy (W1)
Fakhreldine (W1)
Fifth Floor (SW1)
Fino (W1)
Fiore (SW1)
Foliage (SW1)
Franco's (SW1)
Galvin/Windows (W1)
Galvin Bistrot (W1)
Gilgamesh (NW1)
Glasshouse (Kew)
Gordon Ramsay/Claridge's (W1)
Gordon Ramsay/68 Royal (SW3)
Goring Din. Rm. (SW1)
Gravetye Manor (W. Sus)
Greenhouse (W1)
Green's (SW1)
Grill, The (W1)
Grill Room, The (W1)
Il Convivio (SW1)
Imperial City (EC3)
Incognico (WC2)
Indigo (WC2)
I-Thai (W2)
Ivy (WC2)
J. Sheekey (WC2)
Just St. James's (SW1)
Kai Mayfair (W1)
La Genova (W1)
Lanes (W1)
Lanesborough (SW1)
Langan's Bistro (W1)
Langan's Brasserie (W1)
La Noisette (SW1)
La Trompette (W4)
Launceston Place (W8)
Le Café du Marché (EC1)
Le Caprice (SW1)
Le Cercle (SW1)
Ledbury (W11)
Le Gavroche (W1)
Le Manoir/Quat (Oxon)
Le Pont de la Tour (SE1)
L'Escargot (W1)

L'Etranger (SW7)
L'Incontro (SW1)
Locanda Locatelli (W1)
L'Oranger (SW1)
Luciano (SW1)
Malmaison Hotel (EC1)
Manzi's (WC2)
Matsuri (multi. loc.)
Maze (W1)
Memories/China (multi. loc.)
Mirabelle (W1)
Mitsukoshi (SW1)
Miyama (W1)
Mju (SW1)
Nahm (SW1)
Neal Street (WC2)
Nobu Berkeley (W1)
Nobu London (W1)
Odin's (W1)
One-O-One (SW1)
Origin (WC2)
Orrery (W1)
Oxo Tower (SE1)
Papillon (SW3)
Park, The (SW1)
Paternoster Chop (EC4)
Pétrus (SW1)
Pied à Terre (W1)
Plateau (E14)
Poissonnerie (SW3)
Princess Garden (W1)
Prism (EC3)
Providores/Tapa (W1)
Quadrato (E14)
Quaglino's (SW1)
Quirinale (SW1)
Quo Vadis (W1)
Rasa (multi. loc.)
Rasoi Vineet Bhatia (SW3)
Red Fort (W1)
Rhodes 24 (EC2)
Rhodes W1 (W1)
Rib Room (SW1)
Richard Corrigan (W1)
Ritz (W1)
River Café (W6)
Roast (SE1)
Roka (W1)
Rules (WC2)
Santini (SW1)

Savoy Grill (WC2)
Shanghai Blues (WC1)
Shepherd's (SW1)
Sketch/Lecture Rm. (W1)
Smiths/Dining Rm. (EC1)
Smiths/Top Floor (EC1)
Spoon (W1)
Square (W1)
Tamarind (W1)
Tatsuso (EC2)
Terminus (EC2)
Tom Aikens (SW3)
Ubon by Nobu (E14)
Umu (W1)
Vineyard/Stockcross (Berks)
Waterside Inn (Berks)
Wilton's (SW1)
W'Sens (SW1)
Zafferano (SW1)
Zaika (W8)
Zen Central (W1)
ZeNW3 (NW3)
Zuma (SW7)

Celebrity Chefs

Angela Hartnett's (W1), *Angela Hartnett*
Banquette (WC2), *Marcus Wareing*
Belvedere (W8), *Marco Pierre White*
Benares (W1), *Atul Kochhar*
Bentley's (W1), *Richard Corrigan*
Boxwood Café (SW1), *Gordon Ramsay & Stuart Gillies*
Brasserie Roux (SW1), *Albert Roux*
Brian Turner (W1), *Brian Turner*
Café Spice Namasté (E1), *Cyrus Todiwala*
Capital (SW3), *Eric Chavot*
Carluccio's (multi. loc.), *Antonio Carluccio*
Chez Bruce (SW17), *Bruce Poole*
Cinnamon Club (SW1), *Vivek Singh*
Clarke's (W8), *Sally Clarke*
Club Gascon (EC1), *Pascal Aussignac*

Comptoir Gascon (EC1), *Pascal Aussignac*
Drones (SW1), *Marco Pierre White*
Fat Duck (Berks), *Heston Blumenthal*
Fifteen (N1), *Jamie Oliver*
Frankie's Italian (multi. loc.), *Marco Pierre White*
Galvin/Windows (W1), *Chris Galvin*
Galvin Bistrot (W1), *Chris Galvin*
Gilgamesh (NW1), *Ian Pengelley*
Gordon Ramsay/Claridge's (W1), *Gordon Ramsay & Mark Sargeant*
Gordon Ramsay/68 Royal (SW3), *Gordon Ramsay & Mark Askew*
Ivy (WC2), *Mark Hix*
J. Sheekey (WC2), *Mark Hix*
Kensington Pl. (W8), *Rowley Leigh*
Kew Grill (Kew), *Antony Worrall Thompson*
La Noisette (SW1), *Bjorn van der Horst*
Le Caprice (SW1), *Mark Hix*
Le Cercle (SW1), *Pascal Aussignac*
Le Gavroche (W1), *Michel Roux Jr.*
Le Manoir/Quat (Oxon), *Raymond Blanc*
Locanda Locatelli (W1), *Giorgio Locatelli*
Luciano (SW1), *Marco Pierre White*
Maze (W1), *Gordon Ramsay & Jason Atherton*
Moro (EC1), *Sam & Sam Clark*
Nahm (SW1), *David Thompson*
Neal Street (WC2), *Antonio Carluccio*
Nobu Berkeley (W1), *Nobu Matsuhisa & Mark Edwards*
Nobu London (W1), *Nobu Matsuhisa & Mark Edwards*
Notting Grill (W11), *Antony Worrall Thompson*

Origin (WC2), *Adam Byatt*
Pearl (WC1), *Jun Tanaka*
Pétrus (SW1), *Marcus Wareing*
Providores/Tapa (W1), *Peter Gordon*
Racine (SW3), *Henry Harris*
Randall & Aubin (multi. loc.), *Ed Baines*
Rasoi Vineet Bhatia (SW3), *Vineet Bhatia*
Real Greek (N1), *Theodore Kyriakou*
Refettorio (EC4), *Giorgio Locatelli*
Rhodes 24 (EC2), *Gary Rhodes*
Rhodes W1 (W1), *Gary Rhodes*
Richard Corrigan (W1), *Richard Corrigan*
River Café (W6), *Rose Gray & Ruth Rodgers*
Roka (W1), *Rainer Becker*
Savoy Grill (WC2), *Marcus Wareing*
Sketch/Gallery (W1), *Pierre Gagnaire*
Sketch/Lecture Rm. (W1), *Pierre Gagnaire*
Smiths/Dining Rm. (EC1), *John Torode*
Smiths/Top Floor (EC1), *John Torode*
Spoon (W1), *Alain Ducasse*
Square (W1), *Philip Howard*
St. John (EC1), *Fergus Henderson*
St. John Bread/Wine (E1), *Fergus Henderson*
Tamarind (W1), *Cyrus Todiwala*
Tom Aikens (SW3), *Tom Aikens*
Waterside Inn (Berks), *Michel Roux*
W'Sens (SW1), *Jacques & Laurent Pourcel*
Zilli Fish (W1), *Aldo Zilli*
Zuma (SW7), *Rainer Becker*

Cheese Boards

Almeida (N1)
Angela Hartnett's (W1)
Aubergine (SW10)
Aurora (EC2)
Bibendum (SW3)
Bistrotheque (E2)
Bleeding Heart (EC1)
Bonds (EC2)
Caravaggio (EC3)
Chez Bruce (SW17)
Christopher's (WC2)
Clarke's (W8)
Cliveden House (Berks)
Coq d'Argent (EC2)
Cru (N1)
1802 (E14)
Elena's l'Etoile (W1)
Enoteca Turi (SW15)
Fat Duck (Berks)
Fifteen (N1)
Foliage (SW1)
French Horn (Berks)
Glasshouse (Kew)
Gordon Ramsay/Claridge's (W1
Gordon Ramsay/68 Royal (SW3
Goring Din. Rm. (SW1)
Gravetye Manor (W. Sus)
Greenhouse (W1)
Green's (SW1)
Grill Room, The (W1)
Julie's (W11)
La Fromagerie (W1)
Lanesborough (SW1)
La Poule au Pot (SW1)
La Trompette (W4)
La Trouvaille (multi. loc.)
Launceston Place (W8)
Le Boudin Blanc (W1)
Le Café du Jardin (WC2)
Le Cercle (SW1)
Le Colombier (SW3)
Le Gavroche (W1)
Le Manoir/Quat (Oxon)
Le Mercury (N1)
Le Pont de la Tour (SE1)
L'Escargot (W1)
L'Estaminet (WC2)
Les Trois Garçons (E1)
L'Etranger (SW7)
L'Incontro (SW1)
Locanda Locatelli (W1)
Locanda Ottoemezzo (W8)
Lola's (N1)
L'Oranger (SW1)
Lou Pescadou (SW5)
Lucio (SW3)

Lundum's (SW7)
Malmaison Hotel (EC1)
Manicomio (SW3)
Michael Moore (W1)
Mirabelle (W1)
Mju (SW1)
Mon Plaisir (WC2)
One-O-One (SW1)
Orrery (W1)
Oslo Court (NW8)
Osteria dell'Arancio (SW10)
Papillon (SW3)
Paternoster Chop (EC4)
Pearl (WC1)
Petersham (Richmond)
Pétrus (SW1)
Pied à Terre (W1)
Plateau (E14)
Refettorio (EC4)
Richard Corrigan (W1)
Ritz (W1)
River Café (W6)
Roussillon (SW1)
Royal Exchange (EC3)
Rudland & Stubbs (EC1)
Salt Yard (W1)
Sartoria (W1)
Savoy Grill (WC2)
Sketch/Gallery (W1)
Sketch/Lecture Rm. (W1)
Smiths/Top Floor (EC1)
Sonny's (SW13)
Square (W1)
St. John Bread/Wine (E1)
Tamesa@oxo (SE1)
TECA (W1)
Tom Aikens (SW3)
Vineyard/Stockcross (Berks)
Vivat Bacchus (EC4)
Waterside Inn (Berks)
Zafferano (SW1)

Child-Friendly

(Besides the normal fast-food
places; * children's menu
available)
Abbeville (SW4)
Abingdon (W8)
Al Bustan (SW7)
Al Duca (SW1)
Almeida (N1)

Angela Hartnett's (W1)*
Aperitivo (W1)
Archipelago (W1)
Arkansas Cafe (E1)
Asia de Cuba (WC2)*
Ask Pizza (multi. loc.)
Assaggi (W2)
Aubaine (SW3)
Axis (WC2)*
Babylon (W8)*
Baker & Spice (multi. loc.)
Balham Kitchen (SW12)*
Baltic (SE1)*
Bank Aldwych (WC2)*
Banquette (WC2)
Beauberry House (SE21)
Belgo (multi. loc.)*
Benihana (multi. loc.)*
Berkeley Square (W1)*
Bibendum (SW3)
Bibendum Oyster (SW3)
Big Easy (SW3)*
Black & Blue (multi. loc.)
Blandford St. (W1)
Bloom's (NW11)*
Bluebird Brass. (SW3)*
Bluebird Club (SW3)
Blue Elephant (SW6)
Bodeans (multi. loc.)*
Books for Cooks (W11)
Boxwood Café (SW1)*
Brasserie Roux (SW1)*
Browns (multi. loc.)*
Buona Sera (multi. loc.)
Busaba Eathai (multi. loc.)
Café Fish (W1)*
Cafe Pacifico (WC2)*
Café Rouge (multi. loc.)*
Café Spice Namasté (E1)
Cantina del Ponte (SE1)
Canyon (Richmond)*
Caraffini (SW1)
Caravaggio (EC3)
Carluccio's (multi. loc.)*
Carpaccio (SW3)
Casale Franco (N1)
Cecconi's (W1)
Champor (SE1)
Cheyne Walk (SW3)
Chez Bruce (SW17)

Chez Gérard (multi. loc.)
Chez Kristof (W6)*
Christopher's (WC2)*
Chuen Cheng Ku (W1)
Churchill Arms (W8)
Cigala (WC1)
Cinnamon Club (SW1)
Cipriani (W1)
Circus (W1)
Citrus (W1)*
Coach & Horses (EC1)
Daphne's (SW3)
Drones (SW1)
Eagle (EC1)
e&o (W11)
Eat & Two Veg (W1)
Ebury Din. Rm. (SW1)
ECapital (W1)
Edera (W11)
Ed's Easy Diner (multi. loc.)*
Eight Over Eight (SW3)
Electric Brasserie (W11)
Elistano (SW3)
Enoteca Turi (SW15)
Fifteen (N1)
Fifth Floor Cafe (SW1)*
Fino (W1)
fish! (SE1)*
Fish Shop on St. John (EC1)
Fortnum's Fountain (W1)*
Frankie's Italian (SW3)*
Frederick's (N1)*
Friends (SW10)
Gaucho Grill (multi. loc.)
Gay Hussar (W1)
Giraffe (multi. loc.)*
Glasshouse (Kew)*
Gourmet Burger (multi. loc.)*
Great Eastern (EC2)
Grenadier (SW1)
Hakkasan (W1)
Hard Rock Cafe (W1)*
Harlem (W2)*
Indigo (WC2)*
Inn The Park (SW1)*
itsu (multi. loc.)
Jenny Lo's Tea Hse. (SW1)
Jim Thompson's (multi. loc.)*
Joe Allen (WC2)
Joe's Rest./Bar (SW1)

Julie's (W11)*
Kensington Pl. (W8)*
Kettners (W1)
La Brasserie (SW3)*
Ladurée (SW1)
La Famiglia (SW10)
La Fromagerie (W1)
La Porchetta (multi. loc.)
Le Caprice (SW1)
Le Manoir/Quat (Oxon)*
L'Etranger (SW7)
Livebait (multi. loc.)*
Locanda Locatelli (W1)
Locanda Ottoemezzo (W8)
Lola's (N1)
Lucio (SW3)
Lucky 7 (W2)*
Lundum's (SW7)
Made in Italy (SW3)
Mango Tree (SW1)
Manicomio (SW3)
Maroush (multi. loc.)
Masala Zone (multi. loc.)*
Mediterraneo (W11)
Mela (WC2)
Mitsukoshi (SW1)*
Nicole's (W1)
Nobu Berkeley (W1)
Nobu London (W1)
Noura (multi. loc.)
Oliveto (SW1)
Oriel (SW1)
Orso (WC2)
Ottolenghi (multi. loc.)
Oxo Tower (SE1)
Oxo Tower Brass. (SE1)*
Park, The (SW1)*
Patara (multi. loc.)
Pat. Valerie (multi. loc.)
Pellicano (SW3)
Petersham (Richmond)
Pizza Express (multi. loc.)
Pizza Metro (SW11)*
Pizza on Park (SW1)
PJ's B&G (multi. loc.)*
Planet Hollywood (W1)*
Plateau (E14)
Porters (WC2)*
Quadrato (E14)*
Quaglino's (SW1)*

Quality Chop Hse. (EC1)
Quilon (SW1)
Quirinale (SW1)
Rainforest Cafe (W1)*
Randall & Aubin (multi. loc.)
Ransome's Dock (SW11)
Raoul's (multi. loc.)
Rasa (multi. loc.)
Rasoi Vineet Bhatia (SW3)
Real Greek (multi. loc.)*
Red Pepper (W9)
Reubens (W1)*
Riccardo's (SW3)
Richoux (multi. loc.)*
Ritz (W1)*
Riva (SW13)
River Café (W6)
Rocket (multi. loc.)*
Roussillon (SW1)
Royal China (multi. loc.)
Rules (WC2)
Sabor (N1)
Sale e Pepe (SW1)
San Lorenzo (SW3)
Santini (SW1)
Sarkhel's (multi. loc.)*
Seashell (NW1)*
Shepherd's (SW1)
Six-13 (W1)
Smollensky's (multi. loc.)*
Sofra (multi. loc.)*
Solly's (NW11)*
Sonny's (SW13)*
Sophie's Steak (SW10)*
Spiga (W1)
Spighetta (W1)
Sticky Fingers (W8)*
Strada (multi. loc.)*
Tas (SE1)
Tentazioni (SE1)*
Texas Embassy (SW1)*
T.G.I. Friday's (multi. loc.)*
Tiger Lil's (N1)*
Tom's Deli (W11)
Tootsies (multi. loc.)*
Truc Vert (W1)
Tsunami (SW4)
Tuttons Brasserie (WC2)*
Two Bros. Fish (N3)*
202 (W11)

Ubon by Nobu (E14)
Uli (W11)
Vama (SW10)
Villandry (W1)
Vingt-Quatre (SW10)
Wagamama (multi. loc.)*
Waterside Inn (Berks)*
Wòdka (W8)
Wolseley (W1)
Yauatcha (W1)
YO! Sushi (multi. loc.)*
Yoshino (W1)
Zafferano (SW1)
Zen Central (W1)
ZeNW3 (NW3)
Zetter (EC1)*
Zizzi (multi. loc.)*
Zuma (SW7)

Delivery/Takeaway
(D=delivery, T=takeaway)
Alounak (multi. loc.) (D,T)
Arkansas Cafe (E1) (T)
Baker & Spice (multi. loc.) (T)
Beiteddine (SW1) (D,T)
Big Easy (SW3) (T)
Bloom's (NW11) (D,T)
Blue Elephant (SW6) (D,T)
Café Lazeez (multi. loc.) (D,T)
Café Spice Namasté (E1) (D,T)
Cantina del Ponte (SE1) (T)
Carluccio's (multi. loc.) (T)
Chor Bizarre (W1) (T)
Chuen Cheng Ku (W1) (T)
Churchill Arms (W8) (T)
Chutney Mary (SW10) (T)
Cigala (WC1) (T)
Crazy Homies (W2) (T)
Defune (W1) (T)
Eat & Two Veg (W1) (T)
Ed's Easy Diner (multi. loc.) (T)
Esarn Kheaw (W12) (T)
Fairuz (multi. loc.) (D,T)
Fakhreldine (W1) (D,T)
Frankie's Italian (SW3) (T)
Friends (SW10) (T)
Garbo's (W1) (T)
Gaucho Grill (multi. loc.) (T)
Geales Fish (W8) (T)
Giraffe (multi. loc.) (T)
Golden Dragon (W1) (T)

Halepi (W2) (T)
Harbour City (W1) (T)
Harlem (W2) (T)
Ikeda (W1) (T)
Il Falconiere (SW7) (T)
Imperial City (EC3) (T)
Inn The Park (SW1) (T)
Ishbilia (SW1) (D,T)
itsu (multi. loc.) (D,T)
Jenny Lo's Tea Hse. (SW1) (D,T)
Jin Kichi (NW3) (T)
Khan's (W2) (T)
Khan's/Kensington (SW7) (D,T)
Kiku (W1) (T)
Koi (W8) (D,T)
Kulu Kulu Sushi (multi. loc.) (T)
La Fromagerie (W1) (D,T)
La Piragua (N1) (T)
La Porchetta (multi. loc.) (T)
La Porte des Indes (W1) (T)
Levant (W1) (T)
Levantine (W2) (T)
Lucky 7 (W2) (T)
Ma Goa (SW15) (T)
Mandalay (W2) (T)
Mango Tree (SW1) (T)
Mao Tai (SW6) (D,T)
Masala Zone (multi. loc.) (T)
Matsuri (multi. loc.) (T)
Mela (WC2) (T)
Memories/China (multi. loc.) (T)
Moshi Moshi (multi. loc.) (D,T)
Mr. Chow (SW1) (T)
North Sea (WC1) (T)
Noura (multi. loc.) (D,T)
Nyonya (W11) (T)
Oliveto (SW1) (T)
Original Lah. Kebab (multi. loc.) (T)
Ottolenghi (multi. loc.) (T)
Ozer (W1) (T)
Painted Heron (multi. loc.) (T)
Patara (multi. loc.) (T)
Pizza Express (multi. loc.) (T)
Pizza Metro (SW11) (T)
Rasa (multi. loc.) (T)
Red Pepper (W9) (T)
Reubens (W1) (D,T)
Riccardo's (SW3) (T)
Richoux (multi. loc.) (T)

Royal China (multi. loc.) (T)
Salloos (SW1) (D,T)
Santa Lucia (SW10) (T)
Sarkhel's (multi. loc.) (D,T)
Seashell (NW1) (T)
Shanghai Blues (WC1) (T)
Singapore Garden (NW6) (D,T)
Singapura (multi. loc.) (T)
Six-13 (W1) (D,T)
Solly's (NW11) (T)
Spago (SW7) (T)
Spiga (W1) (T)
Spighetta (W1) (T)
Star of India (SW5) (T)
Sticky Fingers (W8) (T)
St. John Bread/Wine (E1) (T)
Strada (multi. loc.) (T)
Tamarind (W1) (D,T)
Tas (SE1) (T)
Thai Square (multi. loc.) (T)
Tom's Deli (W11) (T)
Truc Vert (W1) (D,T)
Two Bros. Fish (N3) (T)
Ubon by Nobu (E14) (T)
Vama (SW10) (D,T)
Veeraswamy (W1) (T)
Villandry (W1) (T)
Vrisaki (N22) (T)
YO! Sushi (multi. loc.) (D,T)
Yoshino (W1) (T)
Zen Central (W1) (D,T)
ZeNW3 (NW3) (D,T)

Dining Alone

(Plus hotels and places with counter service)
Amaya (SW1)
Aubaine (SW3)
Baker & Spice (multi. loc.)
Bibendum Oyster (SW3)
Books for Cooks (W11)
Busaba Eathai (multi. loc.)
Café Rouge (multi. loc.)
Carluccio's (multi. loc.)
Chowki Bar (W1)
Chuen Cheng Ku (W1)
Coach & Horses (EC1)
Comptoir Gascon (EC1)
Eat & Two Veg (W1)
Ed's Easy Diner (multi. loc.)
Fifth Floor Cafe (SW1)

Fino (W1)
Fortnum's Fountain (W1)
Hakkasan (W1)
Inaho (W2)
Inn The Park (SW1)
Jenny Lo's Tea Hse. (SW1)
Joe's Rest./Bar (SW1)
Ladurée (SW1)
La Fromagerie (W1)
Le Colombier (SW3)
Leon (EC4)
Manicomio (SW3)
Matsuri (multi. loc.)
Maze (W1)
Mildreds (W1)
Mitsukoshi (SW1)
Mon Plaisir (WC2)
New Culture Rev. (multi. loc.)
Nicole's (W1)
Obika (W1)
Oriel (SW1)
Ottolenghi (multi. loc.)
Pat. Valerie (multi. loc.)
Ping Pong (W2)
Porters (WC2)
Portrait (WC2)
Providores/Tapa (W1)
Randall & Aubin (multi. loc.)
Richoux (multi. loc.)
Sotheby's Cafe (W1)
St. John Bread/Wine (E1)
Tapas Brindisa (SE1)
Taqueria (W11)
Tate Modern (SE1)
Tom's Deli (W11)
Truc Vert (W1)
Villandry (W1)
Wagamama (multi. loc.)
Wolseley (W1)
Yauatcha (W1)
YO! Sushi (multi. loc.)

Entertainment

(Call for days and times of performances)
Baltic (SE1) (jazz)
Bank Aldwych (WC2) (jazz)
Bank Westminster (SW1) (DJ)
Bengal Clipper (SE1) (piano)
Big Easy (SW3) (bands)
Bluebird Club (SW3) (varies)

Boisdale (multi. loc.) (jazz)
Cantaloupe (EC2) (DJ)
Canyon (Richmond) (jazz/piano)
Cheyne Walk (SW3) (jazz)
Chutney Mary (SW10) (jazz)
Circus (W1) (DJ)
Coq d'Argent (EC2) (jazz)
Efes Kebab (W1) (belly dancing)
1802 (E14) (DJ)
Embassy (W1) (DJ)
Floridita (W1) (Cuban)
Gilgamesh (NW1) (varies)
Globe (NW3) (cabaret)
Hakkasan (W1) (DJ)
Harlem (W2) (DJ)
Ishbilia (SW1) (belly dancing)
I-Thai (W2) (harp)
Joe Allen (WC2) (jazz/piano)
Lanesborough (SW1) (jazz)
Langan's Brasserie (W1) (jazz)
Le Café du Jardin (WC2) (piano)
Le Café du Marché (EC1) (jazz)
Le Caprice (SW1) (piano)
Le Pont de la Tour (SE1) (piano)
Levant (W1) (belly dancing)
Levantine (W2) (belly dancing)
Little Italy (W1) (DJ)
Lola's (N1) (piano)
Maroush (multi. loc.) (varies)
Mash (W1) (DJ)
Meson Don Felipe (SE1) (guitar)
Mirabelle (W1) (piano)
Momo (W1) (varies)
Mon Plaisir (WC2) (accordionian)
Naked Turtle (SW14) (jazz)
Oxo Tower Brass. (SE1) (jazz)
Pigalle Club (W1) (varies)
Pizza on Park (SW1) (varies)
PJ's B&G (WC2) (jazz)
Planet Hollywood (W1) (DJ)
Quaglino's (SW1) (jazz)
Rib Room (SW1) (piano/vocals)
Ritz (W1) (band)
Sartoria (W1) (piano)
Silks & Spice (EC4) (varies)
Simpson's (WC2) (piano)
Smollensky's (multi. loc.) (DJ/ piano)
Soho Spice (W1) (DJ)

Souk (WC2) (belly dancing)
Sugar Reef (W1) (nightclub)
Sumosan (W1) (DJ)
Tas (SE1) (guitar)
Thai Square (multi. loc.) (DJ/
   varies)
Tugga (SW3) (DJ)
Vineyard/Stockcross (Berks)
   (jazz/piano)
Volt (SW1) (DJ)

Fireplaces
Abbeville (SW4)
Admiral Codrington (SW3)
Angela Hartnett's (W1)
Anglesea Arms (W6)
Balham Kitchen (SW12)
Bam-Bou (W1)
Barnsbury (N1)
Bierodrome (WC2)
Bleeding Heart (EC1)
Brunello (SW7)
Builders Arms (SW3)
Bull, The (N6)
Cambio de Tercio (SW5)
Cheyne Walk (SW3)
Christopher's (WC2)
Cicada (EC1)
Clerkenwell (EC1)
Cliveden House (Berks)
Clos Maggiore (WC2)
Cow Din. Rm. (W2)
Crazy Bear (W1)
Daphne's (SW3)
Draper's Arms (N1)
Ebury Din. Rm. (SW1)
Farm (SW6)
French Horn (Berks)
Goring Din. Rm. (SW1)
Gravetye Manor (W. Sus)
Grenadier (SW1)
I-Thai (W2)
Julie's (W11)
La Poule au Pot (SW1)
Le Cercle (SW1)
Le Manoir/Quat (Oxon)
Lemonia (NW1)
L'Escargot (W1)
Living Room, The (W1)
LMNT (E8)
Lundum's (SW7)
Malmaison Hotel (EC1)

Maroush (SW3)
Pacific Bar & Grill (W6)
Palmerston (SE22)
Prince Bonaparte (W2)
Raoul's (W11)
Richard Corrigan (W1)
Rules (WC2)
Salusbury Pub (NW6)
Sonny's (SW13)
Taman gang (W1)
Thomas Cubitt (SW1)
Upstairs Bar/Rest. (SW2)
Waterside Inn (Berks)
Wells (NW3)
Westbourne (W2)

Game in Season
Abbeville (SW4)
Addendum (EC3)
Admiralty (WC2)
Alastair Little (W1)
Albannach (WC2)
Almeida (N1)
Anchor & Hope (SE1)
Andrew Edmunds (W1)
Angela Hartnett's (W1)
Arbutus (W1)
Arkansas Cafe (E1)
Aurora (EC2)
Avenue (SW1)
Axis (WC2)
Baltic (SE1)
Barnsbury (N1)
Belvedere (W8)
Berkeley Square (W1)
Bibendum (SW3)
Bistrotheque (E2)
Blandford St. (W1)
Bleeding Heart (EC1)
Bluebird Brass. (SW3)
Blueprint Café (SE1)
Bonds (EC2)
Boxwood Café (SW1)
Brackenbury (W6)
Brasserie Roux (SW1)
Brass. St. Quentin (SW3)
Brian Turner (W1)
Brunello (SW7)
Butlers Wharf (SE1)
Capital (SW3)
Caraffini (SW1)
Caravaggio (EC3)

Chez Bruce (SW17)
Chez Gérard (SW1)
Chutney Mary (SW10)
Cinnamon Club (SW1)
Cipriani (W1)
Circus (W1)
Cliveden House (Berks)
Clos Maggiore (WC2)
Club Gascon (EC1)
Coach & Horses (EC1)
Comptoir Gascon (EC1)
Eagle (EC1)
Edera (W11)
1802 (E14)
11 Abingdon Rd. (W8)
Embassy (W1)
Enoteca Turi (SW15)
Enterprise (SW3)
Farm (SW6)
ffiona's (W8)
Fifteen (N1)
Fino (W1)
Foliage (SW1)
French Horn (Berks)
Glas (SE1)
Glasshouse (Kew)
Gordon Ramsay/Claridge's (W1)
Gordon Ramsay/68 Royal (SW3)
Goring Din. Rm. (SW1)
Gravetye Manor (W. Sus)
Greenhouse (W1)
Green Olive (W9)
Green's (SW1)
Grenadier (SW1)
Greyhound (SW11)
Grill, The (W1)
Grill Room, The (W1)
Grumbles (SW1)
Il Convivio (SW1)
Il Portico (W8)
Julie's (W11)
Kensington Pl. (W8)
Kew Grill (Kew)
La Famiglia (SW10)
Lanesborough (SW1)
Langan's Bistro (W1)
Langan's Brasserie (W1)
La Poule au Pot (SW1)
La Trompette (W4)
La Trouvaille (multi. loc.)
Launceston Place (W8)

L'Aventure (NW8)
Le Caprice (SW1)
Le Cercle (SW1)
Le Colombier (SW3)
Ledbury (W11)
Le Gavroche (W1)
Le Manoir/Quat (Oxon)
Le Pont de la Tour (SE1)
L'Escargot (W1)
Les Trois Garçons (E1)
L'Etranger (SW7)
Locanda Locatelli (W1)
Lola's (N1)
Lucio (SW3)
Michael Moore (W1)
Mirabelle (W1)
Mon Plaisir (WC2)
Montpeliano (SW7)
Monza (SW3)
Morgan M (N7)
Moro (EC1)
Motcombs (SW1)
Neal Street (WC2)
Notting Grill (W11)
Notting Hill Brass. (W11)
Odette's (NW1)
Olivo (SW1)
1 Lombard St. (EC3)
Orrery (W1)
Oslo Court (NW8)
Osteria Antica (SW11)
Oxo Tower (SE1)
Passione (W1)
Paternoster Chop (EC4)
Pearl (WC1)
Pétrus (SW1)
Pig's Ear (SW3)
Prism (EC3)
Providores/Tapa (W1)
Quadrato (E14)
Quaglino's (SW1)
Quirinale (SW1)
Racine (SW3)
Randall & Aubin (SW10)
Ransome's Dock (SW11)
Rhodes 24 (EC2)
Riccardo's (SW3)
Richard Corrigan (W1)
Ritz (W1)
Riva (SW13)
River Café (W6)

Rivington Grill (multi. loc.)
Roast (SE1)
Rodizio Rico (multi. loc.)
Roussillon (SW1)
Rules (WC2)
Santini (SW1)
Sardo (W1)
Sartoria (W1)
Savoy Grill (WC2)
Simpson's (WC2)
Sketch/Lecture Rm. (W1)
Snows on Green (W6)
Sonny's (SW13)
Square (W1)
St. John (EC1)
Tate Britain Restaurant (SW1)
TECA (W1)
Tentazioni (SE1)
Thomas Cubitt (SW1)
Tom Aikens (SW3)
Villandry (W1)
Vineyard/Stockcross (Berks)
Waterside Inn (Berks)
Wilton's (SW1)
Wolseley (W1)
W'Sens (SW1)
Zafferano (SW1)

Gastropubs

Abbeville (SW4)
Admiral Codrington (SW3)
Anchor & Hope (SE1)
Anglesea Arms (W6)
Barnsbury (N1)
Bountiful Cow (WC1)
Builders Arms (SW3)
Bull, The (N6)
Churchill Arms (W8)
Coach & Horses (EC1)
Cow Din. Rm. (W2)
Draper's Arms (N1)
Duke of Cambridge (N1)
Eagle (EC1)
Ebury Din. Rm. (SW1)
Engineer (NW1)
Farm (SW6)
Grenadier (SW1)
Greyhound (SW11)
Gun (E14)
Ladbroke Arms (W11)
Lansdowne (NW1)

Mash (W1)
Palmerston (SE22)
Pig's Ear (SW3)
Prince Bonaparte (W2)
Salusbury Pub (NW6)
Thomas Cubitt (SW1)
Wells (NW3)
Westbourne (W2)
White Hart (SE11)
White Swan (EC4)
Ye Olde Cheshire (EC4)

Historic Places

(Year opened; * building)
1520 Just St. James's (SW1)*
1550 Fat Duck (Berks)*
1571 Royal Exchange (EC3)*
1598 Gravetye Manor (W. Sus)*
1662 Bleeding Heart (EC1)*
1667 Ye Olde Cheshire (EC4)*
1680 French Horn (Berks)*
1692 Giovanni's (WC2)*
1700 Admiralty (WC2)*
1700 Bellamy's (W1)*
1700 Cru (N1)*
1700 Lanesborough (SW1)*
1700 Ransome's Dock (SW11)*
1740 Richard Corrigan (W1)*
1742 Grenadier (SW1)*
1742 Wilton's (SW1)
1750 Food for Thought (WC2)*
1750 Gun (E14)*
1755 Blandford St. (W1)*
1755 Randall & Aubin (W1)*
1760 Sotheby's Cafe (W1)*
1780 Andrew Edmunds (W1)*
1790 Carluccio's (EC1)*
1790 Chez Gérard (EC2)*
1790 Rowley's (SW1)*
1798 Rules (WC2)*
1800 Anglesea Arms (W6)*
1800 Axis (WC2)*
1800 Churchill Arms (W8)*
1800 Hoxton Apprentice (N1)*
1800 Ladbroke Arms (W11)*
1800 Snows on Green (W6)*
1802 1802 (E14)*
1810 Pig's Ear (SW3)*
1820 Builders Arms (SW3)*
1828 Simpson's (WC2)*

1850 Coach & Horses (EC1)*
1850 El Blason (SW3)*
1855 Baltic (SE1)*
1860 Pepper Tree (SW4)*
1865 Petersham (Richmond)*
1867 Kettners (W1)*
1872 Bistrot 190 (SW7)*
1875 Quality Chop Hse. (EC1)*
1880 Bombay Brasserie (SW7)*
1881 Duke of Cambridge (N1)*
1889 Foliage (SW1)*
1889 Sweetings (EC4)
1890 Aurora (EC2)*
1890 Bradley's (NW3)*
1890 La Fromagerie (W1)*
1890 Maggie Jones's (W8)*
1890 R.S.J. (SE1)*
1896 Elena's l'Etoile (W1)*
1897 Angela Hartnett's (W1)*
1898 J. Sheekey (WC2)*
1900 Annie's (W4)*
1900 Artigiano (NW3)*
1900 Balans (SW5)*
1900 Blakes (SW7)*
1900 Brinkley's (SW10)*
1900 Friends (SW10)*
1900 Frontline (W2)*
1900 La Famiglia (SW10)*
1905 Almeida (N1)*
1906 Ritz (W1)*
1910 Goring Din. Rm. (SW1)*
1911 Bibendum (SW3)*
1911 Bibendum Oyster (SW3)*
1913 Bertorelli (WC2)*
1920 Bloom's (NW11)
1920 Orso (WC2)*
1920 Tamarind (W1)*
1921 Wolseley (W1)*
1923 Bluebird Brass. (SW3)*
1926 Pat. Valerie (W1)
1926 Veeraswamy (W1)
1927 L'Escargot (W1)
1927 Quo Vadis (W1)
1928 Manzi's (WC2)
1931 Grill Room, The (W1)
1930 Sonny's (SW13)*
1933 Sartoria (W1)*
1935 Bistrotheque (E2)*
1935 Lee Ho Fook (W1)*
1939 Geales Fish (W8)

1942 French House (W1)*
1942 Mon Plaisir (WC2)
1946 Daquise (SW7)
1946 Le Caprice (SW1)
1948 Lansdowne (NW1)*
1950 Fortnum's Fountain (W1)
1952 Star of India (SW5)
1953 Gay Hussar (W1)
1953 Guinea Grill (W1)
1954 Troubadour (SW5)
1955 Bertorelli (W1)
1955 Brass. St. Quentin (SW3)*

Hotel Dining

Apex City of London Hotel
    Addendum (EC3)
Baglioni
    Brunello (SW7)
Bentley Hotel
    1880 (SW7)
Berkeley Hotel
    Boxwood Café (SW1)
    Pétrus (SW1)
Blakes Hotel
    Blakes (SW7)
Brown's Hotel
    Grill, The (W1)
Capital Hotel
    Capital (SW3)
City Inn
    City Café (SW1)
Claridge's Hotel
    Gordon Ramsay/Claridge's
    (W1)
Cliveden House Hotel
    Cliveden House (Berks)
Connaught Hotel
    Angela Hartnett's (W1)
Crowne Plaza
    Refettorio (EC4)
Crowne Plaza London St. James
    Hotel
    Quilon (SW1)
Cumberland Hotel
    Rhodes W1 (W1)
Dorchester Hotel
    China Tang (W1)
    Grill Room, The (W1)
Four Seasons Canary Wharf
    Quadrato (E14)

Four Seasons Hotel
Lanes (W1)
French Horn Hotel
French Horn (Berks)
Gore Hotel
Bistrot 190 (SW7)
Goring Hotel
Goring Din. Rm. (SW1)
Gravetye Manor
Gravetye Manor (W. Sus)
Great Eastern Hotel
Aurora (EC2)
Terminus (EC2)
Halkin Hotel
Nahm (SW1)
Hempel Hotel
I-Thai (W2)
Hyatt Regency
Locanda Locatelli (W1)
Jumeirah Carlton Tower Hotel
La Noisette (SW1)
Rib Room (SW1)
Kings Cross Holiday Inn
Rasa (WC1)
Lanesborough
Lanesborough (SW1)
Le Manoir aux Quat'Saisons
Le Manoir/Quat (Oxon)
London Hilton on Park Ln.
Galvin/Windows (W1)
Malmaison Hotel
Malmaison Hotel (EC1)
Mandarin Oriental Hyde Park
Foliage (SW1)
Park, The (SW1)
Manzi's Hotel
Manzi's (WC2)
Metropolitan Hotel
Nobu London (W1)
Millennium Hotel Mayfair
Brian Turner (W1)
Millennium Knightsbridge Hotel
Mju (SW1)
One Aldwych Hotel
Axis (WC2)
Indigo (WC2)
Park Lane Hotel
Citrus (W1)
Petersham Hotel
Petersham (Richmond)

Renaissance Chancery Court
Pearl (WC1)
Ritz Hotel
Ritz (W1)
Royal Lancaster Hotel
Island Rest. (W2)
Sanderson Hotel
Spoon (W1)
Savoy Hotel
Banquette (WC2)
Savoy Grill (WC2)
Sheraton Park Tower
One-O-One (SW1)
Sofitel St. James London
Brasserie Roux (SW1)
St. Martin's Lane Hotel
Asia de Cuba (WC2)
Thistle Hotel
Chez Gérard (SW1)
Threadneedles Hotel
Bonds (EC2)
Vineyard at Stockcross
Vineyard/Stockcross (Berks)
Waterside Inn
Waterside Inn (Berks)
Zetter
Zetter (EC1)

Late Dining
(Weekday closing hour)
Amici/Italian Kitchen (SW17)
  (12 AM)
Annex 3 (W1) (12 AM)
Asia de Cuba (WC2) (varies)
Automat (W1) (1 AM)
Avenue (SW1) (12 AM)
Balans (multi. loc.) (varies)
Banquette (WC2) (12 AM)
Beiteddine (SW1) (12 AM)
Bentley's (W1) (12 AM)
Blakes (SW7) (12 AM)
Blue Elephant (SW6) (12 AM)
Buona Sera (multi. loc.) (12 AM)
Café Lazeez (SW7) (varies)
Cafe Pacifico (WC2) (12 AM)
Cecconi's (W1) (12 AM)
Chelsea Bun (SW10) (12 AM)
Chuen Cheng Ku (W1) (12 AM)
Circus (W1) (12 AM)
Cocoon (W1) (varies)
ECapital (W1) (12 AM)

Efes Kebab (W1) (12 AM)
Electric Brasserie (W11) (1 AM)
Fakhreldine (W1) (12 AM)
Floridita (W1) (1 AM)
1492 (SW6) (12 AM)
Friends (SW10) (12 AM)
Gaucho Grill (NW3) (12 AM)
Gilgamesh (NW1) (12 AM)
Hakkasan (W1) (12 AM)
Halepi (W2) (12 AM)
Hard Rock Cafe (W1) (12:30 AM)
Harlem (W2) (1 AM)
Haz (E1) (12 AM)
Imperial China (WC2) (12 AM)
Ishbilia (SW1) (12 AM)
Ishtar (W1) (12 AM)
Ivy (WC2) (12 AM)
Iznik (N5) (12 AM)
Joe Allen (WC2) (12:45 AM)
J. Sheekey (WC2) (12 AM)
Julie's (W11) (varies)
Kandoo (W2) (12 AM)
Kettners (W1) (1 AM)
La Porchetta (multi. loc.) (12 AM)
Le Café du Jardin (WC2) (12 AM)
Le Caprice (SW1) (12 AM)
Le Deuxième (WC2) (12 AM)
Lee Ho Fook (W1) (12 AM)
Le Mercury (N1) (1 AM)
Levant (W1) (1 AM)
Little Bay (multi. loc.) (12 AM)
Little Italy (W1) (4 AM)
Lou Pescadou (SW5) (12 AM)
L-Restaurant (W8) (12 AM)
Maroush (multi. loc.) (varies)
Meza (W1) (varies)
Mint Leaf (SW1) (12 AM)
Moti Mahal (WC2) (12 AM)
Mr. Chow (SW1) (12 AM)
Mr. Kong (WC2) (2:45 AM)
Naked Turtle (SW14) (12 AM)
New World (W1) (12 AM)
Nobu Berkeley (W1) (1 AM)
Noura (multi. loc.) (varies)
OCCO (W14) (12 AM)
Original Lah. Kebab (multi. loc.) (12 AM)
Orso (WC2) (12 AM)
Ozer (W1) (12 AM)
Papillon (SW3) (12 AM)

Ping Pong (multi. loc.) (12 AM)
Pizza Express (multi. loc.) (varies)
Pizza Pomodoro (SW3) (varies)
PJ's B&G (WC2) (varies)
Planet Hollywood (W1) (1 AM)
Quaglino's (SW1) (12 AM)
Randall & Aubin (SW10) (12 AM)
Sam's Brass. (W4) (12:30 AM)
Saran Rom (SW6) (12 AM)
Scalini (SW3) (12 AM)
Sofra (W1) (12 AM)
Soho Spice (W1) (varies)
Souk (WC2) (12 AM)
Spago (SW7) (12 AM)
Sugar Hut (SW6) (12:30 AM)
Sugar Reef (W1) (1 AM)
Taman gang (W1) (1 AM)
Thai Square (multi. loc.) (varies)
Tokyo Diner (WC2) (12 AM)
Troubadour (SW5) (12 AM)
Vingt-Quatre (SW10) (24 hrs.)
Wolseley (W1) (12 AM)

Noteworthy Newcomers

Addendum (EC3)
Agni (W6)
All Star Lanes (WC1)
Anakana (EC1)
Annex 3 (W1)
Arbutus (W1)
Astor Bar & Grill (W1)
Automat (W1)
Awana (SW3)
Babalou (SW2)
Bar Shu (W1)
Beauberry House (SE21)
Bentley's (W1)
Bountiful Cow (WC1)
Bull, The (N6)
Canteen (E1)
China Tang (W1)
City Café (SW1)
Comptoir Gascon (EC1)
Dans Le Noir (EC1)
Dine (EC4)
Dune (SW1)
11 Abingdon Rd. (W8)
Entrecote Café (W1)
Fire & Stone (WC2)

Fish Hook (W4)
Franco's (SW1)
Galvin/Windows (W1)
Galvin Bistrot (W1)
Gilgamesh (NW1)
Grill, The (W1)
Hosteria del Pesce (SW6)
Imli (W1)
Isarn (N1)
Ladurée (SW1)
La Noisette (SW1)
Le Relais de Venise (W1)
Living Room, The (W1)
L-Restaurant (W8)
Luciano (SW1)
Moti Mahal (WC2)
National Dining Rooms (WC2)
Nobu Berkeley (W1)
Nozomi (SW3)
Obika (W1)
Origin (WC2)
Pacific Bar & Grill (W6)
Papillon (SW3)
Pigalle Club (W1)
Rhodes W1 (W1)
Roast (SE1)
Royal China Club (W1)
Saki Bar/Food (EC1)
Sam's Brass. (W4)
Saran Rom (SW6)
Tamesa@oxo (SE1)
Thomas Cubitt (SW1)
Upstairs Bar/Rest. (SW2)
Volt (SW1)
White Hart (SE11)
Yakitoria (W2)

Offbeat

Albannach (WC2)
All Star Lanes (WC1)
Alounak (multi. loc.)
Annex 3 (W1)
Annie's (multi. loc.)
Aperitivo (W1)
Archipelago (W1)
Arkansas Cafe (E1)
Asia de Cuba (WC2)
Baker & Spice (multi. loc.)
Belgo (multi. loc.)
Benihana (multi. loc.)
Bierodrome (multi. loc.)

Blah! Blah! Blah! (W12)
Bloom's (NW11)
Blue Elephant (SW6)
Boisdale (multi. loc.)
Books for Cooks (W11)
Cambio de Tercio (SW5)
Chor Bizarre (W1)
Chowki Bar (W1)
Club Gascon (EC1)
Cocoon (W1)
Costas Grill (W8)
Crazy Bear (W1)
Crazy Homies (W2)
Cru (N1)
Dans Le Noir (EC1)
Daquise (SW7)
Dish Dash (SW12)
Fat Duck (Berks)
ffiona's (W8)
Fifteen (N1)
FishWorks (W4)
Food for Thought (WC2)
Gilgamesh (NW1)
Hoxton Apprentice (N1)
Inaho (W2)
itsu (multi. loc.)
Jenny Lo's Tea Hse. (SW1)
Jim Thompson's (multi. loc.)
Kulu Kulu Sushi (multi. loc.)
La Fromagerie (W1)
La Porte des Indes (W1)
Le Cercle (SW1)
Les Trois Garçons (E1)
Levant (W1)
Levantine (W2)
LMNT (E8)
Lola's (N1)
Lucky 7 (W2)
Maggie Jones's (W8)
Mju (SW1)
Momo (W1)
Moro (EC1)
Moshi Moshi (EC2)
Nahm (SW1)
Nautilus Fish (NW6)
Obika (W1)
Ottolenghi (multi. loc.)
Petersham Nurseries
   (Richmond)
Pizza Metro (SW11)

Providores/Tapa (W1)
Quality Chop Hse. (EC1)
Rainforest Cafe (W1)
Randall & Aubin (W1)
Ransome's Dock (SW11)
Rasoi Vineet Bhatia (SW3)
Real Greek (EC1)
Richard Corrigan (W1)
Rivington Grill (EC2)
Sabor (N1)
Sale e Pepe (SW1)
Sketch/Gallery (W1)
Solly's (NW11)
Souk (WC2)
Spoon (W1)
St. John (EC1)
St. John Bread/Wine (E1)
Tapas Brindisa (SE1)
Taqueria (W11)
Tate Britain Restaurant (SW1)
Tom's Deli (W11)
Troubadour (SW5)
Truc Vert (W1)
Tsunami (SW4)
Wagamama (multi. loc.)
Wapping Food (E1)
YO! Sushi (multi. loc.)

Outdoor Dining

(G=garden; P=patio;
PV=pavement; T=terrace;
W=waterside)
Abbeville (SW4) (PV)
Abingdon (W8) (PV)
Admiral Codrington (SW3) (P)
Al Hamra (W1) (P)
Anglesea Arms (W6) (P)
Archipelago (W1) (P)
Ark (W8) (T)
Arkansas Cafe (E1) (PV)
Artigiano (NW3) (PV)
Aubaine (SW3) (PV)
Babylon (W8) (T)
Balham Kitchen (SW12) (PV)
Bam-Bou (W1) (T)
Bank Westminster (SW1) (T)
Belvedere (W8) (T)
Berkeley Square (W1) (P)
Blandford St. (W1) (T)
Blueprint Café (SE1) (T,W)
Brackenbury (W6) (P)

Brian Turner (W1) (P)
Brunello (SW7) (T)
Builders Arms (SW3) (PV)
Butlers Wharf (SE1) (P,W)
Cantina del Ponte (SE1) (P,W)
Canyon (Richmond) (T,W)
Caraffini (SW1) (PV)
Casale Franco (N1) (P)
Chez Kristof (W6) (T)
Coq d'Argent (EC2) (G,T)
Eagle (EC1) (PV)
e&o (W11) (PV)
Edera (W11) (P)
Elistano (SW3) (PV)
Embassy (W1) (P)
Engineer (NW1) (G)
Fifth Floor Cafe (SW1) (T)
fish! (SE1) (T)
FishWorks (W4) (G)
Hard Rock Cafe (W1) (T)
Hoxton Apprentice (N1) (T)
Hush (W1) (P)
Inn The Park (SW1) (T)
Ishbilia (SW1) (PV)
Joe's (SW3) (PV)
Julie's (W11) (P,PV)
Kandoo (W2) (G)
La Famiglia (SW10) (G)
La Poule au Pot (SW1) (P)
La Trompette (W4) (T)
L'Aventure (NW8) (T)
Le Colombier (SW3) (T)
Ledbury (W11) (P)
Le Pont de la Tour (SE1) (P,W)
Locanda Ottoemezzo (W8) (PV)
L'Oranger (SW1) (P)
Lundum's (SW7) (T)
Made in Italy (SW3) (T)
Manicomio (SW3) (P)
Mediterraneo (W11) (PV)
Mildreds (W1) (PV)
Mirabelle (W1) (P)
Momo (W1) (T)
Monza (SW3) (PV)
Moro (EC1) (PV)
Motcombs (SW1) (PV)
Notting Grill (W11) (T)
OCCO (W14) (PV)
Odette's (NW1) (G,PV)

Oriel (SW1) (PV)
Orrery (W1) (T)
Osteria Antica (SW11) (PV)
Osteria Basilico (W11) (P)
Oxo Tower (SE1) (T,W)
Oxo Tower Brass. (SE1) (T,W)
Ozer (W1) (PV)
Painted Heron (multi. loc.) (G,T)
Passione (W1) (P)
Pellicano (SW3) (PV)
Petersham (Richmond) (T)
PJ's B&G (WC2) (PV)
Plateau (E14) (T)
Porters (WC2) (PV)
Quadrato (E14) (T)
Ransome's Dock (SW11) (T)
Real Greek (multi. loc.) (PV)
Riccardo's (SW3) (P)
Ritz (W1) (T)
River Café (W6) (P)
Rocket (multi. loc.) (PV,T,W)
Roka (W1) (PV)
Rosmarino (NW8) (T)
Santini (SW1) (T)
Smiths/Top Floor (EC1) (T)
Spoon (W1) (G,P)
Texas Embassy (SW1) (PV)
Tom's Deli (W11) (G)
Toto's (SW3) (G)
202 (W11) (G,PV)
Uli (W11) (P)
Vama (SW10) (P)
Villandry (W1) (PV)
Vineyard/Stockcross (Berks) (T,W)
Wapping Food (E1) (G,P)
Westbourne (W2) (T)

People-Watching

Admiral Codrington (SW3)
All Star Lanes (WC1)
Amaya (SW1)
Angela Hartnett's (W1)
Asia de Cuba (WC2)
Aubaine (SW3)
Avenue (SW1)
Bam-Bou (W1)
Bar Shu (W1)
Bellamy's (W1)
Belvedere (W8)
Bibendum (SW3)
Bibendum Oyster (SW3)
Blakes (SW7)
Boxwood Café (SW1)
Caraffini (SW1)
Carpaccio (SW3)
Cecconi's (W1)
China Tang (W1)
Christopher's (WC2)
Cinnamon Club (SW1)
Cipriani (W1)
Circus (W1)
Club Gascon (EC1)
Daphne's (SW3)
Drones (SW1)
e&o (W11)
Eight Over Eight (SW3)
Electric Brasserie (W11)
Fifteen (N1)
Fino (W1)
Frankie's Italian (multi. loc.)
Galvin/Windows (W1)
Galvin Bistrot (W1)
Gilgamesh (NW1)
Gordon Ramsay/Claridge's (W1)
Gordon Ramsay/68 Royal (SW3)
Grill, The (W1)
Hakkasan (W1)
Hush (W1)
Ivy (WC2)
Joe's (SW3)
J. Sheekey (WC2)
Kensington Pl. (W8)
La Famiglia (SW10)
Langan's Bistro (W1)
Langan's Brasserie (W1)
La Trompette (W4)
Le Caprice (SW1)
Le Cercle (SW1)
Ledbury (W11)
Locanda Locatelli (W1)
Luciano (SW1)
Lucio (SW3)
Manicomio (SW3)
Maze (W1)
Mirabelle (W1)
Momo (W1)
Nicole's (W1)
Nobu Berkeley (W1)
Nobu London (W1)
Orso (WC2)

Papillon (SW3)
Pétrus (SW1)
Pigalle Club (W1)
PJ's B&G (SW3)
Racine (SW3)
Riccardo's (SW3)
River Café (W6)
Roka (W1)
Roundhouse Café (NW1)
San Lorenzo (SW3)
Santini (SW1)
Savoy Grill (WC2)
Sketch/Gallery (W1)
Sketch/Lecture Rm. (W1)
Smiths/Dining Rm. (EC1)
Sophie's Steak (SW10)
Sotheby's Cafe (W1)
Spoon (W1)
Sumosan (W1)
Tartine (SW3)
Tom Aikens (SW3)
Tom's Deli (W11)
202 (W11)
Ubon by Nobu (E14)
Vingt-Quatre (SW10)
Volt (SW1)
Waterside Inn (Berks)
Wilton's (SW1)
Wolseley (W1)
Yauatcha (W1)
Zafferano (SW1)
Zetter (EC1)
Zuma (SW7)

Power Scenes
Angela Hartnett's (W1)
Aurora (EC2)
Avenue (SW1)
Bank Aldwych (WC2)
Belvedere (W8)
Bentley's (W1)
Blueprint Café (SE1)
Boxwood Café (SW1)
Caravaggio (EC3)
China Tang (W1)
Cinnamon Club (SW1)
Cipriani (W1)
Circus (W1)
Club Gascon (EC1)
Daphne's (SW3)
Drones (SW1)

Gordon Ramsay/Claridge's (W1)
Gordon Ramsay/68 Royal (SW3)
Goring Din. Rm. (SW1)
Greenhouse (W1)
Green's (SW1)
Grill, The (W1)
Ivy (WC2)
J. Sheekey (WC2)
Lanes (W1)
Langan's Brasserie (W1)
Launceston Place (W8)
Le Caprice (SW1)
Ledbury (W11)
Le Gavroche (W1)
Le Manoir/Quat (Oxon)
Le Pont de la Tour (SE1)
L'Incontro (SW1)
Luciano (SW1)
Maze (W1)
Mirabelle (W1)
Nahm (SW1)
Neal Street (WC2)
Nobu London (W1)
1 Lombard St. (EC3)
Pétrus (SW1)
Prism (EC3)
Quirinale (SW1)
Rhodes 24 (EC2)
Ritz (W1)
San Lorenzo (SW3)
Savoy Grill (WC2)
Shepherd's (SW1)
Sketch/Lecture Rm. (W1)
Spoon (W1)
Square (W1)
Tom Aikens (SW3)
Umu (W1)
Waterside Inn (Berks)
Wilton's (SW1)
Wolseley (W1)
Zafferano (SW1)
Zuma (SW7)

Pre-Theatre Menus
(Call for prices and times)
Al Duca (SW1)
Almeida (N1)
Angela Hartnett's (W1)
Arbutus (W1)
Asia de Cuba (WC2)
Axis (WC2)

Special Features

Baltic (SE1)
Bank Westminster (SW1)
Benares (W1)
Brasserie Roux (SW1)
Brass. St. Quentin (SW3)
Christopher's (WC2)
Cinnamon Club (SW1)
Clos Maggiore (WC2)
Cocoon (W1)
Dune (SW1)
Gordon Ramsay/Claridge's (W1)
Goring Din. Rm. (SW1)
Grill, The (W1)
Indigo (WC2)
Joe Allen (WC2)
J. Sheekey (WC2)
La Bouchée (SW7)
La Trouvaille (W1)
Le Café du Jardin (WC2)
Le Deuxième (WC2)
L'Escargot (W1)
L'Estaminet (WC2)
L'Etranger (SW7)
Lola's (N1)
Matsuri (SW1)
Mint Leaf (SW1)
Mon Plaisir (WC2)
Neal Street (WC2)
Origin (WC2)
Orso (WC2)
Oxo Tower Brass. (SE1)
Porters (WC2)
Quaglino's (SW1)
Quo Vadis (W1)
Racine (SW3)
Red Fort (W1)
Richard Corrigan (W1)
Ritz (W1)
R.S.J. (SE1)
Savoy Grill (WC2)
Veeraswamy (W1)
Villandry (W1)
Zaika (W8)

Private Rooms

(Call for capacity)
Admiralty (WC2)
Alastair Little (W1)
Albannach (WC2)
Alloro (W1)
All Star Lanes (WC1)
Almeida (N1)

Amaya (SW1)
Angela Hartnett's (W1)
Arkansas Cafe (E1)
Asia de Cuba (WC2)
Babylon (W8)
Baltic (SE1)
Bam-Bou (W1)
Belgo (WC2)
Belvedere (W8)
Benares (W1)
Benihana (multi. loc.)
Bentley's (W1)
Berkeley Square (W1)
Blakes (SW7)
Blue Elephant (SW6)
Bodeans (W1)
Bombay Bicycle (multi. loc.)
Boxwood Café (SW1)
Brasserie Roux (SW1)
Brian Turner (W1)
Brunello (SW7)
Cambio de Tercio (SW5)
Cantina Vinopolis (SE1)
Capital (SW3)
Chez Bruce (SW17)
Chez Kristof (W6)
China Tang (W1)
Christopher's (WC2)
Chuen Cheng Ku (W1)
Chutney Mary (SW10)
Chutney's (NW1)
Cinnamon Club (SW1)
Cipriani (W1)
Circus (W1)
Clerkenwell (EC1)
Cocoon (W1)
Cru (N1)
Daphne's (SW3)
Drones (SW1)
e&o (W11)
Edera (W11)
1802 (E14)
Eight Over Eight (SW3)
Embassy (W1)
Fairuz (W1)
Farm (SW6)
Floridita (W1)
Franco's (SW1)
French Horn (Berks)
Gordon Ramsay/Claridge's (W1)
Gravetye Manor (W. Sus)

Greenhouse (W1)
Green's (SW1)
Greyhound (SW11)
Guinea Grill (W1)
Hakkasan (W1)
Hard Rock Cafe (W1)
Hush (W1)
Il Convivio (SW1)
Ishbilia (SW1)
I-Thai (W2)
itsu (multi. loc.)
Ivy (WC2)
Julie's (W11)
Just St. James's (SW1)
Kai Mayfair (W1)
Kensington Pl. (W8)
La Porte des Indes (W1)
La Poule au Pot (SW1)
La Trouvaille (multi. loc.)
Launceston Place (W8)
Le Cercle (SW1)
Le Colombier (SW3)
Le Manoir/Quat (Oxon)
Le Pont de la Tour (SE1)
L'Escargot (W1)
L'Estaminet (WC2)
Les Trois Garçons (E1)
Le Suquet (SW3)
L'Etranger (SW7)
L'Incontro (SW1)
Lola's (N1)
L'Oranger (SW1)
Lundum's (SW7)
Made in Italy (SW3)
Malmaison Hotel (EC1)
Manicomio (SW3)
Mao Tai (SW6)
Masala Zone (multi. loc.)
Matsuri (multi. loc.)
Memories/China (multi. loc.)
Metrogusto (N1)
Mimmo d'Ischia (SW1)
Mint Leaf (SW1)
Mirabelle (W1)
Mitsukoshi (SW1)
Momo (W1)
Mon Plaisir (WC2)
Montpeliano (SW7)
Morgan M (N7)
Motcombs (SW1)
Mr. Chow (SW1)

Nahm (SW1)
Neal Street (WC2)
Nobu London (W1)
Notting Grill (W11)
Notting Hill Brass. (W11)
Noura (multi. loc.)
Nyonya (W11)
1 Lombard St. (EC3)
1 Lombard Brass. (EC3)
One-O-One (SW1)
Origin (WC2)
Palmerston (SE22)
Pasha (SW7)
Passione (W1)
Patara (multi. loc.)
Patterson's (W1)
Pearl (WC1)
Pellicano (SW3)
Pétrus (SW1)
Pied à Terre (W1)
Plateau (E14)
Poissonnerie (SW3)
Prism (EC3)
Quaglino's (SW1)
Quo Vadis (W1)
Rainforest Cafe (W1)
Rasa (multi. loc.)
Rasoi Vineet Bhatia (SW3)
Real Greek (multi. loc.)
Rib Room (SW1)
Richard Corrigan (W1)
Ritz (W1)
Rivington Grill (EC2)
Rocket (multi. loc.)
Roussillon (SW1)
Royal China (multi. loc.)
Royal Exchange (EC3)
Rules (WC2)
San Lorenzo (SW19)
Santini (SW1)
Sarkhel's (multi. loc.)
Sartoria (W1)
Savoy Grill (WC2)
Shepherd's (SW1)
Six-13 (W1)
Smiths/Dining Rm. (EC1)
Smiths/Top Floor (EC1)
Solly's (NW11)
Square (W1)
Star of India (SW5)
St. John (EC1)

Sumosan (W1)
Tatsuso (EC2)
Tentazioni (SE1)
Texas Embassy (SW1)
Thai Square (multi. loc.)
Thomas Cubitt (SW1)
Timo (W8)
Vasco & Piero's (W1)
Veeraswamy (W1)
Villandry (W1)
Vineyard/Stockcross (Berks)
Vivat Bacchus (EC4)
Waterside Inn (Berks)
Wells (NW3)
White Hart (SE11)
White Swan (EC4)
Wilton's (SW1)
Wòdka (W8)
Ye Olde Cheshire (EC4)
Zafferano (SW1)
Zetter (EC1)
Zuma (SW7)

Pudding Specialists

Alastair Little (W1)
Almeida (N1)
Amaya (SW1)
Angela Hartnett's (W1)
Asia de Cuba (WC2)
Aubaine (SW3)
Aubergine (SW10)
Aurora (EC2)
Baker & Spice (multi. loc.)
Belvedere (W8)
Bibendum Oyster (SW3)
Blakes (SW7)
Boxwood Café (SW1)
Capital (SW3)
Chez Bruce (SW17)
Cipriani (W1)
Clarke's (W8)
Club Gascon (EC1)
Embassy (W1)
Fat Duck (Berks)
Fifth Floor (SW1)
Foliage (SW1)
Fortnum's Fountain (W1)
Galvin/Windows (W1)
Galvin Bistrot (W1)
Glasshouse (Kew)
Gordon Ramsay/Claridge's (W1)
Gordon Ramsay/68 Royal (SW3)

Greenhouse (W1)
Ladurée (SW1)
Lanes (W1)
Lanesborough (SW1)
La Trompette (W4)
Le Cercle (SW1)
Ledbury (W11)
Le Gavroche (W1)
Le Manoir/Quat (Oxon)
Locanda Locatelli (W1)
L'Oranger (SW1)
Maze (W1)
Mirabelle (W1)
Nobu Berkeley (W1)
Nobu London (W1)
Origin (WC2)
Orrery (W1)
Ottolenghi (multi. loc.)
Pat. Valerie (multi. loc.)
Pétrus (SW1)
Pied à Terre (W1)
Plateau (E14)
Providores/Tapa (W1)
Rasoi Vineet Bhatia (SW3)
Richard Corrigan (W1)
Richoux (multi. loc.)
Ritz (W1)
River Café (W6)
Savoy Grill (WC2)
Sketch/Gallery (W1)
Sketch/Lecture Rm. (W1)
Spoon (W1)
Square (W1)
Tom Aikens (SW3)
Ubon by Nobu (E14)
Waterside Inn (Berks)
Wolseley (W1)
W'Sens (SW1)
Yauatcha (W1)
Zafferano (SW1)
Zuma (SW7)

Quiet Conversation

Addendum (EC3)
Al Sultan (W1)
Arbutus (W1)
Aubergine (SW10)
Aurora (EC2)
Axis (WC2)
Banquette (WC2)
Beauberry House (SE21)
Benares (W1)

Bengal Clipper (SE1)
Berkeley Square (W1)
Blakes (SW7)
Brian Turner (W1)
Capital (SW3)
Dine (EC4)
1880 (SW7)
Embassy (W1)
Foliage (SW1)
Goring Din. Rm. (SW1)
Green's (SW1)
Hosteria del Pesce (SW6)
Il Convivio (SW1)
Indigo (WC2)
La Genova (W1)
Lanes (W1)
Lanesborough (SW1)
Launceston Place (W8)
Le Gavroche (W1)
Le Manoir/Quat (Oxon)
L'Oranger (SW1)
L-Restaurant (W8)
Lundum's (SW7)
Mitsukoshi (SW1)
Mju (SW1)
Morel (SW4)
Nahm (SW1)
Odin's (W1)
One-O-One (SW1)
Orrery (W1)
Park, The (SW1)
Pied à Terre (W1)
Quadrato (E14)
Quirinale (SW1)
Rasoi Vineet Bhatia (SW3)
Rhodes W1 (W1)
Ritz (W1)
Roussillon (SW1)
Saki Bar/Food (EC1)
Salloos (SW1)
Sketch/Lecture Rm. (W1)
Stratford's (W8)
Waterside Inn (Berks)
Wilton's (SW1)

Romantic Places

Amaya (SW1)
Andrew Edmunds (W1)
Angela Hartnett's (W1)
Archipelago (W1)
Aurora (EC2)
Babylon (W8)

Beauberry House (SE21)
Belvedere (W8)
Blakes (SW7)
Blue Elephant (SW6)
Brunello (SW7)
Capital (SW3)
Chez Bruce (SW17)
Chutney Mary (SW10)
Cipriani (W1)
Clarke's (W8)
Club Gascon (EC1)
Crazy Bear (W1)
Daphne's (SW3)
Drones (SW1)
Frederick's (N1)
French Horn (Berks)
Galvin/Windows (W1)
Glasshouse (Kew)
Gordon Ramsay/Claridge's (W1)
Gordon Ramsay/68 Royal (SW3)
Gravetye Manor (W. Sus)
Greenhouse (W1)
Hakkasan (W1)
Julie's (W11)
Lanesborough (SW1)
La Poule au Pot (SW1)
La Trompette (W4)
Launceston Place (W8)
L'Aventure (NW8)
Le Café du Marché (EC1)
Le Caprice (SW1)
Le Cercle (SW1)
Ledbury (W11)
Le Gavroche (W1)
Le Manoir/Quat (Oxon)
Le Pont de la Tour (SE1)
Les Trois Garçons (E1)
Locanda Locatelli (W1)
L'Oranger (SW1)
Lundum's (SW7)
Maggie Jones's (W8)
Mirabelle (W1)
Momo (W1)
Nobu London (W1)
Odette's (NW1)
Odin's (W1)
Orrery (W1)
Pétrus (SW1)
Pigalle Club (W1)
Prism (EC3)
Rasoi Vineet Bhatia (SW3)

Richard Corrigan (W1)
Ritz (W1)
River Café (W6)
Roussillon (SW1)
San Lorenzo (SW3)
Sketch/Lecture Rm. (W1)
Snows on Green (W6)
Square (W1)
Tom Aikens (SW3)
Toto's (SW3)
Veeraswamy (W1)
Waterside Inn (Berks)
Zafferano (SW1)
Zuma (SW7)

Senior Appeal

Al Duca (SW1)
Amaya (SW1)
Angela Hartnett's (W1)
Arbutus (W1)
Aubaine (SW3)
Aubergine (SW10)
Beauberry House (SE21)
Bellamy's (W1)
Belvedere (W8)
Bentley's (W1)
Berkeley Square (W1)
Bibendum (SW3)
Bloom's (NW11)
Bonds (EC2)
Boxwood Café (SW1)
Brasserie Roux (SW1)
Brass. St. Quentin (SW3)
Brian Turner (W1)
Capital (SW3)
Cecconi's (W1)
China Tang (W1)
Cipriani (W1)
Citrus (W1)
Cliveden House (Berks)
Dine (EC4)
Drones (SW1)
Elena's l'Etoile (W1)
11 Abingdon Rd. (W8)
Entrecote Café (W1)
Foliage (SW1)
Fortnum's Fountain (W1)
Franco's (SW1)
Galvin/Windows (W1)
Galvin Bistrot (W1)
Glasshouse (Kew)

Gordon Ramsay/Claridge's (W1)
Gordon Ramsay/68 Royal (SW3)
Goring Din. Rm. (SW1)
Gravetye Manor (W. Sus)
Greenhouse (W1)
Green's (SW1)
Grill, The (W1)
Grill Room, The (W1)
Hosteria del Pesce (SW6)
Ivy (WC2)
J. Sheekey (WC2)
Kai Mayfair (W1)
Ladurée (SW1)
La Genova (W1)
Lanes (W1)
Lanesborough (SW1)
Langan's Bistro (W1)
La Poule au Pot (SW1)
Launceston Place (W8)
Le Caprice (SW1)
Ledbury (W11)
Le Gavroche (W1)
Le Manoir/Quat (Oxon)
Le Suquet (SW3)
L'Etranger (SW7)
L'Incontro (SW1)
Locanda Locatelli (W1)
L'Oranger (SW1)
Luciano (SW1)
Lundum's (SW7)
Manzi's (WC2)
Mimmo d'Ischia (SW1)
Mirabelle (W1)
Montpeliano (SW7)
Morel (SW4)
Motcombs (SW1)
Neal Street (WC2)
Noura (multi. loc.)
Odin's (W1)
One-O-One (SW1)
Origin (WC2)
Orrery (W1)
Papillon (SW3)
Park, The (SW1)
Pat. Valerie (multi. loc.)
Pétrus (SW1)
Poissonnerie (SW3)
Quadrato (E14)
Quirinale (SW1)
Racine (SW3)

Red Fort (W1)
Reubens (W1)
Rib Room (SW1)
Richoux (multi. loc.)
Ritz (W1)
Riva (SW13)
Roast (SE1)
Rosmarino (NW8)
Rowley's (SW1)
Rules (WC2)
Santini (SW1)
Sartoria (W1)
Savoy Grill (WC2)
Scalini (SW3)
Shepherd's (SW1)
Simpson's (WC2)
Sketch/Lecture Rm. (W1)
Sotheby's Cafe (W1)
Square (W1)
Stratford's (W8)
Tate Britain Restaurant (SW1)
Tom Aikens (SW3)
Toto's (SW3)
Waterside Inn (Berks)
Wilton's (SW1)
Wolseley (W1)
Zafferano (SW1)
Zen Central (W1)

Set-Price Menus

(Call for prices and times)
Abingdon (W8)
Alastair Little (W1)
Albannach (WC2)
Al Duca (SW1)
Alloro (W1)
Almeida (N1)
Amaya (SW1)
Angela Hartnett's (W1)
Anglesea Arms (W6)
Asia de Cuba (WC2)
Aubergine (SW10)
Aurora (EC2)
Avenue (SW1)
Axis (WC2)
Baltic (SE1)
Bellamy's (W1)
Belvedere (W8)
Benares (W1)
Bengal Clipper (SE1)
Benihana (multi. loc.)

Berkeley Square (W1)
Bibendum (SW3)
Blue Elephant (SW6)
Boxwood Café (SW1)
Brasserie Roux (SW1)
Brass. St. Quentin (SW3)
Brian Turner (W1)
Brunello (SW7)
Butlers Wharf (SE1)
Café Japan (NW11)
Café Spice Namasté (E1)
Capital (SW3)
Caravaggio (EC3)
Champor (SE1)
Chez Bruce (SW17)
Chez Kristof (W6)
Chor Bizarre (W1)
Christopher's (WC2)
Chutney Mary (SW10)
Cigala (WC1)
Cinnamon Club (SW1)
Cipriani (W1)
Citrus (W1)
Clarke's (W8)
Clerkenwell (EC1)
Club Gascon (EC1)
Cocoon (W1)
Coq d'Argent (EC2)
Crazy Bear (W1)
Deya (W1)
Drones (SW1)
ECapital (W1)
1880 (SW7)
Eight Over Eight (SW3)
El Pirata (W1J)
Embassy (W1)
Enoteca Turi (SW15)
Essenza (W11)
Fakhreldine (W1)
Fat Duck (Berks)
Fifteen (N1)
Fino (W1)
Fish Shop on St. John (EC1)
Foliage (SW1)
French Horn (Berks)
Glasshouse (Kew)
Gordon Ramsay/Claridge's (W1)
Gordon Ramsay/68 Royal (SW3)
Goring Din. Rm. (SW1)
Gravetye Manor (W. Sus)

Special Features

Greenhouse (W1)
Grill Room, The (W1)
Ikeda (W1)
Il Convivio (SW1)
Indigo (WC2)
Ivy (WC2)
Joy King Lau (WC2)
J. Sheekey (WC2)
Kai Mayfair (W1)
Kensington Pl. (W8)
Kiku (W1)
Lanes (W1)
Lanesborough (SW1)
Langan's Bistro (W1)
La Poule au Pot (SW1)
Latium (W1)
La Trompette (W4)
Launceston Place (W8)
L'Aventure (NW8)
Le Boudin Blanc (W1)
Le Café du Marché (EC1)
Le Cercle (SW1)
Le Colombier (SW3)
Le Gavroche (W1)
Le Manoir/Quat (Oxon)
Le Pont de la Tour (SE1)
L'Escargot (W1)
Les Trois Garçons (E1)
Le Suquet (SW3)
L'Etranger (SW7)
L'Incontro (SW1)
Livebait (multi. loc.)
Locanda Ottoemezzo (W8)
Lola's (N1)
L'Oranger (SW1)
Lucio (SW3)
Lundum's (SW7)
Malmaison Hotel (EC1)
Matsuri (multi. loc.)
Maze (W1)
Mela (WC2)
Memories/China (multi. loc.)
Mint Leaf (SW1)
Mirabelle (W1)
Mitsukoshi (SW1)
Motcombs (SW1)
Mr. Chow (SW1)
Neal Street (WC2)
Nobu Berkeley (W1)
Noura (multi. loc.)

Olivo (SW1)
1 Lombard St. (EC3)
One-O-One (SW1)
Orrery (W1)
Oslo Court (NW8)
Oxo Tower (SE1)
Ozer (W1)
Painted Heron (SE11)
Patara (multi. loc.)
Patterson's (W1)
Pellicano (SW3)
Pétrus (SW1)
Pied à Terre (W1)
Plateau (E14)
Poissonnerie (SW3)
Porters (WC2)
Princess Garden (W1)
Quadrato (E14)
Quaglino's (SW1)
Quilon (SW1)
Racine (SW3)
Rasa (multi. loc.)
Rasoi Vineet Bhatia (SW3)
Rib Room (SW1)
Richard Corrigan (W1)
Ritz (W1)
Roka (W1)
Roussillon (SW1)
Royal China (multi. loc.)
Sardo Canale (NW1)
Sarkhel's (multi. loc.)
Sartoria (W1)
Savoy Grill (WC2)
Six-13 (W1)
Sketch/Lecture Rm. (W1)
Snows on Green (W6)
Sonny's (SW13)
Sophie's Steak (SW10)
Square (W1)
Taman gang (W1)
Tamarind (W1)
Tatsuso (EC2)
Tentazioni (SE1)
Tom Aikens (SW3)
Toto's (SW3)
Vasco & Piero's (W1)
Veeraswamy (W1)
Vineyard/Stockcross (Berks)
Waterside Inn (Berks)
Wòdka (W8)

Yoshino (W1)
Zafferano (SW1)
Zaika (W8)
Zen Central (W1)
Ziani (SW3)
Zuma (SW7)

Singles Scenes

Admiral Codrington (SW3)
Albannach (WC2)
Amaya (SW1)
Anakana (EC1)
Annex 3 (W1)
Asia de Cuba (WC2)
Astor Bar & Grill (W1)
Avenue (SW1)
Babalou (SW2)
Balans (multi. loc.)
Bank Aldwych (WC2)
Bank Westminster (SW1)
Belgo (multi. loc.)
Bierodrome (multi. loc.)
Big Easy (SW3)
Bistrot 190 (SW7)
Bluebird Brass. (SW3)
Bluebird Club (SW3)
Bountiful Cow (WC1)
Brinkley's (SW10)
Browns (multi. loc.)
Buona Sera (SW3)
Cafe Pacifico (WC2)
Cantaloupe (EC2)
Cecconi's (W1)
Christopher's (WC2)
Circus (W1)
Cocoon (W1)
Collection (SW3)
Dish Dash (SW12)
Draper's Arms (N1)
Dune (SW1)
e&o (W11)
Ebury Wine Bar (SW1)
Eight Over Eight (SW3)
Engineer (NW1)
Enterprise (SW3)
Fifteen (N1)
Fifth Floor Cafe (SW1)
Fino (W1)
First Floor (W11)
Floridita (W1)
Gilgamesh (NW1)

Hakkasan (W1)
Hush (W1)
Just St. James's (SW1)
Kettners (W1)
La Rueda (multi. loc.)
Le Cercle (SW1)
Living Room, The (W1)
Maroush (multi. loc.)
Maze (W1)
Medcalf (EC1)
Momo (W1)
Moro (EC1)
Motcombs (SW1)
Nam Long-Le Shaker (SW5)
Nobu Berkeley (W1)
Nobu London (W1)
Nozomi (SW3)
Oriel (SW1)
Oxo Tower (SE1)
Oxo Tower Brass. (SE1)
Pacific Bar & Grill (W6)
Ping Pong (multi. loc.)
Pizza on Park (SW1)
PJ's B&G (SW3)
Quaglino's (SW1)
Real Greek (multi. loc.)
Roka (W1)
Sabor (N1)
Saran Rom (SW6)
Sketch/Gallery (W1)
Smiths/Dining Rm. (EC1)
Sophie's Steak (SW10)
Spiga (W1)
Spighetta (W1)
Spoon (W1)
Sticky Fingers (W8)
Sugar Reef (W1)
Sumosan (W1)
Tartine (SW3)
Terminus (EC2)
Texas Embassy (SW1)
Tugga (SW3)
Volt (SW1)
White Hart (SE11)
Zinc B&G (multi. loc.)
Zuma (SW7)

Sleepers
(Good to excellent food, but
little known)
Al Waha (W2)
Banquette (WC2)

Café Japan (NW11)
Chutney's (NW1)
Clos Maggiore (WC2)
Defune (W1)
1880 (SW7)
Enoteca Turi (SW15)
Fiore (SW1)
Four Seasons (W2)
French Horn (Berks)
Gate (W6)
Glasshouse (Kew)
Gravetye Manor (W. Sus)
Ikeda (W1)
Jin Kichi (NW3)
Kiku (W1)
La Fromagerie (W1)
Le Cercle (SW1)
L'Etranger (SW7)
Le Vacherin (W4)
Lucio (SW3)
Mandalay (W2)
Mandarin Kitchen (W2)
Metrogusto (N1)
Michael Moore (W1)
Morgan M (N7)
One-O-One (SW1)
Origin (WC2)
Original Lah. Kebab (multi. loc.)
Oslo Court (NW8)
Pearl (WC1)
Quadrato (E14)
Quilon (SW1)
Quirinale (SW1)
Rhodes 24 (EC2)
Rib Room (SW1)
Riva (SW13)
Roussillon (SW1)
Sakura (W1)
Salloos (SW1)
Santini (SW1)
Sonny's (SW13)
St. John Bread/Wine (E1)
Sumosan (W1)
Tatsuso (EC2)
Tentazioni (SE1)
Tsunami (SW4)
Two Bros. Fish (N3)
Umu (W1)
Vasco & Piero's (W1)
Vineyard/Stockcross (Berks)
Wizzy (SW6)

Smoking: No-Smoking Sections

(Current until 2007 when smoking ban goes into effect)

Abingdon (W8)
Almeida (N1)
Amaya (SW1)
Andrew Edmunds (W1)
Anglesea Arms (W6)
Annie's (W4)
Arkansas Cafe (E1)
Ask Pizza (multi. loc.)
Aubergine (SW10)
Automat (W1)
Balans (multi. loc.)
Balham Kitchen (SW12)
Bankside (SE1)
Barnsbury (N1)
Belgo (WC2)
Ben's Thai (W9)
Berkeley Square (W1)
Bertorelli (multi. loc.)
Big Easy (SW3)
Black & Blue (multi. loc.)
Blandford St. (W1)
Bombay Brasserie (SW7)
Brasserie Roux (SW1)
Brian Turner (W1)
Brinkley's (SW10)
Browns (multi. loc.)
Builders Arms (SW3)
Café des Amis (WC2)
Café Lazeez (SW7)
Café Rouge (multi. loc.)
Café Spice Namasté (E1)
Cantina Vinopolis (SE1)
Canyon (Richmond)
Caraffini (SW1)
Carpaccio (SW3)
Casale Franco (N1)
Chez Gérard (multi. loc.)
Chor Bizarre (W1)
Chowki Bar (W1)
Chuen Cheng Ku (W1)
Churchill Arms (W8)
Chutney Mary (SW10)
City Café (SW1)
Clerkenwell (EC1)
Como Lario (SW1)
Daphne's (SW3)
Daquise (SW7)

Defune (W1)
Dim t (multi. loc.)
Dish Dash (SW12)
Don (EC4)
11 Abingdon Rd. (W8)
Enoteca Turi (SW15)
Esarn Kheaw (W12)
Eyre Brothers (EC2)
Fifth Floor Cafe (SW1)
Fiore (SW1)
fish! (SE1)
Fish Shop on St. John (EC1)
1492 (SW6)
Franco's (SW1)
Frederick's (N1)
Getti (multi. loc.)
Ginger (W2)
Giovanni's (WC2)
Grill, The (W1)
Ikkyu (W1)
Indigo (WC2)
Ishbilia (SW1)
Ishtar (W1)
I-Thai (W2)
Jade Garden (W1)
Jim Thompson's (multi. loc.)
Joe Allen (WC2)
Kettners (W1)
Khan's (W2)
Khan's/Kensington (SW7)
La Famiglia (SW10)
Lanes (W1)
Lanesborough (SW1)
La Porchetta (multi. loc.)
Lee Ho Fook (W1)
Le Relais de Venise (W1)
L'Estaminet (WC2)
Little Italy (W1)
Livebait (multi. loc.)
Locanda Ottoemezzo (W8)
Lola's (N1)
Lou Pescadou (SW5)
Malabar Junction (WC1)
Mango Tree (SW1)
Mao Tai (SW6)
Maroush (multi. loc.)
Matsuri (WC1)
Mela (WC2)
Metrogusto (N1)
Meza (W1)
Mitsukoshi (SW1)

Mon Plaisir (WC2)
Motcombs (SW1)
Nautilus Fish (NW6)
New Culture Rev. (multi. loc.)
New World (W1)
Nicole's (W1)
Nobu London (W1)
Notting Grill (W11)
Nozomi (SW3)
Odin's (W1)
One-O-One (SW1)
Oriel (SW1)
Original Tagine (W1)
Orrery (W1)
Orso (WC2)
Osteria dell'Arancio (SW10)
Painted Heron (multi. loc.)
Palmerston (SE22)
Park, The (SW1)
Patara (multi. loc.)
Pat. Valerie (multi. loc.)
Patterson's (W1)
Pescatori (W1)
Phoenix Palace (NW1)
Pizza Express (multi. loc.)
Pizza on Park (SW1)
Pizza Pomodoro (multi. loc.)
PJ's B&G (WC2)
Planet Hollywood (W1)
Portal (EC1)
Porters (WC2)
Prince Bonaparte (W2)
Quadrato (E14)
Randall & Aubin (SW10)
Rasa (WC1)
Real Greek (SE1)
Reubens (W1)
Rhodes W1 (W1)
Richoux (multi. loc.)
Rodizio Rico (multi. loc.)
Rosmarino (NW8)
Royal China (multi. loc.)
Royal China Club (W1)
Rudland & Stubbs (EC1)
Sabor (N1)
San Lorenzo (SW19)
Santa Lucia (SW10)
Sardo (W1)
Sarkhel's (multi. loc.)
Seashell (NW1)
Shanghai Blues (WC1)

Shepherd's (SW1)
Smollensky's (multi. loc.)
Spighetta (W1)
Sticky Fingers (W8)
Strada (multi. loc.)
Sumosan (W1)
Tartine (SW3)
Tas (SE1)
Terminus (EC2)
T.G.I. Friday's (W2)
Thai Square (multi. loc.)
Thomas Cubitt (SW1)
Tootsies (multi. loc.)
Union Cafe (W1)
Verbanella (SW3)
Waterside Inn (Berks)
White Hart (SE11)
W'Sens (SW1)
Zizzi (multi. loc.)

Smoking: Prohibited

(As of summer 2007, all
restaurants will be
nonsmoking)
Abeno (WC2)
Admiralty (WC2)
Agni (W6)
Albannach (WC2)
Alounak (W2)
Amici/Italian Kitchen (SW17)
Angela Hartnett's (W1)
Arbutus (W1)
Awana (SW3)
Babalou (SW2)
Baker & Spice (SW3)
Banquette (WC2)
Bar Shu (W1)
Benares (W1)
Bengal Clipper (SE1)
Benihana (multi. loc.)
Bentley's (W1)
Bibendum (SW3)
Bloom's (NW11)
Bodeans (multi. loc.)
Bombay Bicycle (multi. loc.)
Books for Cooks (W11)
Bountiful Cow (WC1)
Boxwood Café (SW1)
Brackenbury (W6)
Busaba Eathai (multi. loc.)
Café Japan (NW11)
Café Rouge (SW15)

Camerino (W1)
Canteen (E1)
Capital (SW3)
Chez Bruce (SW17)
China Tang (W1)
Chutney's (NW1)
Clarke's (W8)
Cliveden House (Berks)
Clos Maggiore (WC2)
Club Gascon (EC1)
Comptoir Gascon (EC1)
Costas Grill (W8)
Dans Le Noir (EC1)
Deya (W1)
Duke of Cambridge (N1)
Ed's Easy Diner (multi. loc.)
1880 (SW7)
Elistano (SW3)
Enterprise (SW3)
Fat Duck (Berks)
Fifteen (N1)
Fire & Stone (WC2)
Fish Hook (W4)
FishWorks (multi. loc.)
Food for Thought (WC2)
Fortnum's Fountain (W1)
French Horn (Berks)
Frontline (W2)
Galvin/Windows (W1)
Gate (W6)
Giraffe (multi. loc.)
Glas (SE1)
Glasshouse (Kew)
Globe (NW3)
Gordon Ramsay/Claridge's (W1)
Gordon Ramsay/68 Royal (SW3)
Gourmet Burger (multi. loc.)
Gravetye Manor (W. Sus)
Great Eastern (EC2)
Grill Room, The (W1)
Hard Rock Cafe (W1)
Haz (E1)
Hosteria del Pesce (SW6)
Imli (W1)
Inaho (W2)
Inn The Park (SW1)
Isarn (N1)
itsu (multi. loc.)
Jenny Lo's Tea Hse. (SW1)
Kew Grill (Kew)
Kulu Kulu Sushi (multi. loc.)

Ladurée (SW1)
La Fromagerie (W1)
La Noisette (SW1)
La Trompette (W4)
La Trouvaille (W1)
Le Cercle (SW1)
Le Colombier (SW3)
Ledbury (W11)
Le Gavroche (W1)
Le Manoir/Quat (Oxon)
Le Vacherin (W4)
Light House (SW19)
L-Restaurant (W8)
Ma Goa (SW6)
Mandalay (W2)
Masala Zone (multi. loc.)
Maze (W1)
Mestizo (NW1)
Michael Moore (W1)
Mju (SW1)
Morgan M (N7)
Moshi Moshi (multi. loc.)
National Dining Rooms (WC2)
Noto (SW1)
Nyonya (W11)
Obika (W1)
OCCO (W14)
Odette's (NW1)
Origin (WC2)
Ottolenghi (multi. loc.)
Oxo Tower (SE1)
Oxo Tower Brass. (SE1)
Pappagallo (W1)
Pat. Valerie (multi. loc.)
Pearl (WC1)
Pepper Tree (SW4)
Petersham Nurseries
   (Richmond)
Pétrus (SW1)
Pied à Terre (W1)
Ping Pong (multi. loc.)
Pizza Metro (SW11)
Portrait (WC2)
Providores/Tapa (W1)
Quilon (SW1)
Quirinale (SW1)
Racine (SW3)
Rainforest Cafe (W1)
Randall & Aubin (W1)
Ransome's Dock (SW11)
Raoul's (multi. loc.)

Rasa (W1)
Rasoi Vineet Bhatia (SW3)
Real Greek (multi. loc.)
Richard Corrigan (W1)
River Café (W6)
Rivington Grill (SE10)
Roast (SE1)
Rocket (W1)
Roka (W1)
Roundhouse Café (NW1)
Roussillon (SW1)
R.S.J. (SE1)
Rules (WC2)
Saki Bar/Food (EC1)
Sam's Brass. (W4)
Saran Rom (SW6)
Sardo Canale (NW1)
Satsuma (W1)
Savoy Grill (WC2)
Six-13 (W1)
Smiths/Top Floor (EC1)
Smollensky's (E14)
Solly's (NW11)
Sotheby's Cafe (W1)
Square (W1)
Tamesa@oxo (SE1)
Tapas Brindisa (SE1)
Taqueria (W11)
Tate Modern (SE1)
T.G.I. Friday's (SW6)
Timo (W8)
Tom Aikens (SW3)
Tom's Deli (W11)
Tootsies (multi. loc.)
Truc Vert (W1)
Two Bros. Fish (N3)
202 (W11)
Ubon by Nobu (E14)
Umu (W1)
Upstairs Bar/Rest. (SW2)
Villandry (W1)
Vineyard/Stockcross (Berks)
Wagamama (multi. loc.)
Wizzy (SW6)
Yauatcha (W1)
YO! Sushi (multi. loc.)
Zafferano (SW1)
Zuma (SW7)

Special Occasions
Almeida (N1)
Amaya (SW1)

Angela Hartnett's (W1)
Asia de Cuba (WC2)
Aubergine (SW10)
Beauberry House (SE21)
Belvedere (W8)
Bentley's (W1)
Berkeley Square (W1)
Bibendum (SW3)
Blakes (SW7)
Bluebird Club (SW3)
Blue Elephant (SW6)
Boxwood Café (SW1)
Brunello (SW7)
Capital (SW3)
Cecconi's (W1)
Chez Bruce (SW17)
China Tang (W1)
Chutney Mary (SW10)
Cinnamon Club (SW1)
Cipriani (W1)
Clarke's (W8)
Club Gascon (EC1)
Crazy Bear (W1)
Daphne's (SW3)
Drones (SW1)
Fat Duck (Berks)
Fifteen (N1)
Fino (W1)
Floridita (W1)
Foliage (SW1)
French Horn (Berks)
Galvin/Windows (W1)
Galvin Bistrot (W1)
Glasshouse (Kew)
Gordon Ramsay/Claridge's (W1)
Gordon Ramsay/68 Royal (SW3)
Goring Din. Rm. (SW1)
Gravetye Manor (W. Sus)
Greenhouse (W1)
Grill Room, The (W1)
Hakkasan (W1)
Ivy (WC2)
J. Sheekey (WC2)
Lanesborough (SW1)
La Trompette (W4)
Launceston Place (W8)
Le Caprice (SW1)
Le Cercle (SW1)
Ledbury (W11)
Le Gavroche (W1)
Le Manoir/Quat (Oxon)

Le Pont de la Tour (SE1)
Locanda Locatelli (W1)
L'Oranger (SW1)
Luciano (SW1)
Lundum's (SW7)
Maze (W1)
Mirabelle (W1)
Momo (W1)
Morgan M (N7)
Nahm (SW1)
Neal Street (WC2)
Nobu Berkeley (W1)
Nobu London (W1)
Origin (WC2)
Orrery (W1)
Ottolenghi (multi. loc.)
Pétrus (SW1)
Pied à Terre (W1)
Plateau (E14)
Providores/Tapa (W1)
Quaglino's (SW1)
Rasoi Vineet Bhatia (SW3)
Richard Corrigan (W1)
Ritz (W1)
River Café (W6)
Roast (SE1)
San Lorenzo (SW3)
Santini (SW1)
Savoy Grill (WC2)
Sketch/Lecture Rm. (W1)
Smiths/Dining Rm. (EC1)
Smiths/Top Floor (EC1)
Spoon (W1)
Square (W1)
Tom Aikens (SW3)
Ubon by Nobu (E14)
Umu (W1)
Vineyard/Stockcross (Berks)
Waterside Inn (Berks)
Wilton's (SW1)
Wolseley (W1)
Zafferano (SW1)
Zaika (W8)
Zuma (SW7)

Tea Service
(See also Hotel Dining)
Bull, The (N6)
Café Rouge (multi. loc.)
Chor Bizarre (W1)
Cipriani (W1)
1802 (E14)

Fifth Floor Cafe (SW1)
Food for Thought (WC2)
Gilgamesh (NW1)
Inn The Park (SW1)
Joe's Rest./Bar (SW1)
Julie's (W11)
La Brasserie (SW3)
Ladurée (SW1)
La Fromagerie (W1)
Momo (W1)
National Dining Rooms (WC2)
Nicole's (W1)
Pat. Valerie (multi. loc.)
Pizza on Park (SW1)
Porters (WC2)
Portrait (WC2)
Richoux (multi. loc.)
Sotheby's Cafe (W1)
St. John (EC1)
Tate Britain Restaurant (SW1)
Tate Modern (SE1)
Tom's Deli (W11)
Truc Vert (W1)
202 (W11)
Wolseley (W1)
Yauatcha (W1)

Trendy
Admiral Codrington (SW3)
Alloro (W1)
All Star Lanes (WC1)
Amaya (SW1)
Anchor & Hope (SE1)
Annex 3 (W1)
Asia de Cuba (WC2)
Assaggi (W2)
Aubaine (SW3)
Automat (W1)
Avenue (SW1)
Baker & Spice (multi. loc.)
Bam-Bou (W1)
Bar Shu (W1)
Belvedere (W8)
Bibendum (SW3)
Bibendum Oyster (SW3)
Bierodrome (multi. loc.)
Blakes (SW7)
Boxwood Café (SW1)
Busaba Eathai (multi. loc.)
Canteen (E1)
Caraffini (SW1)
Carluccio's (multi. loc.)

Cecconi's (W1)
Cheyne Walk (SW3)
Chez Bruce (SW17)
Christopher's (WC2)
Cicada (EC1)
Cinnamon Club (SW1)
Cipriani (W1)
Circus (W1)
Clarke's (W8)
Club Gascon (EC1)
Cocoon (W1)
Crazy Bear (W1)
Crazy Homies (W2)
Daphne's (SW3)
Drones (SW1)
e&o (W11)
Eight Over Eight (SW3)
Electric Brasserie (W11)
Elistano (SW3)
Enterprise (SW3)
Fifteen (N1)
Fifth Floor Cafe (SW1)
Fino (W1)
fish! (SE1)
Frankie's Italian (multi. loc.)
Galvin/Windows (W1)
Galvin Bistrot (W1)
Gilgamesh (NW1)
Gordon Ramsay/Claridge's (W1)
Gordon Ramsay/68 Royal (SW3)
Hakkasan (W1)
Harlem (W2)
Hush (W1)
itsu (multi. loc.)
Ivy (WC2)
Joe's (SW3)
J. Sheekey (WC2)
Kensington Pl. (W8)
La Fromagerie (W1)
Langan's Brasserie (W1)
La Trompette (W4)
Le Caprice (SW1)
Le Cercle (SW1)
Le Colombier (SW3)
Ledbury (W11)
Les Trois Garçons (E1)
L'Etranger (SW7)
Locanda Locatelli (W1)
Lola's (N1)
Lucky 7 (W2)
Manicomio (SW3)

Special Features

Masala Zone (multi. loc.)
Maze (W1)
Mirabelle (W1)
Momo (W1)
Moro (EC1)
Nam Long-Le Shaker (SW5)
Nicole's (W1)
Nobu Berkeley (W1)
Nobu London (W1)
Nozomi (SW3)
Oliveto (SW1)
Olivo (SW1)
Orso (WC2)
Ottolenghi (multi. loc.)
Oxo Tower (SE1)
Papillon (SW3)
Pasha (SW7)
Pigalle Club (W1)
Ping Pong (W2)
Pizza Metro (SW11)
PJ's B&G (SW3)
Providores/Tapa (W1)
Racine (SW3)
Randall & Aubin (multi. loc.)
Rasoi Vineet Bhatia (SW3)
Real Greek (multi. loc.)
Refettorio (EC4)
Richard Corrigan (W1)
River Café (W6)
Roka (W1)
Salt Yard (W1)
San Lorenzo (SW3)
Sketch/Gallery (W1)
Smiths/Dining Rm. (EC1)
Sophie's Steak (SW10)
Sotheby's Cafe (W1)
Spiga (W1)
Spighetta (W1)
Spoon (W1)
St. John (EC1)
St. John Bread/Wine (E1)
Tapas Brindisa (SE1)
Taqueria (W11)
Tartine (SW3)
Thomas Cubitt (SW1)
Tom Aikens (SW3)
Tom's Deli (W11)
Tsunami (SW4)
Tugga (SW3)
202 (W11)
Ubon by Nobu (E14)

Vama (SW10)
Vingt-Quatre (SW10)
Volt (SW1)
Wagamama (multi. loc.)
Wapping Food (E1)
Wells (NW3)
Wolseley (W1)
Yauatcha (W1)
YO! Sushi (multi. loc.)
Zafferano (SW1)
Zetter (EC1)
Ziani (SW3)
Zilli Fish (W1)
Zuma (SW7)

Views

Addendum (EC3)
Amici/Italian Kitchen (SW17)
Babylon (W8)
Belvedere (W8)
Blueprint Café (SE1)
Butlers Wharf (SE1)
Café Spice Namasté (E1)
Cantina del Ponte (SE1)
Canyon (Richmond)
Cheyne Walk (SW3)
Cocoon (W1)
Coq d'Argent (EC2)
1802 (E14)
Fakhreldine (W1)
Fifth Floor (SW1)
Foliage (SW1)
French Horn (Berks)
Galvin/Windows (W1)
Gaucho Grill (E14)
Gravetye Manor (W. Sus)
Greenhouse (W1)
Gun (E14)
Inn The Park (SW1)
Lanes (W1)
Le Manoir/Quat (Oxon)
Le Pont de la Tour (SE1)
Maze (W1)
Nobu London (W1)
Orrery (W1)
Oxo Tower (SE1)
Oxo Tower Brass. (SE1)
Petersham (Richmond)
Pizza on Park (SW1)
Plateau (E14)
Portrait (WC2)
Quadrato (E14)

ansome's Dock (SW11)
hodes 24 (EC2)
iver Café (W6)
oast (SE1)
ocket (SW15)
oyal China (E14)
aran Rom (SW6)
miths/Top Floor (EC1)
mollensky's (E1)
amesa@oxo (SE1)
ate Modern (SE1)
hai Square (SW15)
bon by Nobu (E14)
Vaterside Inn (Berks)

**Visitors on Expense
Account**

Addendum (EC3)
Almeida (N1)
Amaya (SW1)
Angela Hartnett's (W1)
Arbutus (W1)
Asia de Cuba (WC2)
Astor Bar & Grill (W1)
Aubergine (SW10)
Aurora (EC2)
Bank Aldwych (WC2)
Bank Westminster (SW1)
Belvedere (W8)
Benares (W1)
Bentley's (W1)
Berkeley Square (W1)
Bibendum (SW3)
Blakes (SW7)
Boxwood Café (SW1)
Brian Turner (W1)
Capital (SW3)
Caravaggio (EC3)
Cecconi's (W1)
Chez Bruce (SW17)
China Tang (W1)
Christopher's (WC2)
Chutney Mary (SW10)
Cinnamon Club (SW1)
Cipriani (W1)
Clarke's (W8)
Cliveden House (Berks)
Club Gascon (EC1)
Coq d'Argent (EC2)
Daphne's (SW3)
Deya (W1)
Drones (SW1)

Dune (SW1)
Edera (W11)
1880 (SW7)
Elena's l'Etoile (W1)
Embassy (W1)
Fat Duck (Berks)
Fifteen (N1)
Fifth Floor (SW1)
Fino (W1)
Foliage (SW1)
Galvin/Windows (W1)
Galvin Bistrot (W1)
Glasshouse (Kew)
Gordon Ramsay/Claridge's (W1)
Gordon Ramsay/68 Royal (SW3)
Gravetye Manor (W. Sus)
Greenhouse (W1)
Green's (SW1)
Grill, The (W1)
Grill Room, The (W1)
Hakkasan (W1)
Incognico (WC2)
Ivy (WC2)
J. Sheekey (WC2)
Kai Mayfair (W1)
Lanes (W1)
Lanesborough (SW1)
Langan's Brasserie (W1)
Launceston Place (W8)
Le Caprice (SW1)
Ledbury (W11)
Le Gavroche (W1)
Le Manoir/Quat (Oxon)
Le Pont de la Tour (SE1)
L'Incontro (SW1)
Locanda Locatelli (W1)
L'Oranger (SW1)
Luciano (SW1)
Matsuri (multi. loc.)
Maze (W1)
Mirabelle (W1)
Mitsukoshi (SW1)
Mju (SW1)
Nahm (SW1)
Neal Street (WC2)
Nobu Berkeley (W1)
Nobu London (W1)
Odin's (W1)
One-O-One (SW1)
Origin (WC2)
Orrery (W1)

Oxo Tower (SE1)
Pétrus (SW1)
Pied à Terre (W1)
Plateau (E14)
Poissonnerie (SW3)
Providores/Tapa (W1)
Quaglino's (SW1)
Quirinale (SW1)
Rasoi Vineet Bhatia (SW3)
Red Fort (W1)
Rhodes 24 (EC2)
Ritz (W1)
Riva (SW13)
River Café (W6)
Roast (SE1)
Roka (W1)
San Lorenzo (SW3)
Santini (SW1)
Sartoria (W1)
Savoy Grill (WC2)
Shanghai Blues (WC1)
Sketch/Lecture Rm. (W1)
Smiths/Top Floor (EC1)
Spoon (W1)
Square (W1)
Sumosan (W1)
Tamarind (W1)
Tatsuso (EC2)
Tom Aikens (SW3)
Ubon by Nobu (E14)
Umu (W1)
Vineyard/Stockcross (Berks)
Waterside Inn (Berks)
Wilton's (SW1)
W'Sens (SW1)
Zafferano (SW1)
Zaika (W8)
Zen Central (W1)
Zuma (SW7)

Winning Wine Lists

Andrew Edmunds (W1)
Angela Hartnett's (W1)
Aubergine (SW10)
Aurora (EC2)
Belvedere (W8)
Bibendum (SW3)
Bleeding Heart (EC1)
Boisdale (multi. loc.)
Cantina Vinopolis (SE1)
Capital (SW3)
Caravaggio (EC3)

Chez Bruce (SW17)
Christopher's (WC2)
Chutney Mary (SW10)
Cinnamon Club (SW1)
Cipriani (W1)
Clarke's (W8)
Cliveden House (Berks)
Club Gascon (EC1)
Coq d'Argent (EC2)
Cru (N1)
Drones (SW1)
Ebury Wine Bar (SW1)
ECapital (W1)
Edera (W11)
1880 (SW7)
Embassy (W1)
Enoteca Turi (SW15)
Fat Duck (Berks)
Fifteen (N1)
Fifth Floor (SW1)
Fino (W1)
Foliage (SW1)
Glasshouse (Kew)
Gordon Ramsay/Claridge's (W1
Gordon Ramsay/68 Royal (SW3
Gravetye Manor (W. Sus)
Greenhouse (W1)
Grill, The (W1)
Grill Room, The (W1)
Hakkasan (W1)
Il Convivio (SW1)
Lanes (W1)
Lanesborough (SW1)
Langan's Bistro (W1)
Latium (W1)
La Trompette (W4)
Le Cercle (SW1)
Ledbury (W11)
Le Gavroche (W1)
Le Manoir/Quat (Oxon)
Le Pont de la Tour (SE1)
L'Escargot (W1)
L'Etranger (SW7)
L'Incontro (SW1)
Locanda Locatelli (W1)
Lola's (N1)
L'Oranger (SW1)
Maze (W1)
Mirabelle (W1)
Mju (SW1)
Morgan M (N7)

Nahm (SW1)
Odette's (NW1)
 Lombard St. (EC3)
One-O-One (SW1)
Orrery (W1)
Papillon (SW3)
Pétrus (SW1)
Pied à Terre (W1)
Plateau (E14)
Prism (EC3)
Ransome's Dock (SW11)
Refettorio (EC4)
Rib Room (SW1)
Richard Corrigan (W1)
Ritz (W1)

R.S.J. (SE1)
Sartoria (W1)
Savoy Grill (WC2)
Sketch/Lecture Rm. (W1)
Sotheby's Cafe (W1)
Square (W1)
Tate Britain Restaurant (SW1)
TECA (W1)
Tom Aikens (SW3)
Umu (W1)
Vineyard/Stockcross (Berks)
Vivat Bacchus (EC4)
Waterside Inn (Berks)
Wilton's (SW1)
Zafferano (SW1)

Wine Vintage Chart

This chart is designed to help you select wine to go with your meal. It is based on the same 0 to 30 scale used throughout this *Survey*. The ratings (prepared by our friend **Howard Stravitz**, a law professor at the University of South Carolina) reflect both the quality of the vintage and the wine's readiness for present consumption. Thus, if a wine is not fully mature or is over the hill, its rating has been reduced. We do not include 1987, 1991–1993 vintages because they are not especially recommended for most areas. A dash indicates that a wine is either past its peak or too young to rate.

	'85	'86	'88	'89	'90	'94	'95	'96	'97	'98	'99	'00	'01	'02	'03	'04
WHITES																
French:																
Alsace	24	–	22	27	27	26	25	25	24	26	23	26	27	25	22	–
Burgundy	26	25	–	24	22	–	28	29	24	23	26	25	24	27	23	24
Loire Valley	–	–	–	–	–	20	23	22	–	24	25	26	27	25	23	
Champagne	28	25	24	26	29	–	26	27	24	23	24	24	22	26	–	–
Sauternes	21	28	29	25	27	–	21	23	25	23	24	24	28	25	26	–
German	–	–	25	26	27	25	24	27	26	25	25	23	29	27	25	25
California (Napa, Sonoma, Mendocino):																
Chardonnay	–	–	–	–	–	–	–	–	–	–	24	25	28	27	26	–
Sauvignon Blanc/Sémillon	–	–	–	–	–	–	–	–	–	–	–	–	27	28	26	–
REDS																
French:																
Bordeaux	24	25	24	26	29	22	26	25	23	25	24	28	26	23	25	23
Burgundy	23	–	21	24	26	–	26	28	25	22	27	22	25	27	24	–
Rhône	–	–	26	29	29	24	25	22	24	28	27	27	26	–	25	–
Beaujolais	–	–	–	–	–	–	–	–	–	–	–	24	–	25	28	25
California (Napa, Sonoma, Mendocino):																
Cab./Merlot	27	26	–	–	28	29	27	25	28	23	26	22	27	25	24	–
Pinot Noir	–	–	–	–	–	–	–	24	24	25	24	27	28	26	–	
Zinfandel	–	–	–	–	–	–	–	–	–	–	26	26	28	–		
Italian:																
Tuscany	–	–	–	–	25	22	25	20	29	24	28	24	26	24	–	–
Piedmont	–	–	24	26	28	–	23	26	27	25	25	28	26	18	–	–
Spanish:																
Rioja	–	–	–	–	–	26	26	24	25	22	25	25	27	20	–	–
Ribera del Duero/Priorat	–	–	–	–	–	26	26	27	25	24	26	26	27	20	–	–

On the go.
n the know.

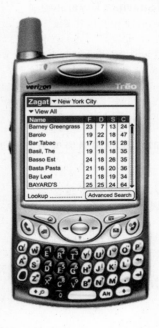

ZAGAT TO GO^{SM}

r Palm OS®, Windows Mobile®, ackBerry® and mobile phones

Unlimited access to Restaurant and Nightlife guides in over 65 world cities.

Search by ratings, cuisines, locations and a host of other handy indexes.

Up-to-the-minute news and software updates.

Available at mobile.zagat.com